International and Foreign Legal Research

International and Foreign Legal Research

A Coursebook
Second Edition

By

Marci Hoffman
Mary Rumsey

MARTINUS
NIJHOFF
PUBLISHERS

LEIDEN • BOSTON
2012

Library of Congress Cataloging-in-Publication Data

Hoffman, Marci.
  International and foreign legal research : a coursebook / by Marci Hoffman, Mary Rumsey.—
2nd ed.
    p. cm.
  ISBN 978-90-04-20480-5 (hardback : alk. paper) 1. Legal research. 2. International law—
Legal research. I. Rumsey, Mary. II. Title.

  K85.H64 2012
  340.042—dc23

2012003895

ISBN 978 90 04 20480 5 (hardback)
ISBN 978 90 04 20481 2 (e-book)

Contents

PART FOUR: FOREIGN AND COMPARATIVE LAW

PART FIVE: INTERNATIONAL ORGANIZATIONS

PART SIX: SELECTED INTERNATIONAL TOPICS

List of Abbreviations and Acronyms

ALI	American Law Institute
ASIL	American Society of International Law
ATCA	Anti-Counterfeiting Trade Agreement
AU	African Union
BIT	bilateral investment treaty
CAFTA	Central American Free Trade Agreement
CEDAW	Convention on the Elimination of All Forms of Discrimination against Women
CERD	Committee on the Elimination of Racial Discrimination
CIEL	Center for International Environmental Law
CIESIN	Center for Earth Science Information Network
CSIG	United Nations Convention on Contracts for the International Sale of Goods
CITES	Convention on International Trade in Endangered Species and Wild Flora and Fauna
CLOUT	Caselaw on UNCITRAL Texts
COE	Council of Europe
CSCE	Conference for Security and Cooperation in Europe
DPI	United Nations Department of Public Information
DSB	Dispute Settlement Body
DSU	Dispute Settlement Understanding
EC	European Community
ECHR	European Court of Human Rights
ECJ	Court of Justice of the European Union
ECOSOC	United Nations Economic and Social Council
ECOWAS	Economic Community of West African States
ECSC	European Coal and Steel Community
EEC	European Economic Community
EFTA	European Free Trade Association
EISIL	Electronic Information System for International Law
EPO	European Patent Office
EU	European Union
EURATOM	European Atomic Energy Community

FAO	Food and Agriculture Organization
GATS	General Agreement on Trade in Services
GATT	General Agreement on Trade and Tariffs
GLIN	Global Legal Information Network
HRC	Human Rights Committee
ICANN	Internet Corporation for Assigned Names and Numbers
ICAO	International Civil Aviation Organization
ICC	International Chamber of Commerce
ICC	International Criminal Court
ICCPR	International Covenant on Civil and Political Rights
ICJ	International Court of Justice
ICSID	International Center for Settlement of Investment Disputes
ICRC	International Committee for the Red Cross
ICTR	International Criminal Tribunal for Rwanda
ICTY	International Criminal Tribunal for the former Yugoslavia
IEL	international environmental law
IFAD	International Fund for Agricultural Development
IGO	intergovernmental organization
ILC	International Law Commission
ILO	International Labour Organization
IMF	International Monetary Fund
IMO	International Maritime Organization
IP	intellectual property
ITLOS	International Tribunal for the Law of the Sea
ITU	International Telecommunication Union
IUCN	World Conservation Union
IUSCT	Iran-United States Claims Tribunal
LCIA	London Court of International Arbitration
LCSH	Library of Congress Subject Headings
NAFTA	North American Free Trade Agreement
NHC	Netherlands Helsinki Committee
NGO	nongovernmental organization
OAS	Organization of American States
OAU	Organization for African Unity
OCLC	Online Computer Library Center
ODS	Official Document System of the United Nations
OHCHR	Office of the High Commissioner for Human Rights
OSCE	Organization for Security and Cooperation in Europe
PCA	Permanent Court of Arbitration
PCIJ	Permanent Court of International Justice
PICT	Project on International Courts and Tribunals

SICE	OAS Foreign Trade Information System (from its Spanish acronym—Sistema de Informacio´n al Comercio Exterior)
SSRN	Social Science Research Network
TEU	Treaty on European Union
TRIPs	Agreement on Trade-Related Aspects of Intellectual Property Rights
UK	United Kingdom
UN	United Nations
UNAT	United Nations Administrative Tribunal
UNCITRAL	United Nations Commission on International Trade Law
UNCLOS	United Nations Convention on the Law of the Seas
UNCTAD	United Nations Conference on Trade and Development
UNESCO	United Nations Education, Scientific and Cultural Organization
UNHCR	United Nations High Commissioner for Refugees
UNIDO	United Nations Industrial Development Organization
UNODC	United Nations Office on Drugs and Crime
UPU	Universal Postal Union
US	United States
WCT	WIPO Copyright Treaty
WHO	World Health Organization
WIPO	World Intellectual Property Organization
WMO	World Meteorological Organization
WORLDLII	World Legal Information Institute
WPPT	WIPO Performances and Phonograms Treaty
WTO	World Trade Organization

About the Authors

Marci Hoffman is the Associate Director and International & Foreign Law Librarian at the University of California, Berkeley Law School. She has been teaching international and foreign legal research since 1994. Ms. Hoffman received her B.A. in Political Science from the University of California, Davis and her M.L.I.S. from the University of California, Berkeley. She served as the foreign, comparative, and international law librarian at the University of Minnesota Law Library from 1993 to 1999 and was the international and foreign law librarian at Georgetown University Law Library. She returned to Boalt in fall 2003 as the international and foreign law librarian.

Ms. Hoffman has done extensive work and written widely on international and foreign legal research. Her work is available on the Web as well as in a variety of publications. Ms. Hoffman also has broad experience working with human rights materials and was the co-director of the University of Minnesota Human Rights Library on the Web. She was also one of the project managers of the American Society of International Law's EISIL project.

Mary Rumsey is the Foreign, Comparative & International Law Librarian at the University of Minnesota. She has taught foreign and international legal research since 2001. Ms. Rumsey received her B.A. degree in Philosophy and Political Science from the University of Wisconsin, her law degree from the University of Chicago, and a master's degree in library and information science from Dominican University.

Ms. Rumsey has written extensively on library and legal research issues, with two of her publications receiving national awards. Her work has been published in *Law Library Journal, Legal Reference Services Quarterly, Spectrum,* the *International Journal of Legal Information,* LLRX.com, and GlobaLex. She also participated as an author in the American Society of International Law's EISIL project.

Part One: Getting Started

Chapter One

Introduction

I. *Basic Concepts*

When researching international and foreign law, you must know two things: (1) the type of law you are researching, and (2) the sources of law. For example, to research how a Nigerian citizen can sue in a US court for violation of international human rights law, you must know that a combination of national and public international law applies. You must further understand the role of treaties and statutes as sources of national and public international law. Both pieces—the type of law and the sources within that type—are necessary components of any research process.

Therefore, it is important to define and understand some basic concepts related to types of law and sources at the outset of any research project. Listed below are some fundamental terms and concepts used throughout this book and when researching international and foreign law generally. Although definitions in other sources may vary slightly, these brief explanations should provide a baseline for understanding these terms and concepts.

A. *National Law*

National law is essentially the domestic or internal law of a country. It defines the role of government to the people and controls relationships between people. It may regulate foreign persons and entities, but it does not usually have effect outside the boundaries of a nation.

> **Sources**: National law is embodied in constitutions, statutes, regulations, and court decisions. Constitutions, statutes, and regulations are primary sources of law for all jurisdictions. Court decisions are also primary sources of law in common law jurisdictions, but they are considered secondary sources of law in civil law jurisdictions. The phrase "foreign law" is sometimes used by US legal researchers when referring to the law of any national or supranational jurisdiction other than the United States. Throughout this book, the term "foreign law" means national law or EU law.

There is some academic dispute over how to classify or group national legal systems.[1] Most scholars seem to agree that there are five types of legal systems: civil law, common law, customary law, religious law, and mixed legal systems. Many systems are mixed because two or more legal systems operate within the same jurisdiction. The following paragraphs provide only a very general overview of legal systems.

The United States, like most former British colonies, has a common law legal system. While the original common law system consisted of judicial precedents and few statutes, modern common law systems usually express much of their law in statutes. Even in these modern common law systems, however, judicial interpretations of the law (i.e., court decisions) are an important source of law. Statutes in common law systems do not usually prescribe comprehensive rules for an entire area of activity (e.g., commerce).

Most civil law systems are based on comprehensive written codes, designed to address an entire area of activity (e.g., criminal law, commerce, civil procedure). Most countries have civil law systems. In these systems, courts ordinarily decide cases only for the parties before them; court decisions do not officially carry any precedential value.[2] Civil law systems originated in Roman law but have evolved in different directions.

Customary law plays a role in some legal systems, though no country operates solely under a customary law system. Customary law tends to govern areas of personal conduct, inheritance, and marriage. Most often, customary law is unwritten and is dispensed by persons with elected or hereditary roles within a small community.

Most religious legal systems are based on Islam, although some communities, and one country (Israel), operate in part based on Judaic law. Generally, religious legal systems operate within countries that also have a civil or common law system. Religious law usually applies to issues of personal status (e.g., marriage) and may apply only to some residents of a country.

Mixed legal systems are not a separate type of legal system. Instead, they are a useful way to characterize countries that include elements of more than one legal system. Because Quebec and Louisiana operate under some elements of civil law systems, for example, you could say that Canada and the United States are mixed legal systems.

---

[1] Jaakko Husa, *Classification of Legal Families Today: Is it Time for a Memorial Hymn?*, 66 R.I.D.C. 11 (2004).

[2] While there are exceptions to this generalization, it is a useful one to begin to understand the difference between common and civil law systems.

For more information about the various legal systems, see the following titles:

- René David & John E.C. Brierly, *Major Legal Systems in the World Today: An Introduction to the Comparative Study of Law* (3d ed. 1985). This is a classic textbook, but a bit dated.
- Mary Ann Glendon et al., *Comparative Legal Traditions in a Nutshell* (3d ed. 2008). In the standard West Nutshell format, this book covers civil and common legal systems, using the British system as a paradigm of common law countries.
- H. Patrick Glenn, *Legal Traditions of the World: Sustainable Diversity in Law* (4th ed. 2010). This book describes various legal traditions rather than systems. It includes aspects of Islamic, Asian, Hindu, Talmudic, and other legal traditions.
- *Introduction to Foreign Legal Systems* (Richard A. Danner & Marie-Louise H. Bernal eds., 1994). Aimed in part at legal researchers, this book covers civil law, Asian, African, and common law systems.
- Frederick H. Lawson, *A Common Lawyer Looks at the Civil Law* (1955). As its title implies, this book examines civil law with a focus on features that differ markedly from those in common law systems.
- John H. Merryman et al., *The Civil Law Tradition: Europe, Latin America, and East Asia* (1994). Although written as a casebook, this 1,278–page text describes the history and modern status of various civil law systems in depth.
- John H. Merryman, *The Civil Law Tradition: An Introduction to the Legal Systems of Europe and Latin America* (3d ed. 2007). A simpler text than the one above, this book discusses general concepts of civil law systems.
- *Mixed Jurisdictions Worldwide: The Third Legal Family* (Vernon Valentine Palmer ed., 2001). This book provides a comparative overview of legal systems in which civil and common law coexist, then it focuses on several examples (e.g., South Africa, Scotland, Louisiana).
- *Mixed Legal Systems at New Frontiers* (Esin Örücü ed., 2010). An introduction to mixed legal systems and includes common law, customary law and other kinds of mixed jurisdictions.

For a quick overview of the major legal systems of the world (civil law, common law, etc.), see World Legal Systems.[3] You can use this website's map to find out what kind of legal system a country has. The site also provides

---

[3] http://www.juriglobe.ca.

some interesting statistical information on the number of civil law systems, mixed systems, etc.

B. *Private International Law*

Private international law governs the choice of which national law to apply when there are conflicts in the domestic law of different countries related to private transactions between private parties. These conflicts arise most often in areas such as contracts, marriage and divorce, jurisdiction, recognition of judgments, and child adoption and abduction. In the United States, Canada, and England, private international law is known as *conflict of laws.*

> **Sources**: Confusingly, the term "private international law" refers primarily to each country's *national* legal rules, which form the main sources of private international law. However, some private international law is also embodied in *public* international law sources, such as treaties and international conventions. For example, the Hague Conventions on Private International Law[4] govern such areas as international service of process, child abduction, and the form of wills. Despite the increasing number of such treaties, however, there is no well-defined body of private international law.

C. *Comparative Law*

Comparative law is "the study of the similarities and differences between the laws of two or more countries, or between two or more legal systems. Comparative law is not itself a system of law or a body of rules, but rather a method or approach to legal inquiry."[5] For researchers who already know how to research US law, comparative legal research ordinarily presents the usual challenges of foreign legal research (as described in Part IV).

> **Sources**: Because comparative law is not a system of law, it does not have its own set of sources. The sources depend on the national law systems being compared.

For more information on comparative law, see the following texts:

- *The Oxford Handbook of Comparative Law* (Reinhard Zimmermann & Mathias Reimann eds., 2008). In 48 chapters, this book describes the current state of comparative law, major approaches to comparative law, and the status of comparative studies in several subjects.
- *Comparative Law: A Handbook* (Esin Örücü & David Nelken eds., 2007). A readable text with a few chapters on comparative law on particular subjects

---

[4] See listing of Hague Conventions at http://www.hcch.net/index_en.php?act=conventions. listing.

[5] Morris Cohen et al., How To Find The Law 565 (9th ed. 1995).

(e.g., administrative law, family law), and several chapters on methods of comparative law.

- Peter De Cruz, *Comparative Law in a Changing World* (3d ed. 2008). In addition to explaining various legal systems, this book covers techniques to answer inquiries of comparative law. It then examines some areas of law using comparative methods.
- *Elgar Encyclopedia of Comparative Law* (2008). This lengthy book offers essays on selected legal topics, treated comparatively, and on several countries' legal systems.
- Mary Ann Glendon, et al., *Comparative Legal Traditions in a Nutshell* (3d ed. 2008).
- Konrad Zweigert & Hein Kötz, *Introduction to Comparative Law* (3d rev. ed. 1998). Often used as a textbook, this book covers the function and methodology of comparative law, major world legal systems, and a few areas of law within those systems.

Books that compare specific systems or specific topics are also available. See, for example:

- Tim Crook, *Comparative Media Law and Ethics* (2010). The focus is on US and UK law, but contains references to several other jurisdictions.
- Maher M. Dabbah, *International and Comparative Competition Law* (2010). Examines anitrust and competition law and policy from the EU, the US, and developing countries.
- Assafa Endeshaw, *Intellectual Property in Asian Emerging Economies: Law and Policy in the Post-TRIPS Era* (2010). A comparative review of intellectual property laws in Asia.
- *The Handbook of Comparative Criminal Law* (Kevin Jon Heller & Marcu D. Dubber eds., 2011). Surveys criminal law in a variety of jurisdictions: Argentina, China, France, Israel, Russia, South Africa, and other countries.
- *Japanese Family Law in Comparative Perspective* (Harry N. Scheiber & Laurent Mayali eds., 2009). Analysis of family law and related issues in Japan; includes comparisons with family law in other countries.
- *The Rule of Law in Comparative Perspective* (Mortimer Sellers & Tadeusz Tomaskewski eds., 2010). Collection of papers from a meeting on legal education.
- Eva Steiner, *French Law: A Comparative Approach* (2010). An account of the French legal system including comparisons to other legal jurisdictions.
- John R. Vaughn, *A Comparative Analysis of Disability Laws* (2010).

You can often find comparative legal works in a library catalog by searching your subject (e.g., family law, contract law) combined with the word "comparative."

D. *Public International Law*

Public international law governs the relationships between national governments, the relationships between intergovernmental organizations (IGOs), and the relationships between national governments and IGOs. It also regulates governments and IGOs across national boundaries.

> **Sources:** The sources of public international law are enumerated below. Their authority is based on Article 38 of the Statute of the International Court of Justice (the ICJ Statute):[6]
>
> * international conventions (treaties);
> * customary law (general practices of states[7] and IGOs that are legally binding and generally recognized by all states);
> * general principles of law; and
> * judicial decisions and the teachings of the most highly qualified publicists[8] of the various nations.

For more information on the sources of public international law, see Thomas Buergenthal, *Public International Law in a Nutshell* (4th ed. 2007). Part III explores the sources of public international law in detail.

E. *Transnational Law*

Transnational law is a broad category that is generally taken "to include all law which regulates actions or events that transcend national frontiers. Both public and private international law are included, as are other rules which do not wholly fit into such standard categories."[9] The focus of this subject "is invariably on the legal relationship between a state and alien individuals or corporations, frequently in commercial, industrial or investment situations."[10]

---

[6] 3 Bevans 1179; 59 Stat. 1031, *available at* http://www.icj-cij.org/documents/index.php?p1=4&p2=2&p3=0.

[7] While US lawyers ordinarily use the word "states" to refer to the 50 US states, in international law, you will often see nations referred to as "states" (as in "state responsibility," "state sovereignty," and "state actors").

[8] Publicists are considered the most important scholars in international law. Although historically they were individual writers, now they are often scholarly organizations such as the American Law Institute, which produced the RESTATEMENT OF THE LAW THIRD, FOREIGN RELATIONS LAW OF THE UNITED STATES.

[9] PHILIP C. JESSUP, TRANSNATIONAL LAW 2 (1956).

[10] PARRY & GRANT ENCYCLOPAEDIC DICTIONARY OF INTERNATIONAL LAW 612 (Craig Barker & John P. Grant eds., 3d ed. 2009).

Sources: Because transnational law encompasses both public and private international law, its sources may include any of the sources for those two types of law.

F. *Supranational Law*

Practically speaking, there is only one supranational legal order—the European Union. A supranational organization (1) has powers that its member states do not have because they surrendered those powers to it; (2) may enact rules that preempt the laws and regulations of its member states; and (3) may grant rights and privileges to the nationals of its member states, which those nationals may directly invoke.

Sources: The European Union has established various sources of law, including its founding treaties ("primary legislation"); other treaties; regulations, directives, and decisions ("secondary legislation"); general principles of law; and treaties between its members.

G. *Soft Law*

Soft law refers to nonbinding documents or instruments (guidelines, declarations, or principles) that may have use politically, but are not enforceable. For example, a UN General Assembly resolution on terrorism[11] constitutes "soft law."[12] It may express the sense of the international community, but it does not obligate even UN members to comply. Soft law has been effective in international economic law and international environmental law. For example, soft law instruments have created an expectation that states will consult with affected states before taking actions that might create a significant risk of transfrontier pollution.[13]

II. *Types of Legal Materials Used in Research*

Legal materials are published in a variety of sources, some official and some unofficial. The outline below highlights some of the most common types of

---

[11] E.g., Declaration to Supplement the 1994 Declaration on Measures to Eliminate International Terrorism, G.A. Res. 210, U.N. GAOR, 51st Sess., Supp. No. 49, at 346, U.N. Doc. A/51/631 (1996).

[12] See Christine M. Chinkin, *The Challenge of Soft Law: Development and Change in International Law*, 38 INT'L COMP. L.Q. 850 (1989).

[13] Pierre-Marie Dupuy, *Soft Law and the International Law of the Environment*, 12 MICH. J. INT'L L. 420, 434 (1991).

legal materials. These materials include books, documents, commercial databases, freely available websites, articles, and people.

The sources cited in this section are used for illustrative purposes only and are not exhaustive lists of what is available. Other sources will be mentioned in the next chapters.

A. *Primary Law Sources*

Primary sources of law contain the law itself. In most jurisdictions, these include constitutions, statutes, codes, and regulations. In some jurisdictions, court decisions are also considered primary law.

In public international law, the sources of law are outlined in Article 38 of the ICJ Statute. They include international conventions, international custom, and general principles of law. While Article 38 does not mention the sources of private international law, these sources include national law, treaties, and customary law.

1. *Constitutions/Charters*

There are many sources for constitutions, both in the vernacular (i.e., the official language of the country) and in English-language translation. One of the well-known sources is *Constitutions of the Countries of the World* (Albert P. Blaustein & Gisbert H. Flanz eds., 1971–). This multivolume print looseleaf is also available in electronic form. A free website with less complete coverage is the International Constitutional Law Project.[14]

One hazard for US researchers is that we assume other countries rarely amend their constitutions. In fact, many countries amend or even replace their constitutions much more often than the United States does. Be careful of relying on outdated versions, especially translations.

2. *Statutes/Codes*

a. Official Gazettes

Many countries publish official (national) gazettes, and they are usually the first official source for laws, regulations, notices, treaties and agreements, and announcements. Gazettes are usually published daily, by the government, in a format similar to the *Federal Register* in the United States. An example of a gazette is the German *Bundesgesetzblatt* (BGBl), published in two parts. Part I contains laws, ordinances, ministerial notices, and decisions of the federal constitutional court. Part II contains international agreements and treaties.

---

[14] http://www.servat.unibe.ch/icl.

You can use various sources to learn whether a country publishes an official gazette. The Government Gazettes Online website provides links to gazettes on the web as well as basic information about the gazette.[15] Thomas H. Reynolds & Arturo A. Flores, *Foreign Law Guide*, available by subscription only, also provides information on country official gazettes.[16]

b. Session Laws

Some countries publish session laws, which are statutes printed chronologically by date of enactment, regardless of the subject. An example is France's *Actualité Législative Dalloz* (1983–). To determine which countries publish session laws, consult Thomas H. Reynolds & Arturo A. Flores, *Foreign Law Guide*. One example is Sweden, which publishes its laws in *Svensk Författningssamling* (1825–). This publication is available online.[17]

c. Codified Law

A codification, or code, is a comprehensive, systematic legislative enactment covering all aspects of a defined subject area. Many countries have enacted five major codifications (civil, civil procedure, criminal, criminal procedure, and commercial). Some countries, like France, have enacted many more codes, including labor, copyright, public health, etc. Codes can be found mostly in the vernacular. However, some English-language translations do exist; for example, *The Mexican Civil Code Annotated* (trans. and updated by Jorge A. Vargas).

d. Compilations or Official Codifications

Some countries publish codes in looseleaf volumes and some in separate annual volumes, arranged by subject. These are usually in the vernacular; for example, Belgium's *Les Codes Larcier* (1995–).

e. Compilations of Specific Laws

Compilations of specific laws are most often from commercial publishers and cover several jurisdictions. They include topic-specific compilations, such as *RIA Worldwide Tax & Commercial Law*, or collections of laws from a particular region, such as *Central & Eastern European Legal Materials* (1990–). Most such compilations appear in English.

---

[15] http://www-personal.umich.edu/~graceyor/doctemp/gazettes/index.htm.
[16] http://www.foreignlawguide.com.
[17] http://www.riksdagen.se/Webbnav/index.aspx?nid=3910.

3. *Administrative Rules/Regulations*

In many jurisdictions, administrative rules and regulations are published in a separate compilation, such as the UK's *Halsbury's Statutory Instruments* (1986–). These are similar to the US *Code of Federal Regulations*. Rules and regulations may also be published in official gazettes. While these laws are considered primary law, they are nearly always in the vernacular, and few are translated into English.

4. *Court Decisions*

a. Decisions of National Courts

National case law comes from a variety of sources. In civil law jurisdictions, case law is referred to as "jurisprudence," which should not be confused with "legal philosophy" as the term is used in the United States.

Decisions of national courts are often published in official reporters, such as the *South African Law Reports* (1947–). However, much more case law is published in commercial or unofficial sources, such as the *All England Law Reports* (1948–). In some jurisdictions, such as France and Germany, more complete reporting is done through commercial journals. Although there is little or no systematic reporting of cases from civil law jurisdictions, more thorough reporting is available from the highest courts. Increasingly, cases from the highest courts are also available on court or other government websites.

There are some sources for case law that publish several jurisdictions together. In these sources, the cases are selected based on topic and jurisdiction. Examples include *Bulletin on Constitutional Case Law* (1993–), *International Labour Law Reports* (1978–), and *Law Reports of the Commonwealth* (1994–).

b. Decisions of International Courts and Tribunals

The decisions of international courts and tribunals are fairly accessible through print publications and official websites. Many of these bodies issue regular publications, such as yearbooks and annual reports, containing summaries or complete decisions. Some case law is published in commercial publications, such as *European Human Rights Reports* (1979–). There are also some compilations, such as *International Law Reports* (1950–) or *Butterworth's Human Rights Cases* (Jeremy McBride ed., 1997–). Websites also provide access to the case law of multiple courts; see the World Legal Information Institute (WorldLII)[18] and WorldCourts.[19]

---

[18] http://www.worldlii.org.
[19] http://www.worldcourts.com.

5. *Treaties and International Agreements*

You will find many sources for treaties and international agreements. These sources include historical collections, such as the *Consolidated Treaty Series* (1969–1981); national collections, such as the *United Kingdom Treaty Series* (1892–); and multijurisdictional collections, such as the *United Nations Treaty Series* (1947–).[20] Some countries also publish treaties and agreements in official gazettes.

Topic-specific collections are also available, usually published by a commercial publisher or an international organization. For example, *International Protection of the Environment* (2d series, 1990–1994) includes treaties on various aspects of environmental law. Collections of basic instruments or documents are also common; for example, *International Economic Law: Basic Documents* (1993).

Many treaties are also available on websites, such as UN organization sites.

6. *Customary Law*

a. Public International Law

Customary law is an important source of public international law (see Chapter 7). These sources include state or diplomatic papers, municipal legislation dealing with international matters, and legislative acts of intergovernmental organizations. To argue that a rule is part of customary international law, you will need to find sources that embody that rule. For example, to argue that customary international law forbids the execution of juveniles, you could cite to the laws of all the countries that do so. Yearbooks and periodicals are particularly good ways to locate this information.

b. Domestic Customary Law

Custom (practices or beliefs, such as tribal law, folk law, or indigenous law) is a source of law in some jurisdictions, but no country operates under a wholly customary legal system. Custom is embodied in the form of practice or belief and is usually not written down. This makes locating this law very difficult. The best way for a researcher to locate this information is in books and articles (i.e., secondary sources) that discuss this law. To learn more about using secondary sources, see Part II.

---

[20] http://treaties.un.org.

B. *Background and Secondary Sources*

Background or secondary sources discuss and analyze the law. On occasion, these sources translate or summarize relevant portions of laws, or reprint actual texts of laws.

1. *Books and Serials*

Secondary sources, such as books and serials, are important research tools. In some jurisdictions, lawyers consult them before looking at the law itself. Common secondary sources include treatises, classics of international law, and periodicals. Compendiums or looseleaf services provide information by topic (e.g., *International Environment Reporter* (1978–)) or cover a nation or region (e.g., *Comparative Law of Monopolies* (2004–), covering the US and the EU). Commentaries are extremely important in some jurisdictions. For example, in Germany, researchers rely on commentaries for subject access to laws and for expert interpretation. Other sources include digests (e.g., *Digest of Commercial Laws of the World* (1998–)), textbooks (some with document supplements), and encyclopedias (e.g., *Encyclopedia del Diritto*—Italy).

2. *Periodicals and Yearbooks*

Some researchers like to review the most important journals every month to learn about new developments in the law and track new legislation and cases. While yearbooks are issued annually, they are excellent sources for locating information on new legislation and legal developments. Publications and proceedings of scholarly organizations, such as Hague Academy of International Law, are also useful because they contain commentary by extremely distinguished contributors.

3. *Dictionaries, Encyclopedias, and Abbreviations*

Researchers focusing on foreign and international law often encounter unfamiliar terms, or familiar terms used in unfamiliar ways. International and foreign law has also spawned its own assortment of abbreviations. When you encounter these terms, you can avoid confusion by turning to dictionaries and lists of abbreviations.

International law dictionaries may be general, such as *Parry & Grant's Encyclopaedic Dictionary of International Law* (J. Craig Barker & John P. Grant eds., 3d ed. 2009),[21] or may focus on a topic within international law (e.g., human rights or trade). Regardless of their focus, they contain more useful information than a general dictionary or even a standard US law dictionary.

---

[21] Also available electronically by subscription, http://www.oxford-internationallaw.com. The electronic version is the same edition as the print.

For foreign law research, you will often rely on bilingual legal dictionaries, such as Henry Saint Dahl, *Dahl's Law Dictionary: Spanish-English/English-Spanish* (4th ed. 2006). It is important to use a bilingual *law* dictionary, as opposed to a regular bilingual dictionary. Regular dictionaries often leave out legal "terms of art" and may give only the most common meaning of a term.

While you can sometimes decode an abbreviation or acronym by entering the term in your favorite web search engine, this won't always work. If it does not, remember that some international law dictionaries include abbreviations.

The online Cardiff Index to Legal Abbreviations[22] helps you find the meaning of abbreviations for English-language legal publications from the United Kingdom, Ireland, Commonwealth countries, and the United States, including those covering international and comparative law. The editors also include some abbreviations for sources not in English, such as "BGB" for the *Burgerliches Gesetzbuch* (German Civil Code).

Another efficient research tool is the legal encyclopedia, which provides an introduction to key legal concepts and lists further sources. For public international law research, the *Max Planck Encyclopedia of Public International Law*[23] is one of your best starting points. It has entries on important legal problems and institutions, and on major international court and tribunal decisions.

C. *Electronic Sources*

The term "electronic sources" refers to online databases and freely available websites. They may contain primary law as well as secondary sources.

In the United States and some other countries, LexisNexis and Westlaw are major sources for law, by subscription only. There are many other companies in other countries that provide similar information for a fee. For example, a service called Indlaw offers access to Indian laws, regulations, cases, etc.[24] Some publishers still publish CD-ROMS for journals and supplements for books, or for publishing cases and legislation.

The web has become one of the primary publishing formats for both domestic and international law. Although many developing countries are not yet able to provide their laws online, you can find recent legislation from most other countries on the web.

---

[22] http://www.legalabbrevs.cardiff.ac.uk.

[23] The Max Planck Encyclopedia of Public International Law is available online by subscription, http://www.mpepil.com. This is a fully updated online edition of the ENCYCLOPEDIA OF PUBLIC INTERNATIONAL LAW published in print between 1991 and 2001 under the general editorship of Rudolf Bernhardt.

[24] http://www.indlaw.com.

D. *Finding Tools*

While not sources of law themselves, finding tools are critical in the research process. These are the tools that allow the researcher to access the primary and secondary sources of law. They include manuals and research guides, bibliographies, indexes, digests, and much more. Part II focuses on these tools and their use.

Legal research guides can help you find information and can also tell you what may be unavailable. If you have to tell a supervising attorney that there is no free online source for Ghana's laws, it is comforting to point to an expert guide on Ghanaian law[25] to back up your statement.

E. *People and Organizations*

Two valuable and often overlooked research sources are people and organizations. While the web has sometimes made personal contacts unnecessary, people remain the best source of information on some topics. Email has become a primary method for contacting people and organizations, replacing costly and difficult international phone calls. To locate useful contacts, you can use directories and guides, available in both paper and electronic formats. Many organizations' websites also list contact information.

III. *Sources of Law*

For quick reference, the chart below lays out the sources of law for major legal systems and international law.

	Common Law	**Civil Law**	**Public International Law**	**Private International Law**
Primary Sources	Constitutions Statutes/Codes Regulations Court Decisions	Constitutions Statutes/Codes Regulations	Treaties Customary Law Generally-recognized Principles of Law	National Law Treaties Customary Law
Secondary Sources	Scholarly Commentary	Court Decisions Scholarly Commentary	Court Decisions Teachings of Publicists (Scholarly Commentary)	Court Decisions Scholarly Commentary

---

[25] http://www.nyulawglobal.org/globalex/ghana1.htm.

Chapter Two

English Translations

This chapter gives important background information on legal translations, and describes strategies for locating them.

I. *About Translations*

For Americans researching foreign law, one of the most common tasks is to look for English translations of foreign legal materials. Even US research-ers who read foreign languages often feel more comfortable with English-language sources. Unfortunately, the comfort of English comes at a high price—the loss of authority. You will find only a few situations in which English versions have the authority of the foreign-language versions. One of those rare examples is Canada's laws, which are published in both Eng-lish and French. If you are not dealing with a jurisdiction like Quebec in which English is an official language, then whenever the English version dif-fers from the original, that original version takes precedence. The original, foreign-language version is called the "authoritative" version.

Even English translations provided by a foreign government, such as the translations of French codes and laws at the Legifrance website,[1] lack the authority of their counterparts in the vernacular. They are, however, considered "official" translations, and as such they are more desirable than other kinds. An "official" translation is one created by or for a governmental organization. Official translations are usually fairly accurate. Intergovernmental organiza-tions (IGOs) also produce translations; for example, UNESCO offers many translated laws on its website. While IGO translations are usually reliable, they are not considered "official."

---

[1] http://www.legifrance.gouv.fr.

The most useful and reliable translation is one that provides the original text next to the translation. Side-by-side translations like these are referred to as "synoptic." Researchers who know the foreign language in question value these because they enable quick comparisons between the original and the translation. Unfortunately, they are expensive to produce and therefore hard to find. Examples include Ian Sumner & H.C.S. Warendorf, *Book 1, Netherlands Antilles Civil Code, Family Law and the Law of Persons* (2005). To see this example, look at a preview of this book on Google Books.[2]

Many translations come from commercial publishers. These unofficial translations vary widely in their accuracy. Without knowing the language in question, you can't evaluate the quality yourself. To get an idea of a translation's quality, check the opinions of experts such as Thomas H. Reynolds & Arturo A. Flores, *Foreign Law Guide* (2000–).[3] Or, if you can afford it, hire your own expert legal translator to evaluate the translation. Other strategies include evaluating the qualifications of the translator (e.g., does she have legal training in addition to language skills?), and the reputation of the publisher. Law librarians can sometimes advise you on the quality or reputation of publishers.

A. *Currentness*

In addition to their lack of authority, translations often suffer from being out-of-date. Legal translation is time-consuming and expensive. Thus, most laws or codes get translated and published only once. Afterwards, or even before the translation is published, governments continue to amend their codes and laws. Civil law countries amend their codes less frequently than do common law countries, but for any translation, you must always find out whether the law you need has been amended since its completion. If you can find a current version of the law in the vernacular, check the beginning and end for dates. Even if you can't read the language, you can often tell by the location of date information that the law has been amended.

For example, here is a Belgian law in French, published in the *Moniteur Belge*, which is available on the web:

Publié le 1998–09–22
MINISTERE DE LA JUSTICE

10 JUIN 1998.—Loi modifiant la loi du 30 juin 1994 relative á la protection de la vie privée contre les écoutes, la prise de connaissance et l'enregistrement de communications et de télécommunications privées

---

[2] http://books.google.com/advanced_book_search.

[3] http://www.foreignlawguide.com. The Foreign Law Guide is available as a subscription database only.

Even if you do not read French, you can pick out the relevant dates, and guess that this is a law from June 10, 1998, modifying a law from June 30, 1994. You will find that dates are an extremely helpful clue in identifying the correct law in a foreign language. Just remember that in many foreign countries, dates appear in day-month-year order, rather than the familiar month-day-year pattern used in the United States.

B. *Online Translators*

You are probably aware of websites that translate webpages or other electronic text; Google Translate[4] is one of the best known. You may be tempted to use these sites to translate foreign laws, cases, or other legal materials. While using online translators may help you decide whether a law is relevant, do not rely on them for much more than that. Unfortunately, they are not good enough to use as a basis for legal analysis. No matter how much you want an English translation of a law, relying on online translators will at best embarrass or confuse you. At worst, it might lead you to provide inaccurate legal advice.

To create Google Translate's translation software, Google used millions of "aligned texts"—examples of human translations between two languages. Many of these texts were legal or quasi-legal in nature, such as European Union and United Nations documents. Google Translate works better than earlier software translators such as Babel Fish, but in the words of one critic, "[f]requently the system has the fluency of a barely competent human translator, one who happens to be both distracted and drunk."[5]

Here is an excerpt from the French code of money and finance, as translated by Google Translate:

Article L122–1
The legal tender of a particular type of notes denominated in Swiss francs may, upon proposal of the Bank of France, be abolished by decree. The Bank is obliged to provide within a period of ten years in exchange for his wickets against other types of legal tender banknotes.

And here is the translation provided by Legifrance,[6] a French government website:

Article L122–1
Legal tender in the form of a specific type of banknotes denominated in francs may be withdrawn by decree on a proposal from the Bank of France.

---

[4] http://translate.google.com.
[5] Lee Gomes, *Google Translate Tangles With Computer Learning*, FORBES, July 22, 2010.
[6] http://www.legifrance.gouv.fr.

For a period of ten years thereafter, the Bank remains bound to exchange them at its branches for other types of banknotes which are legal tender.

The version from Google Translate introduces the incorrect concept of Swiss francs, and provides a remarkably unhelpful translation of "guichets"—as "wickets"—instead of banknotes.

Moreover, online translators perform a mechanical word-substitution process, often interchanging word order and altering the syntax of the original text. Unlike a human translator, they cannot look for the sense of a passage.

From your work with US legal materials, you know how complex legal language is. Because of this complexity, you must not rely on machine translations. Even if ninety percent of the translation is correct, you will never know which ten percent of the translation is misleading.

Nonetheless, researchers sometimes use online translators to get a better sense of the content of a document. For example, if you were looking for a recent German law on genetically modified organisms, you might search English-language websites until you found out the date the law passed and a couple of key words. (Links to German-language materials from English webpages will help you find terms such as "gentechnisch.") With that information, you can search again, perhaps restricting your search to websites in German. Searching with these terms soon retrieves a PDF document that is formatted like a law, and appears to be entitled "Gesetz zur Neuordnung des Gentechnikrechts." At this point, you might use an online translation site. Running the title through Google Translate, for example, yields the phrase "Law for Genetic Engineering Act"—a good sign that you're on the right track. Thus, you might use online translators to obtain the text of a foreign law and then turn to human translators for a useable version of the law.

Another example of using online translators wisely is when you have a reliable citation to a law or case, and you know that a foreign-language website should contain that document. Using Google's translator feature to translate the foreign webpage might be enough to get you through the page's search process.

II. *Finding Translations*

A. *Introduction*

When searching for English translations, the first thing to keep in mind is that the translation might not exist. Most foreign-language statutes do not get translated into English. As a general rule, the more foreign investment money at stake, the more likely a law will be translated into English. So, for example, it is easier to find commercial laws than criminal laws, and it is easier to find intellectual property laws than family laws. By the same token, it is easier to find translations from countries with big economies, like Japan, China, or Germany, than from developing countries like Angola.

Looking for translated court decisions is often a hopeless quest. The market for any particular court decision is likely to be much smaller than for a statute. Also, most jurisdictions that do not use English are civil law jurisdictions, where court decisions play a much smaller role. Because of this smaller role, the market for translations shrinks further.

B. *Translations of Laws and Codes*

1. *Strategies*
You can use several strategies to look for English translations. First, if you have the name of the law you need (e.g., Commercial Code of Japan) search the web using that name. It is fast, and it sometimes works. The following sections identify some of the sources to check if you strike out with a quick web search.

2. *Subject Collections*
Because English-speaking lawyers usually specialize in one area of law, legal publishers tend to sell "subject collections" of translations. In other words, you are more likely to find a book or website that has translations of laws on one topic—such as joint ventures—from several countries, than to find a book that translates several of one country's laws into English. Large law libraries buy many such subject collections, usually in looseleaf or database format. Among the biggest are *Commercial Laws of the World* and *Tax Laws of the World*, both available from Thomson Reuters through the RIA Checkpoint database. Another useful database and print publication is *Constitutions of the Countries of the World* (Albert P. Blaustein & Gisbert II. Flanz eds., 1971–). HeinOnline offers its own collection of foreign constitutions in English, in the World Constitutions Illustrated database. You can also find many subject collections on the web. For example, the World Intellectual Property Organization's WIPO Lex[7] has a huge collection of translated patent, copyright, trademark, and related laws.

3. *Lists of Translations*
Several sources identify English translations of foreign laws. The most comprehensive listing of foreign laws in English is Thomas H. Reynolds & Arturo

---

[7] http://www.wipo.int/wipolex/en.

A. Flores, *Foreign Law Guide* (2000–).[8] *Foreign Law Guide*'s editors describe it as "basically a source to accessible translations of the standard codes and all other available major legislative enactments." To use the *Foreign Law Guide*, first use the drop-down menu to find the country you need. The introduction for each country describes its legal system and history but also gives you a sense of whether legal materials for the country are particularly difficult to find. Usually, the country chapter then lists major codifications, including available translations and sources of new legislation (e.g., government gazettes). Next, you will find an alphabetical list of subjects, with citations to statutes, parts of codes, and English translations if available.

While the authors of *Foreign Law Guide* cover a wide range of material, including web sources, they cannot identify every available translation. If you don't find a translation listed in *Foreign Law Guide*, a good next step is to look at the World Legal Information Institute (WorldLII).[9] WorldLII's home page has a front-page link called "All Countries" that lists countries in alphabetical order. For each country, the editors at WorldLII provide links to available legislation in English. For example, the Albania page includes links to the Criminal Procedural Code of the Republic of Albania (from the Albanian Legal Information Initiative) and the Electoral Code (from the International Foundation for Election Systems). WorldLII also includes links to legislation in the vernacular.

As another approach, you can check for lists of English translations on government, non-governmental, or private websites specific to your jurisdiction. Increasingly, you may find compiled lists of translated laws for particular jurisdictions. For example, English translations of Brazilian laws are collected at a site called Infolegis.[10] Numerous Eastern and Central European laws are available at the Council of Europe's Legislationline site.[11] Try a web search using terms like *translations laws [jurisdiction name]* or *English translations [jurisdiction name] laws*.

4. *Research Guides*
As an alternative, consult legal research guides tailored to the country whose laws you need. A good source for legal research guides is GlobaLex.[12] The guides vary in format and content, but many of them point to sources of English translations.

---

[8] http://www.foreignlawguide.com.
[9] http://www.worldlii.org.
[10] http://www.infolegis.com.br/legbratraduzida-sumario.htm.
[11] http://legislationline.org.
[12] http://www.nyulawglobal.org/globalex.

5. *Government Websites*

If you strike out with the strategies above, don't give up. Check for a website of the relevant foreign ministry or department. Many foreign government websites have small collections of English translations of laws. For instance, some Korean laws are available at the Korean Ministry of Government Legislation site.[13] Check foreign government agencies or ministries focusing on a subject such as intellectual property, trade, immigration, or commerce to find some translated laws and regulations.

6. *Periodical Articles*

Another source of foreign translations is periodical articles. (*Foreign Law Guide* does not include translations that appear in journal articles.) If you have access to full-text databases of law reviews, such as the ones on Lexis-Nexis or Westlaw, try searching for the name of the law. Recent examples of translated statutes are found in Lyombe Eko, 'American Exceptionalism, the French Exception, Intellectual Property Law, and Peer-to-Peer File Sharing on the Web,' *10 J. Marshall Rev. Intell. Prop. L.* 95 (2010) (translating part of a French law on web regulation); Esther Sánchez Torres, 'The Spanish Law on Dependent Self-Employed Workers: A New Evolution in Labor Law,' 31 *Comp. Lab. L. & Pol'y J.* 231 (2010) (translating part of a Spanish law). Even if you don't find a translation of the law you need, you might find a footnote reference to one.

Without access to full-text databases of law reviews, your job is harder. One approach is to use Google Scholar,[14] which enables full-text searching of some law review articles. On the Advanced Scholar Search page, do not choose the "Search all legal opinions and journals" option; this option retrieves too many cases at the top of your results. Instead, click on the button to search "Social Sciences, Arts, and Humanities." So, for example, a search for "Law on the Documents of the State Security Service of the Former GDR" along with the word "translation" leads to an article containing translations of part of this law.[15]

Alternatively, you can find articles using online or paper periodical indexes, such as LegalTrac or *Index to Legal Periodicals and Books*. The index references won't specify whether the article includes a translation, but once you have the article, you can look for translations or references to translations.

---

[13] http://www.moleg.go.kr/english/korLawEng.

[14] http://scholar.google.com.

[15] John Miller, *Settling Accounts with a Secret Police: The German Law on the Stasi Records*, 50 Europe-Asia Stud. 305 (1998).

Moreover, while you search for translations, you may run across useful information such as descriptions or analyses of the law you want. For instance, even if a periodical article doesn't include a translation, the author may give you much more detail about the law's provisions than you had before. This kind of information can be very important, especially if it turns out that no one has translated the law you want.

7. *Library Catalogs*

Keyword searches in library catalogs can sometimes turn up sources not listed elsewhere. You may search by the name of the law (in the vernacular or in English) adding the keywords *English* or *translation*. For example, search *code de commerce* and *english* to find the *French Commercial Code* (2004–);[16] search *handelsgesetzbuch* and *english* to locate *German Commercial Code & Code of Civil Procedure, in English* (2001).

8. *Settling for Summaries*

As suggested above, you may find only a summary of a law. This can still advance your research significantly, so you should know some key sources for summaries of laws. One such source is the Global Legal Information Network (GLIN) database,[17] a project of the Law Library of Congress. This database contains thousands of English-language summaries of laws from countries around the world, but particularly from Latin America. In some cases, the full text of laws is available in the vernacular. To use GLIN, always click on the "More Search Options" link. That link takes you to a page with several drop-down menus permitting you to choose your jurisdiction, type of legal instrument, date range, and so on.

Another useful resource is NATLEX,[18] a database provided by the International Labor Organization. This database focuses on legislation relating to labor, social security, and related human rights. Like GLIN, it provides English-language summaries of laws. NATLEX also links to the full text of laws where possible.

A third source that sometimes yields summaries, and sometimes yields full-text versions of laws, is the WTO's Documents Online database. Depending on the topic of the laws you need, you can choose various "trade topics" from the WTO homepage. Most of the topics have specialized search forms. For example, the intellectual property topics page, called the TRIPS Gateway, allows you to search "reviews of implementing legislation" by country. If you need to find Cameroon's law on geographical indications, you can select Cameroon

---

[16] *French Commercial Code in English* (2004–).

[17] http://www.glin.gov/search.action.

[18] http://www.ilo.org/dyn/natlex/natlex_browse.home.

from the dropdown menu under "Review of legislation on trademarks, geographical indications and industrial designs." The most relevant document this search retrieves, which has the WTO document symbol IP/Q/CMR/1, contains substantial excerpts from the text of Cameroon's law.

C. *Court Decisions*

If you are looking for a translation of a court decision, keep in mind that it is unlikely to exist. Your best strategy is probably to look for references within law review articles, ideally by searching a full-text law review database. Alternatively, look at research guides for the individual country. Also, check available law library catalogs for collections of decisions for the country or court in question. For a few courts, such as the German Constitutional Court, you can find collections of decisions in English: see, for example, Donald P. Kommers, *The Constitutional Jurisprudence of the Federal Republic of Germany* (1997). Other courts for which collections of translated opinions exist include the Japanese, Israeli, and Korean Supreme Courts. Keep in mind, however, that it may take several years for such translations to be published.

D. *Experts*

Experienced researchers will often turn to experts as a last resort. In translation searches, a couple of resources often come in handy. First, you can post a query to an electronic discussion list whose members work in the area needed. The INT-LAW list[19] has law librarians, attorneys, and other members from many countries. Members of the American Association of Law Libraries' section on Foreign, Comparative & International Law have a discussion list open only to members. Other discussion lists, such as those for immigration law attorneys, may be useful depending on the subject matter of the case. You can search the web for relevant electronic discussion lists using terms such as "asylum law" "discussion list" or "listserv."

Second, you can also try contacting a legal research expert who has written about the country in question. Many online research guides, such as most of the GlobaLex[20] guides, include the author's email address.

E. *Translation Services*

Most often, the person seeking a legal translation cannot afford to pay for one. If resources permit, however, you can employ companies or freelance

---

[19] http://listserver.ciesin.columbia.edu/cgi-bin/wa?A0=Int-Law.
[20] http://www.nyulawglobal.org/globalex/index.html.

translators. Numerous companies advertise translation services on the web. Whenever possible, work with a company that is experienced in the language and area of law you need. One example of a well-regarded company is the National Law Center for Inter-American Free Trade,[21] which focuses on Spanish and Portuguese translations to and from English. The Center has a large collection of already-translated statutes and other legal documents. Keep in mind, however, that legal translations are very expensive. For example, in 2011, one well-regarded legal translation company quoted a price of $120.00–$150.00 per page to translate a Japanese patent court opinion.

You may see references to "certified translations." These are translations that the translator has certified, usually under oath, as accurate. Evidentiary rules and agency regulations sometimes require certified translations. In immigration proceedings, for instance, translations must include a certification "that the translator is competent to translate the document, and that the translation is true and accurate to the best of the translator's abilities."[22] Notice that the translator does not have to be a professional.

III. *Conclusion*

Whenever you rely on translated legal materials, you should indicate in your work product the source of the translation, whether it's your own translation, that of a friend or colleague who knows the language, or a translation from a commercial or official source. Also, you should include the date on which the translation was made or published, as well as the full citation of the original document, including its date.

Whether you find a translation or pay for one, the most important thing to remember is that your translation does not have the authority of the original version. It may be cheaper—and it's often safer—to hire a foreign attorney than to get all the relevant materials translated!

---

[21] http://www.natlaw.com.
[22] 8 C.F.R. § 1003.33 (2011).

Chapter Three

Effective Web Research

I. *Introduction*

This chapter covers strategies and tools for effective web research, including some tools for managing sources and citations. The chapter also covers technologies such as blogs, electronic discussion lists, and wikis. Of course, the rest of the book also discusses web research, but in this chapter, you will find specific strategies for improving your search techniques. Unlike other chapters, this one deals primarily with free web resources.

The web has made many aspects of foreign and international legal research much easier. In particular, finding "known items" is often simple. It is usually easy, for example, to find a multilateral treaty on the web just by typing its name into your favorite search engine. Keep in mind, however, that web research creates some new pitfalls for researchers.

The first pitfall is the unreliability of some web information. Traditional publishers acted as a gatekeeper; researching, writing, editing, and publishing a book on paper costs a lot of money. Authors and publishers need to sell their product to recoup these costs. They can't do that if the information isn't reliable. Contrast this model with web publishing—web pages are easy to create. On the web, no one acts as a gatekeeper. To some extent, however, the criteria used by search engines to rank their results have a gatekeeping function. For example, Google ranks pages higher if many other pages link to them. That means Google's top search results show the influence of people's decisions to add links to those pages. However, on controversial topics such as whether the Palestinians or Israelis have committed war crimes, for example, you may still retrieve biased and inaccurate web pages in your top search results. That happens because so many people who feel strongly about the topic have linked to specific pages.

In most jurisdictions, certain legal information resources have always been identified as reliable authority; usually these resources have been books and loose leaf. Robert Berring calls this "cognitive authority"[1] and his metaphor is the "tinkerbell."[2] Like Tinkerbell in *Peter Pan*, who is alive if children believe in her, "[i]f everyone trusts a tool, if everyone uses that tool, then that tool is authoritative." While there are such tinkerbells in the electronic environment, most researchers may not be aware of them.[3] "In contrast, when accessing materials electronically, the researcher is viewing a computer screen, the same screen the person would look at to check e-mail, catch up on the latest blog, check the weather, or shop for shoes. The source is not isolated in a separate location. There is no obvious visual cue to tell the reader that was is being viewed is a source of primary authority, nor are there obvious visual cues that separate legal authority from other authority."[4]

The second pitfall in web research is the tendency to limit information searches to the web. Because researchers can find such a large quantity of free information on the web, they sometimes rely solely on freely available sources found there. Using paper sources and subscription databases can often save time and provide more reliable, useful information.

For example, if you want to understand the international law of treaties, you may already know that the Vienna Convention on the Law of Treaties sets out the basic rules. But it would be much quicker and easier to read about the law of treaties in an introduction to international law, such as Thomas Buergenthal & Sean D. Murphy, *Public International Law in a Nutshell* (4th ed. 2007), than to read the Vienna Convention itself on the web. (This example also illustrates the advantages of using a secondary source rather than going straight to the primary source.)

Limiting your research to the web can also make it impossible for you to find the information you want. Older treaties, bilateral treaties, diplomatic correspondence, and national regulations are a few examples of documents that may be available only in paper sources.

---

[1] Robert C. Berring, *Legal Information and the Search for Cognitive Authority*, 88 CAL. L. REVIEW 1673 (2000).

[2] Robert C. Berring, *A Tinkerbell in Buffalo*, http://www.slaw.ca/2011/04/19/a-tinkerbell-in-buffalo.

[3] The Legal Information Institutes, part of the "Free Access to Law Movement," are considered by many to be tinkerbells: AUSTLII, CANLII, etc., http://www.falm.info. For more information, see Graham Greenleaf, *Free Access to Legal Information, LIIs, and the Free Access to Law Movement, in* THE IALL INTERNATIONAL HANDBOOK OF LEGAL INFORMATION MANAGEMENT HANDBOOK 201 (Richard A. Danner & Jules Winterton eds., 2011).

[4] Ellie Margolis, *Authority without Borders: The World Wide Web and the Delegalization of Law*, 41 SETON HALL L. REV. 909 (2011).

II. *Web Searching*

A. *What's on the Free Web*

The web contains billions of pages.[5] Most of the information was created after 1996, though organizations such as the United Nations have added older documents. The authors of webpages range from distinguished international law scholars (contributors to the American Society of International Law's *ASIL Insights*,[6] for example) to small children. Much of the web, such as the profiles on Facebook, blog postings, or twitter feeds, is non-scholarly, personal information. Thus, to use the web for legal research, you must sift the useful sites from the less useful.

Legal information on the web usually lacks the "added value" of commercially published material. For example, you can often find the text of laws on the web, but this text will lack useful features such as notes about cases that interpret the law. Also, laws on the web are often "uncodified"—in other words, they are published in chronological order and not arranged by topic. Even worse, these laws do not usually reflect later amendments.

B. *Information Quality and Bias*

1. *Quality*

As discussed briefly above, the quality of web information can dip lower than that of traditionally published information. Thus, you must scrutinize the reliability of web information carefully. Check these sources for attribution: Who is the author? What are his or her credentials? Does the source provide citations to support the author's statements? How recent is the information? Much information on the web lacks any date; look for clues such as textual references to dates or even events that may help you figure out when the page was created. Note that it's possible to add code to a web page so that it gives the current date as the date of the last update, even if the page hasn't changed. Thus, don't assume that a page that says "last updated on [today's date]" actually reflects current information.

Another way to improve the quality of your search results is to restrict it to noncommercial pages. Many search engines allow you to limit your results to particular web "domains." For example, Google's advanced search[7] allows

---

[5] "The Indexed Web contains at least 8.58 billion pages" as of Dec. 13, 2011, according to http://www.worldwidewebsize.com, which indexes the size of the web each day.

[6] http://www.asil.org/insights.htm.

[7] If you cannot find the link to the advanced search, click on the gear icon in the top, right-hand corner on the main Google page or go to http://www.google.com/advanced_search.

the user to "Search within a site or domain." You can limit to an entire site, such as "who.int" or to just .org, .edu, or .int sites.

Keep in mind, however, that these options are US-centric. In the United Kingdom, for example, academic or educational sites are indicated by "ac.uk." rather than "edu."

2. *Bias*

While authors of traditionally published information often have biases, the lack of gatekeeping for web information means that webpages are more likely to contain biased information. For instance, nongovernmental organizations may exaggerate the problems on which they focus, either to increase their visibility or to raise funds. To guard against reliance on biased information, try to determine who sponsors a particular website. Look at the other websites to which the site links. Check for inflammatory language, and try to figure out the purpose for which the information is offered (e.g., for fundraising, to elicit political action, or to get clients). If you are still not sure about the reliability of the information, try to confirm it by finding corroborating sources.

C. *Special Problems with International and Foreign Sources*

1. *English as a Second Language*

Often, we tend to judge quality by whether a site is well written, just as you can usually identify phishing scams by the quality of the writing and spelling. (Phishing is a term used in computing to refer to electronic communications that lure ("fish") a person into providing financial information by masquerading as a legitimate entity.)[8] But if an author is writing in a second language, information from her badly written web page may still be reliable. Take the author's language ability into account. For example, Chinese lawyers may provide webpages with summaries of Chinese laws; while these summaries may not read like a law review article, they might be the most current and accurate information available in English.

2. *Style*

Non-Western or non-US websites may not look like what US researchers expect. For example, some webpages on legal information for Thailand have flashing lights, scrolling text, and animated graphics, yet the information itself is reliable. Other sites may have the text of laws in very simple, unprofessional looking pages, without headings, links to other pages, or other

---

[8] For more information, see http://en.wikipedia.org/wiki/Phishing.

features associated with legitimate websites. The page may not look especially sophisticated, but it contains the accurate text of, and citation to, official law. Thus, a researcher would not want to dismiss these sources simply because of their appearance.

3. *Unfamiliarity*

If you are unfamiliar with a region or country, you may not know enough to pick up on bias or to judge credentials. In the United States, there are certain topics where you easily see the potential for bias—for example, a website about abortion law, or gun control. Similarly, you probably know the biases of organizations such as the American Civil Liberties Union, the National Rifle Association, and the John Birch Society. To figure out the biases of a foreign organization, start with what the organization's site tells you about itself. Next, look for information from unaffiliated organizations or individuals. For example, if you are researching the French law on Holocaust denial, called the Fabius-Gayssot law, you will probably retrieve pages from many organizations, some of which are violently anti-Semitic, others that are much more subtly anti-Semitic. You may need to take extra time to determine the reliability of any sites you retrieve. Search the name of the organization, and look at how other web pages treat it.

If you are unfamiliar with other countries' educational systems, you may have trouble judging web authors' academic credentials. For instance, in the United Kingdom and Europe, many well-qualified university teachers are not called professors: they may be called "readers" ("lecteurs" in French), "lecturers," or, in Germany, "Privatdozenten." If you are concerned about the qualifications of an author, you may need to do additional research to learn what the credentials mean.

III. *Using Search Engines Effectively*

A. *Constructing Searches*

Although search engines can sometimes help you with spelling errors, with a "did you mean?" feature, they work in a very literal way. You enter keywords; they retrieve pages that contain those keywords. (Most search engines will also bring back pages that contain only one of your keywords, though they will rank those pages low in your search results.) Because search engines are literal, you need accurate spelling and good search terms. Keep in mind that many international organizations, including the United Nations, use British spellings—e.g., labour, organisation, centre, licence. (While Google has expanded its search function to look for many British and American spelling variants automatically, not all search engines have done so.)

You should be flexible in your search terms. Be prepared to try alternatives—for example, death penalty *or* capital punishment. Scan your results to see whether they contain more specific or more commonly used terms; if so, use them in a new search. If someone tells you to find information about a subject, such as an expert's name, or the name of a treaty, you may need to experiment with dropping pieces out of your search string before you are successful, because often people don't give accurate information. For example, you might be asked to find the "Convention on Endangered Wetlands of International Importance especially as Waterfowl Habitat." This convention does not actually have the word "endangered" in its title, so you might try "convention" with "wetlands of international importance," which would successfully retrieve the treaty.

For similar reasons, although phrase searches are useful when you're confident that your phrase will appear, you may not want to use them with uncertain information. Thus, if someone tells you to find the "Human Rights Council Manual on Special Procedures to Enforce Human Rights," you should enter these search terms without putting them in quotation marks. If, however, you want to find a document specifically referenced in that manual, such as the ICJ opinion on the Difference relating to Immunity from Legal Process of a Special Rapporteur of the Commission on Human Rights, it might be faster to enclose the title in quotation marks, adding "International Court of Justice" or "ICJ" outside the quotation marks. Otherwise, with fairly generic terms like those, you risk retrieving a lot of irrelevant results.

Generally, avoid phrasing your search as a question ("what is an internationally wrongful act"). On the other hand, you can sometimes get good results by phrasing your search as part of an answer (e.g., "an international wrongful act consists of").

Adding search terms that describe the form in which you want the information, such as "report" or "discussion," may decrease the quality of your results. In that situation, you might specify that your results should be in PDF format; many search engines have an advanced feature that lets you do so.

B. *Iterative Searching*

Perhaps the most important concept in constructing searches is "iterative searching." As you search, keep refining or changing your search terms and strategies based on what you find. For example, a law firm associate is asked to find the law that governs incorporating a business in Nigeria. Her first search is simply *nigerian business incorporation*. Although she doesn't retrieve the law, her first result is a summary of the law from the Nigerian Embassy. The summary includes the name of the law: The Companies and Allied Matters Act, 1990. By copying and pasting this name as a new search, she immediately retrieves a copy of the law.

C. *Multiple Search Engines*

Remember that different search engines cover different "territory." In other words, there is surprisingly little overlap in the coverage of major search engines, though they tend to have fairly comparable coverage of major web addresses like the UN and federal government web sites. Thus, if you don't find what you're looking for using your usual search engine, or if you need to perform a particularly comprehensive search, you should use more than one search engine. Useful search engines include Google, Yahoo, Bing, and others.

One situation that you may encounter is research for an asylum claim. Perhaps your client claims to be a member of a group that is subject to persecution in his home country. For some groups and some countries, it is very hard to document persecution. Scouring the web using several search engines is a good approach. Combine this approach with alternative and variant spelling of names and geographic name changes: Ivory Coast or Côte d'Ivoire, Munguki or Mungiki, and Somaliland or Somalia.

D. *Capturing Information and the Invisible Web*

Another aspect of the web that bears remembering is its changeability. If you find useful information, particularly from an unfamiliar site, consider making a paper or electronic copy for your records. Content often disappears from web pages, as their creators remove older information, delete pages, or take down entire websites. If you find yourself in need of information that you found on the web, but can no longer find, look for tools such as the "Wayback Machine" hosted by the Internet Archive.[9] For example, you find the following citation in a law review article: United Nations High Commissioner for Refugees, Comments on Proposed Rules on, "Inspection and Expedited Removal of Aliens; Detention and Removal of Aliens: Conduct of Removal Proceedings; and Asylum Procedures" (February 4, 1997), available at http://unrefugees.org/archives.cfm?ID=122&cat=Archives (last visited Mar. 20, 2006). This site no longer exists on the UN High Commissioner for Refugees website; however, you can locate an April 6, 2005 snapshot of the webpage. Do not rely on the Internet Archive to archive all web content, however; it is much better to keep your own copies of useful web pages.

A large percentage of web content cannot be retrieved by search engines directly; instead, the user must go to the site hosting the content and perform a search or click on links at that site. Some researchers refer to this part of the web as the "invisible web" or "dark matter." One example of this information

---

[9] http://www.archive.org/web/web.php.

is the contents of most library catalogs. While you can go directly to a web catalog and search its contents, a search engine like Google cannot index the catalog's contents—just its first screen. Similarly, search engines cannot access the useful international fisheries law information at "FISHLEX"[10]—the content is dynamically generated when a user enters a query.

To gain access to the invisible web, you can use a couple of approaches. First, think about what nongovernmental organizations, governments, or other organizations might collect the kind of information you need. The United Nations, as one example, has created large databases of statistical information on human development—poverty measures, health, investment, etc. If you need to document investment conditions in connection with a business project, the United Nations, the World Bank, or the International Monetary Fund (IMF) would be reasonable places to look.

A second approach, when you don't know what organization might have helpful information, is to try web searches to find a database that contains the information you need. For example, you might have an international environmental law problem involving toxic substances. You could enter the terms *toxic chemicals database*, and retrieve some useful databases whose contents aren't indexed in search engines. This is also when a web subject directory is a good source to consult. For example, see ipl2[11] or Infomine Scholarly Internet Resource Collections.[12]

E. *Up-to-Date Information*

As you know, search engines don't search actual web pages when you enter a search query. They search their index of pages, based on information they gathered at some earlier time. This method explains why you sometimes retrieve pages that don't contain the search terms you entered. Some search engines, such as Google, may allow you to see the previous version via a "cache." More often, you may be interested in finding newer information than what you have retrieved. With some sites, it's helpful to go from the page you retrieved to the site's main page, and then look for later information.

For example, searching for information on the link between sorts and the trafficking of women. You begin your search by using Google: *trafficking women sports*. This search retrieves a 2009 Briefing Paper entitled *Trafficking in Persons and the 2010 Olympics*, produced by the Global Alliance Against Traffic in Women. Starting with this web document, you can find more recent documents by going to the website of the organization and clicking on Publications. From there, you can read a 2012 publication called *What's the Cost of*

---

[10] http://faolex.fao.org/fishery.

[11] http://www.ipl.org.

[12] http://infomine.ucr.edu.

a Rumour?—a guide that reviews the literature and determines that sporting events do not cause increases in trafficking for prostitution.[13]

Another approach is to use search engines designed specifically to find web news rather than all kinds of webpages. Yahoo, Google, Bing, and other search engines offer this option. Alternatively, you can use advanced search features to restrict your results to pages that have been updated within a certain time period. This approach, however, may retrieve pages of old information to which irrelevant changes have been made. It doesn't guarantee that a page will contain new information.

F. *Advanced Search Features*

1. *Domain and Site Restrictions*

As noted above, you can restrict your search to particular web "domains" or sites. For example, if a searcher is looking for Dominican Republic Law No. 285 on migration, she might use Google's Advanced Search page to restrict her search to the ".gov.do" domain, which would limit the results of the search to government pages from the Dominican Republic.

Another useful way to use this feature is to restrict your search to a particular site, particularly if the site's own search engine or navigation doesn't work well. This technique comes in handy with large sites like intergovernmental organizations, whose sites have huge numbers of documents. For example, a researcher was asked to find an IMF paper discussing (in part) infant and child mortality in Guatemala. While the IMF's own search engine retrieved the document, Google's results ranked the document much higher, making it easier to find.

This same idea applies when using a site's search engine doesn't produce any results. Lets say you need to locate a list of Rwandan bilateral extradition treaties. A logical place to start is the Rwandan Ministry of Foreign Affairs website. However, searching *extradition* doesn't produce any worthwhile results. The "Treaties, Conventions and Protocols" page of this site is not helpful either. Using the Google's Advanced Search, you can limit your search to this website (http://www.minaffet.gov.rw) and search for the term *extradition*. This search retrieves a 1998–2006 list of bilateral treaties (in French) and you can then identify the extradition treaties. While this list may not be as current as you would like, it's a place to start.

2. *Excluding Terms*

Most search engines allow you to exclude terms from your results by prefacing them with a minus sign (e.g., -pharmaceutical). This technique should be

---

[13] http://www.gaatw.org/index.php?option=com_content&view=article&id=107&Itemid=73.

used sparingly, since it excludes documents or web pages that contain your term anywhere. For example, when searching for information on human trafficking in Thailand, you might want to exclude information on drug trafficking: *thailand human trafficking -drug*. Because some organizations are involved in both human and drug trafficking, however, excluding the term "drug" might remove useful results. Excluding terms is probably best used to weed out a meaning of a word that you don't want (e.g., *virus—computer*).

3. *Synonyms*
You can include synonyms in your searches, most often by separating the synonyms with the word "or" in capital letters. For example, searching *capital punishment OR death penalty turkey* gets more complete results than searching only for *capital punishment turkey.*

Google supports the tilde symbol (~) as a way to search for synonyms. Searching *~data patents*, for example, also retrieves documents containing the word "statistics" and patents. This feature can be unpredictable, however; searching for *~canine* retrieves not only documents about dogs, but also about teeth.

4. *Search Operators*
Google does allow you to use some advanced operators when searching.[14] You can limit your search terms to the title of a document by using the following "allintitle:anti-corruption treaties" retrieves webpages with these words in the title (the information usually tagged as the title in the webpage). This operator also works in Google Scholar allowing you to limit your search terms to the title of the materials. Google does offer proximity searching by using "term1 AROUND(n) term2" allowing you to require that webpages include search term1 within a certain number of words of term2. However, some people say this function doesn't work very well and proximity searching on Exalead[15] works more effectively (unfortunately, Exalead isn't as large as Google in content).[16]

IV. *Blogs and Electronic Discussion Lists*

Blogs and electronic discussion lists are two web applications that create smaller online communities with shared information interests. They act as a tool to keep you apprised of new developments and a way to communicate

---

[14] https://sites.google.com/site/gwebsearcheducation/advanced-operators.
[15] http://www.exalead.com/search.
[16] http://lawprofessors.typepad.com/law_librarian_blog/2011/12/google-undocumented-search-operators-out-of-date-and-updated.html.

with other researchers and experts. As you begin to focus on a specific practice area, these will become more important.

A. *Blogs & Twitter*

A blog is a website or page that is updated regularly with "postings" (blog entries) structured in reverse chronological order so that the most recent information appears first. Two or more authors may cooperate to produce a blog, or a blog may be a single author's effort. Usually, postings, or posts, are relatively short and informal. Some blog authors have distinguished academic credentials; for example, several law professors and international law experts collaborate on Opinio Juris[17] and on IntLawGrrls.[18]

Blogs on foreign law have become commonplace too; Prof. Darius Whelan's Irish Law Update[19] is one example, but many are produced in foreign languages.[20] There's a blog on comparative law too.[21]

1. *RSS Feeds and RSS Readers*
Many blogs offer an "RSS feed."[22] These feeds provide an easy way for you to read the headlines of new content in blogs you want to monitor. (The alternative is to visit the site of each blog to see whether you want to read any of the new content—very time consuming!) Using an RSS reader, you can subscribe to RSS feeds. RSS "readers" take RSS feeds and present them on one webpage that you can visit whenever you choose. Practitioners and legal scholars use RSS readers, sometimes called newsreaders or aggregators, to get a quick look at current legal developments in their areas of interest. Postings often link to useful documents—for example, the text of a just-released court decision. People who read a blog posting often have the option of posting a comment on it.

If you are not familiar with RSS feeds and readers, a quick web search will give you enough information to get started.

2. *Finding Useful Blogs*
To identify law-related blogs that interest you, you have several options. First, you can check a site that collects information on available legal blogs.

---

[17] http://opiniojuris.org.
[18] http://intlawgrrls.blogspot.com.
[19] http://irishlawblog.blogspot.com.
[20] E.g., the French law blog Au fil du droit, http://aufildudroit.over-blog.com or the German-language Swiss criminal procedure blog, http://www.strafprozess.ch/.
[21] http://comparativelawblog.blogspot.com.
[22] RSS is usually said to stand for "really simple syndication." It refers to a type of document markup, XML (similar to HTML), which makes it easy to share web content.

One good example is BlawgSearch.[23] This site has a searchable directory of blogs as well as topical categories for browsing. Also, most RSS readers, such as Bloglines, have a search feature that lets you look for blogs by topic. Major search engines like Google offer a search option restricted to blog content; if you find relevant postings on a particular blog, you may want to subscribe to it.

3. *Searching Blog Content*

You can use search engines' blog search features to focus your search on blog content across multiple blogs. RSS readers usually offer a way to search postings across multiple blogs. LexisNexis also offers a couple of databases containing legal blog content,[24] but international and foreign material in these databases is minimal.

Some blogs (a minority) include an index to previous postings, usually on the first screen. Others have a built-in search feature.

4. *Twitter*

Created in 2006, Twitter is a microblogging service that allows users to send and read text-based posts of up to 140 characters, informally known as "tweets."[25] All kinds of people, organizations, and those who write for blogs can be followed on Twitter. It's another mechanism for learning about information and news. For example, you can follow SlawTips (a project of Slaw. ca.) in order to keep up with breaking news in research and technology.[26]

B. *Electronic Discussion Lists*

Electronic discussion lists, or "listservs," can be another source of information on current developments. They are also a good way to seek help from experts.

Unlike blogs, electronic discussion lists do not have centralized authors or editors, though some have moderators who exert some control over content. Persons who share an interest, such as international legal information, subscribe to a list. They then receive email messages sent from other list subscribers to everyone on the list. For example, a subscriber to the INT-LAW list might send the message: "Do any of you know where I can get a copy of the most recent Kuwaiti Labor Code—Law No. 38 of 1964?" Other list subscribers can then reply either to the whole list, or to the person who sent the question.

---

[23] http://blawgsearch.justia.com/. Law-related blogs are sometimes called "blawgs."
[24] Newstex Legal Blogs, American Lawyer Blogs.
[25] For more information, see http://en.wikipedia.org/wiki/Twitter.
[26] http://twitter.com/#!/slawtips.

Subscribers often send messages announcing new information (e.g., that a case has been decided, or that a new database of laws is available). To some extent, then, the functions of blogs and lists overlap.

You can often learn of useful electronic discussion lists from other lawyers or law students. Alternatively, search the web with the terms "electronic discussion list" and your topic of interest. For example, searching *"electronic discussion list" china law* retrieves information about the CHINALAW list, including directions for how to subscribe.

Many electronic discussion lists have online archives. To find whether a list has archives, simply search on the name of the list and the word "archive." For example, searching *intbuslaw archive* retrieves the archives of the International Business Law list. While the traffic on many of these discussion lists has diminished due to blogs and Twitter, some lists are still being used for sharing and obtaining information.

C. *Contacting Experts*

By subscribing to blogs and electronic discussion lists, or just by searching for blog postings and list archives, you can often identify people who are experts on particular subjects. Some—not all—of these experts will respond to requests for help or information. The Foreign, Comparative & International Law Section of the American Association of Law Libraries provides a list, compiled by Lyonette Louis-Jacques and Mary Rumsey, of legal research experts on various international and foreign legal topics (e.g., Swedish law).[27] Generally, experts are more likely to respond if you:

- explain briefly how you found their name,
- clearly identify the information you seek, and
- describe the ways you have already looked for the information.

V. *Wikis*

A. *What is a Wiki?*

You are probably familiar with Wikipedia, and perhaps with other "wikis." A wiki is a collaborative Web site containing information created by its users. Wiki software allows site visitors to add, delete, and otherwise modify entries on the site. While this model has led to a few egregious errors and attempts at manipulation (such as politicians tweaking their own biographies), a 2005

---

[27] http://www.aallnet.org/sis/fcilsis/jumpstart.html.

study comparing the reliability of information on Wikipedia to the Encyclopedia Britannica found that Wikipedia entries were only slightly more prone to error.[28]

B. *Using Wikis in Research*

Wikis do not yet have enough credibility and authority to cite in legal documents, even internal ones. Legal scholars have questioned the practice of citing to Wikipedia and other wikis, pointing out that authors can simply edit a Wikipedia entry to support their contentions.[29] Wikipedia has also been criticized for containing unreliable information, and its credibility has suffered from "contributors" such as congressional staffers who pad their employers' entries with propaganda. Because Wikipedia allowed anyone to edit a section ("free editability"), it was open for spammers, vandals and the like. Consequently, Wikipedia has instituted more barriers to participation (restricting the creation of new articles to registered users, limiting editing of some entries, and blocking certain IP addresses from being able to edit).[30] Thus, when you use wikis, try to verify the accuracy of information on which you rely and follow the footnotes carefully.

You may find, however, that they can be very useful in providing leads for your research. For example, the Wikipedia entry for Salim Ahmed Hamdan, the petitioner in *Hamdan v. Rumsfeld*,[31] contains links to related Department of Defense documents, newspaper stories, and the Supreme Court's opinion in the case.

One of the first significant efforts to create a wiki specifically on law came from Cornell Law School's Legal Information Institute. This wiki, called Wex, aims to be a combined law dictionary and encyclopedia for "law novices." At present, its information on international and foreign law is minimal, but wikis can grow quickly.

VI. *Resource & Citation Management Tools*

A common problem for researchers is managing the information found when doing multiple web searches for research projects, journal articles and

---

[28] Robert Levine, *The Many Voices of Wikipedia, Heard in One Place*, N.Y. Times, Aug. 7, 2006, at C4.

[29] Adam Kolber, posted to PrawfsBlawg, Dec 13, 2006, 10:01 a.m., at http://prawfsblawg.blogs.com/prawfsblawg.

[30] Eric Goldman, *Wikipedia's Labor Squeeze and Its Consequences*, 8 J. Telecomm. & High Tech. L. 157, 164–65 (2010).

[31] 126 S. Ct. 2749 (2006).

research papers. These tools outlined in this section allow you to do many things: organize references, format bibliographies, create your own database of selected resources, import references from library databases, and add full-text articles. There are several fee-based generic bibliographic management tools, like Endnote and Refworks.[32] There are several open source tools to assist you with managing the sources you locate as well as keeping track of citations. One of the most popular is called Zotero,[33] a Firefox add-on that allows the researcher to collect, manage and add citations and notes to sources you find on the web (both freely available sites and subscription databases). Zotero even allows you to set preferences for "Bluebook Law Review Style." There are many step-by-step guides and presentations available on the web for downloading and using Zotero.[34]

Other useful tools for managing your research are noted below. Some are add-ons to web browsers, some will only work with Windows, some are free (or a version of it is free), some allow you to store documents on their server (in the cloud), and some are quite useful.

> iCyte[35] (select and save text from a webpage or an entire page so you don't lose them even if they've been changed or deleted)
> Tinyurl[36] (create shorter and more usable urls; especially useful for those long numerical urls)
> Dropbox[37] (a good web storage service; can share documents with others)
> Sticky-Notes[38] (keep all your notes, web links, addresses, phone numbers, and other information in one place)
> Prezi[39] (presentation tool instead of PowerPoint)
> Delicious[40] (a bookmarking tool; can share your bookmarks)
> Cite-Bite[41] (link directly to quotes in webpages).

---

[32] Many universities offer one or both of these tools to students, faculty and staff. For a comparison of these products and more, see http://en.wikipedia.org/wiki/Comparison_of_reference_management_software.

[33] http://www.zotero.org.

[34] See http://prezi.com/7iy_n-igxl_p/using-zotero-for-legal-research/ or http://brooklaw.word press.com/2011/02/02/zotero. See also, Jason Puckett, *Zotero: A Guide for Librarians, Teachers and Educators* (Chicago: American Library Association, 2011).

[35] http://www.icyte.com (free for students, faculty, librarians).

[36] http://tinyurl.com.

[37] https://www.dropbox.com.

[38] http://www.sticky-notes.net.

[39] http://prezi.com.

[40] http://www.delicious.com.

[41] http://www.citebite.com.

Part Two: Commentary and Analysis

Chapter Four

Introductory and Background Sources

I. *Introduction*

When researching international and foreign law, there are some basic sources that you will use frequently and should get to know. Basic tools or background sources provide a variety of information that may be needed before delving too deeply into a research topic. You may need to:

- find a research guide on your subject;
- define basic international concepts or terms;
- locate the meaning of abbreviations or acronyms;
- find basic background information about an international organization or a specific country;
- locate relevant websites; or
- locate secondary sources (journal articles, treatises) on the topic.

Below is a list of international and foreign legal sources that provide these kinds of information. It is by no means a complete list of essential tools, so you are encouraged to examine these tools yourself and determine which ones are most useful for each research question. Moreover, keep in mind that new tools appear frequently, so checking with a law librarian may lead you to a better approach.

II. *Research Guides and Bibliographies*

Research guides and bibliographies are excellent starting points because they identify the best sources, both print and electronic, and often address research methods and strategies. Fortunately, many research guides are easily accessible on the web, and others are available in books and journal articles. These guides and bibliographies vary in scope and format. Some focus on specific countries, and others concentrate on international topics. Relevant subject headings for locating research guides and bibliographies using an online catalog[1] include the following:

legal research – [geographic area or country]
law – [geographic area or country] – bibliography
legal bibliography – [geographic area]
law – [geographic area or country]
[international organization's name] – bibliography
international agencies – bibliography
[legal topic in Library of Congress form] – [geographic area] – bibliography

Many of these terms can be used as keywords instead of in a subject search when searching an online catalog or a journal database. The *International Journal of Legal Information* regularly publishes bibliographies on countries or specific topics, making it a worthwhile tool to consult. For example, in 2010, this journal published 'Accessing Legal Information in Turkey,' and, in 2009, 'Basic Indian Legal Literature for Foreign Legal Professionals.' The journal is indexed in both LegalTrac and the *Index to Legal Periodicals and Books*, so searching journal indexes for research guides and bibliographies can pay off. (See Chapter 5 for more information on journal indexes.)

A. *Basic Research Guides*

Research guides exist in many forms, print and electronic. For an expanded list of such resources, see Chapter 6 and the topical chapters in Part VI.

- Claire Germain, *Germain's Transnational Law Research* (1991–). This single-volume loose leaf research guide contains chapters on selected international topics and covers some European countries. Each chapter lists basic sources and provides information on where to go further. Not every chapter is up to date. The chapter on French law is available on the web.[2]
- *Guide to International Legal Research* (1992–). This is one of the few paper international legal research guides that are updated annually. It is a good place to start when researching both international legal topics and selected foreign legal jurisdictions. It also provides some historical information.

---

[1] Most libraries provide access to their collections through an online catalog. This is a database that allows the researcher to locate books, journals, and other resources by author, title, subject or keyword.
[2] http://library2.lawschool.cornell.edu/encyclopedia/countries/france.

- J. Paul Lomio et al., *Legal Research Methods in a Modern World: A Coursebook* (3d ed., 2011).
- Thomas Reynolds & Arturo Flores, *Foreign Law Guide* (2000–).[3] This resource is considered one of the most important tools for foreign legal research. Covering over 175 countries and the European Union, it provides brief overviews of the legal system of each jurisdiction, sources for primary law (codes, session laws, etc.), and information on laws by topic. Where possible, it references English-language translations or sources that outline a topic in English. However, the coverage of topics is limited, and it cannot possibly answer each and every foreign legal research problem.

B. *Guides on the Web*

Many research guides are freely available on the web. Many of the sites listed below also link to other useful electronic and print guides.

- American Society of International Law (ASIL), Guide to Electronic Resources for International Law.[4] This electronic resource guide, often called the ERG, has been published online by ASIL since 1997. Since then, it has been systematically updated and continuously expanded. The chapter format of the ERG is designed to be used by students, teachers, practitioners, and researchers as a self-guided tour of relevant, high quality, up-to-date online resources covering important areas of international law.
- GlobaLex.[5] Sponsored by the Hauser Global Law School Program at NYU School of Law, GlobaLex is a website containing numerous guides to foreign and international legal research. For example, Amy Burchfield's International Criminal Courts for the Former Yugoslavia, Rwanda and Sierra Leone: A Guide to Online and Print Resources[6] provides a good listing of available sources, an overview of each court, a chart comparing the scope of each one, and other features useful for research in this area. GlobaLex's homepage divides the available guides into International, Comparative, and Foreign Law Research. Within the Foreign Law Research category, country guides appear in alphabetical order.
- United Nations Documentation: Research Guide.[7] The United Nations Documentation Research Guide can help researchers accomplish several different tasks. First, its quick links provide an easy way for experienced researchers

---

[3] http://www.foreignlawguide.com.
[4] http://www.asil.org/erghome.cfm.
[5] http://www.nyulawglobal.org/globalex.
[6] http://www.nyulawglobal.org/globalex/International_Criminal_Courts1.htm.
[7] http://www.un.org/Depts/dhl/resguide.

to get to useful UN sites, such as the collection of General Assembly resolutions. Second, the Research Guide helps researchers understand the complex UN documentation system, including document symbols and major UN databases. Third, the Research Guide offers sections of Frequently-Asked-Questions for many common research tasks. Fourth, the Research Guide also includes several topical guides (on human rights, international law, the environment, peacekeeping, etc.).

C. *Country-Specific Research Guides*

For in-depth research on a foreign country's legal system, you will benefit from the longer research guides published as books. Generally, these guides include much more detailed information than that appearing in online guides. Some of them also contain introductions to the substantive law of the foreign jurisdictions, thereby jump-starting your research. For example, John Bell's *Principles of French Law* (2d ed., 2008) provides overviews of several areas of French law, including commercial, criminal, family, and employment law. Part III of the book, "Studying French Law," provides a bibliography of French law and explains legal research methods.

To locate these kinds of materials using a library catalog, conduct the following subject search:

law – [name of country]
legal research – [name of country]

Following are selected titles on foreign legal systems. Other titles are available; you can find them by searching library catalogs as shown above.

- Sharifah Suhana Ahmad, *Malaysian Legal System* (2007). Written by a professor of Malaysian law, this book introduces Malaysian legal institutions and summarizes various areas of law, primarily commercial.
- Rose-Marie Belle Antoine, *Commonwealth Caribbean Law and Legal Systems* (2008). This book provides general information about legal systems in the Caribbean, with some discussion of the offshore financial legal sector, a commonly-researched area. The same publisher, Routledge-Cavendish, has produced topical volumes by different authors, such as *Commonwealth Caribbean Civil Procedure* (3d ed. 2009) and *Commonwealth Caribbean Tort Law* (4th ed. 2009).
- William E. Butler, *Russian Law* (3d ed. 2009). Designed as an introductory textbook on Russian law, this book gives an overview of Russian legal institutions and substantive law, but also contains a major section on resource material.

- Richard Chisholm & Garth Nettheim, *Understanding Law: An Introduction to Australia's Legal System* (8h ed. 2012). An introduction to Australia's legal system, including how laws are made, the legal profession, and other topics.
- Nigel Foster & Satish Sule, *German Legal System & Laws* (4th ed. 2010). This book, like others described above, does not address legal research directly. But its description of German law-making institutions and various areas of substantive law (constitutional, administrative, criminal, private law, and business and labor law) will help anyone doing research on German law. Also, each section is followed by a list of German and English-language sources for "Further Reading."
- Jorge A.F. Godinho, *Macau Business Law and Legal System* (2007). This book, while focused on business law (obligations, property, and some aspects of commercial law) also provides an overview of Macau's legal system and constitution.
- *Introduction to Brazilian Law* (Fabiano Deffenti & Welber Barral eds., 2011). Largely an overview of Brazilian law on basic areas of law: constitutional, administrative, property, and so on. One chapter focuses on history and sources of law for Brazil.
- *Introduction to Dutch Law* (Jeroen Chorus et al. eds., 4th rev. ed. 2006). This book combines brief overviews of Dutch legal history, culture, and the Dutch judicial system with detailed descriptions of several areas of law. Topics include private law (family, property, commercial, succession, obligations law, etc.), public law (constitutional, administrative, criminal, tax, and environmental law), and labor law.
- *Introduction to Greek Law* (Konstantinos D. Kerameus & Phaedon J. Kozyris eds., 3d rev. ed. 2008). *Introduction to Greek Law* introduces readers to the history and development of Greek law. It then describes sources and materials for Greek law, including a short "basic bibliography." Later chapters cover nearly every area of Greek law, and include bibliographies (unfortunately for most researchers, the majority of listed materials are in Greek).
- *Introduction to Turkish Law* (Tugrul Ansay & Don Wallace, Jr., eds., 2005). Following an introduction to the sources of Turkish law, including explanations of its legislative and judicial processes, the book covers numerous areas of Turkish law, including constitutional, criminal, administrative, family, property, and more. Although the book does not address legal research directly, each subject section is followed by a bibliography of useful sources (some in English, some in Turkish).
- Lovemore Madhuku, *An Introduction to Zimbabwean Law* (2010). Covers sources of law, the law-making process, courts, the legal profession and statutory interpretation.

- Elena Merino-Blanco, *The Spanish Legal System* (2d ed. 2006). This book introduces the history, sources, institutions, court structures and principles of procedure of the Spanish legal system. While the book does not directly address legal research, its extensive discussion of sources of law in Spain, the court structure, the law-making process, and related topics, will make Spanish legal research much easier to understand and undertake.
- Martin Partington, *An Introduction to the English Legal System* (6th ed. 2008). This textbook, aimed at students, provides an overview of the English legal system.
- Edilenice Passos, *Doing Legal Research in Brazil* (2001).[8] This extensive guide includes some coverage of substantive areas, lists of relevant sources, and information on legal citation. The online version is updated and links to useful web sources.
- Amos Shapira & Keren C DeWitt-Arar, *Introduction to the Law of Israel* (1995). This book outlines the history and sources of Israeli law, and it explains the institutional organization of Israel's legal system. Both of these sections give a researcher useful information with which to devise a research strategy. Subsequent chapters cover several areas of Israeli law, including constitutional, administrative, family, inheritance, tort, property, commercial, and corporate law. Sections include short bibliographies as well as footnotes. The final section is a compiled bibliography for quick reference.
- Ted Tjaden, *Legal Research and Writing* (3d ed. 2010). Unlike most of the other books on this list, *Legal Research and Writing* deals primarily with legal research. It does not cover substantive Canadian law; instead, it focuses on print and online legal research and legal writing.
- Richard Ward et al., *Walker & Walker's English Legal System* (11th ed. 2011). This standard textbook on the English legal system provides an introduction to basic institutions, laws, and legal principles, with some references to leading cases.
- Robert Watt, *Concise Legal Research* (6th ed. 2009). This book is multijurisdictional; it includes Australia, Canada, England, India, New Zealand, the United States, the European Union, and international law. Focusing on research techniques, this book describes how to research laws, cases, and regulations in several jurisdictions. It includes both paper and electronic sources.

III. *Abbreviations and Acronyms*

When using international and foreign legal materials, you will need to decipher unfamiliar acronyms and abbreviations. Below are a few sources that

---

[8] http://www.nyulawglobal.org/Globalex/Brazil1.htm.

are generally useful in solving these pesky problems. A general approach to finding the meaning of an unfamiliar abbreviation is to look first in the source where you found the abbreviation; a full title or name might have been indicated in an earlier footnote or there might be a table of abbreviations in the book or periodical. On the web, the free Cardiff Index to Legal Abbreviations[9] can sometimes provide a quick answer. Other sources to consult include periodical indexes, an index of acronyms for organizations, a legal research guide, an abbreviations list, or a dictionary of legal terms from a particular country. Searching full text law reviews (or even US case law) on LexisNexis or Westlaw can sometimes help determine the meaning of an abbreviation or at least provide some context for figuring out its meaning. Finally, searching the web with the abbreviation and the word *abbreviation* or *abbreviated* may find your answer. For example, searching *BGB abbreviated* on Google retrieves sources explaining that BGB is the abbreviation of the German Civil Code.

A. *Basic Sources*

- Abbreviations of Legal Publications[10] (Monash University). Provided by Monash University Law Library (Australia), this database is helpful for English-language law reports and a few foreign ones (e.g., *Revue de Droit International*, a French legal journal; Entscheidungen des Bundesverfassungsgerichts, a German case reporter).
- *The Bluebook: A Uniform System of Citation* (19th ed. 2010). Table 2, "Foreign Jurisdictions," provides citation rules and examples for several jurisdictions. These citation rules often include common publication abbreviations. The Bluebook is now available online by subscription.[11]
- *Cardiff Index to Legal Abbreviations*,[12] searchable by title or by abbreviation. This web-based database is an up-to-date source giving abbreviations for many English-language legal publications. The editors also include some abbreviations for sources not in English, such as "StGB" for the Strafgesetzbuch (German Criminal Code). The index covers law reports and law periodicals but also includes a few legislative publications and major textbooks.
- *Guide to Foreign and International Legal Citations* (2nd ed. 2009). This guide, created by New York University law students, is one of the most comprehensive attempts to provide standardized foreign and international legal citations.

---

[9] http://www.legalabbrevs.cardiff.ac.uk.
[10] http://www.lib.monash.edu.au/legal-abbreviations.
[11] http://www.legalbluebook.com.
[12] http://www.legalabbrevs.cardiff.ac.uk.

- *Index to Foreign Legal Periodicals* (1960–). The print version of this index includes a section called "Periodicals Indexed by Short Form," which is helpful for some publication abbreviations.
- Hildebert Kirchner, *Abkürzungsverzeichnis der Rechtssprache* (6th ed. 2008). German legal abbreviations, organized by alphabetically by title and abbreviation.
- *Noble's Revised International Guide to the Law Reports* (Scott Noble comp. & ed., 2002). This book is a good resource for case reporters from a variety of jurisdictions.
- Edmund J. Osmanczyk, *The Encyclopedia of the United Nations and International Agreements* (Anthony Mango ed. & rev., 3d ed. 2003). The index at the end of volume 4 lists many abbreviations with cross-references to their corresponding term. The main volumes also contain entries for abbreviations, again with cross-references to the full term. Also available online by subscription through Routledge Politics and International Relations database.[13]
- Donald Raistrick, *Index to Legal Citations and Abbreviations* (3d ed. 2008). This book is a good source for European abbreviations.
- Arturo L. Torres, *Latin American Legal Abbreviations: A Comprehensive Spanish/Portuguese Dictionary with English Translations* (1989). Although somewhat dated, this book is an excellent source when you know you are dealing with Latin American abbreviations.
- *World Dictionary of Legal Abbreviations* (Igor I. Kavass & Mary Miles Prince eds., 1991–). Organized alphabetically by language (German, Spanish, French, etc.), the book also covers some abbreviations by topic (United Nations, environment, maritime, military, taxation, etc.).

IV. *International and Foreign Law Terms and Phrases*

Relevant subject headings for searching online catalogs and other bibliographic databases include:

international law – dictionaries
international relations – dictionaries
law – dictionaries – [language]
international organization – dictionaries
international law – encyclopedias

---

[13] http://www.routledgeonline.com/politics/Book.aspx?id=w032.

A. *English-Language Publications*

Below is a list of books that contain English-language definitions and descriptions of international and foreign legal terms and concepts. There are many dictionaries and encyclopedias devoted to specific international topics as well (e.g., *Dictionary of International Trade* or *Encyclopedia of Human Rights*).

- Gabriel Adeleye, *World Dictionary of Foreign Expressions: A Resource for Readers and Writers* (1999). Although not focused on law, this source offers useful help with abbreviations, words, and phrases from many languages, including Afrikaans, Arabic, Chinese, Dutch, French, Greek, German, Italian, Hebrew, Hindi, Japanese, Latin, Persian, Portuguese, Russian, Spanish, Turkish, and Yiddish.
- Jacques Fomerand & LeRoy Bennett, *Historical Dictionary of the United Nations* (2007). This dictionary offers a brief list of abbreviations and acronyms, short entries on various UN issues, undertakings, entities, and individuals, and a long bibliography.
- Robert L. Bledsoe & Boleslaw A. Boczek, *The International Law Dictionary* (1987). In addition to basic definitions, entries provide the context for and the significance of each term.
- Boleslaw A. Boczek, *International Law: A Dictionary* (2005). This dictionary offers a glossary and a list of acronyms and abbreviations, followed by an unusual subject arrangement (e.g., human rights, law of treaties).
- *Max Planck Encyclopedia of Public International Law* (2008–).[14] This outstanding encyclopedia was published initially (1981–1990) in 12 installments, each of which dealt with particular subject areas. The electronic edition contains in-depth articles, arranged alphabetically by topic, on most aspects of public international law. Each article explains the basic legal principles and concepts and some provide historical information. Each article ends with a short bibliography.
- James R. Fox, *Dictionary of International and Comparative Law* (3d ed. 2003). This is a basic dictionary of international and comparative law terminology. It contains useful resources for quick definitions of unfamiliar terms.
- *Parry & Grant Encyclopaedic Dictionary of International Law* (J. Craig Barker & John P. Grant eds., 3d ed. 2009). A cross between an encyclopedia and a dictionary, this valuable reference defines and explores numerous

---

[14] http://www.mpepil.com.

international law terms, including leading cases, doctrines, jurists, treaties, and other key concepts. This source is now available by subscription.[15]

- Ernest Lindbergh, *International Law Dictionary* (1993). This book defines English, French, and German legal terms relating to international law. It is also published as *Modern Dictionary of International Legal Terms*.
- Edmund J. Osmanczyk, *The Encyclopedia of the United Nations and International Agreements* (Anthony Mango ed. & rev., 3d ed. 2003). This comprehensive, four-volume set defines an extensive list of international law, international relations, and related terms. Some entries include brief bibliographic references or citations to cases, treaties, and statutes. It also contains the text of some agreements. Also available online by subscription through Routledge Politics and International Relations database.[16]
- *United Nations Treaty Reference Guide and Glossary of Terms Related to Treaty Actions.*[17] This site provides useful, authoritative definitions of terms such as "protocol," "modus vivendi," "entry into force," and so on.

B. *Foreign-Language Equivalents*

To locate bilingual or polyglot dictionaries with English as one of the languages, use the following subject headings:

english language – dictionaries – [language]
[language] language – dictionaries – english
law – dictionaries – [language]
english language – dictionaries – polyglot
law – [country or region] – dictionaries
[subject] – dictionaries – [language or polyglot]

- Henry Saint Dahl, *Dahl's Law Dictionary: French to English/English to French: An Annotated Legal Dictionary, including Definitions from Codes, Case Law, Statutes, and Legal Writing = Dictionnaire Juridique Dahl* (3d ed. 2007). This is also available on LexisNexis.
- Henry Saint Dahl, *Dahl's Law Dictionary: Spanish-English/English-Spanish: An Annotated Legal Dictionary, including Authoritative Definitions from Codes, Case Law, Statutes, and Legal Writing = Diccionario Jurídico Dahl* (5th ed. 2010). This is also available on LexisNexis.

---

[15] http://www.oxford-internationallaw.com/?authstatuscode=202.
[16] http://www.routledgeonline.com/politics/Book.aspx?id=w032.
[17] http://treaties.un.org/Pages/Overview.aspx?path=overview/treatyRef/page1_en.xml.

- Duhaime's Legal Dictionary,[18] focus is primarily Canadian legal terminology, but it covers more.
- The English-Chinese Glossary of Legal Terms,[19] by the Department of Justice Bilingual Laws Information System.
- *English-French-Spanish-Russian Manual of the Terminology of Public International Law (Law of Peace) and International Organizations* (1983).
- European Commission, Glossary,[20] focuses on terminology related to justice in the European Union.
- Tony Foster, *Dutch Legal Terminology in English* (3d rev. and enl. ed. 2009).
- Robert Herbst, *Dictionary of Commercial, Financial and Legal Terms* (3 vols., 1998–2003).
- *West's Law and Commercial Dictionary in Five Languages: Definitions of the Legal and Commercial Terms and Phrases of American, English and Civil Law Jurisdictions* (1985).
- See also Dennis Kim-Prieto, 'En La Tierra del Ciego, el Tuerco Es Rey: Problems with Current English-Spanish Legal Dictionaries, and Notes toward a Critical Comparative Legal Lexicography,' 100 *L. Libr. J.* 251 (2008).[21]
- For more titles of multilingual and bilingual legal dictionaries, see Legal Interpreting and Translating: A Research Guide by Don Ford.[22]

V. *Background Information on an International or Foreign Legal Concept*

A. *Some General Sources*

Background information on international and foreign legal issues may be necessary at any point during your research but especially when starting a new project. In addition to the sources listed below, books and articles on the specific topic should be consulted. To locate these items, conduct subject or keyword searches in library catalogs or in periodical indices. Note that sometimes nonlegal sources might be worth checking, depending on the breadth of interest in or the interdisciplinary nature of the topic. Articles are

---

[18] http://www.duhaime.org/LegalDictionary.aspx.

[19] http://www.legislation.gov.hk/eng/glossary/homeglos.htm.

[20] http://ec.europa.eu/justice/glossary/index_en.htm.

[21] http://www.aallnet.org/main-menu/Publications/llj/LLJ-Archives/Vol-100/pub_llj_v100n02/2008-14.pdf.

[22] http://www.law.uiowa.edu/documents/pathfinders/court_interpreter.pdf.

a particularly good source for information on an event or concept, especially if it is a relatively new concept or a recent event.

- *Max Planck Encyclopedia of Public International Law* (2008–). This outstanding encyclopedia was published initially (1981–1990) in 12 installments, each of which dealt with particular subject areas. The electronic edition contains in-depth articles, arranged alphabetically by topic, on most aspects of public international law. Each article explains the basic legal principles and concepts and some provide historical information. Each article ends with a short bibliography. This publication, in a newly-revised edition, is now available online by subscription.[23]
- *Parry & Grant Encyclopaedic Dictionary of International Law* (J. Craig Barker & John P. Grant eds., 3d ed. 2009). A cross between an encyclopedia and a dictionary, this valuable reference defines and explores numerous international law terms, including leading cases, doctrines, jurists, treaties, and other key concepts. This source is now available by subscription.[24]
- *Martindale Hubbell International Law Digest* (1993–). No longer available in print, this title is available on LexisNexis (International Law > Treatises & Analytical Materials). Brief summaries of the law of nearly 70 countries, plus Canadian provinces and the European Union. Generally, each country profile covers basic legal topics such as incorporation, contracts, business regulation, succession, marriage, immigration, etc. For basic questions, such as how to enforce a foreign judgment, this source can be very helpful. The *International Law Digest* is also available free on the web.[25]
- Edmund Jan Osmaczyk, *The Encyclopedia of the United Nations and International Agreements* (Anthony Mango ed. & rev., 3d ed. 2003). This comprehensive, four-volume set defines an extensive list of international law, international relations, and related terms. Some entries include brief bibliographic references or citations to cases, treaties, and statutes. It also contains the text of some agreements.
- *Restatement of the Law, Third, Foreign Relations Law of the United States* (1987, and annual supplement). This is also available on LexisNexis and Westlaw. The *Restatement* represents the attempt of the American Law Institute (ALI) to distill the US practice and policy on foreign relations into black-letter rules. This source is helpful for identifying customary international law.

---

[23] http://www.mpepil.com.
[24] http://www.oxford-internationallaw.com.
[25] http://www.martindale.com/legal-library (select "advanced search" and choose the jurisdiction).

- *Treaties and Alliances of the World* (8th ed. 2007). This one-volume work uses a subject arrangement, dividing coverage by topics such as economic organizations and agreements, the environment, and arms control. Several chapters also take a regional approach (e.g., Africa, the Americas, South and East Asia, and the Pacific). Various entries provide summaries, descriptions, and partial or full text of treaties. If you need information on a specific treaty, start with the index.
- *Yearbook of the United Nations* (1947–). The *Yearbook of the United Nations*, using a broad subject arrangement, details the activities of the United Nations and its organs, programs, and bodies. Entries provide useful references to UN documents. The *Yearbook* is now available free on the web back to its inception.[26]

B. *Legal Encyclopedias*

The titles in this section will focus on publications that are still being published. For a list of historical titles, which may still be useful in today's research, see *Guide to International Legal Research* (2002–).

1. *International and Comparative Law Encyclopedias*

- *A Concise Encyclopedia of the United Nations* (Helmut Volger ed., 2d rev. ed. 2010). As the title suggest, this is a concise volume of UN information, including developments and reforms.
- *Encyclopedia of Human Rights* (David P. Forsythe ed., 2009). This five volume set covers human rights theory, practice, law, and history. Also available electronically.[27]
- *International Encyclopedia of Comparative Law* (1972–). This encyclopedia covers international and comparative law. The National Reports volumes cover many different countries and outline the various legal systems. The other volumes cover specific topics: business and private organizations, civil procedure, copyright and industrial property, labor law, restitution, private international law, transport, torts, and more. Some volumes are a bit dated, but overall, the set is still useful.
- *Modern Legal Systems Cyclopedia* (Kenneth R. Redden ed. 1984–). This multivolume looseleaf provides information on foreign legal jurisdictions, but the quality of the chapters varies. Most of them provide at least a history of the legal system and a description of major law-making institutions.[28]

---

[26] http://unyearbook.un.org.
[27] http://www.oxford-humanrights.com.
[28] Also available on HeinOnline in the World Constitutions Illustrated library.

- *Max Planck Encyclopedia of Public International Law* (2008–). This outstanding encyclopedia was published initially (1981–1990) in 12 installments, each of which dealt with particular subject areas. The electronic edition contains in-depth articles, arranged alphabetically by topic, on most aspects of public international law. Each article explains the basic legal principles and concepts and some provide historical information. Each article ends with a short bibliography. This publication, in a newly-revised edition, is now available by subscription.[29]
- *International Encyclopaedia of Laws* (1991–). This multivolume looseleaf set covers many different topics, including international organizations, civil procedure, commercial and economic law, constitutional law, contracts, corporations and partnerships, criminal law, environmental law, insurance law, medical law, social security law, transport law, torts, etc. Each topic provides chapters on the law for several different countries. The set is now available by subscription.[30]
- *International Encyclopaedia for Labour Law and Industrial Relations* (Roger Blanpain ed., 1977–). This multivolume looseleaf provides information about labor law and industrial relations for many countries and includes legislation. This title is also available by subscription.[31]

2. Foreign Jurisdiction Legal Encyclopedias

Some jurisdictions have comprehensive legal encyclopedias that cover a multitude of topics. They may also have specialized encyclopedias focusing on a particular subject. For more information on the availability of encyclopedias for a particular jurisdiction, consult a research guide for the jurisdiction.

- *Canadian Encyclopedic Digest* (4th ed. 2012–). There are two editions, Ontario and Western. The Ontario edition covers Ontario law, and the Western edition covers the Western provinces, with some emphasis on federal law. Also available on Westlaw Canada.
- *Encyclopédie Juridique* (date varies). This French-language looseleaf encyclopedia covers a variety of subjects in French law: civil law, civil procedure, commercial law, labor law, conflict of laws, criminal law and procedure, and more.
- *Halsbury's Laws of England* (4th ed. 1973–). This source is arranged alphabetically by topic and includes citations to both statutory and case law. The bound volumes are supplemented by annual cumulative supplements and the *Current Service*.

---

[29] http://www.mpepil.com.
[30] http://www.ielaws.com.
[31] http://www.kluwerlawonline.com/iel-laborlaw.

- *Digesto Quarta Edizione* (1988–). See also previous editions such as the *Novissimo Digesto* (1956–). Less scholarly than the *Enciclopedia Del Diritto*, this multivolume set is divided into four "Disciplines"—public law, private commercial law, private civil law, and criminal law and procedure. Topics within each set are alphabetically arranged.
- *Encyclopédie Juridique Dalloz* (edition and publication dates vary depending on topic). This collection is divided into 11 basic topics, each under the title "Répertoire de…" (e.g., *Répertoire de Droit Civil*). Each *Répertoire* is a looseleaf set containing various numbers of volumes.

VI. *Information about Foreign Legal Systems*

Subject headings for locating background information about a foreign country include:

law – [country or region]
comparative law
justice, administration of – [country or region]
legal research – [country]
courts – [country or region]

Searches can be done under specific legal topics using Library of Congress subject headings with the country or region name as a subheading (e.g., *commercial law—latin america*), or by using the country or region as a main subject heading with topical subdivisions provided by the Library of Congress as subheadings (e.g., *australia—politics and government* or *germany—constitutional law* or *italy—law and legislation*). Periodicals are another good source for background information on a country or on a specific topic.

A. *Legal Systems*

- *Accidental Tourist on the New Frontier: An Introductory Guide to Global Legal Research* (Jeanne Rehberg & Radu Popa eds., 1997). A basic research book covering international and foreign law, it includes both print and electronic sources, but treatment of electronic sources is minimal and outdated. A few specific topics are covered, including human rights, treaties, international tax, and environmental law.
- James G. Apple & Robert P. Deyling, *A Primer on the Civil-Law System* (1995).[32] This brief, well-written guide outlines the history of civil law, how

---

[32] http://www.fjc.gov/public/pdf.nsf/lookup/CivilLaw.pdf/$file/CivilLaw.pdf.

it works today, and how it compares to common law systems. Appendices include sample provisions from the French and German codes (in English), and a comparison of how the French and German systems treat a liability question.

- *Elgar Encyclopedia of Comparative Law* (Jan M. Smits ed., 2006). Covering more than 20 different jurisdictions, this book looks at comparative law methodology as well as various legal topics.
- Mary Ann Glendon et al., *Comparative Legal Traditions in a Nutshell* (3d ed. 2008). In the standard West Nutshell format, this book covers civil and common legal systems, using the British system as a paradigm of common law countries.
- H. Patrick Glenn, *Legal Traditions of the World* (2d ed. 2004). This book describes various legal traditions, rather than systems; includes aspects of Islamic, Asian, Hindu, Talmudic, and other legal traditions.
- *Information Sources in Law* (Jules Winterton & Elizabeth M. Moys eds., 2d ed. 1997). This book provides country-by-country descriptions and lists of major legal sources for Western and Eastern European countries, and for the European Union.
- *International Encyclopedia of Comparative Law* (1972–). Some volumes are dated, but it is a useful set. The volumes contain information on foreign legal systems as well as topics.
- *Introduction to Foreign Legal Systems* (Richard A. Danner & Marie-Louise H. Bernal eds., 1994). Aimed in part at legal researchers, this book covers civil law, Asian, African, and common law systems.
- *Law and Judicial Systems of Nations* (Charles S. Rhyne ed., 4th rev. ed. 2002). This book covers 193 nations and provides information about each country's practicing lawyers, hierarchy of courts, and the origins of the legal system.
- *Legal Culture in the Age of Globalization* (Lawrence M. Friedman & Rogelio Pérez-Perdomo eds., 2003). This book provides interesting chapters on the legal systems of various Latin jurisdictions: Argentina, Brazil, Italy, Puerto Rico, etc.
- *Legal Systems of the World: A Political, Social, and Cultural Encyclopedia* (Herbert M. Kritzer ed., 2002). This four-volume set covers more than 400 legal systems and key concepts. Each country profile includes general information about the country, its history, information on the court structure, the evolution of its legal framework, the impact that the legal system has had on the country, and more. It includes references and a bibliography.
- *Mixed Legal Systems at New Frontiers* (Esin Örücü ed., 2010). This title has chapters on mixed systems in general, and then focuses on a few specific systems, including Commonwealth Caribbean, Navajo, Turkey,

South Africa, Sri Lanka, England and Ireland, and the European Union. Treatment in some of the covered jurisdictions is confined to one narrow topic, however, such as intestate secession in South Africa, or trusts in Sri Lanka.

- *Modern Legal Systems Cyclopedia* (Kenneth R. Redden ed., 1984–). This multivolume looseleaf provides information on foreign legal jurisdictions, but the quality of the chapters varies. Most of them provide at least a history of the legal system and a description of major law-making institutions.[33]
- John H. Merryman et al., *The Civil Law Tradition: Europe, Latin America, and East Asia* (1994). Although written as a casebook, this 1,278–page text describes the history and modern status of various civil law systems in depth.
- Thomas Reynolds & Arturo Flores, *Foreign Law Guide* (2000–). This resource is considered one of the most important tools for foreign legal research. Covering over 175 countries and the European Union, it provides brief overviews of the legal system of each jurisdiction, sources for primary law (codes, session laws, etc.), and information on laws by topic. Where possible, it references English-language translations or sources that outline a topic in English. However, the coverage of topics is limited and it cannot possibly answer each and every foreign legal research problem. The *Foreign Law Guide* is available by subscription only.[34]
- United Nations, *Core Document Forming Part of the Reports of States Parties*, U.N. Doc. HRI/Core/[country abbreviation]/[year]. This document provides information on the general constitutional, political and legal structure of the State. See the example at U.N. Doc. HRI/Core/ AGO/2008.[35]
- *Nations of the World.*[36] This Library of Congress site includes some information about the legal system as well as other general country information.
- *JuriGlobe World Legal Systems.*[37] This University of Ottawa website provides a quick overview of the major legal systems of the world (civil law, common law, etc.). You can also use this site's map to find out what kind of legal system a country has. In addition, the site provides some interesting statistical information on the number of civil law systems, mixed systems, etc.
- *Government Gazettes Online.*[38] This site is maintained by the University of Michigan. Each country entry provides the following information: title

---

[33] Also available on HeinOnline in the World Constitutions Illustrated library.
[34] http://www.foreignlawguide.com.
[35] http://www2.ohchr.org/english/bodies/coredocs.htm.
[36] http://www.loc.gov/law/help/guide/nations.php.
[37] http://www.juriglobe.ca/eng/index.php.
[38] http://www-personal.umich.edu/~graceyor/doctemp/gazettes/index.htm.

of the gazette, URL, languages, access (free or fee), dates, searchability, format (HTML, PDF, etc.), and the description of contents of the gazette. Note that this website does not cover every country. One major convenience of the website, however, is its links to online gazettes.

- *Guide to Foreign and International Databases.*[39] The law librarians at New York University maintain this guide, which lists good-quality free and fee-based databases for foreign and international legal research. The section on Foreign Databases by Jurisdiction is particularly useful for learning what resources are available for a particular country.

B. *General Reference Sources*

These sources provide some basic information and brief overviews. While they do not provide detailed information needed for in-depth research, they can answer some basic questions and provide leads for more information.

- *Columbia Gazetteer of the World* (2008). This is an encyclopedia of geographical places and features, including information on country geography, political conditions, and economic information. It is also available electronically.[40]
- *The Europa World Year Book* (1989–). This two-volume set (also available as an online database) covers over 200 countries. Country chapters include basic information about each country's constitution, government, legislature, political organizations, religion, media, finance, trade, industry, transport and tourism. Europa Publications also publishes eight regional surveys, such as *Africa South of the Sahara*, *Central America and the Caribbean*, and *Eastern Europe, Russia and Central Asia*. It is also available electronically by subscription.[41]
- *The Statesman's Yearbook* (1864–). Also available electronically,[42] this annual reference source provides authoritative, basic information about countries of the world. Country profiles include political, economic, demographic, and historical information.
- *The World Almanac and Book of Facts* (1886–). This annual reference work is also available electronically by subscription.[43] Much more focused on the United States than *The Statesman's Yearbook*, above, it contains basic

---

[39] http://www.law.nyu.edu/library/research/foreign_intl/index.htm.
[40] http://www.columbiagazetteer.org/main/Home.html.
[41] http://www.europaworld.com.
[42] http://www.statesmansyearbook.com.
[43] http://www.worldalmanac.com.

statistics about countries and summarizes the world's history (in addition to a lot of non-foreign information).
- *The World Factbook* (1981–). This annual publication from the Central Intelligence Agency is also available without charge on the web.[44] It provides basic information on countries of the world, including form of government, economy, politics, infrastructure, etc.

Some useful websites include:

- *Country Studies* (Library of Congress).[45] This series of profiles of foreign countries offers brief information on each country's historical background, geography, society, economy, transportation and telecommunications, government and politics, and national security. These Country Studies were written between 1988 and 1998; shorter but more current Country Profiles are available for fewer countries.[46]
- *Foreign Governments* (Northwestern University).[47] This site provides links to the official websites of national governments, including selected ministries, departments, offices, etc.

VII. *Background Information on International Organizations*

You can find a great deal of information about international organizations at their own websites. At times, however, you will need more detailed or more impartial information. Subject searches on online catalogs, bibliographic databases, and periodical indexes, using the name of the organization, are useful for finding descriptions of international organizations. Yearbooks and dictionaries are excellent sources to check for this type of information. To locate information and materials by an international organization, use the organization's name as an author. Yearbooks and encyclopedias are also good sources for charters and constituting documents for international organizations.

For more assistance in researching international organizations, see Part V of this text; see also the ASIL Guide to Electronic Resources for International Law, International Organizations.[48]

---

[44] https://www.cia.gov/library/publications/the-world-factbook.

[45] http://memory.loc.gov/frd/cs.

[46] http://memory.loc.gov/frd/cs/profiles.html.

[47] http://www.library.northwestern.edu/libraries-collections/evanston-campus/government-information/international-documents/foreign.

[48] http://www.asil.org/intorg1.cfm.

- *Encyclopedia of Associations: International Organizations* (1989–). This encyclopedia is available electronically by subscription.[49] It gives basic information on over 22,000 multinational, binational, and foreign associations. If you can't find an organization on the Internet, this source is worth checking.
- *The Europa World Year Book* (1989–). This two-volume set (also available as a fee-based online database) covers over 200 countries. Country chapters include basic information about each country's constitution, government, legislature, political organizations, religion, media, finance, trade, industry, transport, and tourism. Europa Publications also publishes eight regional surveys, such as *Africa South of the Sahara, Central America and the Caribbean,* and *Eastern Europe, Russia and Central Asia.*[50]
- *International Information: Documents, Publications, and Information Systems of International Governmental Organizations* (Peter I. Hajnal ed., 2d ed. 1997). This two-volume set lists basic documents and publications of various international organizations, particularly the United Nations. Some citation examples are included.
- *Introduction to International Organizations* (Lyonette Louis-Jacques & Jeanne S. Korman eds., 1996). Written from a researcher's perspective, this book describes the United Nations and other international organizations, including regional ones.
- Giuseppe Schiavone, *International Organizations: A Dictionary and Directory* (6th ed. 2005). Each entry in this book provides a description of the organization, including origin and development, objectives, structure, and activities. Information on the headquarters, web address, and publications is also included.
- Robert V. Williams, *The Information Systems of International Inter-Governmental Organizations: A Reference Guide* (1998). One of the more recent guides, this book covers electronic sources in addition to paper sources. Although the discussion of electronic sources is largely outdated, the book nonetheless offers useful information on IGOs' organization and documentation. Part I discusses the United Nations and many of its subsidiary or related organizations, while Part II is "everything else," including regional organizations as diverse as ECOWAS (Economic Community of West African States) and the International Coffee Organization.
- *Yearbook of International Organizations* (1967–). Also available electronically by subscription,[51] this multivolume set covers both intergovernmental and nonprofit international organizations. Entries usually list contact

---

[49] http://www.gale.cengage.com.
[50] http://www.europaworld.com.
[51] http://www.uia.be/yearbook.

information, including officers if available; date organization was created; aims and activities; members (if the organization is intergovernmental); and other information. It is useful when the organization's website is unavailable or incomplete.

Some relevant websites include:

- EISIL (Electronic Information System for International Law).[52] EISIL, sponsored by the American Society of International Law (ASIL), is a database of carefully annotated links to key sources in international law. It functions as an easy starting point on the web for researchers seeking international legal materials. EISIL allows you to browse the database by topic (such as international economic, criminal, or environmental law) or to search the site using titles, popular names, keywords, dates, or other information. The records in EISIL link to primary documents, the best websites on the topic, and research guides. The "More Information" button by each entry leads to a record that provides considerable added information, such as a legal citation, alternate titles or popular names, a description of the document or website, and relevant dates (signature or entry into force dates).
- International Organizations website (Northwestern University).[53] This site is intended to offer a comprehensive list of links to intergovernmental organizations' (IGOs') websites. It is arranged alphabetically.
- International Organization Information (University of Colorado).[54] This site, like the Northwestern University site above, offers a list of IGOs. Some links connect to guides, but the list of links is not as comprehensive as Northwestern's.
- Materials on International Governmental Organizations (Michigan State University).[55] Written for library patrons at Michigan State University, this guide to IGO materials can also help Internet researchers. It identifies and explains major information sources on IGOs. Its focus is primarily on the United Nations, but some regional IGOs are included.

VIII. *Journal Literature*

Journal literature is a good way to get information on a topic, find a treaty citation, locate the text of a foreign law, learn the meaning of a term, figure

---

[52] http://www.eisil.org.
[53] http://libguides.northwestern.edu/IGO.
[54] http://ucblibraries.colorado.edu/govpubs/int/internat.htm.
[55] http://libguides.lib.msu.edu/internationalgovernmentorganizations.

out what an abbreviation stands for, etc. For more information on locating journal articles using indexes and full-text databases, see Chapter 5.

IX. *Citing International and Foreign Legal Materials*

Unfortunately, there is not a single good source for how to cite to international and foreign legal materials. You can find wide variations in citation styles used even in the "Bluebook journals," such as *Harvard Law Review* and *Yale Law Journal*. Use the sources listed below for some guidance. Keep in mind that the citation should provide enough information to enable someone to find the source being cited. Also, be consistent throughout the document. For more help, ask a librarian for assistance.

- *Australian Guide to Legal Citation* (3d ed. 2010). The AGLC may also be downloaded as a PDF document for viewing only.[56]
- *The Bluebook: A Uniform System of Citation* (19th ed. 2010). This is the standard US legal citation guide, but it also includes basic information on the documentation of international organizations and some foreign jurisdictions.
- *Canadian Guide to Uniform Legal Citation = Manuel Canadien de la Référence Juridique* (7th ed. 2010).
- *Guide to Foreign and International Legal Citations* (2d ed. 2009).
- Shabtai Rosenne, *Practice and Methods of International Law* 23–26, 53–54, 105–07, 121–22 (1984).
- *The Chicago Manual of Style* (16th ed. 2010).

When all else fails, check how others are citing a law or other document by conducting a search in full-text law review files on LexisNexis or Westlaw.

X. *Current Awareness Sources*

Journals and newspapers, blogs, news wires, newsletters, and press releases, are all appropriate sources for keeping abreast of new developments in international and foreign law. International and comparative law journals and looseleaf services are useful for up-to-date information on legal activities worldwide. Looseleaf services on international and foreign law-related topics often include a "current reports" section that contains new information.

---

[56] http://mulr.law.unimelb.edu.au/go/AGLC3.

Many of these services now offer electronic versions with weekly updates. Key subject headings for locating periodicals in catalogs are:

international law – periodicals
comparative law – periodicals
[international organization] – periodicals
law – [country or region] – periodicals
[legal topic in Library of Congress form] – [country or region] – periodicals

- *American Journal of Comparative Law* (1952–). This is also available from HeinOnline.[57]
- *American Journal of International Law* (1907–). This is also available from HeinOnline and JSTOR.[58]
- *ASIL's International Law in Brief.* This is an electronic only newsletter that tracks developments in international law, including case law. Free e-mail subscription.[59]
- *Global Legal Monitor* (Law Library of Congress). Only available electronically, this site tracks legal developments around the world.[60]
- *International Enforcement Law Reporter* (1985–). This is a monthly newsletter that tracks and summarizes key developments in international law and related areas. Topic areas generally include money laundering, drug trafficking, taxation, extradition, asset forfeiture, human rights, cybercrime, and intellectual property. It is also available on LexisNexis.

Blogs and electronic discussion lists are good sources for staying abreast of current topics as well as new laws, resources, and websites. For more information, see Chapter 3.

---

[57] http://heinonline.org.
[58] http://www.jstor.org.
[59] http://www.asil.org/ilibmenu.cfm.
[60] http://www.loc.gov/lawweb/servlet/lloc_news.

Chapter Five

Beyond Background Sources: Books, Journal Articles and More

I. *Introduction*

Researching international, foreign and comparative law can be a confusing mess of treaties, documents, unfamiliar legal concepts, and varied sources. The sources of information range from recognized treaty law to more ephemeral materials from non-governmental organizations to even more hard-to-find foreign regulations. Because of this, it makes sense for you to look for commentary and analysis (books, articles, reports, and other secondary sources) to help set the context and identify relevant law. Reviewing commentary and analysis early in the research process lets you accomplish many key tasks, such as:

- getting an introduction or overview of a topic, often with citations to other sources and relevant laws and regulations;
- familiarizing yourself with terms of art, acronyms, and other vocabulary within your topic;
- verifying or learning pieces of information, such as dates or names; and
- learning about new legal developments.

II. *Bibliographic Databases and Online Catalogs*

International, foreign and comparative law and related commentaries are growing at an amazing rate. While many researchers are turning to the web for access to primary sources, secondary sources are still primarily in print and there is no sign of this changing, even with the major digitization projects that are underway.

To see what's available on a topic, you can search the catalogs of your own library as well as catalogs of libraries from around the country—even around the world. The major bibliographic database in the United States is OCLC (the Online Computer Library Center).[1] OCLC includes the records of academic libraries, law firm libraries, and smaller libraries in the US and a few from other countries. WorldCat is OCLC's catalog of books and other materials. A subscription version with advanced search features is available in many academic and public libraries in the United States. There is also a free web version.[2]

On the free version, the Advanced Search allows you to perform more precise searches than does the main search page. For example, the Advanced Search page lets you look for books published within a specified date range and in a particular language. Researchers may still want to use the version of WorldCat available at major libraries, however, because it allows for even more search options, such as searching for particular publishers or series titles.

Many bibliographic databases and online catalogs use standard Library of Congress Subject Headings (LCSH). The purpose of these standardized headings is to help researchers find all the available catalog entries on their topic. The Library of Congress Classification outline is available on the web.[3] Since the print LCSH volumes are unwieldy, most catalogs provide keyword searching which allows you to locate some materials on your topic and then determine the appropriate subject heading. For example, if you want to locate books on diplomatic immunities, you can start by using this phrase as a keyword search. By doing this search, you can determine that the relevant subject headings are: *diplomats—legal status, laws, etc.; diplomats—protection*; and *diplomatic privileges and immunities*. By looking at the records for books with these subjects, you will also see references to the Vienna Convention on Diplomatic Relations (1961), which you can use as a search term to locate more resources.

Most library catalogs not only offer keyword and subject searching, but also allow you to search by author and title. Therefore, if you know of one book on your topic, you can find others by searching by the subject headings associated with that one source. Most catalogs also allow you to limit your search by language, date, and material type (book, journal, electronic resource, etc.). Some catalogs provide even more advanced features, such as tables of contents, links to electronic versions of the materials, and the ability to download and save records.

Libraries from around the world, including the Library of Congress,[4] have made their catalogs available via the web. See also the European Library (a web

[1] http://www.oclc.org/us/en/default.htm.
[2] http://www.oclc.org/us/en/worldcat/default.htm.
[3] http://www.loc.gov/catdir/cpso/lcco.
[4] http://catalog.loc.gov.

service of Europe's National Libraries) which provides access to the online public catalogs of national libraries in Europe, national bibliographies, and other useful information.[5] Another way to locate a library in another country is to consult Libweb—it "lists over 8000 pages from libraries in 146 countries countries."[6]

Not only can you locate books on point by searching library catalogs, publishers and bookstores make information available on the web as well. For example, Amazon.com permits searching inside some of the books it offers for sale. Many publishers let researchers see tables of contents for books on their websites.

Google Book Search (Google Books)[7] has become an important tool for identifying useful commentary on international and foreign law. One major shortcoming of library catalogs is that their information—subject headings, book titles, and even chapter titles—doesn't always tell the researcher whether the full text of the book contains useful material. To some extent, Google Book Search overcomes those limitations, because researchers can unearth aspects of books (brief discussions, footnotes, case studies, etc.) that may not be reflected in library catalog records.

As with most database interfaces, researchers should select the "Advanced" option for better control of searching. The Advanced Search interface in Google Books provides familiar Google options (phrase searching, excluding terms), but also adds some options specific to book searching. These include an ability to restrict searches to particular subject areas, and to search for particular authors and titles. The author-title options can help researchers figure out if a known book covers the topic in which they're interested.

Of course, Google Book Search does not include every book published. You might find that it has no information on a particular book you'd like to know more about. Or, if you're just searching for books on a topic, such as "ex gratia payments," Google Book Search could give you the false impression that there is no book covering that topic. Google Books can also frustrate researchers by indicating that a book is relevant, but then refusing to show any text from the book, or just a short "snippet." Often, pages or whole chapters are searchable, but not viewable. (These restrictions arise from copyright limitations and publisher decisions.) A final frustration is that Google Books does not permit the user to copy or print text. Nonetheless, researchers should become familiar with Google Book Search and know when to use it.

Searching these catalogs and websites can prove to be overwhelming because of the amount of literature available on any given topic. Therefore, compiled bibliographies and research books and guides can be handy when beginning

---

[5] http://search.theeuropeanlibrary.org/portal/en/index.html.

[6] http://lists.webjunction.org/libweb.

[7] http://books.google.com.

a research project. As noted in Chapter 3, these tools guide researchers to the best sources on a topic or for a particular jurisdiction. Some of these bibliographies are available in print and electronic formats. Here are some sources worth consulting:

> *Public International Law: A Current Bibliography of Articles* (Berlin; New York: Springer-Verlag, 1975–).[8]
> Thomas Reynolds & Auturo Flores, *Foreign Law Guide* (1989–).
> *Szladits' Bibliography on Foreign and Comparative Law: Books and Articles in English* ([1790–APR. 1, 1953]–1998).
> *United Nations Library, Bibliographie Mensuelle = Monthly Bibliography* (1998–).

Concise subject or country specific bibliographies are also available in journal literature. Many journals contain regular sections containing book reviews, lists of books received, and bibliographies. Some examples include:

> *American Journal of Comparative Law* (1952–). See the "book review" and "books received" sections.
> *American Journal of International Law* (1907–). The section called "Recent Books on International Law" contains book reviews and books of briefer notice, and a list of books received.[9]
> *Journal of International Economic Law* (1998–) regularly contains comprehensive bibliographies, an annual book survey that covers more than international economic law, and a web survey of new and important websites.
> *Revue de Droit Africain: Doctrine & Jurisprudence* (2002–). See "recension bibliographique et informations."
> *Revue Internationale de Droit Comparé* ([1949?–]). See the "Informations and Bibliographie" section.
> *Refugee Survey Quarterly* (1994–). Each issue contains a bibliography, selected web sources, abstracts of publications, and publications received.

In addition to these regular publications, you can locate feature articles providing extensive bibliographies on topics, countries, or regions. For example: Ingrid Kost, 'Bibliography on the Katanga Case,' 23 *Leiden J. Int'l L.* 375 (2010) (compiling articles on the ICC case against Congolese warlord Germain Katanga); Karen Willyams, 'Bibliography of Books and Articles on International Law Relevant to New Zealand,' 3 *N.Z. Y.B. Int'l L.* 281 (2006); and William Bradford, 'International Legal Compliance: Surveying the Field,' 36 *Geo. J. Int'l L.* 495 (2005). Searching the journal indexes discussed below is a good way to locate these articles.

---

[8] http://www.mpil.de/ww/en/pub/library/catalogues_databases/doc_of_articles/pil.cfm.
[9] Available on Heinonline and JSTOR.

III. *Journal Literature*

Locating journal articles is an important part of international, foreign and comparative legal research. You should not rely solely on full-text law reviews on LexisNexis and Westlaw. Many journals on international, foreign, and comparative law are not included in either LexisNexis or Westlaw. Thorough research requires using journal indexes to locate relevant literature. Keep in mind that you may find articles on your topic in both law and law-related journal indexes. Many international and foreign law topics are cross-disciplinary in nature and require researching in law-related fields, such as public policy, international relations, economics, etc.

Like books, journal articles will usually point to relevant sources of law, key concepts, and legal developments. One approach to finding articles is to use a full-text database of law journal articles, such as the ones available on LexisNexis and Westlaw. This approach works well if your topic includes a term rarely used in the database (e.g., Ibos, janjaweed).

If you are working with more common terms, however, you may find that searching in full-text databases gets too many irrelevant results. You can limit your results in both LexisNexis and Westlaw Terms and Connectors searching by requiring your search term to appear in the article's title. On LexisNexis, you do this by using the "title" segment. On Westlaw, use the "title" field. You can access these segments and fields by using a drop-down menu on the main search screen.

Another way to increase the relevance of your results in both Westlaw and LexisNexis's database of full-text law reviews is to use the "atleast" feature. You can add an "atleast" restriction to your Terms and Connectors searches, using any number you choose. This feature requires that any document you retrieve uses a term "at least" the specified number of times. Thus, for example, if you are looking for articles that deal with the OECD guidelines for multinational enterprises, you can get better results by searching *OECD w/s "guidelines for multinational enterprises" and atleast 20 (OECD)* than by searching *OECD w/s "guidelines for multinational enterprises."* Articles retrieved by the former search will use the term "OECD" at least twenty times, which means their discussion is likely to be more than just a passing reference or footnote.

When using the "atleast" feature, you should experiment with different numbers to see what number seems to provide the best tradeoff between relevance and precision. In other words, as you increase the number, you will have fewer results to review and fewer irrelevant documents (greater precision), but you might miss some relevant articles. Also, you must be careful to think through your choice of terms to require in the "atleast" feature. Often, authors will use a shorter designation, such as an acronym, for a key term. In the example of the OECD guidelines above, an author might use the full name of the "guidelines for multinational enterprises" in the article's introduction, but then indicate that the guidelines will be referred to as "The Guidelines" for the rest of the article. Similarly, an article about the Convention on the Elimination of All Forms of Discrimination against Women is likely to use the acronym "CEDAW" or even "The Convention" rather than repeat the full title of the treaty. Unfortunately, limiting your search to articles that include your term in their title, or that use your search term a minimum number of times, can cause you to miss relevant articles. Often, a better approach than full-text searching is to use a legal periodical index, such as *Index to Legal Periodicals* (ILP) or LegalTrac, also called *Legal Resource Index* (LRI) or *Current Law Index*. LegalTrac is available on LexisNexis and Westlaw; *Index to Legal Periodicals* is available on the web only. Although paper versions of periodical indexes are still being printed, use an online version whenever possible. Online versions combine records from large time periods; if you use a paper version, you must repeat your search in several volumes.

Periodical indexes can also make up for shortcomings in your search terms. For example, you might search *"corporal punishment" w/p child w/p "human rights"* in Westlaw's JLR database, and miss articles that use the UK/European term "chastisement." In *Legal Resource Index*, however, an indexer has given all these articles the subject heading or descriptor "corporal punishment," so your search would pick them up.

Once you have identified the relevant articles using the indexes, you will need to search a library catalog (by the title of the journal) to determine if an institution owns the print or provides access to the electronic version of a journal or both.

A. *Legal Journal Indexes*

Index to Legal Periodicals and Books (ILP) (1981–present) contains citations from more than 820 legal periodicals from 1981 from the United States, Canada, Ireland, Great Britain, Australia and New Zealand. The print edition covers 1908 to present. The *Index to Legal Periodicals and Books* and *Index to Legal Periodicals Retrospective* (1918–1981) are both available on the web from EBSCO.[10]

Legal Resource Index (LRI) indexes approximately 800 legal publications from the United States, Canada, Great Britain, New Zealand and Australia. It also covers law related articles from more than 1,000 additional business and general interest periodicals. Coverage begins in 1980 and is updated monthly.

---

[10] Wilson has merged with EBSCO and it is unclear if the retrospective collection will be available from EBSCO, http://www.ebscohost.com/public/index-to-legal-periodicals-books.

It is available in print as *Current Law Index,* on LexisNexis and Westlaw, and as Legaltrac on the web.

Index to Foreign Legal Periodicals (IFLP) is a multilingual index to articles and book reviews appearing in approximately 500 legal journals published worldwide. The print edition covers 1960 to present and the electronic version covers 1985 to present. IFLP is available in print and on HeinOnline. The electronic version links to the full-text articles when they are available on HeinOnline and the entire print index is digitized back to 1960.

Legal Journals Index (LJI) indexes approximately 485 journals from the UK & Europe. Coverage is from 1986 on. The print versions of this index (*Legal Journals Index* and *European Legal Journals Index)* were discontinued in 1999. *Legal Journals Index* is available on Westlaw and through Current Legal Information on the web.

Current Index to Legal Periodicals (CILP) provides access to approximately 475 university legal publications and other law journals. It's a good way to update your research since it indexes journals 4–6 weeks before they are picked up by ILP and LRI. It is available on the web through the University of Washington Law Library and Westlaw.

B. *Law-related Journal Indexes*

Other indexes that focus on law-related topics can also be of use when doing international and foreign legal research. These include EconLit (journals on economics), First Search (contains many different databases arranged by topic), International Political Science Abstracts (indexes journals related to political science), Worldwide Political Science Abstracts (another index to political science literature), and PAIS International (covers international relations, political science, and social sciences). Firstsearch provides access to ArticlesFirst and ECO, an OCLC collection of scholarly journals. Most of these indexes are available at college and university libraries.

When you are researching certain areas of human rights, humanitarian law, international trade, and environmental law, to name a few, journal literature from the social sciences can be very useful. For example, when researching humanitarian law, you may need to get some background sources on basic humanitarian principles. This kind of information is easier to locate using PAIS International or a social science index than in the legal literature.

C. *Full-text Journal Articles*

In addition to journal indexes, there are many collections of full-text journal articles. These include databases provided by publishers, like Cambridge University Press or Oxford University Press, which provide access only to the journals they publish. There are specialty collections, including *Contemporary Women's Issues*[11] (provides information on women's issues around the world), *Ethnic NewsWatch* (a collection of the newspapers and journals of the ethnic, minority, and native press), and *GenderWatch* (focuses on the impact of gender across a broad spectrum of subject areas). And there are journal databases such as *HeinOnline* (a retrospective collection of legal journals), *JSTOR* (backfiles of many scholarly journals from a variety of disciplines) and *Project Muse* (access to over 100 scholarly full-text journals in the humanities and social sciences).

Another approach is to start by finding a relevant journal. You can find numerous periodicals on international law topics or the law of a particular country. To find the titles of these periodicals, search your library catalog with subject headings, such as *comparative law—periodicals* or *international law—periodicals*.

Once you identify a relevant periodical, look for an index either specific to the publication, such as an annual end-of-the-year index, or a broader periodical index that covers the periodical you need. The journal indexes listed above allow you to search for the title of a journal to see if it is included.

You can supplement searches in full-text Westlaw and LexisNexis databases, as well as searches in legal periodical indexes, by using Google Scholar. Like Google Book Search, Google Scholar enables full-text searching of content, though it may not allow you to retrieve that content. Use the Advanced Search interface in Google Scholar; like the Advanced Search in Google Books, this interface lets you look for works by particular authors or with particular titles.

D. *Other Web Resources*

A few free indexes (or similar tools) are available on the web. For example, the Max Planck Institute for Comparative Public Law and International Law's OPAC contains information on articles and books since 1996. You can search the catalog or you can browse the classifications for public international law, comparative law, or municipal law.

For example, if you select "Rvgl 2.8.5. Other Basic Rights [Right to Petition see 2.3.; Conscientious Objection see 6.8.4.; Right of Asylum see 5.2.]" from the classification, you can get a list of articles (in a variety of languages) on the topic. When you select one of the articles from the list, you retrieve a complete record for the item, which helps you locate the full article online or in print.

---

[11] http://www.gale.cengage.com.

Washington & Lee Law School also provides a database called "Current Law Journal Content."[12] Here you can search the contents of 1268 journal content pages, although nothing new will be added after May 13, 2011. This database doesn't provide access to the full-text of the articles, but it provides enough information for you to obtain the article either in print or from another electronic source like LexisNexis or Westlaw.

You can also consult the catalogs or recent acquisitions lists from libraries or institutes with reputations for being the leading institutions in a particular field. As noted above, the Max Planck Institute is a good model. Others include the Peace Palace Library[13] and the Swiss Institute for Comparative Law.[14]

IV. *Working Papers, Reports and other Scholarly Publications*

The desire to access working and research papers, reports, and other publications in the social sciences has grown with increased availability of scholarly publishing on the web. Several services have become available, some for a fee, and many academic institutions, think tanks, and international organizations have also made these materials available. Often, these works are a good way to penetrate the research available on current topics. Some working and research papers are available full-text in a variety of formats (PDF, HTML, or Word); others may only have abstracts and the documents must be ordered or located in a library. *Social Science Research Network* (SSRN)[15] provides electronic journal abstracts and working papers for law and social sciences.

Working paper collections provide a good source for commentary on new and fast developing topics. For instance, suppose you want to find recent scholarly articles on the killing of Bin Laden. A quick search using Bin Laden in both the title and the abstract field yields many recent pieces.

Many law schools are posting collections of working papers by their faculty and visiting scholars and students. The Hauser Global Law School Program at NYU provides access to several working paper collections: Global Law Working Papers, Human Rights and Global Justice Working Papers, Jean Monnet Working Papers, and Institute for International Law and Justice Working Papers.[16] Here are a few of the 2010 papers from Jean Monnet Working Papers series, all of which are freely available in PDF: From Expert Administration

---

12 http://lawlib.wlu.edu/cljc.
13 http://www.ppl.nl.
14 http://www.isdc.ch.
15 http://www.ssrn.com.
16 http://www.law.nyu.edu/global/index.htm.

to Accountability Network: A New Paradigm for Comparative Administrative Law; Collective Exit Strategies: New Ideas in Transnational Labour Law; Adjusting Differences and Accommodating Competences: Family Matters in the European Union.

Individual law professors are posting their recent scholarly articles on their own websites, through SSRN, and on their law school's website. In fact, some professors are making articles and other documents freely available on their personal websites.

Think tanks, centers, and institutes also provide access to this kind of literature. The Brookings Institute, the National Bureau of Economic Research, and the Center for Migration and Development are just a few examples of such institutions that provide access to much of their commentary and analysis for free. Since there is no way to list all of the possible collections, use web searches to retrieve these working paper collections.

To learn about new working papers and reports, take a look at DocuTicker, "a hand-picked selection of resources, reports and publications from government agencies, NGOs, think tanks and other public interest organizations."[17] Once you find a new individual document, you might also stumble across an entire collection, such as the bepress Legal Repository.[18]

With so much commentary and analysis available in print, online through subscription databases, and through publicly available websites, there is no way to locate everything with one simple search. A variety of sources and tools—library catalogs, journal indexes, websites, and other databases—all need to be consulted. Nor should you be satisfied with the sources just in law. Once you have identified these secondary sources, you also must be careful to evaluate the information you find, especially from websites. For more information on evaluating what you find on the web, see Chapter 3.

---

[17] http://www.docuticker.com.
[18] http://law.bepress.com/repository.

Part Three: International Law

Chapter Six

Treaties and International Agreements

I. *Introduction*

Treaties can be referred to by a number of different names: international conventions, international agreements, covenants, final acts, charters, protocols, pacts, accords, and constitutions for international organizations. Usually these different names have no legal significance in international law. Treaties may be bilateral (two parties) or multilateral (between more than two parties), and a treaty is usually only binding on the parties to the agreement. An agreement "enters into force" (becomes binding) when the terms for entry into force, as specified in the agreement, are met. Bilateral treaties usually enter into force when both parties agree to be bound as of a certain date.

For assistance with basic treaty law and practice as well as definitions of key terms used in treaties and agreements, see the UN *Treaty Handbook*.[1]

For basic information on treaties, see Thomas Buergenthal & Sean Murphy, *Public International Law in a Nutshell* (4th ed. 2007) or see the chapters on the law of treaties in the *Encyclopedia of Public International Law*.[2]

When researching treaties, you will usually need to find the following information:

1. *The text of the treaty.* If you already know the treaty you want, you will often find it quickly using a web search engine. Finding a treaty by subject, or finding out whether a treaty exists at all, is much harder, and usually requires using secondary sources.

2. *The parties to the treaty* (or at least whether the countries in which you are interested are parties), and the treaty's effective date. This piece of your research is called "status information." For major treaties, such as

---

[1] http://treaties.un.org/pages/Publications.aspx?pathpub=Publication/TH/Page1_en.xml.
[2] Available by subscription, http://www.mpepil.com.

the Geneva Convention, you can find status information fairly easily on the websites of intergovernmental or nongovernmental organizations. It is harder to find accurate status information for less important treaties or for recent ones.

When researching treaty status, you will see countries listed as "signatories" or "parties" or both. Generally, the number of parties to a treaty is more important in international law than the number of signatories.

Signing a treaty, for most countries, means that they will *begin* the process of ratifying the treaty. The United States may sign a treaty but never ratify it, or may sign a treaty and ratify it much later. For example, the United States signed the Genocide Convention in 1948 but did not ratify it for 40 years. If a country signs a treaty but needs to take further steps for ratification, it must in the meantime refrain from acts that would defeat the object and purpose of the treaty.

Interpreting status information takes a little practice. For example, following is partial status information on the United Nations Convention against Illicit Traffic in Narcotic Drugs and Psychotropic Substances, taken from *Multilateral Treaties Deposited with the Secretary-General:*[3]

Participant [i.e., party]	Signature	Ratification, Accession (a), Acceptance (A), Approval (AA), Formal confirmation (c), Succession (d)
Bosnia and Herzegovina		1 Sep 1993 d
Fiji		25 Mar 1993 a
Finland	8 Feb 1989	15 Feb 1994 A
France	13 Feb 1989	31 Dec 1990 AA
Gabon	20 Dec 1989	
Ghana	20 Dec 1988	10 Apr 1990

The negotiating parties concluded the Convention on December 20, 1988. Ghana signed on that date, and ratified it two years later. The Convention was "open for signature" until December 20, 1989. During that period, Finland, France, and Gabon signed it. Subsequently, Finland "accepted" the treaty, and France "approved" it. (Acceptance and approval refer to

---

[3] http://treaties.un.org/pages/ViewDetails.aspx?src=TREATY&mtdsg_no=VI-19&chapter=6&lang=en.

two different internal procedures by which countries can submit to be bound by a treaty.) Gabon, however, has not taken further action. If you were interested in Gabon's status, you would have to investigate whether Gabon law requires such further action.

Fiji has "acceded" to the treaty. Accession, done by notifying the treaty secretariat, is a common way for a country to become a party to a treaty that it did not sign. In fact, the Convention has 87 signatories and 185 parties. As indicated in the table above, most of the parties acceded to it rather than signing the treaty.

Finally, the state of Bosnia and Herzegovina "succeeded" to the treaty, which the former Yugoslavia had signed and ratified. (Succession is usually done by notifying the treaty secretariat, though the subject is complex and disputed in international law.)

3. *Any reservations, understandings, declarations, or other conditions made by the relevant parties.* Reservations are unilateral statements by a country that purport to limit the effect of certain provisions of a multilateral treaty. A country may make a reservation when it signs, ratifies, accepts, or otherwise takes action on a treaty. Countries may also issue "understandings" and "declarations," unilateral statements that do not normally affect the binding nature of the treaty's provisions.

Reservations can significantly limit the effect of a treaty. For example, the United States ratified the International Covenant on Civil and Political Rights (ICCPR), which prohibits the death penalty for juveniles. But the US government made a reservation by which it refused to accept this prohibition. Understandings and declarations clarify a State's position on a particular provision or the scope of the treaty. The US also issued a declaration regarding the ICCPR, stating that the provisions of articles 1 through 27 of the Covenant are not self-executing.

4. *Any subsequent modifications to the treaty* (often made in the form of "protocols"), and whether the relevant parties have become parties to those modifications. Treaties, like laws, may need to be modified to reflect changing circumstances. Usually, treaties include rules for making such changes. It is important to understand that the parties to a treaty are not automatically bound by changes to it. The most common scenario requires parties to undertake the same kind of procedures to agree to amendments as they did for the original treaty. It is not unusual for countries to be parties to a treaty but not to its amendments. For example, the United States is a party to the ICCPR, but it is not a party to its Optional Protocol.

The elements above make up the initial phase of treaty research. Additionally, you may need to research how the treaty should be interpreted. This phase includes two or three components. First, you may want to research the drafting history of a treaty. Its drafting history is referred to as the *travaux préparatoires*, and it consists of early drafts, reports of the drafters, proceedings of the drafters' meetings, and other documents. Like legislative history for statutes, *travaux préparatoires* are used to help interpret the meaning of treaty language.

Second, a country's internal ratification history may be used to interpret treaties. For example, the documents generated by the US Congress as it ratifies a treaty may be useful in understanding how the United States interprets that treaty.

Third, you may want to find how scholars, states parties, and tribunals and courts have interpreted the treaty. This task involves locating commentary, analysis, and interpretations through case law.

With the introduction above in mind, consider the most common task for US researchers—researching treaties to which the United States is a party.

II. *US Treaties and Agreements*

A. *Introduction*

Domestically, treaties to which the United States is a party are equivalent in status to federal legislation, forming part of what the Constitution calls "the supreme Law of the Land." Yet, the word "treaty" has a narrower meaning in the United States than in international law.[4] The Vienna Convention on the Law of Treaties defines a treaty "as an international agreement concluded between States in written form and governed by international law, whether embodied in a single instrument or in two or more related instruments and whatever its particular designation."[5]

United States law, however, distinguishes between the terms "treaty" and "executive agreement":

> In the United States, the word treaty is reserved for an agreement that is made "by and with the Advice and Consent of the Senate" (Article II, section 2,

---

[4] *Treaties and Other International Agreements: The Role of the United States Senate: A Study*, prepared for the Committee on Foreign Relations, United States Senate, S. Print 106-71 (2001), http://www.gpo.gov/fdsys/pkg/CPRT-106SPRT66922/pdf/CPRT-106SPRT66922.pdf. Note that this document is 448 pages long and can take some time to load.

[5] Vienna Convention on the Law of Treaties, 1155 U.N.T.S. 311 (May 23, 1969), art. 2, § 1(a), http://untreaty.un.org/ilc/texts/1_1.htm.

clause 2 of the Constitution). International agreements not submitted to the Senate are known as "executive agreements" in the United States.[6]

Regardless of whether an international agreement is called a convention, agreement, protocol, accord, or anything else, if it is submitted to the Senate for advice and consent, it is considered a treaty under US law. Under international law, however, both types of agreements are considered binding. For a brief overview of this issue, see Frederic Kirgis, 'International Agreements and U.S. Law,' *ASIL Insights*, No. 10 (May 1997).[7] The United States undertakes many more international agreements as executive agreements than as treaties.

The implications of the difference between treaty and executive agreements arise primarily when you explore the history of the instrument. Because of the Senate's involvement in the treaty process, you can find documents such as hearings and reports that shed light on how the United States interprets a treaty. Executive agreements, on the other hand, do not generate these documents and are consequently harder to research. Moreover, until 1945, executive agreements were published separately from treaties, in a series called *Executive Agreements*.

B. *Ratification and Implementation of US Treaties and Agreements*

When conducting US treaty research, it is important to understand the ratification and implementation process. Negotiation of treaties and international agreements is the responsibility of the Executive Branch. The US Department of State provides the Foreign Service with detailed instructions for the negotiation and conclusion of treaties and international agreements. These instructions are part of the *Foreign Affairs Manual*, Circular 175.[8] Circular 175 summarizes the constitutional requirements for determining whether an international agreement should be considered a treaty or an agreement. It outlines the general procedures for negotiation, signature, publication, and registration of treaties and international agreements.

1. *Outline of the Treaty-Making Process*

- Secretary of State authorizes negotiation
- US representatives negotiate
- Agree on terms, and upon authorization of Secretary of State, sign treaty

---

[6] *Treaties and Other International Agreements: The Role of the United States Senate: A Study*, *supra* note 4.

[7] http://www.asil.org/insights/insigh10.htm.

[8] 11 *Treaties and Other International Agreements*, Chapter 720, *Foreign Affairs Manual* (revised Sept. 25, 2006), http://www.state.gov/s/l/treaty/c175/index.htm.

- President submits treaty to Senate
- Senate Foreign Relations Committee considers treaty and reports to Senate
- Senate considers and approves by two-thirds majority
- President signs instrument of ratification
- Treaty enters into force based on the terms of the treaty
- President proclaims entry into force

For more information on the treaty-making process, see *Treaties and Other International Agreements: The Role of the United States Senate: A Study* (2001).[9] This is an excellent study of the treaty-making provisions of the US Constitution. See also Robert E. Dalton, 'National Treaty Law and Practice: United States,' *in National Treaty Law and Practice: Dedicated to the Memory of Monroe Leigh* (Duncan B. Hollis et al. eds., 2005).[10]

2. *Outline of the Agreement-Making Process*

- Secretary of State authorizes negotiation
- US representatives negotiate
- Agree on terms, and upon authorization of Secretary of State, sign agreement
- Three types of agreements[11]
- Agreement enters into force
- President transmits agreement to Congress (pursuant to Case-Zablocki Act)[12]

For an examination of executive agreements, see R.J. Erickson, 'The Making of Executive Agreements by the United States Department of Defense: An Agenda for Progress,' 13 *B.U. Int'l. L.J.* 45 (1995).

Another aspect of implementation concerns domestic legislation that may be passed to implement a treaty. This issue is one of US legal research and will not be covered here. Using an index to an annotated US Code, however, you can often find implementing legislation by looking up the treaty name.

---

[9] Available at http://www.gpo.gov/fdsys/pkg/CPRT-106SPRT66922/pdf/CPRT-106SPRT66922.pdf.

[10] The first edition of this chapter is available on the web, *National Treaty Law and Practice: United States*, in NATIONAL TREATY LAW AND PRACTICE: AUSTRIA, CHILE, COLOMBIA, JAPAN, THE NETHERLANDS, UNITED STATES (1999), available at www.asil.org/files/dalton.pdf.

[11] Agreements based on the president's constitutional authority (executive agreements), agreements pursuant to legislation or congressional-executive agreement, and agreements pursuant to treaty (authorization is based on a treaty previously ratified by United States).

[12] 1 U.S.C. §112b(a), http://www.state.gov/s/l/treaty/caseact/index.htm.

C. Forms of Publication

Until 1950, US treaties appeared regularly after proclamation in *Statutes at Large* (1847–). Pre-1950 treaties can also be found in *Treaties and Other International Agreements of the United States of America, 1776–1949* (Bevans ed., 1968–1976). This 13-volume set is commonly cited by the compilers' name, *Bevans*. In 1950, *United States Treaties and Other International Agreements* (U.S.T.) (1950–) became the official source for all US treaties and agreements. Several volumes are published annually, each with a noncumulative subject and country index. Note that there is almost a 20-year lag time between ratification and official publication in U.S.T.

US treaties first appear in slip form in *Treaties and Other International Acts Series* (T.I.A.S.) (1946–), a set of individually paginated pamphlets, consecutively numbered. This series has a lag time of eight to nine years. Before ratification, you can check on the status of a treaty sent to the Senate for "advice and consent" in *CCH Congressional Index* (1938–).

After ratification, but still well before treaties appear in slip form, selected treaties (after they are cleared for publication by the Senate) are published in the *Senate Treaty Document Series* (Congressional Information Service) (formerly the *Senate Executive Document Series*). If you need to find a recent U.S. treaty, you will probably need to use an online version, unless the treaty has been reprinted in *International Legal Materials*.

D. Indexes and Finding Tools

These tools are useful for locating citations for United States bilateral and multilateral treaties and agreements.

Relevant Library of Congress subject headings include:

> *treaties – indexes*
> *united states – foreign relations – treaties – indexes*

- *Treaties in Force* (TIF) (1950–). This annual publication lists all US treaties and agreements still in force, arranged by country and subject. It includes both bilateral and multilateral treaties and gives references to U.S.T. cites and T.I.A.S. numbers (if they exist). The primary use of TIF is verification of the existence of a treaty. TIF is also available on the State Department's website, but the electronic version is no more current than the print.[13] Since TIF is only published once a year, use Treaty Actions to update TIF. Treaty Actions used to be issued monthly when they were available in print. Now,

---

[13] http://www.state.gov/s/l/treaty/tif/index.htm.

on the web, they are not issued as reliably. Archived issues back to 1997 are also available.[14] TIF is also available on several subscription-only databases: (1) HeinOnline,[15] (2) LexisNexis ("U.S. Treaties in Force" database), and (3) Westlaw ("USTIF" file). Both HeinOnline and Westlaw provide access to some archived volumes.

- *A Guide to the United States Treaties in Force* (I. Kavass & A. Sprudzs, eds., 1982–). This annual publication should be used in conjunction with TIF. Access is by a combined subject index for both bilateral and multilateral treaties, as well as by numerical and country index. The *Guide* contains three parts and a supplement: Part 1 is a numerical list of bilateral and multilateral treaties and agreements listed in TIF; Part 2 provides expanded subject lists of the treaties and agreements; and Part 3 provides a chronological index to US multilateral treaties and agreements in force. The *Guide* is supplemented by *Guide to the United States Treaties in Force: Current Treaty Action Supplement*, which cumulates and indexes the information about treaty developments that have occurred since the cut-off date of the last edition of TIF. HeinOnline provides access to the *Guide* back to 1982.

- *United States Treaty Index* (15 vols.) (I. Kavass, ed., 1991–). This is one of the most comprehensive sources for US treaty information. There are subject, chronological, and country indexes. This set is supplemented by *Current Treaty Index;* see next paragraph. The treaties are available on HeinOnline.

- *Current Treaty Index* (I. Kavass & A. Sprudzs, eds., 1982–). This looseleaf index lists current treaties and agreements published in slip form in T.I.A.S. as well as those treaties without such numbers. It supplements the *United States Treaty Index* (see above). This index is available on HeinOnline from 1982–present.

- *Treaties and International Agreements Online* (Oceana Online, [1999–]).[16] This subscription service is available on the web from Oxford University Press (formerly Oceana Publications). It provides access to over 18,000 treaties and agreements from 1783 to December 2007. It is anticipated that this database will be updated and revamped, but no information is available at this time.

- *CCH Congressional Index* (1937–). This two-volume looseleaf set is issued for each congressional session. The Senate volume of this set contains a

---

[14] http://www.state.gov/s/l/treaty/c3428.htm.

[15] http://heinonline.org, Treaties and Agreements Library.

[16] http://www.oceanalaw.com.

section on treaties pending before the Senate. It provides information on the status of treaties. Look under the tab "Treaties and Nominations."

- *Thomas: Treaties.* This freely available website provides some information for locating treaty documents from the 90th Congress (1968) to the present. Search by Congress, treaty document number, word/phrase, or by type of treaty. Some full-text treaties are available from this site.[17]
- *Congressional Record Index* (1873–). This provides a listing of treaty actions and discussion appearing in the *Congressional Record* under the heading "Treaties" and occasionally under the name of a particular treaty or its subject matter. It may provide the text of a treaty or reservation to a treaty, and it is often a good source for legislative history of a treaty. The *Congressional Record* is available on many websites: (1) via a fee-based service called Proquest Congressional, (2) on the government site called Thomas,[18] and (3) on another government site called GPO's Federal Digital System (FDsys).[19] It is also available on LexisNexis and Westlaw; coverage begins in 1985.
- Journal articles can be a very good source for citations to and information about treaties. Search the full-text journal databases on either LexisNexis or Westlaw.

E. *Full-Text Sources*

One of the tricky aspects of treaty research is that you may have to consult several different sources before locating the text of the document. If you have an exact treaty citation, go directly to the source, such as U.S.T. or T.I.A.S.

Relevant subject headings include:

> *united states – foreign relations – treaties*

1. *Historical Sources*

- *Treaties and Other International Acts of the United States of America* (H. Miller ed., 1931). This eight-volume set contains the text of treaties from 1776–1863. The set also includes legislative history information and commentary. Use the four-volume index called *United States Treaties and Other International Agreements Cumulative Index 1776–1949: Cumulative Index to United States Treaties and Other International Agreements 1776–1949 as Published in Statutes at Large, Malloy, Miller, Bevans, and Other*

---

[17] http://thomas.loc.gov/home/treaties/treaties.html.

[18] http://thomas.loc.gov/home/LegislativeData.php?&n=Record.

[19] http://www.gpo.gov/fdsys/browse/collection.action?collectionCode=CREC.

Relevant Sources (Igor I. Kavass & Mark A. Michael comps., 1975). The entire set is also available electronically in PDF format on HeinOnline,[20] Treaties and Agreements Library.

- *Treaties, Conventions, International Acts, Protocols, and Agreements Between the U.S.A. and Other Powers* (William D. Malloy ed., vols. 1–2; C.F. Redmond & Edward J. Trenwith eds., vols. 3–4, 1910–). This set contains text of treaties from 1776–1937; Volume 4 has a cumulative index and chronological list of treaties. Use the four-volume index called *United States Treaties and Other International Agreements Cumulative Index 1776–1949: Cumulative Index to United States Treaties and Other International Agreements 1776–1949 as Published in Statutes at Large, Malloy, Miller, Bevans, and Other Relevant Sources* (Igor I. Kavass & Mark A. Michael comps., 1975). It is also available electronically in PDF format on HeinOnline, Treaties and Agreements Library.
- *Treaties and Other International Agreements of the United States, 1776–1949* (Bevans ed., 1968–1976). This work supersedes Miller and Malloy; Volumes 1–4 have the text of multilateral treaties and agreements in chronological order by date of signature; Volumes 5–12 includes bilateral treaties and agreements in alphabetical order by country; Volume 13 has a cumulative country and subject index. It covers 1908–September 1929. Use the four-volume index called *United States Treaties and Other International Agreements Cumulative Index 1776–1949: Cumulative Index to United States Treaties and Other International Agreements 1776–1949 as Published in Statutes at Large, Malloy, Miller, Bevans, and Other Relevant Sources* (Igor I. Kavass & Mark A. Michael comps., 1975). It is also available on HeinOnline, Treaties and Agreements Library, and it is commonly referred to as *Bevans*.
- *Treaty Series* (cited as T.S.) (October 1929–1945) (1908–1946). This series provides the text of treaties only. Later, this publication merged with *Executive Agreement Series* to form *Treaties and Other International Acts Series* (T.I.A.S.). Some of this set is available on HeinOnline, Treaties and Agreements Library.
- *Executive Agreement Series* (cited as E.A.S.) (October 1929–1945) (1929–1946). Contains international executive agreements only. This publication later merged with *Treaty Series*. Also available on HeinOnline, Treaties and Agreements Library.
- *Statutes at Large* (cited as Stat.) (1847–). From 1776–1950, treaties and international agreements were published in *Statutes at Large*. Volume 8 contains all treaties between the United States and other countries from

---

[20] http://heinonline.org, Treaties and Agreements Library.

1778–1845. Volume 64, part 3 contains a cumulative list of all treaties and agreements included in Volumes 1–64. The first 18 volumes of Statutes at Large (1789–1875) are available on the web on the Library of Congress, A Century of Lawmaking for a New Nation.[21] Volumes 7 (treaties between the US and Indian Tribes, 1848) and 8 (treaties between the US and other countries, 1867) are available on HeinOnline, Treaties and Agreements Library.

- *Unperfected Treaties of the United States of America, 1776–1976* (1976–1994). This six-volume set includes treaties and agreements concluded by the United States that, for various reasons, never entered into force between 1776 and 1976.

2. Current Sources

- *United States Treaties and Other International Agreements* (cited as U.S.T.) (1950–). This is the cumulative collection of T.I.A.S. (slip copies of treaties) and is the current official collection of US treaties and agreements. There is a considerable lag time with this publication, about 20 years. Volumes 1–35 are also available on HeinOnline, Treaties and Agreements Library.[22] Hein-Online includes all published volumes of the U.S.T. series.
- *Treaties and Other International Acts Series* (cited as T.I.A.S.) (1946–). This series is the first official publication of new treaties and agreements—slip treaties—and are later bound in U.S.T. (see above). There is a lag time of about eight to nine years. T.I.A.S. 11060 to T.I.A.S. 12734 are also available on HeinOnline, Treaties and Agreements Library. The State Department's website provides access to TIAS from 1996–2009.[23]
- Since 2002, treaties and non-treaty acts are available with a new kind of TIAS number. The number is derived from the entry-into-force date of the agreement. For example, a document with the number 02-306 means that this is a 2002 treaty that came into force on March 6, 2002. These documents are available on the State Department's Treaty Affairs website.[24]
- Other international agreements, those reported to Congress under the Case Act, are also available on the State Department's website. 1982–2005 are available on the FOIA site[25] and 2006–2011 are available on the Treaty Affairs website.[26]

---

[21] http://lcweb2.loc.gov/ammem/amlaw/lwsl.html.
[22] http://heinonline.org, Treaties and Agreements Library.
[23] http://www.state.gov/s/l/treaty/tias/index.htm.
[24] http://www.state.gov/s/l/treaty/tias/index.htm.
[25] http://www.state.gov/m/a/ips/c26355.htm.
[26] http://www.state.gov/s/l/treaty/caseact/index.htm.

- *Hein's United States Treaties and Other International Agreements Current Service* [microfiche] (1990–). Use the *United States Treaty Index* and the *Current Treaty Index* to locate the correct microfiche. This set is a good source for recent treaties. This service is also available on Hein-Online, Treaties and Agreements Library, and is called "KAV Agreements" (1987–present).

- *Consolidated Treaties and International Agreements* (cited as C.T.I.A.) (1990–). This set is a continuation of the 231-volume set *Consolidated Treaty Series* (1969–1986) that covers 1648–1918. The continuation set covers from January 1990 to the present (with about a six-month lag). It is available in electronic format as part of *Treaties and International Agreements Online* (see next item).

- *Treaties and International Agreements Online* ([1999–]). This is a subscription database service from Oxford University Press (formerly Oceana Publications). This database contains US treaties and international agreements in force since 1783 to December 2007. You can search by title, parties, date, and the full text of over 15,000 bilateral and multilateral treaties signed by the United States. See the "document details" button for citation and ratification information. See the "source image" button for access to some PDF documents (*Senate Treaty Documents*, T.I.A.S., U.S.T.). It also contains many international tax treaties, including non-US tax treaties. It is anticipated that this database will be updated and revamped, but no information is available at this time.

- *CIS Index to Publications of the United States Congress* [and microfiche] (1970–). Treaties appearing in the *Senate Treaty Document Series* are indexed by CIS. Access is through subject matter of the treaty, title of the treaty, as well as through the heading "Treaties and agreements," and the treaty document number (assigned by the Senate). The index gives a citation to the CIS microfiche set where the full text of the treaty is located. See also CIS, *Senate Executive Documents and Reports* [and microfiche] (1987), a microfiche collection of treaty documents and reports from 1817–1969. There is a two-volume index for accessing the relevant microfiche numbers. See also Proquest Congressional, a subscription database.[27]

- *Senate Treaty Documents* (cited as S. Treaty Doc.) (1981–). Senate, House, and Treaty Documents are available on the web from the 104th Congress forward.[28] These documents include the text of treaties submitted by the Executive Branch to the Senate for its advice and consent, together with supporting documentation. *Senate Treaty Documents* are also available

---

[27] http://cisupa.proquest.com/ws_display.asp?filter=Congressional%20Overview.
[28] http://www.gpo.gov/fdsys/browse/collection.action?collectionCode=CDOC.

through the *Serial Set*, CIS publications, Proquest Congressional, Lexis-Nexis, and Westlaw. Until 1979, these documents were called *Senate Executive Documents*.

- *Senate Executive Reports* (cited as S. Exec. Rep.) (n.d.). *Senate Executive Reports* are available on the web from 104th Congress on.[29] These reports are issued by the Senate Foreign Relations Committee and include the Committee's analysis and recommendations concerning proposed treaties. They also include the text of proposed treaties, together with any conditions (i.e., amendments or reservations) recommended by the Senate Foreign Relations Committee. These documents are also available in the *Serial Set*, *CIS Senate to US Senate Documents and Reports* and Proquest Congressional.
- U.S. Department of State Electronic Reading Room.[30] Pursuant to Pub. L. No. 108–458, 11 Stat. 3638, 3807 (2004), the Secretary of State is required to publish on the State Department's website "each treaty or international agreements proposed to be published in the compilation 'United States Treaties and Other International Agreements' not later than 180 days after the date on which the treaty or agreement enters into force." This collection covers 1982 to 2003.
- *Thomas: Treaties.*[31] This collection provides the text of treaties submitted to the Senate, from the 90th Congress to the present. Search by keyword, Congress, type of treaty (arms control, commercial, etc.), and date.

Both LexisNexis and Westlaw contain US treaties and agreements. Treaties can be located in the USTREATIES file on Westlaw and in US Treaties on LexisNexis. Both of these systems have many topical agreements and treaties: major trade agreements (GATT and NAFTA), International Economic Law Documents, International Environmental Law Documents, and tax treaties.

There are many specialized collections of treaties and agreements, such as *Tax Treaties* (1965–)[32] and *Extradition Laws and Treaties* (1980–). Some of these sets are regularly updated in looseleaf format or available by subscription on the web.

For additional major web sources of US treaties, see the listing at the end of this chapter.

---

[29] http://www.gpo.gov/fdsys/browse/collection.action?collectionCode=CRPT.
[30] http://www.state.gov/m/a/ips/c26355.htm.
[31] http://thomas.loc.gov/home/treaties/treaties.html.
[32] Also available by subscription, CCH Intelliconnect, http://intelliconnect.cch.com.

F. *Status, Updating and Ratification Information, and Amendments*

Once you locate the text of the agreement, you must determine its status. This includes determining the existing parties to a multilateral agreement and its entry into force date. Since status information is ever changing, figuring out the current status of treaties and agreements has always been a challenging task for the researcher. Keep in mind that unratified US treaties do not die at the end of the congressional session; therefore, it is often important to determine where a treaty is in the ratification process.

One of the best ways to get status information is to look for a treaty secretariat or treaty administrator website. Treaty secretariats, like the United Nations, maintain status information for numerous treaties. Many treaties set up organizations to administer the treaty, and these organizations often have websites that post ratification information. For example, the Convention on the Prevention of Marine Pollution by Dumping of Wastes and Other Matter (the London Convention) created an Office for the London Convention through the International Maritime Organization (IMO), which has its own extensive website.[33]

- *Treaties in Force* (TIF) (see Section II.D) is another good source for status information—it lists parties and the entry into force date for the United States. When available, it also lists links to the depositary and status webpages. As for protocols and other amendments, TIF includes protocols after the treaty they affect. It also sometimes has the heading "amendments" after treaties, and under that heading it gives citations to any amendments. For example, TIF's entry for the Nice Agreement concerning the International Classification of Goods and Services for the Purposes of the Registration of Marks is followed by a reference to a 1979 amendment. Its entry for the Convention on Long-Range Transboundary Air Pollution includes four protocols, with parties listed after each one.
- *A Guide to the United States Treaties in Force* (see Section II.D).
- *CCH Congressional Index* (see Section II.D). ˙
- *Current Treaty Index* (see Section II.D).
- The US Senate website, Treaties,[34] provides the following information: a list of treaties received from the President, treaties reported on the Executive Calendar, treaties approved by the Senate, and listings of other recent treaty status actions, including treaties that were rejected by the Senate or withdrawn by the President, during the current Congress. There is also a

---

[33] http://www.imo.org/blast/mainframemenu.asp?topic_id=1488.
[34] http://www.senate.gov/pagelayout/legislative/d_three_sections_with_teasers/treaties.htm.

page of related links and to information about the Senate's treaty-making power.

- *Shepard's Federal Statute Citations* (1996–). Pre-1950 treaties are listed by *Statutes at Large* number and after 1950 they are listed by U.S.T. or T.I.A.S. number. This source provides citations to treaties, cases, and statutes that cite or affect the treaty being shepardized. You cannot shepardize treaties using LexisNexis.
- *Dispatch* (1990–1999) was a weekly newsletter formerly issued by the State Department. It contained a section called "Treaty Actions," which included current information on bilateral and multilateral treaties. This publication ceased in print in 1999, and the Current Treaty Actions information is now available only on the web (updated irregularly).[35] Older editions of the *Dispatch* are available on the State Department's website,[36] on LexisNexis,[37] Westlaw,[38] and on HeinOnline.[39]

Depending on the topic of the treaty or agreement, consult relevant loose-leafs, periodicals, or series on the topic. For example, the *Tax Management International Journal* contains a section called "Current Status of U.S. Tax Treaties and International Tax Agreements." Other topical journals may contain similar information.

If you need status and ratification information for multilateral treaties, use the many treaty secretariat websites and collections on the web. See Section III on multilateral treaties for more information.

If all else fails, call the Department of State's Office of Treaty Affairs at (202) 647–1345 for up-to-date treaty information.

G. *Background Information (Legislative Histories and Treaty Interpretation)*

There are many US government documents that are useful for doing background research. Most of the US government documents mentioned below can be located with the same tools used for researching federal legislative histories, such as the *CIS/Index to Publications* and Proquest Congressional. Also, if it is a multilateral agreement done under the auspices of an international organization, consult the documentation of the organization, the conference materials or website, or the treaty secretariat website. For

---

[35] http://www.state.gov/s/l/index.cfm?id=3428.
[36] http://www.state.gov/www/publications/dispatch/index.html.
[37] US Department of State Dispatch and Bulletin database.
[38] USDPTSTDIS database.
[39] http://heinonline.org.

example, the United Nations Framework Convention on Climate Change website provides background information and documents.[40]

- *Senate Treaty Documents* (see Section II.E.2).
- *Senate Executive Reports* (see Section II.E.2).
- Consult congressional committee hearings, especially the Senate Foreign Relations Committee. See the US Senate website, Treaties, for current information about treaties received from the President, treaties on the calendar, approved treaties, and other recent treaty status actions.[41] See also *CIS/Index to Publications* and Proquest Congressional.
- Consult State Department documents, including *Dispatch* (1990–1999) (See Section II.F) or *Foreign Relations of the United States* (FRUS) (1861–). Some volumes of FRUS are available on the web.[42] The Office of the Legal Advisor publishes an annual *Digest of United States Practice in International Law*. Documents listed in the *Digest* are available on the State Department's website.[43]
- Presidential documents, including *Weekly Compilation of Presidential Documents* (WCPD)[44] and *Public Papers of the Presidents of the United States*[45] can also be useful for ratification statements and other documents. These documents are also available on LexisNexis.
- Christian L. Wiktor, *Treaties Submitted to the United States Senate: Legislative History, 1989–2004* (2006). This book traces the history of 329 treaties; it provides a summary of the history of Senate action, implementing legislation, and annotations.

You can conduct some legislative history research using LexisNexis (Legal > Legislation & Politics-U.S. & U.K. > U.S. Congress > Legislative Histories) and Westlaw (LH database). LexisNexis and Westlaw also include the *Congressional Record* from 1985 onward and more recent congressional hearings.

Look for *travaux préparatoires* or other commentaries in library catalogs or by searching periodical indexes. For example, Vern Krishna, *The Canada-U.S. Tax Treaty: Text and Commentary* (2004). The Library of Congress does not have a *travaux préparatoires* subject heading; instead, use the treaty name as a

---

[40] http://unfccc.int/2860.php.
[41] http://www.senate.gov/pagelayout/legislative/d_three_sections_with_teasers/treaties.htm.
[42] http://history.state.gov/historicaldocuments. See also, http://uwdc.library.wisc.edu/collections/FRUS.
[43] http://www.state.gov/s/l/c8183.htm.
[44] http://www.gpo.gov/fdsys/browse/collection.action?collectionCode=CPD.
[45] http://www.gpo.gov/fdsys/browse/collection.action?collectionCode=PPP.

subject heading, or search the treaty name as keywords, along with the phrase "travaux préparatoires." Finally, instead of "travaux préparatoires," try the treaty name and "commentary" or "history" as keywords, because many commentaries on treaties make extensive references to the *travaux préparatoires*.

- *Shepard's Federal Statute Citations* (1996–). Pre-1950 treaties are listed by Statutes at Large number, and after 1950 they are listed by U.S.T. or T.I.A.S. number. Provides citations to treaties, cases, and statutes that cite or affect the treaty being shepardized.
- *United States Code Service* (1972–). See unnumbered volume "Notes to Uncodified Laws and Treaties." This volume contains interpretive notes and decisions involving multilateral and bilateral treaties. Available on LexisNexis.
- *Treaties and Other International Agreements Online* (Oxford University Press)[37] also provides access to some Senate Treaty Documents (select the "source image" button).[46]

H. *US Treaties and Agreements on the Web*

Listed below are selected treaty collections available on the web. These sites focus on US treaties and agreements.

1. *US Government Websites*

- Bilateral Agreements [International Aviation] (Federal Aviation Administration).[47]
- Bilateral Investment Treaties and Related Agreements (US Department of State).[48]
- Indian Affairs: Laws and Treaties (Electronic version of the treatise compiled and edited by Charles J. Kappler).[49]
- International Antitrust and Consumer Protection Cooperation Agreements (Federal Trade Commission).[50]
- International Judicial Assistance, Notarial Services, and Authentication of Documents (US Department of State).[51]

---

[46] http://www.oceanalaw.com.
[47] http://www.faa.gov/aircraft/air_cert/international/bilateral_agreements.
[48] http://www.state.gov/e/eb/ifd/bit/index.htm.
[49] http://digital.library.okstate.edu/kappler.
[50] http://www.ftc.gov/oia/agreements.shtm.
[51] http://travel.state.gov/law/judicial/judicial_702.html.

- Income Tax Treaties (Internal Revenue Service).[52]
- Private International Law (US Department of State).[53]
- Trade Agreements (US Department of Agriculture).[54]
- Trade Agreements (Office of the US Trade Representative).[55]
- Trade and Related Agreements (US Department of Commerce, International Trade Administration).[56]
- US Bureau of Nonproliferation, Treaties, and Agreements (US Department of State).[57]
- US Bureau of Arms Control-related Treaties and Agreements (US Department of State).[58]
- US International Social Security Agreements (Social Security Administration).[59]

2. *Other Websites*

- Avalon Project (Documents in Law, History, and Diplomacy) (Yale Law School).[60]
- Trade Agreements (OAS, Foreign Trade Information System).[61]
- HeinOnline, Treaties and Agreements Library.[62]
- US Treaties on LexisNexis (International Law > Treaties & International Agreements > U.S. Treaties on LEXIS).[63]
- Westlaw, U.S. Treaties and Other International Agreements (International/ Worldwide Materials > Multi-National Materials > Legislation > U.S. Treaties and Other International Agreements).[64]

---

[52] http://www.irs.gov/businesses/international/article/0,,id=96739,00.html.
[53] http://www.state.gov/s/l/c3452.htm.
[54] http://www.fas.usda.gov/itp/agreements.asp.
[55] http://www.ustr.gov/trade-agreements.
[56] http://tcc.export.gov/Trade_Agreements/index.asp.
[57] http://www.state.gov/t/isn/trty.
[58] http://www.state.gov/t/avc/trty.
[59] http://www.ssa.gov/international/agreements_overview.html.
[60] http://avalon.law.yale.edu/default.asp.
[61] http://www.sice.oas.org/agreements_e.asp.
[62] http://www.heinonline.com.
[63] http://lexisnexis.com.
[64] http://www.westlaw.com.

III. *Treaties where the United States is not a Party and Multilateral Treaties*

Much of the information in Sections I and II also applies to treaty research where the United States is not a party.

When researching treaties to which the United States is not a party, or multilateral treaties, you will be interested in finding the following:

- the text of the treaty,
- status and ratification information for specific countries,
- reservations and declarations,
- any subsequent modifications to the treaty (often made in the form of "protocols"), and whether the relevant parties have become parties to those modifications,
- background documents that may explain the intent of the treaty,
- commentary and analysis.

A. *General Sources for Treaties and Agreements*

There are many sources for locating the full text of treaties and agreements in print. Listed below are some general sources where treaties (both bilateral and multilateral) are published.

- Official country treaty series—for example, the *Canada Treaty Series* (1928–). These series can be identified by using the *List of Treaty Collections* by the United Nations Office of Legal Affairs (1956). Also check a country legal research guide or search under the Library of Congress subject heading:

  [country] – foreign relations – treaties

Official treaty series are usually slower in publication than other treaty sources, and not all countries have treaty series. These series are especially important for locating bilateral treaties.

- International governmental organization (IGO) treaty series, such as the *League of Nations Treaty Series* (1919–1945) or the *United Nations Treaty Series* (1946–). Locate these sets by using the subject *treaties—collections* or by checking a bibliography or publications catalog for the IGO. These sets are usually slow in publication—the United Nations is about two or three years behind. This series is the most important compilation for locating multilateral treaties.

- Official gazettes—often the first official source—for example, *Bundesgesetz-blatt*, Part II for Germany. See Government Gazettes Online,[65] or conduct a subject search using *gazettes*—[country] to locate the title of the publication. The EU's *Official Journal* is often the easiest place to find a treaty in print first.
- Statutory compilations (arranged chronologically)—for example, *Statutes at Large of the United States* (1847–) used to publish all US treaties. Volume 8 of the *Statutes at Large* has treaties from 1778–1845; later volumes have treaties annually until 1951. To find statutory compilations for another country, search under the country's name or check a legal research guide (see Chapter 8).
- Looseleaf services. There are numerous such services; to find a service on the subject matter of the treaty, consult *Legal Looseleafs in Print* (1981–) or a legal research guide. The frequency of updating for looseleafs varies from every week to every year to every two to three years. These publications can be a good source for recent treaties and agreements. For example, *ICSID's Investment Promotion and Protection Treaties* (1983–). Some treaty collections in looseleaf format have been converted to subscription websites, like tax treaties from the International Bureau of Fiscal Documentation.[66]
- Electronic sources, including websites and subscription databases. To identify relevant electronic sources, use database directories, catalogs, and legal research guides. Electronic sources are good for locating very recent treaties. An example is the United Nations Treaty Collection.[67]
- Periodical literature, such as *International Legal Materials* (I.L.M.) (1962–). Some periodicals regularly reprint major treaties and others contain articles to which the text of a treaty being discussed might be appended.

Other sources of treaty texts include proceedings of international conferences (sometimes, the treaty is the "final act" of the conference); documents of international organizations and national government bodies, such as the US Congress (*Senate Treaty Documents*); monographic subject compilations (e.g., *Basic Documents on Human Rights*); newspapers (e.g., *New York Times*); governmental bodies (US State Department or foreign consulates); and press releases.

Some treaties are separately published (not part of a set); you can find these by doing a search on an online catalog using the name of the treaty

---

[65] http://www-personal.umich.edu/~graceyor/doctemp/gazettes/index.htm.

[66] http://www.ibfd.org.

[67] http://treaties.un.org.

as a keyword or as the subject heading. To find compilations, add the word 'treaties' to a subject search, as in *taxation, double—united states—treaties*. You may also use other subject searches, such as *commercial treaties* or *european economic community countries—commercial treaties*.

B. *Bilateral Treaties (Where United States is Not a Party)*

Relevant subject headings include:

> *[country] – foreign relations – treaties*

Bilateral agreements can be difficult to locate, especially if the agreement is between small countries or if it is an older treaty. Moreover, if neither party is an English-speaking country, you are unlikely to find an English-language version. Sources to consult include the treaty series, statutory compilation, or official gazette of one of the country parties. Some examples include *United Kingdom Treaty Series* or *Australian Treaty Series*. Some governments make their treaties available on the web, in free databases such as the Australian Treaties Library.[68] France has an excellent online treaty collection called Base Pacte.[69] This collection includes citations to France's *Journal Officiel*, the *United Nations Treaty Series*, and to other publications. To locate other such country treaty series, see the WorldLII web directory of treaties and agreements by country.[70] Country research guides (see Chapter 8) and web searches are also effective ways to locate bilateral treaties.

- *International Legal Materials* (I.L.M.) (1962–) reprints selected treaties based on their importance. It is often the first place a treaty appears in a paper publication. I.L.M. is also available on LexisNexis, Westlaw, and HeinOnline.[71]
- Since there are not very good indexes or finding tools for bilateral treaties, use the *World Treaty Index* (1983)[72] or the *United Nations Treaty Series Index* (1946–) for a citation to bilateral treaties. The full text of the treaty might be available in U.N.T.S.
- International yearbooks (e.g., *African Yearbook of International Law*) or other international law periodicals provide some information on treaties and agreements for selected countries. While the full text is not usually available, you may find a citation or other information that will let

---

[68] http://www.austlii.edu.au/au/other/dfat.

[69] http://basedoc.diplomatie.gouv.fr/Traites/Accords_Traites.php.

[70] http://www.worldlii.org/catalog/2322.html.

[71] http://www.heinonline.com.

[72] This index is available in beta at http://worldtreatyindex.com.

you verify the existence of the treaty and locate it elsewhere. For more yearbooks and related periodicals, search an online catalog using subject searches: *international law—periodicals or international law—[geographic area or country]—periodicals*. HeinOnline provides access to many such yearbooks; see the Foreign & International Law Resources Database.[73]

Another possible source for bilateral agreements includes compilations of documents from an international organization, topical compilations of treaties or websites. For example, the two series of *International Protection of the Environment: Treaties and Related Documents* (1975–1982 and 1990–1994) and *Investment Promotion and Protection Treaties* (1983–) both contain bilateral treaties. A very comprehensive collection of bilateral investment treaties is available from the UNCTAD website.[74]

As a last resort, try emails or phone calls to interested parties (organizations), embassies, the Department of State's Office of Treaty Affairs, or the UN Office of Legal Affairs, Treaty Section.

C. *Multilateral Treaties*

1. *Indexes and Finding Tools*

Relevant subject headings include:

> *treaties – indexes*

- *Multilateral Treaties Deposited with the Secretary General* (1982–). This is a good source for citations and a list of the parties to an agreement, although it is limited to those treaties deposited with the United Nations. This source is also available on the United Nations Treaty Collection on the web.[75] For the most recent information about treaties registered with the UN Secretariat, such as whether a treaty has in fact been registered, see *Statement of Treaties and International Agreements Registered or Filed and Recorded with the Secretariat during…*(1947–). This information is also available on the UN Treaty Collection website as the *Monthly Statement of Treaties and International Agreements.*[76] Be careful, as documents are not cumulative. If you need to confirm the existence of a treaty, or whether a treaty has recently been registered, you may need to look at several months' worth of statements.

---

[73] http://heinonline.org.
[74] http://www.unctadxi.org/templates/docsearch____779.aspx.
[75] http://treaties.un.org.
[76] http://treaties.un.org/Pages/Publications.aspx?pathpub=Publication/MS/Page1_en.xml.

- *World Treaty Index* (Peter H. Rohn ed., 1983). This index covers bilateral and multilateral treaties between 1900–1980. A beta version of this index is available on the web.[77]
- Christian L. Wiktor, *Multilateral Treaty Calendar = Répertoire des Traités Multilatéraux, 1648–1995* (1998). This index is considered the best multilateral index available. It is very complete for the time period it covers, but it lacks ratification information.
- *Multilateral Treaties: Index and Current Status* (M.J. Bowman & D.J. Harris eds., 1984) used to be the best source for citations and status information for multilateral treaties. This can be a useful source for older multilateral treaties. With each passing year, however, the information is less and less useful. It has a vague subject and keyword index, and all of the entries are arranged in chronological order. There is a cumulative supplement, but it is also quite dated.
- *Index to the United Nations Treaty Series* (1946–). This index accompanies U.N.T.S. Some of the index volumes are available on the United Nations Treaty Collection on the web.
- *United Nations Cumulative Treaty Index* (1999). A 15-volume set in the same format as the *United States Treaty Index,* this set is also supplemented periodically. This is much more useful than the U.N.T.S. Index, mentioned above; however the print version of this index is no longer current. For current information, see the *United Nations Treaty Index on CD-ROM,* issued twice a year from Hein. You can also use recent volumes of the Index through the UN Treaty Collection on the web, but they are large, noncumulative PDF documents and offer only the usual PDF search function. You may have to consult several documents to encompass the entire time span you need to cover.
- Flare Index to Treaties.[78] A searchable database of basic information on over 2,000 multilateral treaties and some bilateral treaties concluded between 1353 and the present, including citation information and links to the electronic versions.

2. *Full-Text Sources*

Relevant subject headings include:

> *[name of individual treaty]*
> *treaties – collections*

---

[77] http://worldtreatyindex.com.
[78] http://193.62.18.232/dbtw-wpd/textbase/treatysearch.htm.

- *Consolidated Treaty Series* (cited as C.T.S.) (1969–1986) covers 1648–1918.
- *League of Nations Treaty Series* (cited as L.N.T.S.) (1920–1946) covers 1920–1944. The complete set is available on the United Nations Treaty Collection website.[79]
- *United Nations Treaty Series* (cited as U.N.T.S.) (1944–). This series covers both bilateral and multilateral treaties from 1944 to date. The United Nations Treaty Collection website provides access electronically.
- *International Legal Materials* (cited as I.L.M.) (1962–). I.L.M. publishes selected treaties and agreements. It is available on LexisNexis, Westlaw, and HeinOnline.[80]

Since not all treaties are deposited with the United Nations, there are many regional organizations that publish the treaties done under the auspices of those organizations. For example, the Council of Europe publishes the *Council of Europe Treaty Series* (2004–). Other European IGO treaties can be found in the *European Yearbook* (1955–). The Organization of American States publishes (sporadically) a *Treaty Series* (1954–) as well. Many IGOs have websites that contain the text of these regional treaties; see the Treaty Collections on the Web in Section III.G.

Other useful sources include periodicals, loose leaf services, or subject compilations, such as *International Law & World Order: Basic Documents* (1994–) or *International Documents on Children* (2d ed. 1998).

And, as with bilateral conventions, country treaty series or official gazettes contain multilateral treaties as well. See Government Gazettes Online for more information.[81]

LexisNexis and Westlaw have selected treaties on various topics (trade, taxation, environment, etc.). For Lexis, look in the directory under "Find Treaties & International Agreements."[82] For Westlaw, use the "Search for a database" function in Classic Westlaw to find relevant databases. E.g., entering *intellectual property treaties* shows that Westlaw has a separate database for these treaties.

The web is a great resource for multilateral treaties; see Treaty Collections on the Web in Section III.G and the research guides mentioned at the end of this chapter.

---

[79] http://treaties.un.org/Pages/LONOnline.aspx.

[80] http://www.heinonline.com.

[81] http://www-personal.umich.edu/~graceyor/doctemp/gazettes/index.htm.

[82] Environmental law treaties, however, are not listed under this heading. Find them by searching for the source Environmental Law Reporter Environmental Statutes and Treaties.

D. *Signatories, Status, Ratification, Reservations*

Relevant subject headings include:

> *treaties – ratification treaties – reservations*

This can be the most difficult information to locate for many treaties. The UN's *Status of Multilateral Treaties Deposited with the Secretary-General* includes status information and reservations, but it covers only a small proportion of the world's treaties. For treaties not covered, the best place to start is with a database or website, such as the sites provided by treaty secretariats and depositories. To date, there is no one collection of links that provides access to all of the relevant treaty information. Some of the useful sites are listed below. This is only a sampling of what is out there on the web.

- ECOLEX.[83]
- Environmental Treaties and Resource Indicators.[84]
- FAO Conventions, Agreements and Treaties.[85]
- Council of Europe, European Treaties.[86]
- Hague Conventions on Private International Law.[87]
- ICRC, International Humanitarian Law: Treaties and Documents.[88]
- ILOLEX (International Labour Organization).[89]
- Inter-American Treaties (Organization of American States).[90]
- NATO Basic Texts.[91]
- Peace Agreements Digital Collection (USIP).[92]
- UN, International Human Rights Treaties.[93]
- UNEP, Environmental Law Instruments.[94]
- WIPO-Administrated Treaties.[95]

---

[83] http://www.ecolex.org/start.php.
[84] http://sedac.ciesin.org/entri/treatySearch.jsp.
[85] http://www.fao.org/Legal/treaties/treaty-e.htm.
[86] http://conventions.coe.int.
[87] http://www.hcch.net/index_en.php?act=conventions.listing.
[88] http://www.icrc.org/ihl.
[89] http://www.ilo.org/ilolex/english.
[90] http://www.oas.org/dil/treaties.htm.
[91] http://www.nato.int/ifor/general/home.htm.
[92] http://www.usip.org/publications-tools/latest?filter1=**ALL**&filter0=**ALL**&filter2=2223 &filter3=**ALL**&filter4=.
[93] http://www2.ohchr.org/english/law/index.htm.
[94] http://www.unep.org/law/Law_instruments/index.asp.
[95] http://www.wipo.int/treaties/en.

For some treaties, the treaty indexes, such as *Treaties in Force* (1950–), *Multilateral Treaties Deposited with the Secretary General* (1982–), or *Multilateral Treaties: Index and Current Status* (M.J. Bowman & D.J. Harris eds. 1984), may be the only source available.

Depending on the topic of the treaty or agreement, you can consult relevant looseleafs, periodicals, or series on the topic. For example, for human rights treaties, see the *Human Rights Law Journal* (1980–); for Hague conventions, see the *Netherlands International Law Review* (1975–). These are just a few of the many sources available.

Sometimes a call to the US State Department's Treaty Affairs Office or the UN treaty information office can be useful.

E. *Implementing Legislation*

Some treaties are "self-executing"; these do not require implementing legislation and become effective as domestic law as soon as they enter into force. Other treaties are non-self-executing and require "implementing legislation." Implementing legislation may require a new domestic law or changes to an existing law (technically, the legislation is the domestic law and not the treaty).

It is important to note that it is not always clear whether a treaty is self-executing or requires implementing legislation. Some treaties contain a provision calling for implementing legislation. The Executive Branch often decides whether or not a treaty requires such legislation. However, on occasion, the Senate includes an understanding in the resolution of ratification that certain provisions are not self-executing or that the President is to exchange or deposit the instrument of ratification only after implementation legislation has been enacted.[96]

To locate implementing legislation, you may need to consult sources of domestic legislation for the country in question. Some treaty secretariats provide such information. For example, see the secretariat's website for the Chemical Weapons Convention[97] or the OECD's Anti-Bribery Convention: National Implementing Legislation.[98]

---

[96] *Treaties and Other International Agreements: The Role of the United States Senate: A Study*, prepared for the Committee on Foreign Relations, United States Senate, S. Print 106-71 (2001), http://www.gpo.gov/fdsys/pkg/CPRT-106SPRT66922/pdf/CPRT-106SPRT66922.pdf.

[97] http://www.opcw.org.

[98] http://www.oecd.org/document/30/0,2340,en_2649_34859_2027102_1_1_1_1,00.html.

F. *Background Information (Commentary, Treaty Interpretation and* Travaux Préparatoires*)*

Researching the background or history of non-US treaties is challenging, especially for bilateral treaties. For the most part, you will not have access to materials for a legislative history for other countries. If you are researching the background of a multilateral treaty, there are many more resources available.

For relatively few treaties, but including some of the most important ones, experts have compiled and published the *travaux préparatoires* as books; for example, Sharon Detrick, *The United Nations Convention on the Rights of the Child: A Guide to the "Travaux Préparatoires"* (1992). Look for these publications, or for history and commentaries in library catalogs and journal indexes. For more information on the nature of this documentation and how to locate these documents, see Jonathan Pratter, A la Recherche des Travaux Préparatoires: An Approach to Researching the Drafting History of International Agreements.[99]

If the treaty or agreement was concluded pursuant to an international conference, look for conference documents using the name of the conference as an author or subject in a library catalog. If it is a recent conference, try searching for the conference on the web.

If the treaty or conference was done under the auspices of an international organization, such as the United Nations, look for documents using tools for locating such documents. See United Nations Documentation: Research Guide for assistance with such documents.[100] See also the ASIL Guide to Electronic Resources for International Law: International Organizations for tips on researching intergovernmental organizations on the web.[101] The UN website also has a collection of proceedings from several diplomatic conferences, such as Law of the Sea, Conference on the Law of Treaties, and Conference on the Establishment of the International Criminal Court.[102]

To research how treaties are implemented or interpreted in domestic legal systems, the most useful tools include international law yearbooks and *International Law Reports* (1919–)[103] (cited as I.L.R.). I.L.R. is a compilation of selected international and domestic court decisions, all translated into English. Another useful tool is a database called *International Law in Domestic Courts* (ILCD).[104]

---

[99] http://www.nyulawglobal.org/globalex/Travaux_Preparatoires.htm.

[100] http://www.un.org/Depts/dhl/resguide.

[101] http://www.asil.org/erg/?page=io.

[102] http://untreaty.un.org/cod/diplomaticconferences/index.html.

[103] Also available by subscription from Justis, http://www.justis.com.

[104] ILDC is part of Oxford Reports on International Law (ORIL), a subscription database, http://www.oxfordlawreports.com/.

ILDC is a regularly updated collection of domestic cases in international law from over 70 jurisdictions. Each document contains headnotes, analysis, and the text of the decision in English as well as in the vernacular.

Since locating case law can be difficult, try looking at collections based on a specific treaty.

- CISG Database (UN Convention on Contracts for the International Sale of Goods).[105]
- UNILEX (CISG and UNIDROIT Principles).[106]
- Case Law on UNCITRAL Texts (CLOUT).[107]
- International Child Abduction Database (Hague Convention on the Civil Aspects of International Child Abduction) (1980).[108]

G. *Treaty Collections on the Web*

- Electronic System for International Law (EISIL).[109]
- Flare Index to Treaties.[110]
- Multilaterals Project.[111]
- United Nations Treaty Collection.[112]

H. *Treaties by Popular Name*

Often treaties and agreements are referred to by popular names, which can cause some frustration for the researcher trying to locate them in indexes and finding tools. Using a search engine on the web, such as Google, can often provide clues to the complete names of treaties. If not, the following sources may be helpful in deciphering the official name of the document.

- *Treaties and Other International Agreements of the United States of America, 1776–1949* (Charles I. Bevans ed., 1968–1976). Available on HeinOnline.
- Edmund Jan Osmanczyk, *Encyclopedia of the United Nations and International Agreements* (3d ed. 2003). The index in Volume 4 includes many popular names and acronyms.[113]

---

[105] http://www.cisg.law.pace.edu.
[106] http://www.unilex.info.
[107] http://www.uncitral.org/uncitral/en/case_law.html.
[108] http://www.incadat.com.
[109] http://www.eisil.org.
[110] http://193.62.18.232/dbtw-wpd/textbase/treatysearch.htm.
[111] http://fletcher.tufts.edu/multilaterals.
[112] http://treaties.un.org.
[113] Also available electronically by subscription, http://www.routledgeonline.com/politics/Book.aspx?id=w032.

- UN Treaty Collection; see the section of the UNTS Database called "International Agreement by Popular Name."[114]

Searching full-text sources (especially law review articles) on LexisNexis and Westlaw can often lead to the full title of a treaty or agreement, and even a citation.

I. *Treaty Citations*

- *The Bluebook: A Uniform System of Citation* (19th ed. 2010)[115] requires that treaty citations include the name of the agreement; date of signing; parties; the subdivision referred to, if applicable; and the source(s) for the text of the treaty (see rule 21.4). The treaty sources will vary depending upon the parties. See *The Bluebook* for guidance on appropriate sources. Keep in mind that many "official sources" can take a long time for publication, so you may not be able to cite to the sources listed in *The Bluebook*.
- The *ALWD Citation Manual* (4th ed. 2010) has more lenient rules on treaty citation, and permits web citations at the writer's discretion, see Part 21.
- *Guide to Foreign and International Legal Citations* (2d ed. 2009). The first edition of this guide is available online.[116]
- Frequently-Cited Treaties and Other International Instruments includes a handy list of treaties with complete citations, in Bluebook format.[117]

J. *Research Guides*

These guides are good places to begin when researching treaties and agreements. Most contain information on both print and electronic sources.

- *Guide to International Legal Research* (2002–).
- Jeanne M. Rehberg, 'Finding Treaties and Other International Agreements,' *in Accidental Tourist on the New Frontier: An Introductory Guide to Global Legal Research* 123 (Jeanne M. Rehberg & Radu Popa eds., 1998).
- *Sources of State Practice in International Law* (Ralph Gaebler & Maria Smolka-Day eds., 2002–). This set covers selected countries and includes information on general treaty collections, treaty indexes, topical treaty collections, and state practice materials for each country.

---

[114] http://treaties.un.org/pages/UNTSOnline.aspx?id=1.

[115] The electronic version is available by subscription, http://www.legalbluebook.com/ and contains the 18th and 19th editions.

[116] http://www.law.nyu.edu/ecm_dlv1/groups/public/@nyu_law_website__library/documents/documents/ecm_dlv_006388.pdf.

[117] http://library.law.umn.edu/researchguides/most-cited.html.

- Suzanne Thorpe, 'A Guide to International Legal Bibliography,' in *Contemporary Practice of Public International Law* 17 (Ellen G. Schaffer & Randall J. Snyder eds., 1997).

In addition to the print guides mentioned above, there are many web guides on treaty research. Here are some of the ones that provide good coverage and link to other relevant guides.

- ASIL Guide to Electronic Resources for International Law: Treaties.[118] See also the other topical chapters for subject-specific treaties (environment, human rights, private international law, etc.).[119]
- Researching U.S. Treaties and Agreements (LLRX).[120]

---

[118] http://www.asil.org/erg/?page=treaties.
[119] http://www.asil.org/erg.
[120] http://www.llrx.com/features/ustreaty.htm.

Chapter Seven

Customary International Law, Generally Recognized Principles, and Judicial Decisions

I. *Introduction*

Like treaties, customary international law can bind states and individuals. For example, nationals of a state (e.g., Taiwan) that has not ratified the 1949 Geneva Conventions are nonetheless subject to prosecution for violations of common Article 3 committed during an armed conflict such as an insurgency. The basis for prosecution would not be the Conventions themselves, but the customary law evidenced by common Article 3.[1]

Even a powerful state can be bound by customary international law. The United States, for example, has not ratified the Vienna Convention on the Law of Treaties (VCLT). The *Restatement of the Law, Third, the Foreign Relations Law of the United States*, however, concludes that the VCLT dominates customary law on that topic, and that the United States is bound by at least some parts of its rules.

According to Article 38 of the International Court of Justice Statute,[2] custom and general principles of law are two primary sources of international law. These sources of public international law are difficult to research because they are not easy to identify and locate. It is important to remember that there is no one collection of all of the sources of customary international law since these are available in a variety of sources: treaties, national law, state papers, etc. The aim of this section is to provide some overall guidance to the sources for custom and principles and to provide ideas on what to look for to support the contention that a rule or principle is customary international law.

---

[1] Jordan J. Paust, *The Importance of Customary International Law during Armed Conflict*, 12 ILSA J. INT'L & COMP. L. 601, 601 (2006).

[2] Statute of the International Court of Justice, June 26, 1945, art. 38(1), 59 Stat. 1031.

Article 38 also mentions judicial decisions and the teachings of publicists as "subsidiary means for the determination of rules of law." It is important to remember that decisions and teachings are not authorities themselves, but they are authoritative *evidence* of the state of international law.

For more information about customary international law and its complexities, see David J. Bederman, *Custom as a Source of Law* (2010), Vladimir Djuro Degan, *Sources of International Law* (1997) and Mark Eugene Villiger, *Customary International Law and Treaties: A Manual on the Theory and Practice of the Interrelation of Sources* (rev. 2d. ed. 1997).

A. *Research Guides*

There are not many guides that are aimed specifically at researching customary international law. Guides that cover researching public international law generally can be helpful when researching international custom. These guides have been mentioned in other chapters and include *Guide to International Legal Research* (2002–), Claire M. Germain, *Germain's Transnational Law Research* (1991–), and Columbia Law Library's Researching Public International Law (unlike most such research guides, this one does provide some guidance on researching custom and state practice as well as general principles).[3]

There are a few research books that do provide more detailed information on researching custom and state practice. These include Shabtai Rosenne, *Practice and Methods of International Law* (1984), an excellent research guide that refers to the classic resources for international law research, although the sources are dated; *Contemporary Practice of Public International Law* (Ellen G. Schaffer & Randall J. Snyder eds., 1997), one of the only guides that specifically addresses customary international law research, see chapter 4; and *Sources of State Practice in International Law* (Ralph Gaebler & Maria Smolka-Day eds., 2001–), a source providing detailed information on state practice sources for selected countries.

B. *Customary International Law*

To locate materials in a library collection, search a library catalog using the subject: *customary law international.* This search will retrieve books and other items that specifically address customary international law. However, many of the materials used as evidence of customary international law will not be retrieved by this search. For example, diplomatic correspondence and records of diplomatic conferences, although they often evidence customary

---

[3] http://library.law.columbia.edu/guides/Researching_Public_International_Law.

international law, do not get this subject heading. Instead, they are likely to be given a subject heading such as *World War, 1939–1945—Sources*, or the name of the conference in question. The subject heading may also relate to the international topic in question, e.g., *German reunification question (1949–1990)*.

Rather than search for the subject *customary law international*, or for types of sources, you may want to start your search by reading about your international topic (e.g., the right to an education in international law). Books and articles on this topic will probably address claims of customary international law, with reference to sources that support the claim.

Some principles of customary international law are themselves Library of Congress subject headings, such as the *precautionary principle* in international environmental law. Other concepts are not subject headings themselves but have a closely-related term assigned as a subject heading; e.g., the concept of diplomatic immunity has the subject heading *diplomatic privileges and immunities*. Finally, some principles of customary international law are "buried" under much more general headings; for example, works on the concept of universal jurisdiction get the subject heading *jurisdiction (international law)*, and the environmental law concept of "polluter pays" is associated with the subject heading *liability for environmental damages*. Use the technique of trying various keyword searches in your library catalog, and looking at subject headings to refine your search.

Another effective approach to researching customary international law is to use Westlaw and LexisNexis full-text databases of law review articles. For example, to find articles discussing whether the precautionary principle has risen to the level of customary international law, search the law review databases with terms such as *"precautionary principle" w/s "international custom" OR CIL OR "customary international law"*. If your topic of interest is part of a specialized area of international law, considering modifying "customary international law" to reflect that specialization. For instance, if you are researching the humanitarian law concept of "responsibility to protect" (also called R2P), considering searching *R2P OR "responsibility to protect" w/s CIL OR "international custom" OR "customary international law" OR "customary international humanitarian" OR "customary humanitarian."*

1. What Is Customary International Law?

"It consists of rules of law derived from the consistent conduct of States acting out of the belief that the law required them to act that way."[4]

The elements of customary international law include:

---

[4] SHABTAI ROSENNE, PRACTICE AND METHODS OF INTERNATIONAL LAW 55 (1984).

1. widespread repetition by states of similar international acts over time (referred to as *state practice*);
2. acts occurring out of sense of obligation (referred to as *opinio juris*); and
3. acts taken by a significant number of states and not rejected by a significant number of states.

> Customary international law develops from the practice of States. To international lawyers, "the practice of states" means official governmental conduct reflected in a variety of acts, including official statements at international conferences and in diplomatic exchanges, formal instructions to diplomatic agents, national court decisions, legislative measures or other actions taken by governments to deal with matters of international concern.[5]

You should also be aware of peremptory norms (also called *jus cogens*). These are international law rules or principles that are accepted and considered binding by the international community. There is no agreement on what norms are peremptory. However, these norms generally include the following: prohibitions on use of force, crimes against humanity, war crimes, piracy, genocide, and slavery. For a thorough discussion of this issue, see Alexander Orakhelashvili, *Peremptory Norms in International Law* (2006). This book states that "custom is the most commonly recognized source of peremptory norms."[6]

For a good analysis of customary international law, see Anthea E. Roberts, 'Traditional and Modern Approaches to Customary International Law: A Reconciliation,' 95 *Am. J. Int'l L.* 757 (2001). This article contains references to many standard sources of customary international law. For information on the relationship between peremptory norms and "erga omnes" obligations,[7] see *The Fundamental Rules of the International Legal Order: Jus Cogens and Obligations Erga Omnes* (Christian Tomuschat & Jean Marc Thouvenin eds., 2006).

2. *Evidence of State Practice*

When doing research in this area, your objective is to find evidence of state practice. Evidence of state practice is found in a variety of primary source materials. In 1950, the International Law Commission listed the following sources as forms of evidence of customary international law: treaties,

---

[5] THOMAS BUERGENTHAL & SEAN D. MURPHY, PUBLIC INTERNATIONAL LAW IN A NUTSHELL 22–23 (4th ed. 2007).

[6] ALEXANDER ORAKHELASHVILI, PEREMPTORY NORMS IN INTERNATIONAL LAW 113 (2006).

[7] "Erga omnes" obligations are those owed to the whole international community. For a thorough treatment of the topic, see MAURIZIO RAGAZZI, THE CONCEPT OF INTERNATIONAL OBLIGATIONS ERGA OMNES (1997).

decisions of national and international courts, national legislation, opinions of national legal advisors, diplomatic correspondence, and practice of international organizations.[8] This list was not intended to be exhaustive, nor is there agreement among international legal scholars "on the forms of evidence that must be used to demonstrate state practice."[9] A good starting point for locating sources of state practice for a number of countries is *Sources of State Practice in International Law* (Ralph Gaebler & Maria Smolka-Day eds., 2001–).

For example, suppose you are researching the legality of a country taking military action to protect another country's residents from attacks by their own government. It is helpful to think of similar situations in which countries, regional, or international organizations have intervened, have chosen not to intervene, or have objected to intervention or the lack of intervention. So, for instance, you would research international reaction to NATO countries' attacks on Libya, including UN, NATO, and Arab League resolutions; statements by government officials from intervening and non-intervening countries; and the actual actions taken or not taken by those governments. You might also look at the situation in Syria, where the government has used force against its own citizens, killing at least a few thousand of them. (In this case, unlike Syria, states have not intervened as of late 2011.) Again, statements by IGOs, regional organizations, and various countries would be relevant.

a. Records of a State's Foreign Relations and Diplomatic Practices

Among the records of a state's foreign relations and diplomatic practices, a state's official treaty publication is perhaps the most important. One example is Canada's *Treaty Series*, published by the Office of External Affairs and International Trade. To look for evidence of Canada's practice relating to an issue, you would consult subject indexes to the series.

Another useful type of resource is a collection of diplomatic documents. These collections are published by a government entity, an independent organization, or an individual. For example, Swiss practice in foreign relations is documented in a publication entitled *Diplomatische Dokumente der Schweiz*, published by the Swiss National Commission for the Publication of

---

[8] [1950] 2 Y.B. INT'L L. COMM'N 367, U.N. Doc. A/CN.4/Ser.A/1950/Add.1 (1957), available at http://untreaty.un.org/ilc/publications/yearbooks/Ybkvolumes(e)/ILC_1950_v2_e.pdf.

[9] MARK VILLAGER, CUSTOMARY INTERNATIONAL LAW AND TREATIES 17 (rev. 2d ed. 1997). *See also* ANDREW T. GUZMAN, *Saving Customary International Law*, 27 MICH.J. INT'L L. 115, 125 (2005).

Diplomatic Documents. The Commission has also created an online database of diplomatic documents.[10]

To locate compiled state papers and diplomatic archives, search a library catalog under the following subject headings:

> *[country] – foreign relations*
> *[country] – history – sources*

The sources cited below focus on the United States; while other countries may publish these kinds of materials, access to them can be difficult. To locate the titles of sources for some other countries, check *Sources of State Practice in International Law* (Ralph Gaebler & Maria Smolka-Day eds., 2001–).

Of course, locating state and diplomatic papers for the United States is a much easer task for the researcher since there are several published compilations.

- *American State Papers: Documents, Legislative and Executive, of the Congress of the United States* (38 vols., reprint, 1998). In particular, see the six volumes on foreign relations, covering the 1st Cong.–20th Cong., 1st Sess., Apr. 30, 1789–May 24, 1828. This is available on the web.[11]
- *Papers Relating to the Foreign Relations of the United States* (1861–1931) covers 1789–1931 and contains documents, letters, etc.
- *Foreign Relations of the United States* (1861–). This set provides retrospective coverage with more than a 20-year lag time. Some volumes are available on the web.[12]
- *A Decade of American Foreign Policy: Basic Documents, 1941–1949* (1985).
- *American Foreign Policy: Current Documents* (1959–1969). This book covers 1956–1967 and contains full text documents on microfiche (official messages, reports, press statements).
- *American Foreign Policy: Basic Documents* (1983–). Documents cover 1977–1980.
- *American Foreign Policy: Current Documents* (1984–1991). Documents cover 1981–1991.
- U.S. Department of State, *Department of State Bulletin* (1939–1989) and *Dispatch* (1990–1999). These periodicals contained monthly updates on foreign relations. Though no longer published, the *Dispatch* is available on

---

[10] http://www.dodis.ch/en/home. This site links to other national collections of state papers, see http://www.dodis.ch/en/links.

[11] http://memory.loc.gov/ammem/amlaw/lwsp.html.

[12] http://digicoll.library.wisc.edu/FRUS; http://www.state.gov/www/about_state/history/frusonline.html.

Westlaw and LexisNexis. Archived issues of the *Dispatch* are available on the State Department's website and on HeinOnline.[13] Because both of these publications have been discontinued, use the State Department's website to locate information and documents related to foreign relations.

Other countries have similar collections, but they may not be as easy to access and the documents are most likely not available in English. However, some collections are available on the web. For example, as noted above, Swiss Diplomatic Documents (DDS) provides access to thousands of documents and pieces of information. A collection of British Foreign Office documents, grouped by topic, is available online.[14] To locate other such collections, consult a good list[15] of foreign ministries or conduct a web search using the name of the country and *foreign ministry* or *foreign affairs*.

b. Legislation Concerning a Country's International Obligations

A country's domestic laws also provide evidence of international custom. For example, a scholar examining a possible customary international law norm of universal jurisdiction for drug trafficking analyzed the laws of numerous states:

> When viewed as a whole, state practice indicates that while several states have enacted legislation embracing universal jurisdiction over drug trafficking, that trend is not yet firmly enough established to suggest that states feel compelled to recognize universal jurisdiction over drug traffickers as a matter of course.[16]

To find relevant materials, look at session laws, gazettes, statutory laws, and compilations of laws. Cumulative or yearly subject indexes to these publications will include some international topics. Yearbooks are helpful in identifying legislation; see Section I.B.3.c below. To find session laws and statutory compilations of individual states, search a library catalog under the subject headings:

gazettes – [country]
[country] – law; session laws – [country]

---

[13] http://www.heinonline.org. The *Dispatch* is also available on Westlaw (USDPTSTDIS database) and LexisNexis (US Department of State Dispatch and Bulletin database).

[14] http://www.fco.gov.uk/en/about-us/our-history/historical-publications/documents-british-policy.

[15] http://www.usip.org/publications/foreign-affairs-ministries-web.

[16] Anne H. Geraghty, *Universal Jurisdiction and Drug Trafficking: A Tool for Fighting One of the World's Most Pervasive Problems*, 16 FLA.J.INT'L L. 371, 391 (2004).

To identify official gazettes and their availability on the web, consult Government Gazettes Online.[17] To locate specific laws or sources for legislation, see Thomas H. Reynolds & Arturo A. Flores, *Foreign Law Guide*.[18]

Another useful source is the *United Nations Legislative Series* (1951–).[19] It contains a collection of national laws concerning various areas of international law, though it is not complete for every country. Researchers interested in international custom relating to terrorism, for example, could consult *National Laws and Regulations on the Prevention and Suppression of International Terrorism* (2002–). In this case, the UN Office on Drugs and Crime also provides a legislative database containing laws and provisions relating to the implementation of international anti-terrorism instruments as well as relevant national case law.[20]

Some national legislation is freely available on the web or through subscription databases like LexisNexis and Westlaw. For more assistance researching foreign law, see Part IV of this book.

c. Practice of Intergovernmental Organizations

One of the best-known examples of the use of international governmental organization (IGO) practice to show customary international law is found in the *Nicaragua* case before the International Court of Justice (ICJ).[21] In that case, the ICJ found that acceptance of certain UN resolutions on the use of force evidenced a norm of customary international law. UN resolutions about nuclear weapons were cited in the ICJ's advisory opinion on the *Legality of the Threat Or Use of Nuclear Weapons*, although in that case the resolutions failed to prove the existence of customary international law.[22]

The aim is to locate resolutions, decisions, and other legislative acts of IGOs. While these instruments are generally nonbinding instruments, they can reflect the acceptance of international norms. International practice of states is evident in these documents through voting practices and through the positions taken by states during negotiations. Official records contain the relevant acts and documents, and yearbooks are good for identifying the

---

[17] http://www-personal.umich.edu/~graceyor/doctemp/gazettes/index.htm.

[18] http://www.foreignlawguide.com.

[19] Also available on HeinOnline, http://www.heinonline.org, see United Nations Law Collection.

[20] https://www.unodc.org/tldb/en/index.html.

[21] Military and Paramilitary Activities (Nicar. v. U.S.), 1986 I.C.J. 14 (June 27), available at http://www.icj-cij.org/docket/index.php?p1=3&p2=3&code=nus&case=70&k=66&p3=0.

[22] Legality of Threat or Use of Nuclear Weapons, Advisory Opinion, 1996 I.C.J. 226 (July 8), *available at* http://www.icj-cij.org/docket/index.php?p1=3&p2=4&code=unan&case=95&k =e1&p3=0.

documents and acts within the official records. For a list of yearbooks and other tools, see Section I.B.3.c.

For example, resolutions and decisions of the UN General Assembly are good indicators of customary international law. (On some issues requiring significant resources, such as the use of nuclear weapons, smaller countries have few other ways to demonstrate their state practice.) General Assembly official records contain the resolutions for each session.[23] An easier method for accessing these documents is the Official Documents System (ODS)[24] and the UN website.[25] UNBISnet, the UN Bibliographic Information System,[26] is a good source for identifying relevant resolutions and for obtaining voting records. UNBISnet allows you to limit your search results to resolutions, using the drop-down menus; it also offers a separate search feature for finding voting records. AccessUN, a subscription database, is another useful tool for locating resolutions and provides access to some full-text documents.[27]

Other IGOs issue similar types of resolutions and decisions. For more information on the practice of international organizations, see the yearbooks listed in Section I.B.3.c. To learn more about researching the documentation of international organizations, see Part V of this book.

3. Locating the Evidence

Using the sources listed above to find the relevant evidence of customary international law can be challenging. Use international law digests, repertories, yearbooks, and the other sources listed below to identify evidence contained in the primary sources. Search a library catalog under the subject headings:

> *law reports, digests, etc.*
> *law reports, digests, etc. - [country]*

a. International Digests

- John L. Cadwalader, *Digest of the Published Opinions of the Attorneys-General and of the Leading Decisions of the Federal Courts, with Reference to International Law, Treaties, and Kindred Subjects* (1877). This is a subject

---

[23] RESOLUTIONS AND DECISIONS ADOPTED BY THE GENERAL ASSEMBLY (New York: United Nations, 1976–).

[24] http://documents.un.org/.

[25] http://www.un.org/en/documents.

[26] http://unbisnet.un.org.

[27] http://infoweb.newsbank.com.

guide to documentary sources (mostly quotations) taken from court cases and attorney general opinions. Also available on HeinOnline.[28]

- Francis Wharton, *Digest of the International Law of the United States* (1886). This is a subject guide to official statements of President and Secretary of State, court decisions and attorney general opinions.
- John Bassett Moore, *Digest of International Law* (1906). This book supersedes *Cadwalader* and *Wharton*; it is more like a treatise.
- Green Haywood Hackworth, *Digest of International Law* (1940–1944). This book continues the 1906 edition through 1939.
- Marjorie M. Whiteman, *Digest of International Law* (1963–1973). This covers 1940–1960, but topics have different coverage.
- *Digest of United States Practice in International Law* (1973–1980; 2001–). This series continues *Whiteman* (noted above). It does not use the complete approach of its predecessors; instead, it includes only calendar year material. The earlier edition was continued by *Cumulative Digest of United States Practice in International Law* (1981–), which covered 1981–1988. This source is supplemented monthly by the *American Journal of International Law* (column: "Contemporary Practice of the United States Relating to International Law"). The new edition of the *Digest* began with 2000 and is issued annually. Some source documents that are cited in the *Digest* are available on the State Department's website.[29]
- Sean D. Murphy, *United States Practice in International Law* (2002–). Volumes 1 and 2 cover 1999–2004. This new series is a thorough survey of US international law practice arranged by topic. It includes citations to US statutes and cases, US documents, international documents, and materials.
- *Restatement of the Law, Third, Foreign Relations* (1987–, plus annual supplement). This is an unofficial but authoritative outline of the law and a digest to US practice. It is also available on Westlaw and LexisNexis.
- Charles C. Hyde, *International Law Chiefly as Interpreted and Applied by the United States* (1945).
- *International Law, Chiefly as Interpreted and Applied in Canada* (Hugh M. Kindred et al., eds., 7th ed. 2006).[30]
- *British Digest of International Law* (1965–). This set covers materials from the British Foreign Office from 1860 on.

---

[28] HeinOnline's Foreign & International Law Resources database contains searchable versions of *Wharton, Moore, Hackworth, Whiteman* and the *Digest of United States Practice in International Law.*

[29] http://www.state.gov/s/l/c8183.htm.

[30] The website provides links to treaties and cases, http://www.emp.ca/index.php/international-law-chiefly-as-interpreted-and-applied-in-canada.

- *National Treaty Law and Practice: France, Germany, India, Switzerland, Thailand, United Kingdom* (Monroe Leigh & Merritt R. Blakeslee eds., 1995).
- *National Treaty Law and Practice: Austria, Chile, Colombia, Japan, The Netherlands, United States* (Monroe Leigh & Merritt R. Blakeslee eds., 1999).
- *National Treaty Law and Practice: Canada, Egypt, Israel, Mexico, Russia, South Africa* (Monroe Leigh et al. eds., 2003).
- *National Treaty Law and Practice: Dedicated to the Memory of Monroe Leigh* (Duncan B. Hollis ed., 2005). This set covers Austria, Canada, Chile, China, Colombia, Egypt, France, Germany, India, Israel, Japan, Mexico, The Netherlands, Russia, South Africa, Switzerland, Thailand, United Kingdom and the United States.

Many country foreign offices or ministries, similar to the US Department of State, have good websites: for example, the United Kingdom's Foreign and Commonwealth Office,[31] Australia's Department of Foreign Affairs and Trade,[32] and Germany's Auswärtiges Amt.[33] Information varies from country to country.

b. Repertories
These are considered the digests to the practice of international organizations.

- *Repertory of Practice of United Nations Organs* (1958–). This digest provides a comprehensive summary of the decisions of UN bodies, organized by the articles of the UN Charter. It deals with the application and interpretation of the Charter. It is kept up with supplements, but nothing new has been issued in quite some time. It is available on the UN's website.[34]
- *Repertoire of the Practice of the Security Council* (1946–). This digest provides the "ways and means for making the evidence of customary international law readily available." For example, if you are researching the Palestinian bid for statehood, you would want to research the Security Council's practice of recommending states for membership in the United Nations. For such research, this is one of the best sources. The *Repertoire*

---

[31] http://www.fco.gov.uk/en.
[32] http://www.dfat.gov.au.
[33] http://www.auswaertiges-amt.de.
[34] http://www.un.org/law/repertory. Searchable from the United Nations Legal Publications Global Search device, http://untreaty.un.org/cod/globalsearch/dtSearch/Search_Forms/dtSearch.html.

is an analytical record of the practice of the Security Council, kept up with supplements. It is also available on the UN website from 1946–2009.[35]

c. Yearbooks of States, Organizations and Topics

Yearbooks provide surveys of state practice arranged by treaty and international activities, and provide one of the best ways to access this information. They note important legislation, case law, and diplomatic practice dealing with matters of international law. However, the nature of yearbooks mean that they are not issued for a year or more after the close of the specific year. To locate yearbooks and similar periodicals, search a library catalog using the subject headings:

> international law – yearbooks
> international law – periodicals

HeinOnline offers a large collection of yearbooks available electronically via its Foreign and International Law Resources Database;[36] check whether your library subscribes to this collection.

State and Regional Yearbooks

Most yearbooks contain similar types of information: articles on international law topics, summaries of national legislation, case law, and practice as it relates to international law, information about new treaties and international case law. Some of these sources focus on the countries in the region and some provide information on the activities of international organizations. Many of these yearbooks are available on HeinOnline and are also indexed by the *Index to Foreign Legal Periodicals*.

- *African Yearbook of International Law = Annuaire Africain de Droit International* (1994–).
- *Annuaire Européen = European Yearbook* (1955–). This yearbook is in French and English.
- *Annuaire Français de Droit International* (1955–).
- *Anuario Mexicano de Derecho Internacional* (2001–).
- *Asian Yearbook of International Law* (1993–).
- *Australian Year Book of International Law* (1966–).
- *Baltic Yearbook of International Law* (2002–).

---

[35] http://www.un.org/en/sc/repertoire/index.shtml. Searchable from the United Nations Legal Publications Global Search device, http://untreaty.un.org/cod/globalsearch/dtSearch/Search_Forms/dtSearch.html.
[36] http://heinonline.org.

- *British Year Book of International Law* (1921–).
- *Canadian Yearbook of International Law = Annuaire Canadien de Droit International* (1963–).
- *Chinese Yearbook of International Law and Affairs* (1981–).
- *Czech Yearbook of International Law* (2010–).
- *Czech Yearbook of International Law* (2010–).[37]
- *Finnish Yearbook of International Law* (1990–).
- *German Yearbook of International Law = Jahrbuch für Internationales Recht* (1948–). The table of contents is in English; articles are in German, French, and English. The Max Planck Institute for Comparative Public Law provides the text of German practice from the Yearbook from 1993–2003 (in German).
- *Irish Yearbook of International Law* (2008–).
- *The Italian Yearbook of International Law* (1975–).
- *Japanese Annual of International Law* (1957–2008), continued by *Japanese Yearbook of International Law* (2009–).
- *Netherlands Yearbook of International Law* (1970–).
- *New Zealand Yearbook of International Law* (2004–).
- *The Palestine Yearbook of International Law* (1984–).
- *The Polish Yearbook of International Law* (1967–).
- *Schweizerisches Jahrbuch für Internationales Recht = Annuaire Suisse de Droit International* (1944–1990). In German and French.
- *Schweizerische Zeitschrift für Internationales und Europaisches Recht = Revue Suisse de Droit International et de Droit Européen* (1991–).
- *Singapore Year Book of International Law* (2004–). It is also available on HeinOnline.
- *South African Yearbook of International Law = Suid-Afrikaanse Jaarboek vir Volkereg* (1975–).
- *Sovetskii Ezhegodnik Mezhdunarodnogo Prava = Soviet Year-Book of International Law* (1958–1994). The table of contents is in English, French, and German. Articles are summarized in English.
- *Spanish Yearbook of International Law* (1994–).
- *Rossiiskii Ezhegodnik Mezhdunarodnogo Prava = Russian Yearbook of International Law* (1994–). Summaries and table of contents are in English.
- *Yearbook of Islamic and Middle Eastern Law* (1995–).

---

[37] Available online, http://www.cyil.eu. This publication is also called *Czech Yearbook of Public & Private International Law*.

Intergovernmental Organization Yearbooks
Individual IGOs publish yearbooks that provide an annual survey of activities. Some yearbooks cover the international law activities of various organizations.

- *Annual Review of United Nations Affairs* (1957–). ARUNA provides the text of important documents from the five key UN bodies.
- *Anuario Juridico Interamericano* (1948–1986). Reports on activities of the Organization of American States (OAS) are included; it includes legal studies and essays.
- *Global Community: Yearbook of International Law and Jurisprudence* (2001–). This yearbook contains substantive articles on international law issues, decisions of international courts and tribunals (such as ICJ, ITLOS, WTO, ICTY, and more), and a section on contemporary practice of international law.
- *Hague Yearbook of International Law = Annuaire de La Haye de Droit International* (1988–). This yearbook contains articles on international law issues and a section on the activities of international law institutions at the Hague (ICJ, ICTY, PCA, etc.).
- *Max Planck Yearbook of United Nations Law* (1998–). This annual focuses on UN activities in the field of international law.[38]
- *United Nations Juridical Yearbook* (1962–). This yearbook provides coverage of judicial decisions of international and national tribunals, and it includes unpublished legal opinions of the Secretariat.[39]
- United Nations International Law Commission, *Yearbook of the International Law Commission* (1949–). This body is charged with codifying international law. The *Yearbook* includes summaries of reports and documents of ILC and UN General Assembly, records of current session (commentaries on draft articles, articles under consideration), and record of annual session. This is a very important tool because often the views of the member states are sought on draft treaties. See the ILC website for access to yearbooks and documents.[40]
- *Yearbook of European Law* (1981–). This yearbook focuses on the European Union.

---

[38] Volumes 1–13 are freely available at http://www.mpil.de/ww/en/pub/research/details/publications/institute/mpyunl.cfm. Volumes 1–12 are available on HeinOnline, http://www.heinonline.org.

[39] Also available at http://www.un.org/law/UNJuridicalYearbook/index.htm and on HeinOnline, http://www.heinonline.org.

[40] Available on the ILC website, 1949–, http://untreaty.un.org/ilc/publications/yearbooks/yearbooks.htm. Also available on HeinOnline from 1949–2004, http://www.heinonline.org.

- *Yearbook of the United Nations* (1947–). Proceedings and activities of UN organs and bodies are described.[41]

Topical Yearbooks
Topical yearbooks are certainly a source for articles and can also provide information on the practice of states (legislation, treaties, and cases) and international organizations (including international courts and tribunals). Many of these yearbooks are indexed by the *Index to Foreign Legal Periodicals.*

- *African Yearbook on International Humanitarian Law* (2006–).
- *European Yearbook of Disability Law* (2009–).
- *European Yearbook of Minority Issues* (2003–).[42]
- *International Maritime and Commercial Law Yearbook* (2002–).
- *International Yearbook of Minority Issues* (2002–).
- *ISIL Year Book of International Humanitarian and Refugee Law* (2001–).
- *Yearbook of Cultural Property Law* (2006–).
- *Yearbook of European Environmental Law* (2000–).
- *Yearbook of International Environmental Law* (1991–).
- *Yearbook of International Humanitarian Law* (1998–).
- *Yearbook of Polar Law* (2009–).

d. Some Specific Sources
Some books that compile state practice have been published recently. The most comprehensive and long-awaited book is the one on international humanitarian law. Search for books and articles using the following search terms: international custom or rule, *customary international law*, or *state practice.*

- Jean-Marie Henckaerts & Louise Doswald-Beck, *Customary International Humanitarian Law* (2005). This is a detailed three volume set; Volume 1 contains the rules and Volumes 2 and 3 contain examples of state practice.[43]
- *Customary International Law on the Use of Force: A Methodological Approach* (Enzo Cannizzaro & Paolo Palchetti eds., 2005).
- Brian D. Lepard, *Customary International Law: A New Theory with Practical Applications* (2010).

---

[41] Available from 1946 onwards at http://unyearbook.un.org.
[42] Also available on HeinOnline, http://www.heinonline.org.
[43] Also available from the Customary IHL website by the ICRC, http://www.icrc.org/customary-ihl/eng/docs/home.

- Charles Quince, *The Persistent Objector and Customary International Law* (2010).
- Birgit Schlütter, *Developments in Customary International Law: Theory and the Practice of the International Court of Justice and the International Ad Hoc Criminal Tribunals for Rwanda and Yugoslavia* (2010).
- *State Practice Regarding State Immunities* (Council of Europe ed., 2006).

C. *General Principles*

Article 38 of the International Court of Justice Statute includes "general principles of law recognized by civilized nations" as another source of international law. General principles of law are doctrines of fairness and justice that are applied universally in legal systems around the world (e.g., laches, good faith, *res judicata*, impartiality of judges). General principles may be embodied in a treaty provision or become part of customary international law. They frequently involve procedural matters. International tribunals rely on these principles when they cannot find authority in other sources of international law.

There is no one collection of general principles, but they can be identified by reference in decisions of international tribunals and national courts and in the writings (or teachings) of publicists. Search for the following phrases in decisions and writings: *established principle, general concept of law, general principle*, or *universal or absolute principle of international law*. Another clue may be references to Article 38 of the ICJ Statute. The sources for locating these materials are detailed in Section I.D.

There are a few sources that provide information on general principles; see, for example, Bin Cheng, *General Principles of Law, as Applied by International Courts and Tribunals* (1953) and Fabián O. Raimondo, *General Principles of Law in the Decisions of International Criminal Courts and Tribunals* (2008).[44]

D. *Judicial Decisions and Writings of Publicists*

Along with general principles, Article 38 of the ICJ Statute also mentions "judicial decisions and the teachings of the most highly qualified publicists of the various nations, as subsidiary means for the determination of rules of law." These are not considered authorities according to Article 38, but they are persuasive evidence of a customary rule. Decisions can also contribute to

---

[44] There is also an earlier article on this topic by this author, Fabián O. Raimondo, *General Principles of Law as Applied by International Criminal Courts and Tribunals*, 6 L. & PRAC. INT'L. COURTS & TRIB. 393 (2007).

the emergence of a rule of customary law. Use decisions and writings to find references to and recognition of rules in other sources (treaties, customary law, and general principles).

1. *Judicial Decisions of International Tribunals*
You will often find citations to decisions of international tribunals while reading secondary sources. To find the actual decisions in paper sources, use a library catalog, and search under the author: [name of court]; or under the subject heading:

> *international law – cases*

a. Permanent Court of International Justice (PCIJ)

- *Recueil des Arrêts = Collection of Judgments* [Series A] (1923–1930).
- *Recueil des Avis Consultatifs = Advisory Opinions* [Series B] (1922–1930). Later merged with Series A into *Arrêts Ordonnances et Avis Consultatifs = Judgments, Orders, and Advisory Opinions* [Series A/B] (1931–1940).
- *Actes et Documents Relatifs aux Arrêts et aux Avis Consultatifs de la Cour = Acts and Documents Relating to Judgments and Advisory Opinions* [Series C] (1922–1930).
- Permanent Court of International Justice (1922–1946) decisions and the documents from Series A–F are available on the ICJ website.[45]

b. International Court of Justice (ICJ)

- *Recueil des Arrêts, Avis Consultatifs et Ordonnances = Reports of Judgments, Advisory Opinions and Orders* (1947–). Reports are also available on LexisNexis and Westlaw.
- *Memoires, Plaidoiries et Documents = Pleadings, Oral Arguments and Documents* (1947–). Motions, briefs, and oral arguments are contained in French and English.
- *Yearbook* (1947–). Provides summaries of Court's work each year.
- *World Court Reports* (Reprint of the 1934 ed. 1969). This includes commentary and summaries.
- *Case Law of the International Court* (1952–). This provides a digest of cases and includes a bibliography.

---

[45] http://www.icj-cij.org/pcij/index.php?p1=9.

- *Répertoire de la Jurisprudence de la Cour Internationale de Justice (1947– 1992) = Repertory of Decisions of the International Court of Justice (1947– 1992)* (50 vols).
- *World Court Digest* (1993–). This digest covers 1986–2005 so far. It is available on the website of the Max Planck Institute.[46] Earlier editions are under the title *Fontes Iuris Gentium*.[47]
- Official ICJ website provides access to documents, cases, practical information and related publications.[48]
- HeinOnline also contains many documents, cases, and other information from the Court.[49]
- Westlaw.[50]

c. Court of Justice of the European Union (ECJ)

- *Reports of Cases Before the Court* (1959–).
- *Digest of Case-Law Relating to the European Communities* (1981–1990).
- LexisNexis[51] and Westlaw.[52]
- The ECJ's website.[53]

d. European Court of Human Rights (ECHR)

- *Publications de la Cour Européenne des Droits de l'Homme. Série A, Arrêts et Décisions = Publications of the European Court of Human Rights. Series A, Judgments and Decisions* (1961–1996).
- *Publications de la Cour Européenne des Droits de l'Homme. Série B, Mémoires, Plaidoiries et Documents = Publications of the European Court of Human Rights. Series B, Pleadings, Oral Arguments, and Documents* (1962–1995).
- *Recueil des Arrêts et Décisions = Reports of Judgments and Decisions* (1996–).

---

[46] http://www.mpil.de/ww/en/pub/research/details/publications/institute/wcd.cfm.
[47] Also available electronically by subscription, http://www.springerlink.com and http://www .mpil.de/ww/en/pub/research/details/publications/institute/wcd.cfm.
[48] http://www.icj-cij.org/homepage/index.php.
[49] See the United Nations Law Collection, http://www.heinonline.org.
[50] INT-ICJ database.
[51] Legal > Find Laws by Country or Region > Foreign Laws & Legal Sources > European Union > Caselaw > EUR-Lex European Union Cases.
[52] EU-CS database.
[53] http://curia.europa.eu/jcms/jcms/j_6.

- *European Human Rights Reports* (1979–). These reports are also available on LexisNexis.[54]
- European Court of Human Rights website.[55]

e. Permanent Court of Arbitration (PCA)

- *Hague Court Reports* (1916–1932).
- *Reports of International Arbitral Awards* (1948–).
- *International Commercial Arbitration* (1979–).
- PCA's website.[56]

f. Other International Courts and Tribunals

There are several other international courts and tribunals, all of which issue decisions. To locate print versions of judgments from these courts, do an author search, using the name of the court, on a library catalog. For more information on researching information and cases from other international courts and tribunals, see Chapter 22.

- Iran-United States Claims Tribunal.[57]
- Inter-American Court of Human Rights.[58]
- International Criminal Court.[59]
- International Criminal Tribunal for the former Yugoslavia (ICTY).[60] These decisions are also available on Westlaw.
- International Criminal Tribunal for Rwanda (ICTR).[61] These decisions are also available on Westlaw.
- International Tribunal for the Law of the Sea (ITLOS).[62]
- Khmer Rouge Trials.[63]
- Serious Crimes Unit, East Timor.[64]
- Special Court for Sierra Leone.[65]

---

[54] International Law > Find Cases > Human Rights Cases.
[55] http://www.echr.coe.int/echr.
[56] http://www.pca-cpa.org.
[57] http://www.iusct.org.
[58] http://www.corteidh.or.cr/index.cfm?CFID=1444444&CFTOKEN=12385462.
[59] http://www.icc-cpi.int/Menus/ICC/Home.
[60] http://www.icty.org.
[61] http://www.unictr.org.
[62] http://www.itlos.org.
[63] http://www.unakrt-online.org.
[64] http://socrates.berkeley.edu/~warcrime/Serious%20Crimes%20Unit%20Files/default.html.
[65] http://www.sc-sl.org.

g. Other Useful Websites
These sites provide access to many other international courts and tribunals, as well as other related information.

- African Human Rights Case Law Analyser, a collection of decisions from the African Human Rights System.[66]
- African International Courts and Tribunals.[67]
- Commonwealth and International Human Rights Case Law Databases (Interights).[68] Contains summaries of human rights decisions from both domestic Commonwealth courts and from international courts and tribunals.
- DomCLIC Project, a database of domestic jurisprudence relating to international criminal law.[69]
- Hague Justice Portal provides access to information and selected court documents from various judicial bodies located in the Hague.[70]
- *International Justice Tribune* is an e-journal that covers international criminal justice and publishes investigative articles and interviews about worldwide efforts to try war criminals, from the International Criminal Court to domestic courts. An archive of past articles is also available.[71]
- Project on International Courts and Tribunals.[72]
- World Courts.[73] This site allows you to search the decisions of many international courts and tribunals.
- WorldLII: International Courts & Tribunals Project.[74] This site allows for searching across a variety of courts and tribunals and provides links to these bodies.

h. Print Collections and Digests
These compilations reprint selected cases from a variety of courts and tribunals.

---

[66] http://caselaw.ihrda.org.
[67] http://www.aict-ctia.org. Hard to determine if this site has been updated, but still provides some useful information.
[68] http://www.interights.org/commonwealth-and-international-law-database/index.html.
[69] http://www.asser.nl/default.aspx?site_id=36.
[70] http://www.haguejusticeportal.net.
[71] http://www.rnw.nl/international-justice/dossier/international%20justice%20tribune.
[72] http://www.pict-pcti.org/. Hard to determine if this site has been updated, but still provides some useful information.
[73] http://www.worldcourts.com.
[74] http://www.worldlii.org/int/cases.

- *The Annotated Digest of the International Criminal Court* (2007–).
- *Annotated Leading Cases of International Criminal Tribunals* (1999–).[75]
- *Digest of International Cases on the Law of the Sea* (2007).[76]
- *Digest of Jurisprudence of Special Court for Sierra Leone, 2003–2005* (2007).
- *Genocide, War Crimes and Crimes Against Humanity: Topical Digests of the Case Law of the International Tribunal for Rwanda* (2010).[77]
- *Global War Crimes Tribunal Collection* (1997–).
- *International Human Rights Reports* (I.H.R.R.) (1994–). Cases from the UN Human Rights Committee, the UN Committee against Torture, CERD, the Inter-American Commission on Human Rights, the Inter-American Court of Human Rights, the African Commission on Human and Peoples' Rights, the Yugoslav and Rwanda War Crimes Tribunals, and the Bosnian Human Rights Chamber are reproduced.
- *International Law Reports* (1919–). This contains full text of cases, translated into English, from both national and international tribunals.[78]
- *International Legal Materials* (1962–). This is also available on HeinOnline, LexisNexis[79] and Westlaw.[80] Reprints selected cases from international courts and tribunals.
- *The International Criminal Law Reports* (2000–).
- *International Environmental Law Reports* (1999–).
- *International Labour Law Reports* (1978–).[81]
- *The International Trade Law Reports* (1996–).
- *The Jurisprudence on Regional and International Tribunals Digest* (2007).

2. Court Decisions of an Individual State (Country) Concerning Its International Obligations

Look at court reports and special collections of court reports concerning international law. Search a library catalog under the subject headings:

> *international law – cases*
> *[country] – law reports, digests, etc*

The yearbooks mentioned in Section I.B.3.c are also a good source for this information.

---

[75] Available electronically by subscription, http://www.annotatedleadingcases.com.
[76] Also available electronically by subscription, http://www.heinonline.org.
[77] http://www.hrw.org/reports/2010/01/12/genocide-war-crimes-and-crimes-against-humanity.
[78] Available electronically by subscription, http://www.justis.com.
[79] International Law > Find Treaties & International Agreements > International Legal Materials.
[80] ILM database.
[81] Available electronically by subscription, http://www.heinonline.org/.

- *International Law Reports* (1919–). The set contains full text of selected cases, translated into English, from both national and international tribunals.
- *British International Law Cases* (1964–1970). This is a collection of British decisions on international law.
- Malgosia Fitzmaurice & Eric Heinze, *Landmark Cases in Public International Law* (1998).
- *International Law in Domestic Courts.* This collection is part of the Oxford University Press subscription database called Oxford Reports on International Law. It includes selected national court decisions that address international law, along with commentary on each decision.[82]

3. *Writings of Publicists*

Although a publicist is defined simply as an "international law scholar" in *Black's Law Dictionary*,[83] keep in mind that the ICJ Statute refers to "the most highly qualified publicists" of various nations. Thus, when you look for writings of publicists, do not assume that any law professor who writes about international law can provide evidence of customary international law. The list below identifies some such publicists. Increasingly, a "publicist" is a scholarly organization, such as the American Law Institute, which publishes the *Restatement of the Law, Third, Foreign Relations.* To determine whether a certain author is a highly qualified publicist, consider such factors as the author's number of publications and how often he or she is cited.

a. Treatises

The writings of publicists abound, and some of the most important works are listed below. If looking for more works, search a library catalog under the subject heading:

> international law

To locate such treatises in other languages, select the appropriate language from a keyword search or limit the original search by language.

- J.L. Brierly, *Law of Nations: An Introduction to the International Law of Peace* (6th ed. 1963).
- Ian Brownlie, *Principles of Public International Law* (6th ed. 2003).
- Thomas Buergenthal & Sean D. Murphy, *Public International Law in a Nutshell* (4th ed. 2007).

---

[82] Available by subscription, http://www.oxfordlawreports.com/.
[83] BLACK'S LAW DICTIONARY 1350 (9th ed. 2009).

- Louis Henkin, *International Law: Cases and Materials* (3d ed. 1993).
- *Oppenheim's International Law* (9th ed., Robert Jennings & Arthur Watts ed., 1992).
- Peter Malanczuk, *Akehurst's Modern Introduction to International Law* (7th rev. ed. 1997).
- Malcolm N. Shaw, *International Law* (5th ed. 2003).
- Georg Schwarzenberger, *A Manual of International Law* (6th ed. 1976).
- Gerhard Von Glahn, *Law Among Nations: An Introduction to Public International Law* (7th ed. 1996).
- *Max Planck Encyclopedia of Public International Law.*[84]

b. Periodicals
Search a library catalog under the subject heading:

international law – periodicals

These are just a few of the relevant journals, but don't forget to search periodical indexes. International journals and yearbooks provide surveys of state practice by treaty bodies as well. For more information about searching periodicals and periodical indexes, see Chapter 5.

- *American Journal of International Law* (1907–). This journal is also available on HeinOnline, JSTOR, LexisNexis, and Westlaw.
- Hague Academy of International Law, *Recueil des Cours* (1923–).[85]
- *International and Comparative Law Quarterly* (1952–). This journal is also available on HeinOnline, Cambridge University Press Current, LexisNexis, and Westlaw.
- *Annuaire de l'Institut de Droit International* (1877–).
- *European Journal of International Law* (1990–).

c. Publications of Scholarly International Law Associations
Search a library catalog under the author:

[name of the organization]

- International Law Association, *Report of the… Conference* (1873–). This provides reports of working committees, as well as names and addresses of

---

[84] http://www.mpepil.com and print editions.
[85] Available electronically by subscription, http://www.nijhoffonline.nl/pages/recueil and http://www.heinonline.org.

members. It often summarizes the state of customary law on a particular subject. Also available on HeinOnline.[86]

- Institute of International Law, *Annuaire de l'Institute de Droit International* (1877–). Reports of the annual meeting and texts of resolutions are provided.
- Hague Academy of International Law, *Recueil des Cours* (1923–).[87]
- *United Nations International Law Commission, Yearbook of the International Law Commission* (ILC) (1949–). This body is charged with codifying international law. This is a very important tool because often the views of the member states are sought on draft treaties. See the ILC website.[88]

[86] International Law Association Reports of Conferences, in the Foreign and International Library.

[87] Available electronically by subscription, http://ejil.oxfordjournals.org, http://www.heinonline.org.

[88] http://www.un.org/law/ilc/index.htm.

Part Four: Foreign and Comparative Law

Chapter Eight

Foreign Law

I. *Introduction*

As noted in Chapter 1, foreign or national law is essentially the domestic or internal law of any country. For the purposes of this book, it is national law of any jurisdiction other than the United States. Comparative law is "the study of the similarities and differences between the laws of two or more countries, or between two or more legal systems. Comparative law is not itself a system of law or a body of rules, but rather a method or approach to legal inquiry."[1]

Research methods will vary depending on the country you are researching. When beginning to research a legal system, you usually need to do the following:

1. Understand the structure of the foreign legal system.
   a. Is it a civil law system based upon codes, a common law system (such as the United States), or a mixed system? Some legal systems are influenced by religious law or by a political structure, like a socialist system. For a quick look at the legal system of a particular country, see the JuriGlobe World Legal System website.[2] For more information on legal systems generally, see *Patrick H. Glenn, Legal Traditions of the World* (3d ed. 2010).

   For example, if you need to research German law, you should know that Germany is a civil law system. Its civil code lays out highly detailed rules for legal relationships. Because of Germany's legal system, your research will probably involve looking at a commentary on the civil

---

[1] MORRIS L. COHEN ET AL., HOW TO FIND THE LAW 565 (9th ed. 1995).

[2] http://www.juriglobe.ca/eng/index.php.

code, and the text of some code sections, but you are unlikely to spend much time looking at court decisions.

b. Begin your research with a source that explains the legal system, such as Thomas H. Reynolds & Arturo R. Flores, *Foreign Law Guide*,[3] *Modern Legal Systems Cyclopedia* (Kenneth R. Redden ed., 1984–), or *Introduction to Foreign Legal Systems* (Richard A. Danner & Marie-Louise H. Bernal eds., 1994).

c. Determine if a specific research guide or overview exists for the country of interest.

For example, if you're asked to research New Zealand law, it makes sense to start with a research guide, such as Margaret Greville's *An Introduction to New Zealand Law & Sources of Legal Information*.[4] You can find this guide online by using search terms such as *legal research new zealand*.

2. Identify exactly what you need—the constitution, a specific statute or law, a case, or general information.

a. Do you have a citation to the law, article, etc.? Many research requests start with the name of a law, as referred to in a news article, a legal document, or on a webpage. For example, you may come across a reference to the "Loi Toubon," a French law requiring advertisements to be written in French. The citation might look like this: Law no. 94–665, *Journal Officiel de la République Française*, Aug. 4, 1994, p. 11392. You would then start your search by checking whether your library has the *Journal Officiel*. By checking a research guide, you would also learn that the French official gazette is available on the web.[5]

b. What are the dates?

c. Do you need the complete text of the law, a summary, an English translation, or a detailed explanation or commentary? Some sources offer full-text versions of laws, while others just summarize key features of a law.

d. Will an electronic version be sufficient?

3. Use a secondary source to start your research since these sources describe the law or legal issue, provide commentary, and put the issue into context. See Part II for more information on locating such sources.

4. Identify the sources of law for the country.

a. Does the country publish codes, compilations of statutes, or case reporters?

---

[3] http://www.foreignlawguide.com.
[4] http://www.nyulawglobal.org/Globalex/New_Zealand1.htm.
[5] http://www.nyulawglobal.org/globalex/france1.htm.

b. A good source for gathering this information is Reynolds & Flores, *Foreign Law Guide.*[6]

c. Once you have identified the sources, consult a web database, library catalog or other bibliographic databases to determine if the item is available.

For example, if you need to research Canadian law, *Foreign Law Guide* informs you that the most current set of consolidated statutes is the *Revised Statutes of Canada*. Enter this title into your library catalog to find out whether your library owns it.

II. *Locating Primary Law*

The sources of law can vary from country to country. In civil law systems, statutes and codes are primary law, and court decisions are less important. Consult the "Sources of Law" outline in Chapter 1 for a refresher on primary and secondary sources of law. Keep these concepts in mind when doing foreign law research.

A. *Where to Start*

When researching the law of another country, it is important to start with a relevant research guide, bibliography, or some other tool for determining the sources that are available for a particular country. To locate relevant guides, search a library catalog using subject headings:

> *legal research – [country]*
> *law – [country] – bibliography*
> *law – [country]*

Research guides and bibliographies may be contained in journal articles or in a chapter of a more general book.

A relevant research guide or an introductory source often provides an outline of the legal system and identifies the relevant sources for law. Chief among these tools is Thomas H. Reynolds & Arturo R. Flores, *Foreign Law Guide* (2000–). There is a chapter for each country represented, and each chapter includes the following components: an introduction to the legal system of the country, including legal history; major publications, which outline the sources for major codes, official gazettes, compilations or official codifications, session laws, court reports, and some web sources; subject arrangement, an alphabetical arrangement of subjects with references

---

[6] http://www.foreignlawguide.com.

to specific laws; and a bibliography at the end of the chapter. There is also a list of materials indexed. Keep in mind that this source does not cover every country or every subject.

Other useful sources include:

- Government Gazettes Online.[7] This website identifies and describes national official gazettes. Many countries have made these gazettes available online, and gazettes are a good source of recent foreign laws in the vernacular. Another useful source for information on legal gazettes is a 2009 study called *Access to Legislation in Europe: Guide to the Legal Gazettes and Other Official Information Sources in the European Union and the European Free Trade Association*. There is also a companion website, European Forum of Official Gazettes.[8]
- *Introduction to Foreign Legal Systems* (Richard A. Danner & Mary-Louise H. Bernal ed., 1994). This text provides a good introduction to the basics for a number of different legal systems, including France, Mexico, Japan, African countries, and other Asian countries.
- Claire M. Germain, *Germain's Transnational Law Research* (1991–). Country guides focus on Europe.
- *Modern Legal Systems Cyclopedia* (Kenneth R. Redden ed., 1984–). This comprehensive multivolume set provides general information about the legal system of most countries in the world. Also available electronically.[9]
- *Guide to International Legal Research* (2002–). This softcover annual guide contains general information on "geopolitical regions" (e.g., Africa), but provides detailed information on one country (e.g., Nigeria) within each region.
- *International Encyclopedia of Comparative Law* (1973–). The National Reports volumes provide an outline of a country's legal system, and there are also topical volumes. Some sections are dated, but it is still a useful source.
- *A Bibliography on Foreign and Comparative Law: Books and Articles in English* (1955–1989); *Szladits' Bibliography on Foreign and Comparative Law: Books and Articles in English* (1990–1998). These are useful for locating English-language secondary sources; they are organized by topic and country.

---

[7] http://www-personal.umich.edu/~graceyor/doctemp/gazettes/index.htm.

[8] Study: http://circa.europa.eu/irc/opoce/ojf/info/data/prod/data/pdf/AccessToLegislationInEurope GUIDE2009.pdf and companion website: http://circa.europa.eu/irc/opoce/ojf/info/data/prod/html/index.htm.

[9] Available by subscription from HeinOnline in the World Constitutions Illustrated library, http://www.heinonline.org/HOL/Index?index=cow/mlsc&collection=cow.

- *Accidental Tourist on the New Frontier: An Introductory Guide to Global Legal Research* (Jeanne Rehberg & Radu D. Popa eds., 1998). This is a basic research guide.
- *Information Sources in Law* (2d ed. 1997). The focus of this book is Europe.
- *Introductions* or *Doing Business In…* guides are very useful places to start. See, e.g., *Doing Business in Mexico, Introduction to Chinese Law, Introduction to Dutch Law, Doing Business in Asia,* or *Doing Business in Argentina.* These sources can be located by using keyword searches on a library catalog. Several "Doing Business" guides are available on LexisNexis, and a few on Westlaw.

B. *Introductory Works on Specific Countries*

The researcher is well advised to look for an introductory work on the country in question. There are many print sources that provide excellent information on the legal system, the structure of legal materials, and information and tips on subject areas. Some of these sources are listed below.

To locate these materials, search catalogs using the subject headings:

> *law – [name of country]*
> *justice, administration of – [name of country]*

See also the introductions for each country in the *Foreign Law Guide* (see Section II.A).

- Adineh Abghari, *Introduction to the Iranian Legal System and the Protection of Human Rights in Iran* (2008).
- Emmanuel Akomaye Agim, *The Gambian Legal System* (2009).
- John Bell et al., *Principles of French Law* (2d ed. 2008).
- Alexander Biryukov & Inna Shyrokova, *The Law and Legal System of Ukraine* (2005).
- William Burnham et al., *Law and Legal System of the Russian Federation* (2009).
- Jennifer Corrin & Don Paterson, *Introduction to South Pacific Law* (2007).
- Wan Arfah Hamzah, *An Introduction to the Malaysian Legal System* (2003).
- *Introduction to the Law of South Africa* (C.G. van der Merwe & Jacques E. du Plessis eds., 2004).
- *Introduction to Turkish Law* (Tugrul Ansay & Don Wallace, Jr. eds., 5th ed. 2005).
- *The Law and Legal System of Uzbekistan* (Ilias Bantekas ed., 2005).

- Wei Luo, *Chinese Law and Legal Research* (2005).
- Adefi M. Olong, *The Nigerian Legal System: An Introduction* (2007).
- Charlotte Villiers, *The Spanish Legal Tradition: An Introduction to the Spanish Law and Legal System* (1999).
- Ian Ward, *A Critical Introduction to European Law* (2d ed. 2003).
- George Wille, *Wille's Principles of South African Law* (9th ed. 2010).
- Guanghua Yu, *The Development of the Chinese Legal System: Change and Challenges* (2011).
- Reinhold Zippelius, *Introduction to German Legal Methods* (2008).

Consider sources on the region when looking for laws or information on a specific legal system. Sources on the region may contain sections or chapters on the country in question. See, for example, *Legal Aspects of Doing Business in Africa* (2d ed. 2011–) or *Doing Business in Asia* (1991–).

Many research guides are available on the web:

- An Annotated Guide to Web Sites around the World (Harvard Law Library) covers regional and national law sites.[10]
- A Selective List of Guides to Foreign Legal Research (Columbia Law Library) provides a list of guides available in print and electronic sources.[11]
- LLRX.com country guides provides many guides on researching the law of foreign jurisdictions, such as Argentina, Canada, China, Germany, Israel, and the United Kingdom.[12] Note that the GlobaLex site, below, may have a more recent guide.
- Legal Research Guide for China, Taiwan, Korea and Japan (University of Washington).[13] The University of Washington has a historically-strong collection of East Asian legal materials, and its guides, while tailored to its library's holdings, can be useful to researchers elsewhere.
- Globalex.[14] Globalex includes a large collection of country-specific research guides. The scope and format vary considerably from country to country, but they are generally a very useful resource.
- Global Legal Information Catalog (Library of Congress).[15] The Global Legal Information Catalog lists items which reprint the laws and regulations of international jurisdictions on a particular legal topic, comparative

---

[10] http://www.law.harvard.edu/library/research/guides/int_foreign/web-resources/index.html.
[11] http://library.law.columbia.edu/guides/A_Selective_List_of_Guides_to_Foreign_Legal_Research.
[12] http://www.llrx.com/category/857.
[13] http://lib.law.washington.edu/eald/eald.html.
[14] http://www.nyulawglobal.org/Globalex/#.
[15] http://www.loc.gov/lawweb/servlet/Glic?home.

in nature. The purpose of the database is to provide additional identifying information about titles, beyond that which is provided in the Library's online catalog. For example, if you want to find out whether *Investment Laws of the World* covers the country of Chad, you can select the Jurisdiction box and enter "Chad." You will then get a list of all the multijurisdictional collections that have an entry for Chad.

- NYU's Collection of Foreign Databases by Jurisdiction is an annotated collection of foreign law databases by jurisdiction. It is a good place to consult when trying to locate law for a particular country.[16]
- Many law libraries post country research guides on their websites. A search using "legal research guide" and the name of the country will usually provide some links.

C. Constitutions

One of the most important texts to locate when doing foreign and comparative research is a country's constitution. Luckily, this is one of the easier legal sources to locate in both the vernacular as well as in English. Relevant subject headings include:

> *constitutions*
> *constitutions – [country]*
> *constitutional history – [country]*
> *constitutional law – [country]*
> *constitutional courts – [country]*
> *judicial review*
> *judicial power*

1. Collections of Constitutions

- *Constitutions of the Countries of the World* (Philip Raworth & G. Alan Tarr eds., 2012–). Each chapter provides some historical information, and the older versions help the researcher track changes to the language. It is available electronically from the publisher's website, by subscription.[17] The electronic version of this collection allows you to do comparative constitutional law research with ease. For example, if you want to determine which national constitutions contain the right to freedom of expression, you can search this phrase and limit it to current constitutions. This search

---

[16] http://www.law.nyu.edu/library/research/foreign_intl/foreigndatabasesbyjurisdiction/index.htm.

[17] http://www.oxfordonline.com.

allows you to locate over 90 national constitutions containing this particular right.

- A new subscription database is now available from HeinOnline, World Constitutions Illustrated.[18] This collection contains current national constitutions in the original language and in English translation. It also has constitutional histories of selected countries including Brazil, Colombia, France and the United Kingdom, as well as related full-text periodicals and books.
- *Constitutions of Dependencies and Territories* (Philip Raworth ed., 1975–) (former title, *Constitutions of Dependencies and Special Sovereignties*). This book is similar in format to *Constitutions of the Countries of the World* and also available electronically from the publisher.[19]
- *Constitutions of the World: 1850 to the Present* (2003–). This microfiche set contains past versions of constitutions at the state and federal level, in both the vernacular and English, where possible. It is quite useful for historical research.
- *Constitutions of the World from the Late 18th Century to the Middle of the 19th Century* (2006–). This multivolume set contains about 1,000 constitutions, human rights declarations, and drafts of constitutions that never came into force from this period. These early constitutional documents were collected from archives and libraries worldwide. The set supplements the microfiche edition of *Constitutions of the World: 1850 to the Present.*
- *Central & Eastern European Legal Materials* (1990–). This title contains constitutions and related documents for this region.
- *Global Constitutional Law Collection* (1996). Volume 1, Europe—A-Est.; Volume 2, Europe—Finland-Liechtenstein; Volume 3, Europe—Lithuania-Romania; Volume 4, Europe—Russian Federation-Federal Republic of Yugoslavia.

Many constitutions are available from free websites.

- The Constitution Finder.[20] This site offers links to current and some historical constitutions, in both English and the vernacular.
- International Constitutional Law.[21] The International Constitutional Law Project offers html versions of numerous foreign constitutions, translated

---

[18] http://home.heinonline.org.
[19] http://www.oxfordonline.com.
[20] http://confinder.richmond.edu.
[21] http://www.servat.unibe.ch/icl.

into English. For some countries, background on constitutional history and structure is provided.

- National Constitutions.[22] This site has a limited number of constitutions, and links to constitutions, for various countries, including some historical versions. Various languages, mostly the vernacular but some in English.
- Constitutions of the Americas.[23] Part of Georgetown University's Political Database of the Americas, this site includes versions of Caribbean and Latin American constitutions in the vernacular.
- Rise of Modern Constitutionalism, 1776–1849.[24] This site seeks to include all constitutions that these scholars consider part of the constitutional movement during these years. There is limited material at this time, but offers images and translations of 18th- and 19th-century materials. Some material is free; the rest requires a subscription.

2. Relevant Journals

The journals listed below focus on constitutional law issues in a variety of countries or regions. Many of these journals are indexed in the *Index to Foreign Legal Periodicals* (IFLP); check this index to locate relevant articles (see Chapter 5 for more information). To find other relevant journals, search a library catalog using the following subject headings:

> *constitutional law – [country] – periodicals*
> *[country] – politics and government – periodicals*

- *Anuario Iberoamericano de Justicia Constitucional* (1997–).
- *Archiv des Öffentlichen Rechts* (1886–).
- *Bulletin on Constitutional Case-law* ([1993]–).
- *Constitutional Court Review* (2009–).
- *Constitutional Law & Policy Review* (1998–).
- *Cuestiones Constitucionales: Revista Mexicana de Derecho Constitucional* (1999–).
- *East European Constitutional Review* (1992–2003).
- *European Constitutional Law Review: EUConst* (2005–).
- *Gaceta Constitucional* (1999–2006).
- *International Journal of Constitutional Law: I-CON* (2003–).
- *Journal of Constitutional Law in Eastern and Central Europe* (1994–).
- *Les Cahiers du Conseil Constitutionnel* (1996–).

---

[22] http://www.constitution.org/cons/natlcons.htm.
[23] http://pdba.georgetown.edu/Constitutions/constitutions.html.
[24] http://www.modern-constitutions.de.

- *National Journal of Constitutional Law = Revue Nationale de Droit Constitutionnel* (1991–).
- *Review of Constitutional Studies = Revue d'études Constitutionnelles* (1993–).
- *Revista Española de Derecho Constitucional* (1981–).
- *Revue Française de Droit Constitutionnel* (1990–).
- *The Supreme Court Law Review* (1980–).
- *University of Pennsylvania Journal of Constitutional Law* (1998–).
- *Vesnik Kanstytutsyinaha Suda Respubliki Belarus: VKS* (1994–).
- *Vestnik Konstitutsionnogo Suda Rossiiskoi Federatsii* (1993–).

D. Legislation

There are generally two approaches for looking for foreign law—by subject or by jurisdiction. If you are looking for a piece of legislation for a specific country, the tools mentioned in Sections II.A and II.B (research guides and introductory books) are very useful. The *Foreign Law Guide*[25] is particularly useful since it contains a section of laws arranged by subject for each country. Country research guides may not provide guidance for all specific laws, but they will provide information on compilations of laws or specific codes.

Be sure to look for subject compilations; for example, European commercial laws are contained in *Commercial Laws of Europe* (1978–). One drawback of library catalogs is their failure to identify all the countries covered in subject compilations. For example, if you need to find investment law for Djibouti, you might try searching keywords in your catalog: *Djibouti, investment, law.* You might conclude that your library owns nothing on the topic, even if your law library owns the multivolume subject compilation *Investment Laws of the World* (1972–), which includes a chapter on Djibouti investment law. Extend your research, either by checking the Law Library of Congress's Global Legal Information Catalog[26] or the *Foreign Law Guide*, or by asking a reference librarian.

Other sources include:

- Claire Germain, *Germain's Transnational Law Research* (1991–). Last updated 2006. See Section 3.01 of this book for lists of subject compilations or the sections on particular topics.
- Amber Smith, 'Foreign Law in Translation,' *in Introduction to Foreign Legal Systems* ch. 14 (Richard A. Danner & Marie-Louise H. Bernal eds.,

---

[25] http://www.foreignlawguide.com.
[26] http://www.loc.gov/lawweb/servlet/Glic?home.

1994). While this chapter is now a bit dated, it does list many compilations of foreign laws in translation.

- *The International Lawyer's Deskbook* (Lucinda A. Low et al. eds., 2d ed. 2002) focuses on areas of interest to practicing lawyers, like arbitration, family law, and litigation.
- *Accidental Tourist on the New Frontier: An Introductory Guide to Global Legal Research* (Jeanne Rehberg & Radu D. Popa eds., 1998). Chapter 4, 'Finding Foreign Law,' is particularly helpful. The chapter describes strategies for foreign legal research, and then provides an annotated list of useful sources.
- Martindale Hubbell International Law Digest. For selected countries, it provides brief outlines of the law and references to codes and legislation. It available on LexisNexis and on the web.[27]
- *International Encyclopaedia of Laws* (date varies). Arranged by topic (civil procedure, contracts, environmental law, family and succession, social security, etc.), it summarizes the law in many jurisdictions. This excellent publication is now available online, by subscription.[28]

Look for subject compilations, digests, or periodicals, such as *Tax Laws of the World, Commercial Laws of the World, Digest of Commercial Laws of the World,* and *China Law and Practice. Foreign Law Guide*[29] has a good listing of subject compilations under the section called "materials indexed." Remember to use Global Legal Information Catalog (Library of Congress)[30] (see Section II.B) to help locate relevant sources and the jurisdictions covered by these sources. You can locate periodicals by doing a subject search of:

> *law – [country] – periodicals*

E. *LexisNexis and Westlaw*

While these databases provide exhaustive coverage of American law, they do not provide comprehensive coverage of other jurisdictions. Some of the country files provide coverage of statutory law, some cover case law, and some provide only access to news sources. Be sure to check the scope of coverage for any file on these databases.[31]

---

[27] http://www.martindale.com/legal-library.
[28] http://www.ielaws.com.
[29] http://www.foreignlawguide.com.
[30] http://www.loc.gov/lawweb/servlet/Glic?home.
[31] The scope or database information can be checked by clicking on the "i" next to the title of the source.

LexisNexis is a useful source for the laws of many different countries. The extent of coverage varies from country to country. See the section of the website labeled "Find Laws by Country or Region." Some of the countries include Argentina (archival laws), Australia, Canada, Hong Kong, France (official journal 2000–2008), Ireland, Israel (some translated cases), Malaysia (cases, statutes), Mexico (codes, cases to Feb. 2011), New Zealand, Northern Ireland, Russia (selected laws, some archival), Scotland, South Africa (some cases, laws through March 2011), and the United Kingdom. LexisNexis tends to retain archival material for foreign countries without reflecting the database's archival status in the file name; make sure to check the scope of coverage to make sure the database is still being updated.

LexisNexis has begun to include references in its database directory, under individual countries, to subject compilations that cover the country in question. For example, if France's estate planning law is covered in the database International Estate Planning, the listings under France will include that database. For some countries in the directory, these listings will appear when you click on the country name; for others, you must click the link for "Commentaries & Treatises" after clicking on the country name. LexisNexis also offers databases of foreign news sources; check under News & Business > Country & Region (excluding United States).

Westlaw's coverage of foreign law has waxed and waned. It contains law for the United Kingdom, Australia, Canada, and Hong Kong. Westlaw also contain news and business information. To check Westlaw's current coverage of foreign legal materials, select "International Worldwide Materials" from the database directory, and then the desired region.

F. *English-Language Sources*

When using translations, keep in mind the information provided in Chapter 2 of this book. Generally speaking, there are many English language compilations, especially in the areas of taxation, trade, intellectual property, commercial and business law.

1. *Topical Collections*

Listed below is a sampling of the many English-language sources available. Some contain full translations of laws; others merely have summaries and excerpts. Many of the sources below are looseleafs, a publication format that allows for frequent updating. Not all looseleafs, however, are frequently updated.

- *Citizenship and the State: A Comparative Study of Citizenship Legislation in Israel, Jordan, Palestine, Syria and Lebanon Edition* (1997).

- *Commercial Laws of Europe* (1978–).
- *Commercial Laws of the World* (dates vary) (available online by subscription).[32]
- *Comparative Environmental Law and Regulation* (1997–).
- *Copyright throughout the World* (2008–).
- *Doing Business* (World Bank).[33]
- *International Encyclopaedia of Laws* (dates vary) (topics vary: civil procedure, contracts, corporations, family law, insurance, etc.) (also available electronically).
- *International Franchising* (2d ed. 2011–).
- *International Immigration and Nationality* (2d ed. 2011–).
- *Investment Laws of the World* (1972–).
- *International Protection of Foreign Investment* (2d ed. 2010–).
- *International Securities Law and Regulation* (2d ed., 2010–).
- *Tax Laws of the World* (dates vary) (available online by subscription).[34]
- *World Arbitration Reporter: International Encyclopaedia of Arbitration Law and Practice* (2d ed. 2010–).
- *World Patent Law and Practice* (1974–).

2. *Country or Region Collections*
There are some English-language collections of national laws organized by country or region. Some individual codes and laws are also available in translation.

- *Arbitration in Asia* (2d ed. 2008–).
- *Business Law: The Polish Law Collection* (2000–).
- *Central & Eastern European Legal Materials* (1990–).
- *China Laws for Foreign Business* (1985–) (also available electronically, by subscription).[35]
- *EHS Law Bulletin* [Japan] (dates vary).
- *Islamic Law and Civil Code: The Law of Property in Egypt* (2010).
- *Mexican Commercial Code Annotated* (2009).
- *Russia and the Republics: Legal Materials* (2d series, 2006–).
- *Securing and Enforcing Judgments in Latin America* (rev. ed. 2011–).

---

[32] http://riacheckpoint.com.
[33] http://www.doingbusiness.org/law-library.
[34] http://riacheckpoint.com.
[35] http://www.chinalawandpractice.com.

3. *Selected Websites*
In addition to the databases mentioned in Sections II.A through II.F.2, many websites provide access to foreign law in translation. Note the breadth of subjects covered and that some of the sources below are provided by inter-governmental organizations (IGOs), such as FAO, WIPO, and the ILO. IGOs can be a good source for translated laws and information. Also note, unfortu-nately, that sites like the ones below sometimes get abandoned, and are either removed or no longer updated. Never assume the contents are current.

- Annual Review of Population Law (covers a variety of topics: abortion, fam-ily planning, domestic violence, etc.) (Harvard School of Public Health).[36]
- Centre for German Legal Information (CGerLI).[37]
- CODICES (includes laws relating to courts) (Council of Europe, Venice Commission).[38]
- WIPO Lex (laws on copyright, patent, trademark, geographical indica-tions, unfair trade practices, etc.) (WIPO).[39]
- Criminal Law Resources on the Web. Criminal codes; no longer updated, but still a good source. (Buffalo Criminal Law Center).[40]
- Electoral Knowledge Network (laws pertaining to elections; see "Electoral Materials" tab) (Ace Project).[41]
- Foreign Trade Information Center (OAS) (trade laws and related issues; under individual countries, see link for "Disciplines").[42]
- FAOLEX (FAO) (national laws and regulations on food, agriculture and renewable natural resources).[43]
- International Constitutional Law (constitutions and a few related laws).[44]
- International Digest of Health Legislation (WHO).[45]
- Legislationonline.org (legislation dealing with the rule of law, human rights and fundamental freedoms) (OSCE).[46]
- NATLEX (labor law, social security) (ILO).[47]

---

[36] http://www.hsph.harvard.edu/population/annual_review.htm.
[37] http://www.cgerli.org.
[38] http://www.venice.coe.int/site/main/CODICES_E.asp.
[39] http://www.wipo.int/wipolex/en.
[40] http://wings.buffalo.edu/law/bclc/resource.htm.
[41] http://aceproject.org/regions-en.
[42] http://www.sice.oas.org.
[43] http://faolex.fao.org.
[44] http://www.servat.unibe.ch/icl.
[45] http://apps.who.int/idhl-rils/frame.cfm?language=english.
[46] http://www.legislationline.org.
[47] http://www.ilo.org/dyn/natlex/natlex_browse.home.

- UNHCR Legal Information, REFWORLD (law relating to refugees, asylum seekers, stateless persons).[48]
- UNODC Legal Library (drug and related legislation).[49]
- World Trade Organization (good source for laws associated with trade topics; see the trade topics page and the official documents database).[50]

IGO websites can be useful for getting translations for free. For example, if you need antidumping regulations for China, the WTO website is an excellent place to check. Select the country you need from the link called "150 Members" and then select "China" from the list. Scroll down the page to the section called "Notifications from China." Select "antidumping" from the topic and click on search. A search for notifications for China will be run by the database. Notifications contain the text of national laws pursuant to various WTO agreements.

To locate more foreign laws on the web, see the guides mentioned in Sections II.A and II.B, and Foreign and International Law Resources: An Annotated Guide to websites around the World[51] (Harvard Law Library), or WorldLII by country[52] or subject.[53] Keep in mind that some national government websites provide selected laws in English (trade, intellectual property, and finance in particular).

III. *Case Law*

A good place to find out if the country of interest produces compilations of court decisions is through the sources mentioned above. Keep in mind that in many countries, court decisions are not considered primary law, and there may not be any official publication of decisions. Also, in some countries, only the country's highest court will issue its decisions for publication. Periodicals and journals may be the best source for decisions.

Relevant library catalog subject headings include:

> *law reports, digests, etc. – [country]*
> *[topic] – [country] – cases*

---

[48] http://www.unhcr.org/refworld/category,LEGAL,,,,,0.html.
[49] http://www.unodc.org/enl/index.html.
[50] http://www.wto.org.
[51] http://www.law.harvard.edu/library/research/guides/int_foreign/web-resources/index.html.
[52] http://www.worldlii.org/countries.html.
[53] http://www.worldlii.org/catalog/272.html.

For example, to find out whether your library collects court decisions from Germany, use the subject search *law reports, digests, etc. Germany.*

Check the sections on "Court Reports" in *Foreign Law Guide.*[54] This section will tell you whether the country issues official reports or if you must look in other sources, such as periodicals.

LexisNexis contains summaries or the full text of some case law from Australia, Canada, England, Ireland, the EU, Mexico, and a few others. See the "Find Laws by Country or Region" section on the website. Westlaw also contains some case reporters for Canada, the United Kingdom and the EU; check in the Directory under International/Worldwide Materials.

To determine the full title of an unfamiliar case citation, try the following resources:

- Cardiff Index to Legal Abbreviations.[55]
- Donald Raistrick & David Edmond Neuberger, *Index to Legal Citations and Abbreviations* (3d ed. 2008).
- *Guide to Foreign and International Legal Citations* (2d ed. 2009).
- *Noble's Revised International Guide to the Law Reports* (Scott Noble ed., 2002).
- Abbreviations of Legal Publications (Monash University).[56]

For example, you might run across this citation while reading an article about international copyright law: [2004] E.C.D.R. 16. Using the "Search by Abbreviation" feature of the Cardiff Index to Legal Abbreviations, you can see that E.C.D.R. stands for *European Copyright and Design Reports.* With the name of the reporter, you can use WorldCat[57] to search for libraries that own the title.

Note that in many countries, legal periodicals act as unofficial sources for case decisions. For instance, many German cases appear in the weekly periodical *Neue Juristische Wochenschrift.*

It is much easier to locate case law on the web than ever before. While some courts put up large collections, other courts may be more selective. Here are a few selected websites for case law:

- American Law Sources Online.[58]
- Centre for German Legal Information (CGerLI).[59]

---

[54] http://www.foreignlawguide.com.
[55] http://www.legalabbrevs.cardiff.ac.uk.
[56] http://www.lib.monash.edu.au/legal-abbreviations.
[57] http://www.worldcat.org.
[58] http://www.lawsource.com/also.
[59] http://www.cgerli.org.

- CODICES, Constitutional Case Law from Europe and a few other countries (Council of Europe, Venice Commission).[60]
- LII: Legal Information Institute, Law by Source: Global.[61]
- Global Courts: Supreme Court Decisions from Around the World.[62]
- Institute of Global Law (selected French, German, Austrian and Israeli cases).[63]
- Links to Constitutional Courts and Equivalent Bodies (COE).[64]
- NYU's Collection of Foreign Databases by Jurisdiction.[65]
- World Law Guide (collection of links to courts/cases).[66]

Some of the sites noted above provide access to cases in the vernacular, while others provide some English translations. For example, the Global Courts website allows you easily locate the Supreme Court decisions for courts from 129 countries, such as the Dominican Republic's Supreme Court. This site provides information about the Court as well as its jurisprudence, statistical data, and other relevant information regarding the Court.[67]

The Institute for Transnational Law provides users with access to selected German, French, Italian, Austrian, and Israeli cases in English in the areas of constitutional law, administrative law, tort law, contracts, and restitution law.[68] While other cases may be relevant, note that only those that have been translated are available on this website. The site also indicates the origin of the translation.

While there are many publications that provide translated text of foreign laws, there are relatively few sources for case law.

- *Arbitration Law Reports and Review* (2010–).
- *International Law Reports* (1919–) (now available online by subscription from Justis).[69]
- *Bulletin on Constitutional Case Law* (1993–). See also CODICES,[70] the infobase on Constitutional Case-Law of the Venice Commission.

---

[60] http://www.codices.coe.int/NXT/gateway.dll?f=templates&fn=default.htm.
[61] http://www.law.cornell.edu/world/.
[62] http://www.globalcourts.com.
[63] http://www.utexas.edu/law/academics/centers/transnational/work_new.
[64] http://www.venice.coe.int/site/dynamics/N_court_links_ef.asp.
[65] http://www.law.nyu.edu/library/research/foreign_intl/foreigndatabasesbyjurisdiction/index.htm.
[66] http://www.lexadin.nl/wlg/legis/nofr/legis.php.
[67] http://www.suprema.gov.do.
[68] http://www.utexas.edu/law/academics/centers/transnational/work_new.
[69] http://www.justis.com/data-coverage/international-law-reports.aspx.
[70] See footnote 60, above.

- *The International Criminal Law Reports* (2000–).
- *International Environmental Law Reports* (1999–2007).
- *International Labour Law Reports* (1978–). Also available via HeinOnline.
- *The International Trade Law Reports* (1996–).
- *Law Reports of the Commonwealth* (1980/85–) (contains cases from many Commonwealth jurisdictions; topics include constitutional law, administrative law, commercial law and criminal law).

To locate compilations of cases in English, try library catalog searches using relevant subject headings or keyword searches (e.g., *Korea* and *translat?* and *case?* OR *opinion?* OR *decision?*) (using whatever character is used for truncation in your catalog). You may retrieve texts such as *The First Ten Years of the Korean Constitutional Court: 1988-1998* (2001)—or, with minor variations on your search, *The Constitutional Jurisprudence of the Federal Republic of Germany* (2d ed. 1997), or *Israel Law Reports* (2002–), or Aharon Layish, *Sharīa and Custom in Libyan Tribal Society: An Annotated Translation of Decisions from the Sharīa Courts of Adjābiya and Kufra* (2005).

Journal articles are an especially good source for summaries of and citations to case law. For example: Kenneth L. Port, 'Japanese Intellectual Property Law in Translation: Representative Case and Commentary,' 34 *Vand. J. Transnat'l L.* 847 (2001); 'Case Law, Z. G. v. The Federal Republic of Germany,' 23 *Int'l J. Refugee L.* 113 (2011) (providing a translation of a recent decision of the German Bundesverwaltungs-gericht, Germany's highest administrative court).

As noted throughout this chapter, country websites can provide needed laws. Since a Google search may not always work or cannot produce the information you need, remember to consult a directory, like WorldLII,[71] to see if a national court has a site. For instance, you want to determine if a Canadian case has been appealed to a higher court. The citation you have is Commission Scolaire Marguerite-Bourgeoys v. Singh Multani, 241 DLR (4th) 33. A Google search for the citation or case name does not yield the desired information. However, if you use WorldLII, you will find out that there is a freely available collection of Canadian cases called CANLII.[72] Within that collection, a search by the name of the case will produce this case as well as a link to the relevant Canadian Supreme Court decision.

---

[71] http://www.worldlii.org/countries.html.
[72] http://www.canlii.org.

IV. *Other Sources of Law*

You will sometimes need to find secondary legislation, regulations (sometimes called statutory instruments or delegated legislation), and administrative decisions. These sources may be even more elusive than statutory law and case law. Start by using the sources mentioned in the above sections. Relevant subject headings include:

delegated legislation – [country]

Secondary sources may be another way to track down relevant sources or citations. If a country publishes an official gazette (as most civil law systems do), you have a better chance of locating regulations, notices, circulars, etc. See the collection of links to online gazettes[73] or *Foreign Law Guide*[74] for more information. As noted in Section III for cases, the WorldLII collection is a good directory for locating government agency websites or collections of regulations. Keep in mind that translated secondary legislation is extremely difficult to obtain.

V. *Foreign Law Subscription Databases*

Throughout this chapter, many databases have been mentioned in relation to a print source or a topic, country or region. However, many databases are available by subscription for specific countries, regions and topics. For more information on these and other subscription sources, please see the database website and country or topical research guides (see Section II.B. of this chapter). Many of these databases are briefly outlined in the Guide to Foreign and International Legal Database from NYU.[75] See the Appendix to this book for the websites for all of the databases listed herein.

Beck-Online (German law)
China Laws for Foreign Business (English & Chinese)
ChinaLawInfo (English & Chinese)
DataCenta (Ghanaian law)
DeJure (Italian law, no English translations)
Editions Dalloz (French law)

---

[73] http://www-personal.umich.edu/~graceyor/doctemp/gazettes/index.htm.
[74] http://foreignlawguide.com.
[75] http://www.law.nyu.edu/library/research/foreign_intl/index.htm.

HeinOnline: World Trials (selected national trials)
INDLAW (India)
Inter-Am Database (Latin & South American law, some English translations)
International Bureau of Fiscal Documentation (IBFD) (commentary on taxa-
    tion and investment)
International Law Report (selected international and national cases, in English)
iSinolaw (English & Chinese)
JURIS (German law)
JurisClasseur Lexis/Nexis (French law)
Justis (English law)
JUTASTAT (South Africa)
KluwerArbitration (national statutes, cases, and commentary—arbitration)
Kodeks Law Databases (Russian and English)
Lawafrica.com (Kenya)
LexisNexis Argentina
LexisNexis Butterworths (Canada, South Africa, Australia and New Zealand)
LexisNexis Quicklaw (Canada)
Manupatra (India)
Oxford Reports on International Law (selected international and national
    cases, in English)
RIA Checkpoint (taxation and investment laws from around the world)
Swisslex (Swiss law)
Takdin (Israeli High Court)
Transnational Dispute Management (national laws re arbitration)
Vietnam Laws Online (English)
vLex Global (various countries, legislation and cases)
Westlaw China (English & Chinese)
Westlaw Gulf (UAE and other countries)

VI. *Citing to Foreign Law*

Consult *The Bluebook: A Uniform System of Citation* (19th ed. 2010), Rule 20
and Table 2, for assistance with citing to foreign law. Unfortunately, not all
jurisdictions are listed in Table 2, so follow the general guidelines noted in
Rule 20. To locate proper abbreviations, consult *Noble's International Guide
to the Law Reports* (2002), *World Dictionary of Legal Abbreviations* (1991–),
or other sources of abbreviations (see Chapter 4).

Some countries have their own citation manuals, such as *the Canadian
Guide to Uniform Legal Citation* (7th ed., 2010) or the *Australian Guide to*

Legal Citation (2d ed., 2002).[76] For guidance on a number of countries, see *Guide to Foreign and International Legal Citations* (2d ed., 2009).

VII. *Periodical Literature and Other Sources*

Periodical literature is a good way to obtain background information, locate the text of a foreign law or a citation, or locate information about a subject. To obtain the best results, use periodical indexes to locate relevant articles. For more assistance with locating journal literature, see Chapter 5.

Other databases that compile a variety of sources (newsletters, news articles, reports) can be good places to find the text of a law, a summary, or an explanation. Some good sources for these kinds of materials include *Gender-Watch*, *Ethnic NewsWatch*, *World News Connection* (formerly FBIS), and INTNEWS on Westlaw (which includes full-text, English-language articles and English-language abstracts for non-English-language newspapers, magazines, trade journals, newsletters, and news services). Some countries have English-language newspapers that may contain the text of a new law or some information—for example, *South China Morning Post*.[77]

---

[76] http://mulr.law.unimelb.edu.au/files/aglcdl.pdf.
[77] Available on LexisNexis and Westlaw, and at http://www.scmp.com.

Chapter Nine

Comparative Law

I. *Introduction*

Comparative law is "the study of the similarities and differences between the laws of two or more countries, or between two or more legal systems. Comparative law is not itself a system of law or a body of rules, but rather a method or approach to legal inquiry."[1] In order to compare legal systems and laws, you should have some knowledge on how systems, legal rules and institutions function. To understand how they function, you need an awareness of the legal, economic and social context. Comparative analyses vary from broad reviews of legal systems, for example, *Common Law, Civil Law and the Future of Categories* (Janet Walker & Oscar G. Chase eds., 2010), to targeted study of specific laws or topics, like *Comparative Constitutional Law* (Tom Ginsburg & Rosalind Dixon eds., 2011).

II. *Secondary Sources*

A. *General Works*

Comparative law books and materials present information in a couple of different ways. Some focus on comparing legal families or traditions (civil law versus common law, ancient law, etc.). Some books compare specific countries (German law as compared to French law). Others focus on comparing topics within laws and within countries (constitutional law in Germany and the United States). And some sources do all of the above. Books are not the only sources. Much comparative work can be found in journal literature; see Chapter 5 on searching for journal articles.

---

[1] MORRIS L. COHEN ET AL., HOW TO FIND THE LAW 565 (9th ed. 1995).

To locate books on comparative law generally, use the subject heading:

comparative law

Since this is such a broad subject heading, search for books and articles using keywords: comparative, international, world, worldwide, transnational, harmonize, uniform laws, conflict of laws, region, global (or globalization). *ALR International* can be a useful place to start comparative law research since the annotations cover international topics and cite to legislation and cases from around the world. For example: *Recovery of Paintings and Other Artworks Lost During World War II—Global Cases*, 4 ALR INT. 287 (2011). This report cites to legislation and cases from Russia, Germany, Switzerland, France, and other jurisdictions.

Listed below are some examples of the above-mentioned sources.

- *Comparative Law: An Introduction* (Vivian Grosswald Curran ed., 2002).
- *Comparative Law in the 21st Century* (Andrew Harding & Esin Örücü eds., 2002).
- Peter De Cruz, *Comparative Law in a Changing World* (2d ed. 1999).
- *Foundations of Comparative Law: Methods and Typologies* (William E. Butler ed., 2011).
- Mary Ann Glendon et al., *Comparative Legal Traditions in a Nutshell* (3d ed. 2008).
- James T. McHugh, *Comparative Constitutional Traditions* (2002).
- John Henry Merryman et al., *The Civil Law Tradition: Europe, Latin America, and East Asia* (1994). Successor edition to John Henry Merryman & David S. Clark, *Comparative Law: Western European and Latin American Legal Systems* (1978).
- *Mixed Legal Systems at New Frontiers* (Esin Örücü ed., 2010).
- *New Directions in Comparative Law* (Antonia Bakardjieva Engelbrekt ed., 2009).
- Werner Menski, *Comparative Law in a Global Context: The Legal Systems of Asia and Africa* (2d ed. 2006).
- Alan Watson, *Comparative Law: Law, Reality and Society* (3d ed. 2010).
- Raymond Youngs, *English, French, and German Comparative Law* (2d ed. 2007).
- Konrad Zweigert & Hein Kötz, *Introduction to Comparative Law* (3d rev. ed. 1998).

B. *Specific Works*

Beyond comparing legal systems or jurisdictions, many comparative works focus on specific laws, topics, or regional comparisons. There is no useful subject heading for locating these materials in a catalog since they usually won't have a "comparative law" subject heading, unlike the titles noted above. Sometimes these materials will have "comparative" in the title, like Kevin Jon Heller & Markus Dirk Dubber, *The Handbook of Comparative Criminal Law* (2011); or *Indigenous Peoples and the Law: Comparative and Critical Perspectives* (Benjamin J. Richardson et al. eds., 2009). To locate comparative works on a specific topic, you will need to search using the subject heading for the topic or keywords. In some cases, a regional comparison will have the name of the region in the title or as part of the subject heading.

For example, suppose you are interested in tort law comparisons. Here are a few of the many titles that deal with comparative tort law issues.

- *Punitive Damages: Common Law and Civil Law Perspectives* (Helmut Koziol, Vanessa Wilcox eds., 2009). The subject heading is *exemplary damages*, but the tip-off that this is a comparative work is the phrase "common law and civil law perspectives."
- Gert Brüggemeier, *Modernising Civil Liability Law in Europe, China, Brazil and Russia: Texts and Commentaries* (2011). The subject headings are *liability (law)—Europe, liability (law)—China, etc.* Also, the title indicates the author is comparing several jurisdictions.
- *The Development of Product Liability* (Simon Whittaker ed. 2010). The subject heading is: *products liability—Europe, Western.*

C. A Few Good Compilations

As mentioned in Chapter 8, there are many print and electronic resources that compile the laws of several jurisdictions on a particular topic. These topical compilations make comparative research much more effective because each chapter is usually organized similarly, making comparison easy to do across jurisdictions. To locate these resources, use a library catalog to search by topic or check the Global Legal Information Catalog (Library of Congress).[2] A few of the most well known collections are listed here:

- *International Encyclopaedia of Laws* (date varies). Covers foreign law of selected jurisdictions by topic: civil procedure, commercial and economic Law, competition law, constitutional Law, contracts, corporations and partnerships, criminal law, cyber law, energy law, environmental law, family and succession law, insurance law, intellectual property, intergovernmental organizations, labor law, media law, medical law, migration law, private

---

[2] http://www.loc.gov/lawweb/servlet/Glic?home.

international law, property and trust law, religion law, social security law, sports law, tort law, and transport law.

- *International Encyclopedia of Comparative Law* (1973–). The National Reports volumes provide an outline of a country's legal system, and there are also topical volumes. The topical volumes include a variety of subjects: private international law, persons and family, succession, contracts, civil procedure, and more. Some sections are dated (especially the National Reports), but it is still a useful source especially if you are looking for an explanation of the law in effect during a specific point in time.
- *Investment Laws of the World* (1972–). Contains texts in English, French, or Spanish of investments laws and regulations for more than 150 countries; updated bi-annually.
- *International Bureau of Fiscal Documentation.* This database contains comprehensive information on tax legislation, regulations, case law and tax treaties. You can also create comparative tables allowing you to easily compare different aspects of taxation between countries. For example, you can compare corporate or individual tax rates on outbound payments (i.e. patent royalties, dividends or interest) between the source country and residence country.
- *International Franchising* (2d ed. 2011–). Covers 48 countries and includes topics on franchise trade practices and regulation of franchising, including the treatment of foreign-owned and foreign-directed businesses, nature of exchange controls, use of trade and service marks and the effect of anti-trust regulation.
- *International Immigration and Nationality Law* (2d ed. 2011–). This loose-leaf volume compiles laws for 42 jurisdictions. Each chapter (by jurisdiction) has information on government policies and attitudes towards immigration and naturalization, visa requirements, procedures for business and non-business visitors, work permits, property ownership, taxation, immigration requirements, citizenship, and deportation.
- *International Survey of Family Law* (1994–). This annual provides a review of major developments in family law and usually covering about 20 countries in each volume. A recent volume covered marriage and sexual orientation in Argentina, gender mainstreaming in the family law of China, and matrimonial property and its contractual regulation in Kazakhstan.
- *International Trust Laws and Analysis* (William H. Byrnes & Robert J. Munro, eds., 1995–). Covers legal, tax and estate planning information for 60 jurisdictions.

Beyond these larger compilations or regular reviews, there are many books and articles available covering more narrow topics or aspects of law and practice. Keep in mind that even if an article or book is not particularly current, it can provide a good place to start and allow you to identify the laws you need to update.

- Halley & Rittich, 'Critical Directions in Comparative Family Law: Gene-alogies and Contemporary Studies of Family Law Exceptionalism,' 58 *Am. J. Comp. L.* 753 (2010).
- Kadir, 'The Scope and the Nature of Computer Crimes Statutes—A Criti-cal Comparative Study,' 11 *German L.J.* 609 (2010).[3]
- *Judiciaries in Comparative Perspective* (H.P. Lee ed., 2011).
- *The Regulation of Genetically Modified Organisms: Comparative Approaches* (Bodiguel & Cardwell eds., 2010).
- *The Rule of Law in Comparative Perspective* (Mortimer Sellers & Tadeusz Tomaszewski eds., 2010).

D. *Selected Comparative Law Journals*

Articles about comparative law can be found in many different law journals, including international and foreign journals. There are some journals that focus on comparative law; some of these are listed below.

Locate relevant articles by searching journal indexes[4] (the *Index to Foreign Legal Periodicals* indexes many comparative law journals) or by searching a library catalog for relevant journals using the subject heading:

comparative law – periodicals

You can also search Westlaw and LexisNexis full-text law review databases, perhaps narrowing your results by limiting searches to the title field (West-law) or name segment (LexisNexis). Some of these journals are available on HeinOnline.[5]

- *American Journal of Comparative Law* (1952–).
- *Annual Survey of International & Comparative Law* ([1994]–).
- *Arizona Journal of International and Comparative Law* (1982–).
- *Boston College International and Comparative Law Review* (1979–).
- *Cardozo Journal of International and Comparative Law* (1995–).
- *Duke Journal of Comparative & International Law* (1991–).
- *Electronic Journal of Comparative Law* (1997–).[6]

---

[3] http://www.germanlawjournal.com/pdfs/Vol11-No6/PDF_Vol_11_No_06_609-632_RM_kadir.pdf.
[4] See Chapter 5.
[5] http://heinonline.org.
[6] Available only online, http://www.ejcl.org.

- *European Journal of Comparative Law* (2002–).
- *European Journal of Legal Studies* (2007–).[7]
- *The Georgia Journal of International and Comparative Law* (1970–).
- *Hastings International and Comparative Law Review* (1978–).
- *ILSA Journal of International & Comparative Law* (1995–).
- *Indiana International & Comparative Law Review* (1991–).
- *The International and Comparative Law Quarterly* (1952–).
- *The Journal of Comparative Law* (2006–).
- *Loyola of Los Angeles International & Comparative Law Review* (1999–).
- *Maastricht Journal of European and Comparative Law* (1994–).
- *Transnational Legal Theory* (2010–).
- *Washington University Global Studies Review* (2002–).
- *Zeitschrift für Europarecht, Internationales Privatrecht und Rechtsvergleichung* (2008–).

The journal *International Lawyer* (1966–)[8] has an annual volume called "International Legal Developments in Review" and the topics range from antitrust to international litigation to arbitration to human rights. There are also regional reports on significant legal developments throughout the world. If you want to survey the changes in financial products and services due to the financial crisis in 2008, the 2009 edition of this journal has an article comparing the developments in several jurisdictions.

For a more comprehensive list of comparative law journals, organized by region and country, see Teresa M. Miguel, 'Comparative Law: Academic Perspectives, Appendix A: Currently Published Comparative Law Journals', in *IALL International Handbook of Legal Information* 327 (Richard A. Danner & Jules Winterton eds., 2011).

III. *In Practice*

Comparative legal research is not simply an academic endeavor. Calls and emails come in regularly from practicing lawyers needing to conduct comparative research for clients.

Example: You want to understand how to commence class actions by private litigants (i.e., not by government agencies) in a variety of European countries. Generally, you need to understand how class actions operate in Europe. Start

---

[7] An Open Access journal, http://www.ejls.eu/index.php.
[8] Also available on HeinOnline.

with a keyword search on a library catalog using the terms "class actions" and "Europe." This search retrieves several useful books on point: Christopher J.S. Hodges, *The Reform of Class and Representative Actions in European Legal Systems: A New Framework for Collective Redress in Europe* (2008) and Linda Willett, *U.S.-Style Class Actions in Europe: A Growing Threat?* (2005). These sources clue you into a few other phrases to use when searching, such as "multi-party actions," "collective redress," and "mass litigation."

Example: You need to compare dual citizenship laws in Mexico and Korea. Looking at the constitution is one of the first steps you think of when researching citizenship. However, before jumping right to the constitution, take a look at *International Immigration and Nationality Law* (2d ed. 2011–). Each chapter has a section on "citizenship and nationality" and it refers to the relevant articles of the constitution as well as any relevant legislation or case law. In this case, this title only covers Mexico and not Korea. A quick check of *Foreign Law Guide* reveals another useful secondary source, *Nationality and International Law in Asian Perspective* (1990). *Foreign Law Guide* also identifies relevant Korean laws translated in *Statutes of the Republic of Korea* (1997–).

Example: You want to know about how tort law in other countries compensates for what US lawyers call pain and suffering damages, or non-economic loss, or general damages. A search using the *Index to Foreign Legal Periodicals* retrieves a recent article called *The Recovery of Non-Pecuniary Damages in Europe: A Comparative Analysis*, 34 ANNALS AIR & SPACE L. 311 (2009). To locate more information for other regions, try *The International Encyclopaedia of Laws: Torts* (2001–) which covers several non-European countries.

IV. *Research Guides*

Globalex, a collection of research guides on the web, has a section on comparative law.[9] See Paul Norman, Comparative Law or Radu D. Popa & Mirela Roznovschi, Comparative Civil Procedure: A Guide to Primary and Secondary Sources. The resources and research guides noted in Chapter 8 will also be useful when doing comparisons.

---

[9] http://www.nyulawglobal.org/globalex/index.html#.

Part Five: International Organizations

Chapter Ten

International Organizations

I. *Generally*

According to the *Yearbook of International Organizations* (1983–), as of 2011 there are over 55,000 international organizations (intergovernmental organizations (IGOs), nongovernmental organizations (NGOs), and other bodies).[1] The sheer number of organizations makes it impossible for this chapter to cover all or even a small percentage of these organizations. Some organizations, like the United Nations and the European Union, play a major role in international law, so these organizations will be covered in greater detail. Other organizations will be covered more generally in this chapter as well as in the topical chapters of this book. Moreover, understanding how a few IGOs work will help you understand how any IGO works.

A. *Definitions*

What is an intergovernmental organization (IGO)?
Generally, an IGO is a public or governmental organization created by treaty or agreement between states. Examples include the United Nations, the European Union,[2] the Council of Europe (COE), and the Organization of American States (OAS). Countries usually become members of these organizations by signing a treaty or agreement. Here is a basic outline of the legal characteristics of an IGO:

---

[1] *Yearbook of International Organizations* (1983–). Also available at http://www.uia.be/login.
[2] The European Union is considered a supranational organization, which is a specific type of IGO; see Chapter 1 for a definition of a supranational organization.

- An IGO has international legal status (privileges, immunities, rights, and duties) that is based upon its founding charter, constitution, or statute. As such, an IGO can enter into agreements with other IGOs or with states.
- An IGO usually has a legislative body that creates legal acts (decisions, resolutions, directives, etc.) that may bind the IGO and its member states under international law. Most of these legislative acts do not supersede national law (with the exception of the European Union).
- An IGO may have a dispute resolution mechanism or body that is empowered to resolve disputes among its member states.
- The IGO may have an executive body (a secretariat) that facilitates the operations of the IGO.

The World Trade Organization (WTO), for example, has all of these characteristics:

1   It was created by the Final Act Embodying the Results of the Uruguay Round of Multilateral Trade Negotiations.[3]
2   Its legislative body or the top-level decision-making body is the Ministerial Conference which meets at least once every two years.
3   There is a Dispute Settlement Body for resolving trade disputes between member States.
4   There is a WTO Secretariat headed by a Director-General.

See the WTO website for basic information and an organizational chart for more details.[4]

What is a nongovernmental organization (NGO)?
Organizations established by individuals or groups of individuals are considered NGOs. NGOs are not endowed with governmental powers or the same legal status as IGOs.[5] NGOs vary in size, structure, and influence; and some of the larger organizations, such as Amnesty International and Greenpeace, exercise considerable pressure in national and international policy debates. You may see references to NGOs as part of "civil society" (non-state, non-market institutions).

Many NGOs have consultative status with international organizations like the United Nations. Consultative status means that an NGO has been

---

[3] Apr. 15, 1994, 1867 U.N.T.S. 14, *reprinted in* 33 I.L.M. 1143 (1994).
[4] http://www.wto.org/english/thewto_e/whatis_e/tif_e/org2_e.htm.
[5] Parry & Grant Encyclopaedic Dictionary of International Law 416–17 (3d ed. 2009). Now available online by subscription.

admitted to participate or contribute to the work of the United Nations. NGOs can serve as technical experts, advisors and consultants to governments and the secretariat.[6] More information on consultative status is available on the ECOSOC website and on the UN DPI-NGO website.[7]

For more information on the legal nature of international organizations and the role these organizations play in international law, see the sources listed below. To locate similar books, search an online catalog using *international organization, international agencies, non-governmental organizations,* or *non-governmental organizations—law and legislation* as the subject.

- José Alvarez, *International Organizations as Law-makers* (2005).
- José Alvarez, *International Organizations: Then and Now*, 100 AM. J. INT'L. L. 324 (2006).
- Chittharanjan F. Amerasinghe, *Principles of the Institutional Law of International Organizations* (2d rev. ed. 2005).
- Steve Charnovitz, *Nongovernmental Organizations and International Law*, 100 AM. J. INT'L. L. 348 (2006).
- Frederick H. Gareau, *The United Nations and Other International Institutions: A Critical Analysis* (2002).
- Jan Klabbers, *International Organizations* (2005).
- Jan Klabbers, *An Introduction to International Institutional Law* (2nd ed. 2009).
- *The Legitimacy of International Organizations* (Jean-Marc Coicaud & Veijo Heiskanen eds., 2001).
- Anna-Karin Lindblom, *Non-governmental Organisations in International Law* (2005).
- Robert McCorquodale, *International Law beyond the State: Essays on Sovereignty, Non-State Actors and Human Rights* (2011).
- *Research Handbook on the Law of International Organisations* (Jan Klabbers & Åsa Wallendahl eds., 2011).
- Ingrid Rossi, *Legal Status of Non-Governmental Organizations in International Law* (2010).
- Philippe Sands & Pierre Klein, *Bowett's Law of International Institutions* (6th ed. 2009).
- Henry G. Schermers & Niels M. Blokker, *International Institutional Law: Unity within Diversity* (5th rev. ed. 2011).

---

[6] http://csonet.org.

[7] http://www.un.org/esa/coordination/ngo; http://www.un.org/wcm/content/site/dpingorelations/index.html.

- Paul C. Szasz, *Selected Essays on Understanding International Institutions and the Legislative Process* (2001).
- Anton Vedder et al., *NGO Involvement in International Governance and Policy* (2007).

B. *Background Information*

This section includes sources that contain a variety of information about organizations, such as history, structure and function, addresses, names of member countries, and a short list of publications produced by international organizations. Relevant subject headings include:

> *international agencies – periodicals*
> *international law – sources*
> *international organization – Periodicals*

See also Chapter 4 for more background sources and information.

Although IGOs often provide a lot of information on their websites, it can be useful to consult an independent source. In addition to providing a more impartial assessment of the organization, another advantage of using a source like the *Europa World Year Book* is that it provides well-organized summaries of organizational history, structure, and publications. For example, the *Europa World Year Book* entry for the Inter-American Development Bank includes a "Publications" section with which you can quickly identify the Bank's major publications.

- *Encyclopedia of Associations: International Organizations* (1989–).[8]
- *Max Planck Encyclopedia of Public International Law* (updated ed., 2008–) and previous editions.
- *Europa Directory of International Organizations* (1999–).[9]
- *Europa World Year Book* (1989–). This yearbook provides detailed information on selected international organizations. It also includes the text of the UN Charter and other documents.[10]
- *International Organizations: A Dictionary and Directory* (7th ed. 2008).
- *International Organization* (1947–). This journal covers the legal and political aspects of international organizations.[11]

---

[8] Also available online by subscription, http://www.gale.cengage.com.
[9] Also available online by subscription, http://www.europaworld.com.
[10] Also available online by subscription, http://www.europaworld.com/welcome.
[11] Also available online by subscription from JSTOR, http://ww.jstor.org, and Westlaw.

C. *Bibliographies and Research Guides*

Bibliographies and guides will help you determine what kinds of documents and publications an organization produces and how to locate them. Since the web is not always adequate for locating documents issued before 1995, or documents with limited distribution, these sources can be helpful in determining where (and whether) a document was published.

Some of these tools are listed below or you can search a library catalog using the subject headings:

> *international agencies – bibliography*
> *international agencies – information services*
> *[name of organization] – bibliography*

- George W. Baer, *International Organizations, 1918–1945: A Guide to Research and Research Materials* (1991).
- Claire M. Germain, *Germain's Transnational Law Research* (1991–).
- *Guide to International Legal Research* (2002–). Updated annually, this book covers researching a variety of international organizations: UN, EU, WTO, and regional organizations.
- *International Bibliography: Publications of Intergovernmental Organizations* (1983–1991).
- *International Information: Documents, Publications, and Electronic Information of International Governmental Organizations* (Peter I. Hajnal, 2d ed. 1997–). This two-volume work covers a few organizations in great detail.
- *Introduction to International Organizations* (Lyonette Louis-Jacques & Jeanne S. Korman eds., 1996).
- Shabtai Rosenne, *Practice and Methods of International Law* (1984).
- Robert V. Williams, *The Information Systems of Inter-Governmental Organizations: A Reference Guide* (1998).
- Jeroen Vervliet, 'International Organizations and Legal Information,' in *The IALL International Handbook of Legal Information Management* 281 (Richard A. Danner & Jules Winterton eds., 2011).

Web guides and resources:

- ASIL Guide to Electronic Resources for International Law: International Organizations. This chapter of the guide has some handy tips on locating documents and information.[12]

---

[12] http://www.asil.org/erg/?page=io.

- Non-Governmental Organizations Research Guide (Duke University) is one of the few guides that focuses on NGOs.[13]
- Non-Governmental Organizations (University of Michigan) offers information on finding NGO information, with sections on human rights NGOs, think tanks, and NGOs focused on economic and social development.[14]
- International Governmental Information (UC Berkeley).[15]
- EISIL (Electronic Information System for International Law), a good tool for locating international organizations and related resources.[16]

As an example, suppose you are asked to find out what international organizations regulate the use of nuclear power in the international arena. EISIL includes a section on Nuclear Energy[17] under its Environmental Law category, and you can quickly identify two international organizations that make international policy on this subject: the International Atomic Energy Agency and the Nuclear Energy Agency.

D. *Publications and Information*

Many IGOs issue publications and documents that may be of interest to the legal researcher: founding documents (treaties, charters, statutes); treaties where the IGO is a party; treaties where the IGO is the sponsor; legal acts, proceedings, and documents issued by the IGO's legislative body; and decisions of the IGO's adjudicative body. IGOs also produce reports that provide information on a country's laws and legal system. For example, the World Bank has a series of reports called "Legal and Judicial Sector Assessments."[18] These reports provide a detailed analysis of the legal and judicial system of particular countries, including information on key legal and judicial system institutions, legal education and training, availability of laws and regulations, access to justice, and more.

NGOs tend to publish reports, newsletters, and documents that may not have a great deal of legal weight, but that are valuable because they document conditions within countries and provide current analyses of problems and issues. The most effective method for locating these materials is to consult the

---

[13] http://guides.library.duke.edu/ngo_guide.
[14] http://guides.lib.umich.edu/ngo.
[15] http://www.lib.berkeley.edu/doemoff/govinfo/intl.
[16] http://www.eisil.org.
[17] http://www.eisil.org/index.php?sid=403234415&t=sub_pages&cat=446.
[18] To locate these, go to http://www-wds.worldbank.org; then select Documents & Reports > All Documents > By Doc Type, Legal and Judicial Sector Assessment.

NGO's website. Documents may be listed on the website under "Research," "Publications," "Library," "Topics," or other headings. Most NGO websites have a search function too, though often not a good one. You may get better results by using Google to search the site instead. To do so, add a site restriction to your search terms. You can add a site restriction in one of two ways. First, you can use Google Advanced Search and put the root of the URL in the box called "Search within a site or domain." For example, if you want to search the website of Advocates for Human Rights, you would put theadvocatesforhumanrights.org in that box. Alternatively, in a regular Google search, just add the prefix "site:"—i.e., *site:theadvocatesforhumanrights.org* along with your other search terms.

For older and harder to locate documents, try searching a library catalog and secondary sources. Many law reviews and books will cite to documents published by NGOs, especially in the area of human rights, refugees, asylum, and environmental protection. A few collections of NGO documentation also exist. In the area of human rights, see the online fee-based collection from IDC/Brill, *Online Human Rights Documents*; it contains the documents for 483 organizations, from 1980–2008.[19] Columbia University's Center for Human Rights Documentation & Research, a free website, is the official designated repository for the archives of some human rights NGOs, including Amnesty International USA, the Committee of Concerned Scientists, Human Rights First, and Human Rights Watch.

1. How to Find Documents

When searching an online catalog or database, use the name of the organization in an author search to locate the materials published under the auspices of that organization. A subject search using the name of the organization will produce materials about that organization. Be sure to note spelling variations when searching by name or keywords, such as organization and organisation or labor and labour.

Use the research guides listed above to find out what kinds of documents organizations publish as well as descriptions of how the documents are organized. Such a guide may explain the official documents of the organization as well as information on other related publications; for example, see the organization-specific guide for WTO and GATT research at http://nyulaw.libguides.com/wto_gatt. Topical guides may contain sections on the documentation of specific organizations; for example, see the ASIL topic-specific guide to human rights at http://www.asil.org/erg/?page=ihr.

---

[19] http://hrd.idcpublishers.info/hrd (also available on microfiche).

The "International Organizations" section of EISIL provides links to many research guides for individual organizations and topics.[20]

Many unofficial sources contain reproductions or compilations of important legal documents from international organizations. However, some of these may only provide access to portions of documents or only selected documents. Subject compilations, like *International Protection of the Environment: Conservation in Sustainable Development* (Wolfgang E. Burhenne & Nicholas A Robinson eds., 1995–), are good sources for documents from a variety of environmental organizations. Journals and yearbooks are another useful source. They sometimes reprint documents from IGOs and NGOs, or at least provide citations that can lead you to relevant ones. If you find a useful citation that includes a URL, but the link no longer works, remember to try the Internet Archive ("Wayback Machine"),[21] which archives web pages.

See Section I.D.3 for some tips on searching the web for international documents or contact the IGO or NGO directly. Consult the *Yearbook of International Organizations* (1983–)[22] or the *Encyclopedia of Associations: International Organizations* (1989–)[23] for more information.

For publications about international agencies generally, use the subject headings:

> *international agencies – dictionaries*
> *international agencies – encyclopedias*
> *international agencies – yearbooks*

2. *Journal Articles*

As noted above, journal articles are a good source for information about international organizations and current developments. They are also good for getting citations to international documents or information about other publications issued by IGOs and NGOs. To find articles in legal and nonlegal journals, use periodical indexes. You may also search online catalogs to find relevant periodicals using the subject headings:

> . *international agencies – periodicals*
> *international law – periodicals*
> *international organization – periodicals*

See Chapter 5 for more information on researching journal articles. Some useful journals to review on a regular basis include:

---

[20] http://www.eisil.org/index.php?sid=725989758&t=sub_pages&cat=15.
[21] http://www.archive.org.
[22] http://www.uia.be/yearbook.
[23] Also available online by subscription, http://www.gale.cengage.com.

- *International Journal of Legal Information* (1982–) (also available on HeinOnline,[24] and free on the web back to volume 33).[25]
- *International Organization* (1947–) (also available online from a variety of sources).
- *Journal of International Affairs* (1952–) (also available online from a variety of sources).
- *Government Information Quarterly* (1984–) (also available online from a variety of sources).
- *International Community Law Review* (2006–) (also available on HeinOnline).
- *International Organizations Law Review* (2004–) (also available online).
- *The Review of International Organizations* (2006–) (also available online).
- *Journal of International Organizations Studies* (2010–) (also available online).

3. *The Web*

The web is a valuable vehicle for obtaining needed documents. Many international organizations are using websites as a distribution mechanism or as a tool to alert the researcher to new publications and information. As noted in the ASIL Guide to Electronic Resources for International Law, International Organizations,

> [W]hen searching the Web for the sites of international organizations, utilize the advanced features on search engines to limit your results to sites ending in the domain name .int which is reserved for organizations established by international treaties between or among national governments. For example, in Google's Advanced Search mode,[26] enter ".int" in the domain box to limit your results.[27]

Note, however, that not all international organizations use ".int" as part of their web addresses. For example, the African Union uses ".org." It is best to locate the organization's website first, and check what its higher-level domain name is.

For instance, assume that you need to locate the *OECD Best Practices on Competition in Telecommunications* (2002). While you can search the OECD website using the site's search engine, you can also search Google using the advanced search mechanism and limiting the search to the OECD domain. (If you do a quick search for the OECD website, you will find that it uses the

---

[24] http://heinonline.org.
[25] http://scholarship.law.cornell.edu/ijli.
[26] http://www.google.com/advanced_search.
[27] http://www.asil.org/erg/?page=io.

domain name ".oecd.org.") The first three links on this list will all retrieve the appropriate OECD document, though it does not appear in the top results using the OECD's own search engine.

Web directories and compilations of sites help you locate the correct website for an IGO or NGO:

- International Governmental Organizations (Northwestern University).[28]
- Official website Locator for the United Nations Systems Organizations.[29]
- International Governmental Organizations (IGOs): Guide by Organization (Michigan State University), with sections on many UN organizations as well as regional organizations.[30]
- Union of International Associations, Database of International Organization websites.[31] Many portions of this site are available by subscription only.

You can also try searching the web for relevant NGOs using keywords and the words "nongovernmental organization" or NGO. For example, perhaps you need to research the emerging international doctrine of the "responsibility to protect." If you use the Google search *"responsibility to protect" NGO*, your top search results will include pages from the site of The International Coalition for the Responsibility to Protect,[32] a group of NGOs actively promoting the doctrine. Many NGOs will also link to other organizations working on the same issue.

Google also offers a Custom Search Engine for international organizations[33] and non-governmental organizations.[34] These search engines enable researchers to search across the websites of hundreds of IGOs or NGOs at once. You can also create your own Custom Search Engine, using Google,[35] and specify which websites you want it to search. Thus, for example, if you are researching the condition of migrant workers in the Middle East, you might identify sites such as the International Labour Organization, the International Organization for Migration, Human Rights Watch, and other IGOs and NGOs with information about the topic. This approach is particularly

---

[28] http://libguides.northwestern.edu/IGO.

[29] http://www.unsystem.org.

[30] http://libguides.lib.msu.edu/internationalgovernmentorganizations.

[31] http://www.uia.be/s/or/en/igo.

[32] http://www.responsibilitytoprotect.org.

[33] http://www.google.com/cse/home?cx=006748068166572874491%3A55ez0c3j3ey.

[34] http://www.google.com/cse/home?cx=012681683249965267634%3Aq4g16p05-ao.

[35] http://www.google.com/cse.

helpful if you need to run multiple queries (e.g., a list of related groups or sub-topics) against a group of websites.

4. *LexisNexis and Westlaw*

Neither of these databases provides access to much in the way of IGO and NGO documentation. However, for selected IGOs, some materials are available, such as GATT and WTO panel reports. Both LexisNexis and Westlaw provide full-text law reviews and indexes to periodical literature.

5. *Words of Caution*

Finding documents produced by IGOs and NGOs can be difficult and frustrating. There is a general lack of good indexing, abstracting, and bibliographies for these documents. Many organizations have their own classification schemes for documentation, or, even worse, no classification or numbering scheme. Even if you have what you think is a valid citation, the document may not actually be available on the organization's website or in a library's collection. For example, even a recent African Union document, with an official AU document number,[36] is not available on the web, and apparently in no library. And, while official documents are preferable, the publication of these documents can be quite slow.

Other chapters will focus on the United Nations, the European Union, the African Union, the Council of Europe, the Organization of American States, and the Organization for Security and Cooperation in Europe.

---

[36] African Union, Summary Report of the Working Group on the Draft Single Instrument Relating to the Merger of the African Court on Human and Peoples' Rights and the Court of Justice of the African Union, UA/EXP/Fusion.Cours/Rpt.1 (2007).

Chapter Eleven

United Nations

I. *Introduction*

The United Nations is the best-known and largest intergovernmental organization. The United Nations is the successor organization to the League of Nations, which was established in 1919 under the Treaty of Versailles 'to promote international cooperation and to achieve peace and security.'[1] The constituting document, the UN Charter,[2] was signed on June 26, 1945, at the Conference on International Organization in San Francisco.[3] The UN's mandate includes peace and security, economic and social development, human rights, decolonization, and international law. It is composed of six principal organs: the General Assembly (GA), the Security Council (SC), the Economic and Social Council (ECOSOC), the Trusteeship Council, the International Court of Justice (ICJ), and the Secretariat. With the admission of South Sudan in 2011, currently there are 193 member states.[4]

The Security Council, General Assembly, Economic and Social Council, and the Secretariat are all responsible for many other bodies, commissions, and committees within the UN system; see the Organization Chart.[5] Of particular interest to legal researchers are the autonomous organizations called "Specialized Agencies." These include the following: ILO, FAO, UNESCO, WHO, World Bank Group, IMF, ICAO, IMO, ITU, UPU, WMO, WIPO, IFAD, UNIDO, and WTO (tourism).[6] Each specialized agency has its own membership, governing bodies, budgets, and secretariats. Being a member of

---

[1] http://www.un.org/aboutun/unhistory.
[2] 3 Bevans 1153, UN Yearbook, http://www.un.org/aboutun/charter/index.html.
[3] http://www.un.org/en/aboutun/history/sanfrancisco_conference.shtml.
[4] http://www.un.org/en/members/growth.shtml.
[5] http://www.un.org/en/aboutun/structure.
[6] http://www.un.org/Overview/uninbrief/institutions.shtml.

the United Nations does not make a country a member of these independent organizations.

In addition to these organizations, there are a number of UN offices, programs, and funds, such as the Office of the UN High Commissioner for Refugees (UNHCR), the UN Development Program (UNDP), the UN Children's Fund (UNICEF), and many more.

II. *Research Guides*

Since navigating through all of the documents and information issued by the United Nations can be challenging, you should probably start with a research guide. Listed below are a few guides that deal with the United Nations specifically, but they may also be helpful for researching other intergovernmental organizations.

- *Accidental Tourist on the New Frontier: An Introductory Guide to Global Legal Research* (Jeanne Rehberg & Radu Popa eds., 1997); see chapter 7.
- Brenda Brimmer et al., *A Guide to the Use of United Nations Documents* (1962). This is good for historical research.
- Claire Germain, *Germain's Transnational Law Research* (1991–); see IV-346.
- *Guide to International Legal Research* (2002–); see § 5.06[3].
- Peter I. Hajnal, *Guide to United Nations Organization, Documentation and Publishing for Students, Researchers, Librarians* (1978).
- *International Information: Documents, Publications, and Information Systems of International Governmental Organizations* (2 vols., Peter I. Hajnal ed. 1988); chapter 2 is on the United Nations.
- *Introduction to International Organizations* (Lyonette Louis-Jacques & Jeanne S. Korman eds., 1996); see pp. 207–391.

Some of the best guides are available on the web:

- ASIL Guide to Electronic Resources for International Law: United Nations.[7]
- United Nations Documentation: Research Guide (UN Dag Hammarskjöld Library).[8]

---

[7] http://www.asil.org/erg/?page=un.
[8] http://www.un.org/Depts/dhl/resguide/index.html.

- United Nations System Pathfinder.[9]
- Research Guide: The United Nations (Columbia University).[10]
- Research Guide to League of Nations Documents and Publications (Northwestern University).[11]

> **Example**: You are asked to find a General Assembly resolution from the 2010 session, relating to measures to prevent terrorists from acquiring weapons of mass destruction. Pulling up the United Nations Documentation: Research Guide (by a web search for *united nations research guide* or by entering the URL provided in this chapter), you see "Quick Links." The "Quick Links" let you go immediately to a list of General Assembly resolutions for the 65st session (2010). By using your browser's "Find" function (Control f) to look for the terms *mass destruction*, you quickly locate the title of the resolution, along with a link to the PDF version.

> **Example**: You are beginning a project on international intellectual property law. Because you don't know what international agency is most active in this area, you start with the UN System Pathfinder. By choosing the headings "International Law," then "Intellectual Property," you see that the World Intellectual Property Organization (WIPO) is the key organization. The pathfinder also offers a link to WIPO's annual reports.

III. *Background Information*

Basic information about the United Nations is available on its official website—see "UN at a Glance."[12] This page provides an introduction to the structure and work of the United Nations. For more detailed information, check out the many books about the United Nations and its work. Some of these include the following:

- *Annual Review of United Nations Affairs* (1957–). ARUNA provides the text of important documents from the five key UN bodies, though publication lags.
- *Basic Facts about the United Nations* (various editions, latest is 2011). This is a basic handbook providing information about the organization.
- *Everyone's United Nations* (1979–1986). This book describes the structure, history, and procedures of the UN organs and specialized agencies; it contains text of the Charter of the United Nations, the Statute of the International Court of Justice, and the Universal Declaration of Human Rights.

---

[9] http://www.un.org/depts/dhl/pathfind/frame/start.htm.
[10] http://library.law.columbia.edu/guides/United_Nations.
[11] http://digital.library.northwestern.edu/league/background.html.
[12] http://www.un.org/en/aboutun/index.shtml.

- Edward Osmancyzk, *Encyclopedia of the United Nations and International Agreements* (2003). This four-volume set provides brief explanations of terms related to the United Nations as well as international law and economics.[13]
- *United Nations Handbook* (1973–). This handbook provides up-to-date information on all of the organs of the United Nations as well as the specialized agencies. This is a good source for information on the purpose and structure of a particular body or agency.
- *The United Nations System and Its Predecessors* (1997). This book contains a collection of important documents, including some League of Nations materials.
- *Yearbook of the United Nations* (1946/47–). This yearbook includes full text of resolutions and gives useful references to important reports and documents. Many UN bodies and institutions issue their own yearbooks, such as the *Yearbook of the International Law Commission*. Now available free on the web.[14]
- *UN Chronicle* (1975–). This is a good source for current information; it also provides cites to important resolutions and documents. An online edition is also available on the UN website.[15]

> **Example:** To get a quick introduction to the international law instruments governing the treatment of prisoners, check the *Encyclopedia of the United Nations and International Agreements* (2003). The entry for "Prisoners" lists some key international instruments, including a Body of Principles for the Protection of All Persons under Any Form of Detention or Imprisonment,[16] and it sets out the text of those principles.

For some sources more focused on international law, see:

- *Charter of the United Nations: A Commentary* (Bruno Simma ed., 2d ed. 2002). This is the most detailed commentary on the UN Charter, with relevant citations to other documents.
- Benedetto Conforti, *The Law and Practice of the United Nations* (4th rev. ed. 2010). This book provides a legal analysis of membership, structure, origins, and practice.
- Simon Chesterman et al., *Law and Practice of the United Nations: Documents and Commentary* (2008).

---

[13] Also available online by subscription, http://www.routledgeonline.com/politics/Book.aspx?id=w032.

[14] http://unyearbook.un.org.

[15] http://www.un.org/wcm/content/site/chronicle.

[16] G.A. Res. 43/173, annex, 43 U.N. GAOR Supp. (No. 49) at 298, U.N. Doc. A/43/49 (1988).

- *Max Planck Yearbook of United Nations Law* (1998–). This yearbook focuses on the activities of the United Nations in the field of international law.[17]

To locate more books about the United Nations and its work, search a library catalog. For example, search UNBISnet, the catalogue for the UN Dag Hammarskjöld Library,[18] and the Library of the UN Office at Geneva.[19] While the *United Nations* is a valid Library of Congress subject heading for locating books, it is not very specific. Keyword searching is more effective, e.g., *states* and *united nations*.

IV. *Documents and Publications*

There are four basic types of UN documents: periodicals, sales publications, mimeographed/masthead documents, and official records. Periodicals (like the *UN Chronicle*) can be located by searching the indexes mentioned above.

Periodicals generally report on the activities of the United Nations and its subsidiary organizations.

Sales publications include yearbooks and annuals (*Yearbook of the United Nations* and *Yearbook on Human Rights*) serials, monographs, and special studies. They are classified as "sales publications" because the United Nations feels the public (libraries, researchers, schools, etc.) has enough interest in them to purchase them. Any type of UN document can end up as a sales publication.

Mimeographed[20] (now more commonly called "masthead") documents include provisional records of meetings, reports, resolutions, and other working documents of the UN organs. Some are republished in final corrected form in the official records or sales publications. Official records contain the meeting records of the UN organs (usually summary records, with the exception of the records of General Assembly and First Committee and Security Council meetings which are verbatim—*procès-verbaux*). Annexes contain the text of agenda items (papers submitted to the organs for discussion), and supplements contain reports of subsidiary organs and resolutions.

---

[17] Some volumes freely available on the web, http://www.mpil.dc/ww/en/pub/research/details/publications/institute/mpyunl.cfm#volumes. Also available on HeinOnline by subscription, http://www.heinonline.org/HOL/Index?index=intyb/maxpyb&collection=intyb.

[18] http://unbisnet.un.org.

[19] http://www.unog.ch/library.

[20] "Mimeographed" refers to an old method of making multiple copies of documents.

For more information on types of UN documents, see Section II on research guides.

A. *UN Legal Documentation*

An excellent overview of UN legal materials is contained in the United Nations Documentation: Research Guide, International Law chapter.[21] The chapter defines the principal UN bodies working in the area of international law; identifies the document series symbols attached to their working documents, as well as the major types of documents and publications they produce; and gives some basic tips for conducting topical searches in the Library's online database UNBISnet.[22]

The principal legal bodies of the United Nations are the Sixth Committee of the General Assembly, the International Law Commission (ILC), and the United Nations Commission on International Trade Law (UNCITRAL). See the United Nations Documentation: Research Guide, noted above, for an understanding of the documents and publications issued by these principal legal bodies, and use UNBISnet to locate documents and publications.[23] ODS allows you to search the full-text of UN documents; UNBISnet does not.

The UN website is a good tool for locating the full text of selected documents. See UN Documents[24] for access to documents·from the General Assembly, the Security Council, the Economic and Social Council, and the Secretariat. However, not all UN documents are available from this site.

The UNBISnet database should be used to locate legal documents (more details below). For access to more documents, see ODS (Official Document System of the United Nations),[25] which covers all types of official UN documentation beginning in 1993, and is updated daily. The system does not contain press releases, UN sales publications, or the UN Treaty Series. The most efficient way to locate documents through ODS is by using a UN document symbol. If you don't have a symbol, use UNBISnet to help you locate the correct symbol. Most UN documents collections are arranged by the document symbol. The basic principle is that documents are identified by the issuing body and are composed of capital letters and numbers. The first letter(s) indicates the main body of the UN (A/ is the General Assembly, E/ is

---

[21] http://www.un.org/depts/dhl/resguide/specil.htm.
[22] See Maureen Ratynski Andersen, *Where to Begin…When You Don't Know How to Start: Tips for Researching UN Legal Materials*, 31 INT'L J. LEGAL INFO. 264 (2003).
[23] http://unbisnet.un.org.
[24] http://www.un.org/en/documents/index.shtml.
[25] http://www.un.org/en/documents/ods.

ECOSOC, etc.). Specific symbols after the first slash indicate the sub-body within the main body (/CN is a commission, /WP is working party, etc.).

The classification system of the United Nations is explained (with lists of the abbreviations) in many of the research guides mentioned above. The *UNDOC: Current Index* lists new document symbols. See also the Document Symbols section of the UN website.[26]

Examples of Document Symbols:[27]

A/64/1	General Assembly, 64th session, document no. 1
A/CONF.157/PC/63/Add.4	General Assembly, World Conference on Human Rights, Preparatory Committee, document no. 63, addendum no. 4
E/CN.4/Sub.2/2003/38/Rev.2	Economic and Social Council, Commission on Human Rights, Subcommission on the Promotion and Protection of Human Rights, year: 2003, document no. 38, revision no. 2

By the way, many UN documents can be retrieved in a simple web search by entering the document symbol along with a couple of other keywords.

Example: You can retrieve the General Assembly resolution A/RES/53/243 or the CEDAW report CEDAW/C/DEN/CO/6 simply by entering those document symbols into Google. Other document symbols are not sufficiently unique; for example, if you are searching for Security Council Resolution S/RES/1216, that document will rank high in your search results only if you add "Security Council" to the symbol for your search: i.e., *S/RES/1216 security council.*

B. *Document Indexes*

Over the years, there have been many UN document indexes. A good overview of UN document indexes is available on the UN Dag Hammarskjöld Library website.[28]

For most UN research, you will probably be able to find what you need on the web. If you are doing some historical research, however, you may need to consult some of the older UN document indexes. These include: *United*

---

[26] http://www.un.org/Depts/dhl/resguide/symbol.htm#symbols.

[27] http://www.un.org/depts/dhl/resguide/symbol.htm#symbols.

[28] http://www.un.org/Depts/dhl/resguide/itp.htm.

Nations Documents Index (UNDI) (1950–1962), *United Nations Documents Index* (UNDI) (1963–1973), *UNDEX* (1973–1978), and *UNDOC: Current Index* (1979–1996). The last paper index is *United Nations Documents Index* (1998–2007). Issued quarterly, this index provided broad subject access to UN documents; UNBISnet is the online version.

AccessUN[29] is a commercial electronic index to UN documents including Official Records, masthead documents, draft resolutions, meeting records, UN Sales Publications, and the UN Treaty Series citations. It also includes the full text of several thousand UN documents. AccessUN covers 1944 to the present and is available by subscription only, but many academic libraries make this index available to users.

UNBISnet (UN Bibliographic Information System) is a valuable index of UN publications and publications held in the two main UN libraries, since 1979 (or earlier for selected documents).[30] Not only can you search for UN documents, but you can also search voting records, speeches, and publications held by these two libraries, including non-UN publications. Some records are linked to the full text of the document (usually in PDF format from ODS). Use the UNBIS Thesaurus for assistance with subject searches. UNBISnet also offers date restriction options through boxes near the bottom of the screen. By default, results appear in reverse chronological order, but researchers can specify other ranking options.

> **Example:** A research assistant was asked to locate the recent UN Convention on Corruption. She went to UNBISnet, and entered "corruption" as a subject heading. She took advantage of the options for minimizing irrelevant results by specifying that she wanted only UN documents, in English, and selecting "treaties, etc." as the "type of material." She retrieved four results, with the Convention included as part of the first and second documents.

C. Resolutions

Resolutions of the major organs of the United Nations are often sought after by legal researchers. General Assembly resolutions are compiled in the last supplement of its official records. Between 1946 and 1975, resolutions were numbered consecutively; those adopted after 1975 include the session as the third component of the symbol.

Resolutions of the General Assembly and the Security Council are all on the web back to the first year of the United Nations. Economic and Social

---

[29] http://www.newsbank.com/schools/product.cfm?product=159.
[30] http://unbisnet.un.org.

Council resolutions currently only extend back to 1992.[31] Some common sources for GA resolutions include:

- *Resolutions and Decisions Adopted by the General Assembly...* (1976–). This press release is sometimes available seven to eight months before the official record supplement.
- *Yearbook of the United Nations* (1946/47–). This is not a good source for current resolutions.
- AccessUN. This is a subscription database described in Section IV.B.
- ODS. This is a freely available source described in Section IV.A.
- UNBISnet.[32]
- UN Documents website.[33]

The resolutions of the Security Council appear in an unnumbered supplement to its official records. Unlike GA resolutions, SC resolutions are numbered in one continuous sequence since 1946. These documents are available in the SC official records and all of the sources mentioned above. Resolutions are published in the first numbered supplement of the official records of the Economic and Social Council (ECOSOC) and of the Trusteeship Council. Some ECOSOC documents and resolutions are available on the UN website.[34] See also UNBISnet for access to Economic and Social Council resolutions from 1946 to present.

D. *Treaties*

Start by consulting the United Nations Documentation: Research Guide on Treaties.[35] This guide outlines major UN publications related to treaty research.

- *United Nations Treaty Series* (U.N.T.S.) (1946/1947–). U.N.T.S. contains both bilateral and multilateral treaties in the language of the original treaty, as well as English and French. The United Nations makes the full text of the published UN treaty series—as well as new, unpublished treaties—available on the web through the United Nations Treaty Collection.[36]

---

[31] http://www.un.org/esa/documents/ecosocmainres.htm.
[32] http://unbisnet.un.org.
[33] http://www.un.org/en/documents/index.shtml.
[34] http://www.un.org/en/ecosoc/docs/docs.shtml.
[35] http://www.un.org/depts/dhl/resguide/spectreat.htm.
[36] http://treaties.un.org.

Multilateral Treaties Deposited with the Secretary General (1982–).[37] This is a very useful tool for locating the citation to a treaty (often including cites to conference proceedings if the treaty is not yet available in U.N.T.S.). The participating parties with the dates of signature and ratification are also included. This source is also available through the United Nations Treaty Collection on the web, where it is updated more frequently than the print version.

Collections of multilateral treaties are accessible through many UN and specialized agency websites; here is a sampling of what's available:

- FAO Conventions and Agreements (Food & Agriculture Organization).[38]
- ILOLEX (International Labor Organization).[39]
- UNESCO Legal Instruments.[40]
- Office of the High Commissioner for Human Rights.[41]
- WIPO-Administered Treaties.[42]

E. *International Court of Justice*

The International Court of Justice (ICJ or World Court) is the principal judicial organ of the United Nations. The ICJ Statute[43] is an annex to the Charter of the United Nations. Information on the history, composition, jurisdiction, procedure, and decisions of the Court is available on the ICJ website.[44] If you need more assistance with ICJ documents, see Germain's International Court of Justice Research Guide.[45] To locate books about the ICJ, do a subject search using *International Court of Justice*. See also Chapter 22 of this book, on International Courts and Tribunals.

There are many publications containing ICJ documents.

- *Reports of Judgments, Advisory Opinions and Orders* (1947–).
- *Pleadings, Oral Arguments, Documents* (1949–). This series contains motions, briefs, and oral arguments.

---

[37] http://treaties.un.org/pages/ParticipationStatus.aspx.
[38] http://www.fao.org/Legal/treaties/treaty-e.htm.
[39] http://www.ilo.org/ilolex/english.
[40] http://portal.unesco.org/en/ev.php-URL_ID=12025&URL_DO=DO_TOPIC&URL_SECTION=-471.html.
[41] http://www2.ohchr.org/english/law.
[42] http://www.wipo.int/treaties/en.
[43] http://www.icj-cij.org/documents/index.php?p1=4&p2=2&p3=0. (Cited as Statute of the International Court of Justice, 3 Bevans 1179, 59 Stat. 1055, T.S. No. 993.)
[44] http://www.icj-cij.org/court/index.php?p1=1.
[45] http://library.lawschool.cornell.edu/WhatWeDo/ResearchGuides/ICJ.cfm.

- ICJ, *Yearbook* (1947–). This contains summaries of judgments, advisory opinions, and orders of the Court.

To see whether your library carries these publications, search by title, or enter *International Court of Justice* as an author search.
Several tools exist to help the researcher locate relevant decisions.

- *Digest of the Decisions of the International Court of Justice* (1978) (summaries of cases from 1959–1975).
- *Digest of the Decisions of the International Court of Justice, 1976–1985* (1978).
- *Répertoire de la Jurisprudence de la Cour Internationale de Justice* (1947–1992) = *Repertory of Decisions of the International Court of Justice (1947–1992)* (2 vols., 1995).
- *World Court Digest* (1993–) (1986–2000). See the Max Planck website for an electronic version of the *World Court Digest*.[46]

Full-text judgments are also available on the web, including the ICJ official website, which has full text for most of its decisions and summaries of the rest.[47] See also Westlaw (full coverage of ICJ decisions in INT-ICJ) and LexisNexis (full coverage in Legal > Area of Law -By Topic > International Law > Cases). ICJ decisions and pleadings are searchable on WorldLII's International Courts & Tribunals Project.[48] Decisions are also available on the Project on International Courts and Tribunals (PICT), along with basic documents and biographies of the judges.[49]

For judgments and documents from the Permanent Court of International Justice (PCIJ), the ironically-named predecessor to the ICJ, conduct an author search on a library catalog using *Permanent Court of International Justice*. PCIJ decisions are also available on the ICJ website, on HeinOnline,[50] and on a site called worldcourts.com.[51]

F. *Other Tribunals*

Decisions and documents from other international courts under the authority of the United Nations include the sites listed below. See also the United

---

[46] http://www.mpil.de/ww/en/pub/research/details/publications/institute/wcd.cfm.
[47] http://www.icj-cij.org/docket/index.php?p1=3&p2=3.
[48] http://www.worldlii.org/int/cases/ICJ.
[49] http://www.pict-pcti.org.
[50] http://www.heinonline.org.
[51] http://www.worldcourts.com.

Nations Documentation: Research Guide on International Law for guidance on researching these tribunals.[52]

- International Criminal Court (ICC).[53]
- International Criminal Tribunal for the former Yugoslavia (ICTY).[54]
- International Criminal Tribunal for Rwanda (ICTR).[55]
- International Tribunal for the Law of the Sea (ITLOS).[56]
- United Nations Administrative Tribunal (UNAT).[57]

Other tribunals created wholly or in part by the United Nations, but not directly under its control, include

- Special Tribunal for Lebanon.[58]
- Extraordinary Chambers in the Courts of Cambodia for the Prosecution of Crimes Committed during the Period of Democratic Kampuchea.[59]
- Special Court for Sierra Leone.[60]

International criminal tribunals are discussed more fully in Chapters 16 (international criminal law) and 22 (International Courts and Tribunals). Westlaw offers databases of decisions from the Yugoslavia[61] and Rwanda[62] tribunals. Many libraries collect the print resources for these tribunals as well as books and materials about these bodies. Search library catalogs using the tribunal name as a keyword, an author, or a subject.

G. *Journal Literature*

Journal literature is a good way to locate information on the United Nations and international law issues, especially for current topics. See Chapter 5 for more information on researching journal articles. UNBISnet also indexes some non-UN publications, including journal articles. When searching for

---

[52] http://www.un.org/depts/dhl/resguide/specil.htm.
[53] http://www.icc-cpi.int.
[54] http://www.icty.org.
[55] http://www.unictr.org.
[56] http://www.itlos.org.
[57] http://untreaty.un.org/UNAT/main_page.htm.
[58] http://www.stl-tsl.org.
[59] http://www.eccc.gov.kh/en.
[60] http://www.sc-sl.org.
[61] INT-ICTY database.
[62] INT-ICTR database.

articles about UN subsidiary and specialized agencies, keep in mind that the terms "united nations" may not appear in the article or index entry.

> **Example:** If you are searching for information about the World Intellectual Property Organization, use "WIPO" and the organization's full name as alternative search terms.

H. *Current Awareness*

You can monitor many different sources to learn about what's going on at the United Nations or to learn about new reports and documents.

- *UN Chronicle* is a good source for current information and also provides cites to important resolutions and documents. Selected articles are available on the web.[63]
- The UN News Centre provides access to the Daily News, press releases, briefings, etc.[64]
- Recent Additions on the UN website keeps you informed about new documents and information on the UN website, including new websites and webcasts.[65]
- UN Pulse alerts you to selected UN online information, major reports, publications, and documents. This blog, created and maintained by a team of reference librarians at the UN Dag Hammarskjöld Library in New York, is updated as new information is published and received.[66]

Other non-UN groups provide information about UN activities and monitor the work of the organization. UN Wire is an independent news briefing about the United Nations available by free subscription[67] and UN Watch monitors the performance of the United Nations with a focus on human rights.[68]

I. *Other Websites*

Listed below are some sites which are good starting points for locating other UN sites, documents, and related information. Many of the documents

---

[63] http://www.un.org/wcm/content/site/chronicle.
[64] http://www.un.org/news.
[65] http://www.un.org/en/additions/index.shtml.
[66] http://un-library.tumblr.com/.
[67] https://www.smartbrief.com/un_wire/index.jsp.
[68] http://www.unwatch.org.

prepared before and after UN conferences are now available on the web before they are issued in paper.

- Official UN websites includes specialized topical sites, such as International Law, Peace and Security, Economic and Social Development, Human Rights and Humanitarian Affairs.[69]
- Official website Locator for the United Nations System of Organizations provides alphabetical and thematic indexes of UN websites.[70]

Each specialized agency has its own website; link to these sites from the Structure and Organization page of the United Nations[71] or consult a directory of international governmental organizations.[72] You should consult these websites for history, membership, documents, treaties, reports, and other information prepared under the auspices of the specialized agency. For assistance with researching specialized agencies, see the guide prepared by the Stanford University Library, United Nations Specialized Agencies.[73]

---

[69] http://www.un.org/en.
[70] http://www.unsystem.org.
[71] http://www.un.org/en/aboutun/structure/index.shtml.
[72] See Section I.B., this chapter, for information on such directories.
[73] http://www-sul.stanford.edu/depts/jonsson/collections/intl/spec.html.

Chapter Twelve

The European Union

I. *Introduction*

The European Union holds a unique place among IGOs because it is a supranational organization. Its member states have given up some of their sovereignty in return for the advantages of a common market. The relationship between a member state and the European Union creates a rough landscape for the legal researcher. You must identify relevant EU law in addition to national laws, and you must understand the relationship between the two kinds of law. Moreover, EU documentation is voluminous; it takes practice to sort out the key documents.

The EU evolved from the 1951 founding of the European Coal and Steel Community (ECSC), which led the way for the European Atomic Energy Community (EURATOM) and the European Economic Community (EEC), formed in 1957. These three separate institutions merged in 1967. The term "European Union" (EU) appeared in 1992, with the Treaty of Maastricht. The Treaty of Maastricht also removed the term "Economic" from "European Economic Community," which is why you may see materials referring to the EC. Don't worry much about the terminology, but keep it in mind if you are searching library catalogs or other databases for older materials.

A. *Sources of EU Law*

The primary source of EU law is the set of treaties that establish the European Union and its powers. The treaties provide authority for secondary EU law and take precedence over the law of member states. Written in fairly broad language, the treaties have been fleshed out by EU regulations, directives, and decisions—these instruments comprise the EU's secondary legislation. (Note that regulations and directives are much more important than decisions.) Treaties and secondary legislation are roughly analogous to US federal laws and regulations.

1. *Treaties (Primary Legislation)*

The European Union began with a fairly limited treaty in 1951. Later treaties expanded its powers. The main "founding" treaties you should know are the following:

- Treaty Establishing the European Coal and Steel Community, April 18, 1951 (also called the ECSC Treaty or Treaty of Paris). This treaty expired in 2002; its main importance is that it was the first of the EU treaties.
- Treaty Establishing the European Economic Community, March 25, 1957 (also called the Rome Treaty).
- Treaty Establishing a Single Council and a Single Commission of the European Communities, April 8, 1965 (also called the Merger Treaty).
- Single European Act, February 17, 1986.
- Treaty on European Union, February 7, 1992 (also called the Maastricht Treaty or TEU).
- Treaty of Amsterdam Amending the Treaty on European Union, the Treaties Establishing the European Communities and Certain Related Acts, October 2, 1997 (also called the Treaty of Amsterdam).
- Treaty of Nice Amending the Treaty on European Union, the Treaties Establishing the European Communities and Certain Related Acts, 2001 (also called the Treaty of Nice).
- Treaty of Lisbon amending the Treaty on European Union and the Treaty establishing the European Community, 2007 (also called Treaty of Lisbon or Lisbon Treaty). The Treaty of Lisbon incorporates the Charter of Fundamental Rights and the European Convention on Human Rights into EU law, although a few member states are exempted.

These treaties are easily found by searching their names on the Internet, but most of the time you will want to work with a consolidated version.[1] A web search such as *consolidated treaty european union* quickly retrieves the text. For a useful summary of the main goals of each treaty except the 2007 Treaty of Lisbon, see Marylin Raisch, European Union Law: An Integrated Guide to Electronic and Print Research.[2]

The Treaty of Amsterdam renumbered the articles from the earlier treaties; thus, if you're reading EU documents or commentary from before 1998, those sources may refer to different article numbers from the current ones. Some post-Amsterdam sources include both article numbers—in the format, for example, Article 81 (ex Art. 85). Article 85 is the old treaty article

---

[1] The founding treaties and consolidated versions are available at http://eur-lex.europa.eu/en/treaties/index.htm.
[2] http://www.llrx.com/features/eulaw2.htm.

on Restraint of Competition; Article 81 is the new number. If you need a conversion chart, search on the Web for "Table of Equivalences Referred to in Article 12 of the Treaty of Amsterdam," or consult the *Official Journal*, at 1997 O.J. (C 340) 85. The Treaty of Lisbon added new articles; for a comprehensive Table of Equivalences, see the *Official Journal*, at 2008 O.J. (C 115) 362.[3]

Other types of EU treaties include "accession treaties," marking the addition of a new country to the EU;[4] and treaties made between the EU and other entities, such as other countries or intergovernmental organizations.[5]

2. Regulations (Secondary Legislation)

European Union "regulations" resemble federal statutes or regulations. They apply directly to all member states. An example of a regulation is Commission Regulation No. 297/2011, imposing special conditions governing the import of feed and food from Japan following the accident at the Fukushima nuclear power station, 2011 O.J. (L 80) 5 (EU). Regulations and other EU legislation used to have "(EC)" in parentheses after the citation; starting in 2010 they have "(EU)" after them.

3. Directives (Secondary Legislation)

"Directives" also apply to all member states, but they allow states to devise their own means of complying with the policy goals prescribed in the directives. Usually, the European Union acts through directives, rather than regulations, leaving member states more flexibility regarding implementation. An example of a directive is Council Directive 2001/29 on the Harmonisation of Certain Aspects of Copyright and Related Rights in the Information Society, 2001 O.J. (L 167) 10 (EC). EU members have adopted varying national legislation in compliance with this Directive.

Directives contain time limits giving member states a certain amount of time to comply, whether by enacting legislation, regulations, or even constitutional amendments. It is not unusual, however, for member states to fail to meet these deadlines.

4. Decisions (Secondary Legislation)

"Decisions" have narrower scope than regulations and directives. They bind only the parties to which they are addressed. A decision may be addressed to one member state or to a corporation. More often, decisions simply address some internal EU procedure. An example is Council Decision appointing

---

[3] http://eur-lex.europa.eu/LexUriServ/LexUriServ.do?uri=OJ:C:2008:115:0361:0388:EN:PDF.

[4] Accession treaties are available at http://eur-lex.europa.eu/en/treaties/index.htm#accession.

[5] http://eur-lex.europa.eu/en/treaties/index.htm#other.

two Irish members and an Irish alternate member of the Committee of the Regions, 2011 O.J. (L 261) 25 (EU).

B. *EU Law-Making Institutions*

Three main bodies play key roles in the EU legislative process; they are described briefly below.

1. *European Commission*[6]

The European Commission drafts legislative proposals. In some respects, the Commission acts like the Executive Branch of the US government: it administers and implements the law, and it negotiates treaties. The Commission is organized into Directorates-General (DGs), which have responsibility in various areas of the law (e.g., competition, taxation and customs, fisheries). The DGs draft legislation and administer the law in their portfolio areas.

2. *European Parliament*[7]

After a weak start, the Parliament has played an increasingly important role in the legislative process. Parliament now adopts most legislation in "codecision" with the Council of Ministers.[8] While the Parliament cannot initiate legislation, it can amend or veto it in most policy areas.

3. *Council of Ministers (Council of the European Union)*[9]

The Council of Ministers has final legislative authority. It can amend legislative proposals from the Commission, but only by unanimous vote.

It is composed of government ministers from member countries. The composition of the Council, however, varies depending on the subject matter that the Council is addressing. For example, member states' finance ministers meet together as the Council to consider matters of economy and finance. This consideration includes voting on proposed legislation.

C. *European Court of Justice*[10]

The European Court of Justice plays an informal but important law-making role, filling in gaps in the EU's treaties and legislation. The Court has created

---

6 http://ec.europa.eu/index_en.htm.

7 http://www.europarl.europa.eu/portal/en.

8 For a brief explanation of the three procedures used for EU lawmaking, see RALPH H. FOLSOM, EUROPEAN UNION LAW IN A NUTSHELL 59–61 (7th ed. 2011). The EU's explanation of the codecision procedure is here: http://ec.europa.eu/codecision/index_en.htm.

9 http://www.consilium.europa.eu/homepage.aspx?lang=en.

10 http://curia.europa.eu/jcms/jcms/j_6.

an EU "common law" consisting of general principles of law, such a duty to respect fundamental human rights or a right to contractual certainty.

Decisions of the European Union's courts—the European Court of Justice and the Court of First Instance—lack precedential value. The courts' verdicts bind only the parties to whom they are addressed. Previous court decisions may be used as *persuasive* authority.

One important aspect of the Court of Justice's jurisprudence, however, is its ruling that EU law has primacy over member states' laws.[11] This doctrine has enabled the Court of Justice to invalidate numerous national laws.

D. Research Strategies and Information Sources

This section will address some common research scenarios in EU law.

1. Finding a Known EU Document

a. Legislation

If you have a citation to the *Official Journal*, your task will be fairly easy. EU legislation is published in the *Official Journal of the European Communities*, usually referred to as "O.J." This journal is divided into the "L" series and the "C" series (including CE and CA). Final legislative acts and treaties appear in the "L" series. The "C" series contains preparatory acts, information, and notices. The O.J. is available on the web from 1968,[12] and on both LexisNexis and Westlaw back to 1952 for the "L" series.

Official Journal:	2011 O.J. L 281/1	2011 = Year L281 = Issue in L Series 1 = page # in Issue L281
Regulations:	(EU) 1083/2011	EU = European Union initials 1083 = number of regulation numbered consecutively 2011 = year
Other legal acts:	2011/76/EU	2011 = year 76 = number of decision or directive EU = European Union initials

Official Journal Citations

---

[11] Case 6/64, Costa v. ENEL, 1964 E.C.R. 1251.

[12] http://eur-lex.europa.eu/JOIndex.do. The English version starts in 1973 online; note that there is a special English edition in print (or at many libraries, microfiche) that contains English translation of acts adopted before the UK acceded to the EU.

The O.J. website has drop-down boxes into which you can put the year, series, and issue number. Clicking "Search" will take you into the table of contents for that issue.

b. Cases

Finding an EU case with a known citation—for example, 2009 E.C.R. I-2665—is also fairly straightforward; you can use the "Find" function on Westlaw. LexisNexis's "Get a Document" feature does not work with citations to the *European Court Reports*, but you can search the "CITES" segment in Legal > Global Legal > European Union > Case Law > EUR-Lex European Union Cases. The CITES segment search doesn't work perfectly for ECR citations. For best results, drop the year and the "ECR"—search only on the page number (e.g., I-2665), and add a date restriction.

You can also find cases on the website of the European Court of Justice, Curia.[13] However, you will have to use the case number rather than the E.C.R. citation. You can often find the case number (or the case itself) just with a Google search; if not, use EUR-LEX search of ECJ cases by E.C.R. citation to retrieve the case.[14]

The official case reports for the ECJ and the Court of First Instance are the *Reports of Cases before the Court of Justice and the Court of First Instance*. These reports are also called the *European Court Reports*, and are abbreviated as E.C.R. (e.g., 2004 E.C.R. I-5039). Unofficial paper reporters, which are more current, include the *European Community Cases*, part of the *European Union Law Reporter*, and the *Common Market Law Reports*, which has selected cases (this publication is also on Westlaw as CML-RPTS). As in the US, some court decisions are "unpublished"—starting in 2004, some decisions are available only via online sources such as Curia.[15] Unpublished decisions are available only in the language of the deliberation and of the decision; thus, you may not be able to find them in English.

2. *Finding Relevant Law*

One easy way to identify relevant EU law is to use the subject approach of the Summaries of EU Legislation website.[16] This site has a hierarchical organization starting with broad subject categories (e.g., Consumers, Environment, or Energy). You can click on increasingly specific subjects; at the lower levels, Summaries of EU Legislation lists relevant EU legislation. For example, to

---

[13] http://curia.europa.eu/jurisp/cgi-bin/form.pl?lang=en.

[14] http://eur-lex.europa.eu/RECH_recueil.do.

[15] http://curia.europa.eu/jcms/jcms/Jo2_14954.

[16] http://europa.eu/legislation_summaries/index_en.htm (formerly "SCADPLUS").

find EU regulations on the labelling of "organic" food, start with Consumers. One subcategory is "Product Labeling and Packaging," which includes the even more specific category "Production and labelling of organic products." Clicking on this category retrieves a web page that identifies, summarizes, and links to the governing EU regulation. The page also identifies related legislation and provides links to those documents.

Using secondary sources is another good way to find relevant legislation. In addition to treatises, websites, and journal articles, many researchers use the Sweet & Maxwell *European Union Law Reporter* (2000–). This publication summarizes and identifies governing EU law in major subject areas.

Current EU law is available on the free EU website Europa,[17] but it can be confusing to navigate this huge site. One resource for current legislation is the Directory of European Union consolidated legislation[18]—an outline of all EU law. You can navigate from broad to narrow subject headings, eventually reaching the text of actual instruments. For many researchers, however, it is hard to tell where a topic falls within the broad groups: for example, intellectual property legislation falls under the heading "Law relating to undertakings."

Another useful tool for locating EU law by topic is the A–Z Index of the European Commission.[19] This convenient index leads you to the pages on the Europa website that provide information about a topic as well as the relevant legislation. You can also use the Directorates-General websites, which are roughly equivalent to US federal agency sites. To find the relevant Directorate-General for your topic of interest, see the Directorates General and Services page, which offers an alphabetical list of topics, linked to the appropriate site.[20]

3. *Tracking a Legislative Proposal*

Most EU legislation is adopted through a procedure called "codecision." The codecision process gives a role to both the Parliament and to the Council. The European Union has created a website, called PreLex, to help researchers track proposals through this process.[21] PreLex allows researchers to search by keyword. The results screen has a section called "Events" that shows the status of a proposal.

For example, perhaps you are told that the EU has considered changing the requirements for limited liability companies set out in Council Directive 77/91/EEC. You can search this directive as a keyword in PreLex.

---

[17] http://europa.eu/index_en.htm.

[18] http://eur-lex.europa.eu/en/consleg/latest/index.htm.

[19] http://ec.europa.eu/atoz_en.htm.

[20] http://ec.europa.eu/about/ds_en.htm.

[21] http://ec.europa.eu/prelex/apcnet.cfm?CL=en.

The search retrieves a "Proposal for a Directive of the European Parliament and of the Council amending Council Directive 77/91/EEC, as regards the formation of public limited liability companies and the maintenance and alteration of their capital." The proposal, "COM" document COM (2004) 730, is linked to the summary page.

The PreLex summary page, under "Events," also indicates that the proposal gained the approval of the Council and the Parliament. The summary page provides a link to the final Directive as published in the *Official Journal.*

PreLex is made up of "dossiers," each linked to the adoption of a Commission proposal. Each dossier tracks events up to and including final adoption. For each event PreLex show the dates, the departments or individuals responsible, links to the relevant document, and OJ citations. Because PreLex offers links to related documents through every step of the EU legislative process, PreLex can also be used to find the "legislative history" of EU instruments. COM documents contain proposed legislation, along with an explanatory memorandum. They are analogous to the congressional committee reports used for US federal legislative histories. Coverage begins in 1975, although links to full-text documents are limited to what is in EUR-Lex's Official Journal database. For early documents, PreLex provides the citations, but you will have to find the actual documents in paper.

An alternative way of finding legislative history is to use EUR-Lex to retrieve the directive or regulation in question, and then look in the "Bibliographic Notice" for the "Procedure" section. This section includes a "Legislative History Section" with citations to relevant documents, but without links. However, by clicking the link to "European Parliament—OEIL," you can retrieve a centralized legislative history summary with links to relevant documents.

4. *Finding National Implementing Laws*

Because most EU law appears in the form of a directive, which requires member states to enact legislation that complies with the directive, you must often find whether a country has enacted such legislation. For example, to understand the copyright law of France, you must not only find the EU directives on copyright, but you must find France's laws that implement the directives. This part of the research process can be difficult.

One database that can help is LexisNexis's National Provisions Implementing Directives database.[22] While this database is neither comprehensive nor up-to-date, it does note some national legislation for directives. For example,

---

[22] Legal > Find Laws by Country or Region > Foreign Laws & Legal Sources > European Union > Legislation & Regulations > EUR-Lex EU Law Database: National Provisions Implementing Directives.

searching on the European water quality directive 2008/105/EC in this database retrieves citations to the laws of several member countries.

Westlaw also lists the "national measures" by member states at the end of directives (see International/Worldwide Materials > European Union).

The EUR-Lex database also provides similar information to that provided by LexisNexis and Westlaw. From the Simple Search screen,[23] click the box for "Legislation," then for "Directives," and search by keyword or directive number. From your search result list, click on the "Bibliographic Notice," and scroll down to "Display the national execution measures—MNE." Clicking on "MNE" will retrieve a list of hyperlinks to countries. You can then click on the country name to see the citation(s) to implementing legislation.

None of these databases provide links to the relevant laws themselves, but you will be able to identify the name of the law, the number, the source, and the date. With this information you can use the sources outlined in the chapter on researching foreign law (see Chapter 8) to locate the text of the needed legislation.

Eur-Lex also provides access to a database called N-Lex: A Common Gateway to National Law.[24] The aim of this database is to provide a single access point to the legislation of EU Member States. For most of the countries, the search interface is the same and you are actually searching the official legal database for each jurisdiction. In some cases, you can search consolidated legislation or the official gazette. Since most of the national legislation is not available in English, you can use EuroVoc,[25] the EU's multilingual thesaurus, to locate the proper term in the vernacular for a language you do not know. For example, if you want to search "arbitration clause" in German legislation, use the thesaurus to locate the proper term in German, "schiedsklausel." Because N-Lex is still experimental, it does not always produce satisfying results. However, it does help you identify the proper online database for national legislation for the EU Member States.[26]

Other strategies include searching secondary sources, including EU news sources (see below) and national news sources from the country of interest. You can also search in national legislation databases, using the number or title of the directive. Not all countries, however, refer to the title or number

---

[23] http://eur-lex.europa.eu/RECH_menu.do?ihmlang=en.

[24] http://eur-lex.europa.eu/n-lex/pri/pri_en.htm.

[25] http://eurovoc.europa.eu/drupal/.

[26] For more information about the database, see Access to Legislation in Europe: Guide to the Legal Gazettes and Other Information Sources in the European Union and the European Free Trade Association, http://circa.europa.eu/irc/opoce/ojf/info/data/prod/data/pdf/AccessToLegislationInEuropeGUIDE2009.pdf.

of the directive in their implementing legislation. If these methods fail, attack the problem like an ordinary problem of finding foreign law (see Chapter 8).

Remember, in searching for national legislation, do not assume that countries will abide by deadlines in the directives. Often, member states fail to enact legislation by the deadline prescribed in a directive. In such cases, the Commission sometimes sues the noncompliant member state in the European Court of Justice.

5. *Finding EU Court Decisions by Topic*

The European Union makes decisions of the European Court of Justice (ECJ) and the Court of First Instance back to 1997 available online, at the Curia section[27] of the Europa site. The cases are also available on the EUR-Lex website[28] back to 1954. From the EUR-Lex Simple Search screen, select "EU case-law." Most law students prefer to use LexisNexis[29] or Westlaw[30] to search these decisions because they're familiar with the LexisNexis and Westlaw search engines. Both databases include decisions back to 1954 (the inception of the ECJ).

The *European Union Law Reporter* (2000–) refers to important EU cases, though it is not a comprehensive digest. On the Curia website, you will find a digest, but it is available only in French.[31]

One important piece of EU case research that US law students should be aware of is the "Advocate-General opinion." The ECJ relies in part on a lawyer called the Advocate-General, who reads the parties' submissions and writes a recommendation (opinion) for the justices. These opinions are published along with the Court's opinion in the Court's official reports, the *Reports of Cases before the Court of Justice and the Court of First Instance* (1990–), but they are not included in LexisNexis's and Westlaw's databases of EU cases. Often, the Advocate-General's opinion is more detailed than the ECJ opinion. EUR-Lex allows you to search only the Advocate-General opinions; choose "EU case-law" from the Simple Search menu, and you will get a screen offering restrictions such as Advocate General Opinions, Court of First Instance decisions, etc.

To find a case by name in either Westlaw or LexisNexis, the most efficient approach is to use a "field" or "segment" search. Using the drop-down menu, select the "title" field on Westlaw or the "name" segment on LexisNexis: for example, on Westlaw, title(microsoft); on LexisNexis, name(microsoft).

---

[27] http://curia.europa.eu/jurisp/cgi-bin/form.pl?lang=en.

[28] http://eur-lex.europa.eu/RECH_menu.do?ihmlang=en.

[29] Legal > Find Laws by Country or Region > Foreign Laws & Legal Sources > European Union > Caselaw > EUR-Lex European Union Cases.

[30] EU-CS.

[31] http://curia.europa.eu/jcms/jcms/Jo2_7046.

E. *Other Useful EU Research Sources*

- Delegation of the European Commission to the United States.[32] This website includes the *European Union—A Guide for Americans*, which provides an overview of the European Union, including its history and institutions.
- *Encyclopedia of European Union Law* (Neville March Hunnings ed., 1996–).
- Ralph H. Folsom, *European Union Law in a Nutshell* (7th ed. 2011).
- Ralph H. Folsom, *Principles of European Union Law* (3d ed. 2011).
- P.S.R.F. Mathijsen, *A Guide to European Union Law: As Amended by the Treaty of Lisbon* (10th ed. 2010).
- *Smit & Herzog on the Law of the European Union* (2d ed. 2005–).
- Jo Steiner and Lorna Woods, *EU Law* (10th ed. 2009).
- Alan Dashwood & Derrick Wyatt, *Wyatt and Dashwood's European Union Law* (6th ed. 2011).

Publications on the European Union have exploded in the last ten years. To locate additional materials in your library, use subject headings:

> *law – european union countries*
> *european union – law and legislation*

Many law libraries also have books on specific areas of EU law; e.g., energy, environment, business, competition; you can find them in your online catalog by combining relevant keywords.

F. *Guides to EU Research*

One of the most useful and thorough guides is New York University Law Library, European Union Research.[33] This guide gives detailed advice on many aspects of EU research, including how to find older materials and EU statistics. Many law students also like Duncan Alford, Update, European Union Legal Materials: An Infrequent User's Guide.[34] This guide provides key background information for researchers who have not worked with EU documents or who have done so only rarely. A useful print guide is Frederic Eggermont & Stefaan Smis, *Research Guide to Instruments of European Regional Organizations* (2010).

---

[32] http://www.eurunion.org/eu.
[33] http://www.law.nyu.edu/library/research/researchguides/europeanunionresearch/index.htm.
[34] http://www.nyulawglobal.org/Globalex/European_Union1.htm.

Chapter Thirteen

Regional International Organizations

I. *Council of Europe*

A. *Introduction*

The Council of Europe (COE) calls itself "Europe's oldest political organization."[1] With more members than the European Union, its goals are narrower. One of its key goals is to promote human rights in Europe. This goal led the COE to recognize human rights in various treaties and to create a mechanism to enforce them. The European Court of Human Rights is the most important part of this mechanism. From 1954–1998, the European Commission on Human Rights formed another part, but the COE abolished the Commission in 1998.

The key bodies of the COE include the Council of Ministers, the Parliamentary Assembly, and European Court of Human Rights. The Committee of Ministers, comprising the Foreign Affairs Ministers of all the member states, is the Council of Europe's decision-making body. The Parliamentary Assembly provides a forum for debate and discussion on the COE's values and programs. Each of these three bodies has its own section on the COE website (look under the "Organisation" tab). A fourth body, the Congress of Local and Regional Authorities of Europe, promotes parliamentary democracy; it also has its own section on the website. Like many intergovernmental organizations, the COE also has a secretariat to run its day-to-day operations.

Researchers may sometimes confuse COE bodies with those of the European Union; the names of these bodies are similar. Confusion is frequent enough that the COE offers a webpage to sort out the various institutions.[2]

---

[1] Council of Europe, Committee of Ministers, COE Doc. CM/AS(2005) 4 (May 2, 2005).
[2] Council of Europe, Do Not Get Confused, http://www.coe.int/aboutCoe/index.asp?page=nepasconfondre&l=en.

For more information on researching the Council of Europe's human rights system, see Chapter 15.

Unlike most IGOs, the Council of Europe provides older documents on its website. Researchers can find documents back to the creation of the Council of Europe in 1949. For specialized research, see Sophie Lobey, Update: History, Role, and Activities of the Council of Europe: Facts, Figures and Information Sources,[3] and Frederic Eggermont & Stefaan Smis, *Research Guide to Instruments of European Regional Organizations* (2010).

B. *Committee of Ministers and Its Documentation*

The Committee of Ministers issues several types of documents, including declarations, recommendations, resolutions, and decisions. It also produces various working and informational documents. The most important of the Committee of Ministers' documents are referred to as its "adopted texts." Adopted texts and other documents are available from the Committee of Ministers' section of the COE website (see the "Documents" link).[4]

Declarations have no binding force and are used simply to express the opinion of the Committee of Ministers to the world at large. For example, in 2011, the Committee of Ministers adopted a Declaration on Internet Governance Principles. Like many other IGOs, the COE assigns a document symbol: this declaration is Decl-21.09.2011_2E (2011). As with other document symbols, the cryptic abbreviations and numbers can be translated into useful information. In this case, "Decl." stands for declaration, and the numeric portion represents the date on which the declaration was adopted.

Recommendations, like declarations, have no binding force. They are directed to member states and provide general guidance on issues. A recent example is the Resolution on Quality and Safety Assurance Requirements for Medicinal Products Prepared in Pharmacies for the Special Needs of Patients (2011) CM/ResAP(2011)1E. Resolutions may address various subjects. Some address internal administrative matters such as finances. Another common type of resolution involves the Committee of Ministers' responsibility to ensure that European Court of Human Rights judgments are enforced and to pressure member countries to protect human rights. Resolutions of this type are searchable within the HUDOC database (select "Resolutions" from the left-hand side of the screen).[5] All other resolutions can be searched at

---

[3] http://www.nyulawglobal.org/globalex/Council_of_Europe1.htm.

[4] http://www.coe.int/t/cm/home_en.asp.

[5] http://cmiskp.echr.coe.int/tkp197/search.asp?skin=hudoc-en.

the Committee of Ministers' site by keyword, date, and broad subject matter (e.g., social security, national minorities).[6]

"Decisions" are Committee of Ministers documents by which other kinds of documents are adopted. Decisions are binding on all entities subject to the Committee of Ministers' authority. Thus, for example, when the Council of Ministers concludes a treaty, agrees on a budget, or makes a recommendation, the underlying item is adopted as a decision.

The Committee of Ministers has spearheaded the drafting and adoption of over 200 treaties on subjects ranging from torture to data protection.[7] The core human rights treaty in the COE system is the Convention for the Protection of Human Rights and Fundamental Freedoms; it also includes several protocols. The most convenient way to access COE treaties is through the dedicated section of its website.[8] This section provides the full text; status information, including reservations, declarations, and understandings; signing and effective dates; and other useful information. COE treaties were also published in the *European Treaty Series* (1949–2003),[9] which was continued by the *Council of Europe Treaty Series* (2004–).

C. Parliamentary Assembly and Its Documentation

The Assembly can adopt three different types of texts: recommendations, resolutions, and opinions. Like the Council of Ministers, it also generates other documents, such as working documents and verbatim records of its debates. Again, the "adopted texts" are the most important ones, and you can find them on the Parliamentary Assembly site back to 1949.[10] Recommendations contain proposals addressed to the Committee of Ministers. Resolutions express the views of the Assembly on various questions. Opinions are, for the most part, responses by the Assembly to specific questions posed to it by the Committee of Ministers, on topics such as the admission of new member states to the COE.

D. European Court of Human Rights and Its Documentation

The European Court of Human Rights (ECHR), created in 1959, has established an extensive body of decisions. While the ECHR does not follow the rule of *stare decisis* (i.e., its past decisions do not bind its future ones), this

---

[6] http://www.coe.int/t/cm/WCD/fulltextSearch_en.asp#.

[7] http://www.conventions.coe.int.

[8] Id.

[9] Cited as E.T.S.; the new series is cited as C.E.T.S.

[10] http://assembly.coe.int/defaultE.asp.

body of decisions has nonetheless become an important source of persuasive human rights jurisprudence. Its decisions, and those of the now-defunct European Commission of Human Rights, are available online in the searchable database HUDOC.[11]

Westlaw and LexisNexis have less complete coverage. Decisions of the ECHR from 1979 and selected decisions of the Commission are available on Westlaw.[12] LexisNexis offers ECHR decisions from 1960.[13]

ECHR decisions from 1996 are published in *Reports of Judgments and Decisions* (1996–). (Until 1995, the ECHR decisions were published in *Publications of the European Court of Human Rights*, Series A.) According to the Court, the *Reports of Judgments and Decisions* contain "a selection of judgments and decisions…sometimes in the form of extracts." Thus, not all decisions are published in hard copy. Other paper reports of European human rights jurisprudence include:

- *European Commission of Human Rights, Decisions and Reports* (1975–1998) (cited as D & R).
- *European Human Rights Reports* (1979–) (also available on LexisNexis and Westlaw).
- *Human Rights Case Digest* (1990–) (also available on HeinOnline[14] and Ingenta).[15]
- Council of Europe, *Yearbook of the European Convention on Human Rights* (1960–).

The COE also publishes books, pamphlets, reports, and other documents on topics such as human rights, law, health, society, and the environment. A full catalog of its publications for the last several years is available on its website.[16] You can also search library catalogs for publications that have the Council of Europe as their author or publisher.

E. *Venice Commission*

The Venice Commission, formally known as the European Commission for Democracy through Law, is the Council of Europe's advisory body on constitutional matters. It offers assistance to emerging or reforming states that

---

[11] http://cmiskp.echr.coe.int/tkp197/search.asp?skin=hudoc-en.
[12] EHR-RPTS database.
[13] International Law > Cases > Human Rights Cases.
[14] http://home.heinonline.org.
[15] http://www.ingentaconnect.com.
[16] http://book.coe.int/EN (select "Catalogue" link).

have constitutional drafting problems. The Venice Commission has emerged as a "think tank" on constitutional issues, and has published numerous studies and reports on constitutional law and fundamental rights. One important research tool offered by the Venice Commission is its CODICES database.[17] This database contains laws and summaries of court decisions relating to constitutional rights within COE member countries. CODICES has a search engine that permits searching by country, date, index term, and other features.

F. *Additional Research Strategies*

To find out whether the COE has been concerned with a particular issue, such as human trafficking, check the COE site's extensive A-Z index.[18]

Alternatively, you can use the site's search engine. The search engine provides the option of searching several categories of information; for example, you can search the treaties, or all documents from the European Committee for the Prevention of Torture and Inhuman or Degrading Treatment or Punishment, an organization similar to the UN Committee against Torture. You may also want to consult the COE's annual reports on its own activities, called variously "Activities of the Council of Europe...report" or "Council of Europe...activity report."

To find outside evaluations of the COE's work, search library catalogs using *council of europe* as a subject. Depending on your area of interest, you may want to add keywords, such as *minorities* or *constitutions*.

II. *African Union*

A. *Introduction*

The African Union (AU) was launched in 1999 as a successor to the Organization for African Unity (OAU). Dissatisfaction with the OAU, including its perceived lack of democracy and its protection of despotic rulers, sparked the creation of the new organization. In a series of summit conferences beginning in 1999, representatives of member states created the framework for the African Union, launching it in 2002. The African Union promotes the socioeconomic integration of African states and peoples. In contrast to IGOs such as the Council of Europe, the African Union is a new organization, underfunded and not yet fully developed. Therefore, you will find it much harder

---

[17] http://www.codices.coe.int/NXT/gateway.dll?f=templates&fn=default.htm.
[18] http://www.coe.int/t/dc/General/indexAZ/default_en.asp.

to research. The AU's website[19] contains documents pertaining to both the African Union and to its predecessor, the OAU, but the site is sometimes unavailable.

As of 2011, 53 African countries make up the African Union; on the African continent, this excludes only Morocco.

B. *Organization*

The main organs of the African Union include the Assembly of Heads of State and Government, the Executive Council, and the Commission. The African Union has many other organs, including the Permanent Representatives' Committee, the Peace and Security Council (PSC), the Pan-African Parliament, the Economic, Social and Cultural Council, Specialized Technical Committees, and the Court of Justice and Human Rights, though not all of these organs are fully operational yet.

The Commission has control over the day-to-day operations of the African Union, but the Assembly is the supreme organ of the African Union. The Executive Council is responsible to the Assembly and is supposed to present the work of the Permanent Representatives' Committee to it.

The Pan-African Parliament, composed of legislators from member states, began operations in 2004. Currently, this parliament has consultative powers only, though eventually it is supposed to have full legislative capacity.

In 2008, the AU's Court of Justice merged with the African Court of Human and People's Rights to become the African Court of Justice and Human Rights.[20] The new Court has two chambers; one for general legal matters, and the other for human rights.

C. *Research*

The African Union does not publish official documentation of activities at its sessions in a paper format. Nor does it publish its official documents such as treaties and decisions in any systematic way. Thus, the best way to find official AU documents is on the organization's website. The AU site also includes some documents from the OAU. Documents from its 2002 summit are also available at a separate website[21] maintained by the South African government. Neither Westlaw nor LexisNexis offers databases of AU or OAU documents.

---

[19] http://www.au.int/en.
[20] http://www.africa-union.org/root/au/organs/court_of_justice_en.htm.
[21] http://www.au2002.gov.za.

Most of the key AU materials on its website are found under the "Legal Documents" link, or from the Legal Affairs page. These include treaties (with ratification information), decisions and declarations, and a few reports. As with many organizations that conduct business in more than one language, the different language versions of the site do not contain the same information. For example, in late 2011, on the English side, the "Decisions and Declarations" portion of the "Legal documents" section is updated through July 2011. On the French side, the latest information is from January 2011.

You will probably need to rely on information sources beyond the African Union's own site. To find news stories about the African Union, you can use Westlaw and LexisNexis; each service offers databases of African newspapers and articles relating to Africa.[22] Your library may also provide access to useful indexes to literature on the African Union, such as the International Index to Black Periodicals (which includes some full-text articles), South African Studies, the World News Connection,[23] and PAIS International.[24] If you don't have access to these subscription databases, you may want to try allAfrica.com.[25]

In library catalogs, use *african union* as a subject heading to find materials about the organization. You can also search the subject *african union* in the Index to Legal Periodicals[26] and LegalTrac.[27]

D. *Research Examples*

In 2011, political unrest in North Africa displaced many citizens of North African countries, with some moving within their home country borders, and some moving across borders. You are asked to find out how the AU has addressed the problem of internal displacement, and whether certain North African countries are involved in that effort. Starting with secondary sources (law review articles, in this case), and using Westlaw's JLR database, you search *"african union" au /s "internally-displaced" idp* (if you are not sure whether a term such as "internally displaced" is hyphenated, use a hyphen as

---

[22] In Westlaw, choose the AFRNEWS database. In LexisNexis, use News & Business > Country & Region (excluding U.S.) > Middle East & Africa > News > Global News Wire -Middle East & Africa Stories, or use News & Business > Country & Region (excluding U.S.) > Middle East & Africa > News > Middle East/Africa News Information Sources.

[23] http://wnc.fedworld.gov.

[24] http://www.csa.com/factsheets/pais-set-c.php.

[25] http://allafrica.com.

[26] http://www.ebscohost.com/academic/index-to-legal-periodicals-books.

[27] http://www.gale.cengage.com/pdf/facts/legal.pdf (LRI on Westlaw; Find a Source > Legal Resource Index on LexisNexis).

shown; with that technique, Westlaw will also retrieve documents in which the term has a space instead of a hyphen).

This search retrieves an article[28] discussing the African Union Convention for the Protection and Assistance of Internally Displaced Persons (also referred to as the Kampala Convention). This convention was opened for signature on October 23, 2009—quite recently—so it will be particularly important to get current status information. Both the "Legal Affairs" page and the "Legal Documents" link on the AU website offer a list of AU treaties. Scrolling down the list or using the control-Find function with a key term (e.g., internally or displace), you will see a link to the treaty text in PDF and a link to status information. The status information shows that some of the key North African countries, such as Libya, Egypt, and Tunisia, have not become parties to the treaty. Thus, trying to find remedies against those countries under these treaties is a dead end.

Another current issue in African law and politics is cooperation with the International Criminal Court (ICC). Leaders of African nations have noted that the ICC has concerned itself overwhelmingly with investigating potential defendants from Africa. One touchy question has been the extent to which African nations are obligated, as parties to the Rome Statute, to arrest the Sudanese president, Omar al-Bashir, for whom the ICC has issued two arrest warrants. A quick search of the news databases listed in Section C above (or even a quick web search) shows that the African Union has objected to the ICC's pursuit of al-Bashir.

Notice that al-Bashir's name is sometimes spelled differently (e.g., Umar instead of Omar, el-Bashir instead of al-Bashir). The same problem arises with searches on Muammar Gaddafi's name, which is notorious for its wide variety of spelling variations (e.g., Moammar el-Qaddafi). It's important to look for spelling variants while using some online databases, such as Westlaw and LexisNexis news databases, library catalogs, and periodical indexes. Usually, a quick Google search with the name, adding terms like "also spelled" or "sometimes spelled" will bring up the variants you need.

To find the official documents issued by the AU on the question of al-Bashir's prosecution, you can try using the search function on the AU website. Unfortunately, this method retrieves only a couple of documents. A better approach is to use Google Advanced Search, looking for *al-bashir OR el-bashir OR bashir*, and confining the search to the AU website (either by using Google's Advanced Search boxes, or by adding *site:.au.int/en* to your search terms). This search retrieves many more documents, including

---

[28] Won Kidane, *Managing Forced Displacement by Law in Africa: The Role of the New African Union IDPS Convention*, 44 Vand. J. Transnat'l L. 1 (2011).

a document from December 2011, entitled "The African Union Reiterates Its Commitment to the Respect of the Immunity of Incumbent African Heads of State."[29]

As you can see, to research issues relating to the African Union, you need to be particularly flexible. If your research involves human rights, you will also need to look at the African Commission on Human and Peoples' Rights (see Chapter 15). Another useful source is Rachel Murray, *Human Rights in Africa: From the OAU to the African Union* (2004). The relationship between the AU and the African Commission on Human and Peoples' Rights is complicated; for a useful discussion, see Curtis F.J. Doebbler, 'A Complex Ambiguity: The Relationship between the African Commission on Human and Peoples' Rights and Other African Union Initiatives Affecting Respect for Human Rights,' 13 *Transnat'l L. & Contemp. Probs.* 7 (2003).

Finally, don't forget to search the *Index to Foreign Legal Periodicals* for articles from journals published in Africa, such as Karen Stefiszyn, 'The African Union: Challenges and Opportunities for Women,' 5 *Afr. Hum. Rts. L.J.* 358 (2005).

III. *Organization for Security and Co-Operation in Europe*

A. *Introduction*

The Organization for Security and Cooperation in Europe (OSCE) is the world's largest regional security organization, with 56 member states. Founded as the Conference for Security and Cooperation in Europe (CSCE) in 1975, it began as a tool to reduce Cold War tensions. Meetings between member states led to the "Final Act of the Conference on Security and Cooperation in Europe," also known as the Helsinki Final Act, or Helsinki Accords. This document articulated several principles such as respect for human rights, peaceful dispute resolution, and rights to self-determination. Some organizations used the document as the baseline for monitoring Soviet and Eastern bloc countries' adherence to human rights norms. After the end of the Cold War, the CSCE refocused its efforts on promoting good governance and democratization in Europe, particularly in Eastern Europe. In 1995, its name changed to the Organization for Security and Co-operation in Europe (OSCE). Its membership includes Canada and the United States. The OSCE

---

[29] African Union, Communique, The African Union Reiterates Its Commitment to the Respect of the Immunity of Incumbent African Heads of State, Dec. 4, 2011, http://www.au.int/en/sites/default/files/Communique%20of%20the%20Chairperson%20Sudan-04–12–11.pdf.

also includes some states with the status of "Partners for Cooperation"—these include Asian and Middle Eastern states.

B. *Organization*

Negotiating and decision-making bodies include the Summit and Ministerial Council, the Permanent Council, the Forum for Security Cooperation, and the Economic Forum. The day-to-day governance is handled by the Secretariat. The Parliamentary Assembly has the power to issue resolutions, but they are nonbinding.

The OSCE holds periodic "summits" during which members set long-range priorities. Between summits, the Ministerial Council, which meets once a year, officially holds decision-making power. The Permanent Council, however, is the main regular decision-making body of the Organization. It meets weekly at the OSCE's Vienna headquarters to confer and to take action. The Forum for Security Cooperation also meets weekly to discuss and make decisions regarding military aspects of security in the OSCE area. The Economic Forum meets only yearly and focuses on post-Soviet transitions to market economies.

C. *Research*

1. *OSCE Website*

Like the Council of Europe, the OSCE has a highly developed website,[30] with extensive documentation available even back to the 1975 founding of the organization. The Documents Library[31] section of the site (listed under "Resources") organizes documents primarily by issuing body; for example, the Permanent Council's documents comprise a separate category. Clicking on the name of a body, such as the Permanent Council, leads to a separate search page. This page offers a Search box for keyword searching, with a choice of document types. Thus, for example, you can search for *"human trafficking" children* and specify that you want only reports on that topic.

Most of the OSCE organs issue "decisions." These decisions usually deal with minor procedural matters, but some of them express OSCE policy and could be used to evidence customary international law. For example, Permanent Council Decision No. 683, Countering the Threat of Radioactive Sources (2005), urges member states to take certain steps with regard to controlling import and export of radioactive sources. This decision has the document

---

[30] http://www.osce.org.
[31] http://www.osce.org/library.

symbol PC.DEC/683. Like other IGO documents, this one indicates the body issuing the document (PC for Permanent Council), indicates the document type (DEC for Decision), and provides a number for a unique citation (this is the Permanent Council's 683rd decision).

Periodically, the OSCE publishes an Index of Permanent Council Decisions[32] as a PDF document. With this index, and by using a combination of the OSCE-assigned topics and keyword-finding enabled in PDF documents, you can identify all the relevant decisions on a particular topic. You can retrieve the index by searching (in quotation marks) *"Index of Permanent Council Decisions."* You can then either browse the document or use control-find to look for terms (e.g., terrorism, trafficking). The OSCE publishes its decisions in a print series called (not surprisingly) *OSCE Decisions* (1995–), though not many US libraries subscribe to this title.

Some of the OSCE organs also issue journal documents, which are procedural documents regarding the agenda for, and outcomes of, organizations' meetings. These journal documents often reference underlying documents of more importance, such as reports and decisions. They are useful for tracking OSCE activities. Clicking on the OSCE site's "What We Do" tab gives you a list of its major areas of activity. Once you select a topic, however, such as "Arms Control," it is often most helpful to look for the OSCE office listed under the "Links" heading. The individual offices, such as the Secretariat— Conflict Prevention Centre, usually have more detailed information than the topic pages. Moreover, they often have their own "Documents" link with a list of topics you can use to filter the results.

2. *Beyond the Website*

As with other IGOs, you can find the OSCE's publications by using its name as an author or publisher search in your library catalog. To find materials *about* the OSCE, use its name as a Library of Congress subject heading. The Index to Legal Periodicals[33] and LegalTrac[34] also recognize *organization for security and cooperation in europe* as a subject or index heading. You can combine this subject heading with keywords to retrieve materials on your area of interest. Frederic Eggermont & Stefaan Smis, *Research Guide to Instruments of European Regional Organizations* (2010), also has a section on the OSCE.

---

[32] See, e.g., http://www.osce.org/pc/70160.
[33] http://www.ebscohost.com/academic/index-to-legal-periodicals-books.
[34] http://www.gale.cengage.com/pdf/facts/legal.pdf (LRI on Westlaw; Find a Source > Legal Resource Index on LexisNexis).

Some large libraries subscribe to the OSCE Yearbook, *Yearbook on the Organization for Security and Co-operation in Europe* (1996–), which is an excellent resource for tracking the OSCE's activities. You can see the tables of contents for all issues online, along with the full text of older articles.[35]

Another useful website, which is published and maintained by the OSCE Office for Democratic Institutions and Human Rights, is called Legislationline.[36] You can access domestic legislation (usually in English) and international standards on human rights and related issues at this site.

A few NGOs monitor the OSCE itself. Perhaps the best known of these NGOs is the Netherlands Helsinki Committee (NHC).[37] In addition to publishing the quarterly journal *Security and Human Rights* (formerly *Helsinki Monitor*),[38] which reports on the OSCE and its activities, the NHC engages in research and monitoring projects related to human rights in the OSCE area. A few years' worth of *Security and Human Rights* issues are freely available at the NHC's website, but most are available only by subscription.

IV. *Organization of American States*

A. *Introduction*

The Organization of American States (OAS) was founded in 1948 with the adoption of its charter.[39] The OAS now includes all 35 independent countries of the Americas, although Cuba was suspended from 1962 to 2009 and now declines to participate. The OAS cooperates on democratic values, defends common interests, and confronts problems such as poverty, terrorism, illegal drugs, and corruption. There is also a related process, called the Summit of the Americas process, that brings together heads of countries in the Americas to set goals and discuss common issues.[40] While the Summit process began as an alternative forum to the OAS, the OAS now takes a lead role in organizing these periodic forums.

B. *Organization*

The OAS General Assembly, which consists of member countries' ministers of foreign affairs, meets annually to set major policies and goals. The

---

[35] http://www.core-hamburg.de/CORE_english/pub_osce_yearbook.htm.
[36] http://legislationline.org.
[37] http://www.nhc.nl.
[38] http://api.ingentaconnect.com (by subscription).
[39] http://www.oas.org/en/about/who_we_are.asp.
[40] http://www.summit-americas.org/default_en.htm.

Permanent Council, which is made up of ambassadors from each member state, provides ongoing guidance. As with many IGOs, the organization's secretariat carries out the day-to-day functions.

Two important human rights bodies, the Inter-American Commission on Human Rights and the Inter-American Court of Human Rights, apply Inter-American law on human rights. These two bodies report directly to the Secretary-General of the OAS.

C. Research

As usual when researching an IGO, you can search your library catalog using the name of the organization as a keyword, author, or subject search. Some recent works on the OAS include:

- Andrew Fenton Cooper & Thomas F. Legler, *Intervention without Intervening?: The OAS Defense and Promotion of Democracy in the Americas* (2006).
- Klaas Dykmann, *Philanthropic Endeavors or the Exploitation of an Ideal?: The Human Rights Policy of the Organization of American States in Latin America* (1970–1991) (2004).
- Mônica Herz, *The Organization of American States (OAS): Global Governance away from the Media* (2011).
- Betty Horwitz, *The Transformation of the Organization of American States: A Multilateral Framework for Regional Governance* (2010).
- Carolyn M. Shaw, *Cooperation, Conflict, and Consensus in the Organization of American States* (2004).
- Christopher R. Thomas & Juliana T. Magloire, *Regionalism versus Multilateralism: The Organization of American States in a Global Changing Environment* (2000).

Key OAS documents can be found on the OAS website; select "Documents" from the home page.[41] Several types of documents are available from the Documents page; a few of the more important ones are discussed below.

1. Resolutions and Declarations
Resolutions and declarations of the various OAS organs are organized according to the body that produced them. The website does not yet have these documents back to the beginning of the OAS; coverage varies depending on

---

[41] http://www.oas.org/en.

the body. These documents are available at some US libraries as "Proceedings," or as "Documentos oficiales de la OEA."

Although the resolutions and declarations are not searchable, the OAS Department of International Legal Affairs has identified resolutions on a few topics for easier reference.[42] Thus, if you are searching for evidence of international legal norms on these particular topics, such as humanitarian law, you can quickly find related resolutions. The OAS site offers a "Document Search,"[43] but it does not permit full-text searching (you can search document titles, restrict by date, and specify document symbols).

2. *Treaties*

The OAS site has a collection of treaties and agreements.[44] The collection is split into bilateral and multilateral agreements, although some treaties are only listed, with no text available at the site. A separate page, "Recent actions regarding multilateral treaties," is a good source for brief information on recent treaty actions.

You can look for multilateral treaties by year[45] or by subject, but bilateral treaties are arranged only alphabetically by the name of state parties or other entity (e.g., African Telecommunications Union). Note that in the bilateral index, countries are listed by their Spanish names, so, for example, while there is no listing for "Germany," treaties with Germany are listed under "Alemania."

The OAS site also provides status information, in a section called "Signatories and Ratifications," linked to the text of each treaty. You should also check the "Recent actions regarding multilateral treaties"[46] page, however, because the status information associated with a treaty may not include the most current actions.

The OAS also has a sporadically published treaty series, entitled *Inter-American Treaties and Conventions: Signatures, Ratifications, and Deposits with Explanatory Notes* (1954–).[47] Generally, it is easier to use other sources, such as the OAS website, for these treaties.

---

[42] http://www.oas.org/DIL/international_law.htm.

[43] https://www.apps.oas.org/publicsearch/default.asp.

[44] http://www.oas.org/DIL/treaties_and_agreements.htm.

[45] As of late 2011, the most recent multilateral treaty concluded within the OAS was done in 2003; thus, while the Multilateral Treaties by Year stops at 2003, it is not out-of-date.

[46] http://www.oas.org/DIL/recentactionstreaties.htm.

[47] INTER-AMERICAN TREATIES AND CONVENTIONS: SIGNATURES, RATIFICATIONS, AND DEPOSITS WITH EXPLANATORY NOTES (1954–).

3. *Documents of Inter-American Court of Human Rights and*
Inter-American Commission on Human Rights
Materials from the OAS human rights bodies can be difficult to find online
or on paper. Furthermore, decisions are often available in Spanish before
they are available in English. To find materials in your library, search *Inter-*
American Commission and the *Inter-American Court* as authors and as keywords and subjects. See also Chapter 15 for more information on human
rights research.

a. Inter-American Court of Human Rights
The Court's decisions are available on its website,[48] and on the University
of Minnesota Human Rights website, though the latter site does not have
recent decisions.[49] Paper versions are published in *Inter-American Court of*
Human Rights, Series A: Judgments and Opinions (1982–) (none published
since 2004), *Series B: Pleadings, Oral Arguments and Documents* (1983–)
(only a few ever published), and *Series C: Decisions and Judgments* (1987–)
(none published since 2006). For summaries of the Court's activity, see *Inter-*
American Court of Human Rights, Annual Report (1981–). Annual reports
from 1980 onwards are available on the Court's website.[50]

The Inter-American Human Rights Digest Project at American University
offers an index to the Court's jurisprudence from 1980–1997, but this index
is in Spanish only.[51] Currently one of the best ways to find relevant cases by
topic is to consult this book: Laurence Burgorgue-Larsen & Amaya Ubeda
de Torres, *The Inter-American Court of Human Rights: Case-Law and Com-*
mentary (2011). The book covers major human rights and discusses key cases
for each right.

b. Inter-American Commission on Human Rights
Like the Court, the Commission's work is summarized in its annual report:
the *Inter-American Commission on Human Rights Annual Report* (1977–).
Many annual reports are available on the Commission's website. The annual
reports contain reports of decisions of the Commission. Documents from
the annual reports are also available on Westlaw[52] and on the University of
Minnesota Human Rights Library website.[53]

---

[48] http://www.corteidh.or.cr/index.cfm?&CFID=1388470&CFTOKEN=19583031.
[49] http://www1.umn.edu/humanrts/iachr/series_A.html.
[50] http://www.corteidh.or.cr/informes.cfm.
[51] http://www.wcl.american.edu/humright/repertorio/indice.cfm.
[52] IACHR-OAS database.
[53] http://www1.umn.edu/humanrts/cases/commissn.htm.

The Inter-American Human Rights Database[54] at American University provides online access to Commission documents from its inception, but it has not been updated since 1998.

c. Inter-American Human Rights System Generally
Inter-American Yearbook on Human Rights (1968–) provides background information, key instruments, documents, and a discussion of human rights practices in selected OAS countries. Several books are available that explore various human rights issues as well as the Inter-American system. Some of these books include:

- Clara Burbano Herrera, *Provisional Measures in the Case Law of the Inter-American Court of Human Rights* (2010).
- Jo M. Pasqualucci, *The Practice and Procedure of the Inter-American Court of Human Rights* (2003).
- *The Inter-American System of Human Rights* (David J. Harris & Stephen Livingstone eds., 1998).
- Diego Rodríguez-Pinzón & Claudia Martin, *The Prohibition of Torture and Ill-treatment in the Inter-American Human Rights System: A Handbook for Victims and their Advocates* (2006).

4. *Other Documents*
The OAS site contains numerous other documents, such as documents relating to the organization and its functioning. These organizational documents, such as the rules of procedure for the General Assembly, are easily accessed from the Department of Legal Services page.[55] Remember that the OAS site, like many sites available in more than one language, may have different information available depending on which "side" of the website you check. For example, the English and Spanish sides have more up-to-date press releases than the French or Portuguese sides.

---

[54] http://www.wcl.american.edu/humright/digest.
[55] http://www.oas.org/legal/intro.htm.

Part Six: Selected International Topics

Chapter Fourteen

Introduction to Researching International Topics

I. *Researching International Topics Outline*

A. *Introduction*

Research in international and foreign law usually involves researching a particular topic or issue. As you can imagine, these topics are varied: human rights, taxation, environmental law, criminal law, litigation, trade, etc.

When researching an international law topic, you are usually looking for several bodies of law and sources of information:

- public international law (usually treaties and documents);
- private international law (sometime treaties, usually foreign law);
- foreign law (national laws or case law);
- uniform laws, guidelines or principles (materials from intergovernmental organizations (IGOs) and nongovernmental organizations (NGOs)); and
- commentary, explanatory materials, or forms.

A savvy international legal researcher will consult materials in other related disciplines, such as political science, public policy, health, economics, etc. (see Part II for more information). Since many international issues cross over into other fields, useful materials can be found in law-related resources.

While you will not necessarily research all topics in the same manner, there are some common approaches when you start researching an unfamiliar topic. The steps outlined below provide some general guidance and will vary depending on your topic, the amount of time you have to research the topic, and what resources are available to you.

B. *Research Steps*

1. *Start with a research guide.* Use chapters in this book to identify relevant guides, both print and electronic, or search the web for a research guide (e.g.,

try searching *researching law of the sea* [or other search terms], *"research guide" law sea*, or *pathfinder law sea*). Two useful collections of online legal research guides are the LLRX site[1] and GlobaLex.[2] (Generally, GlobaLex has more recent guides.) Another source for guides is the Electronic Information System for International Law (EISIL) database;[3] choose your topic from the hierarchical listings, then look under Research Resources.

> **Example**: In EISIL, the path Home > International Economic Law > GATT/ WTO System leads to a section on "Research Resources" that includes two excellent guides and a bibliography.

2. *Use secondary sources for an overview or introduction to the subject and for citations to primary law and other sources.* Look for books, articles, working papers, documents, etc. Use library catalogs and research guides to identify the tools that will aid you in locating relevant materials. See Part II for more help with searching for sources.

> **Example**: If you were researching international sports law, you might start by looking for a research guide. The Google search *researching "international sports law"* retrieves as its first result this guide: Amy Burchfield, Update: International Sports Law (2011).[4] This guide includes a "References" section that lists several useful treatises on international sports law. You could then search for these titles in your library catalog.

3. *Identify any terms of art, keywords or phrases.* Use dictionaries, encyclopedias, etc., to help define words and phrases. Consult Chapter 4 to help identify such items.

> **Example**: In disputes that involve transnational shipping, you may encounter terms such as "air waybill," "clean bill of lading," and "ocean bill of lading." While *Black's Law Dictionary* provides brief definitions of these terms, you may also want to consult more specialized sources, such as Edward G. Hinkelman, *Dictionary of International Trade: Handbook of the Global Trade Community* (6th ed. 2005), Raj Bhala, *Dictionary of International Trade Law* (2008), or John J. Capela & Stephen W. Hartman, *Dictionary of International Business Terms* (3d ed. 2004).

4. *Locate the relevant law: international treaties and agreements, international decisions (including jurisprudence and other dispute resolution decisions), international soft law, national legislation, and national case law.* Consult individual sections of this book, such as International Law (Part III) and

---

[1] http://www.llrx.com/category/1050.
[2] http://www.nyulawglobal.org/globalex/index.html.
[3] http://www.eisil.org.
[4] http://www.nyulawglobal.org/globalex/International_Sports_Law1.htm.

Foreign and Comparative Law (Part IV), in order to locate relevant law. Secondary sources, such as those mentioned in the previous section (see Section I.A), will usually identify relevant sources of law.

> **Example**: You are asked to research the international framework governing transboundary movement of waste. One approach is to start with a secondary source such as Philippe Sands, *Principles of International Environmental Law* (2d ed. 2003). The chapter on "Waste" lets you quickly identify relevant treaties, and points to some of the relevant cases.

> If you want to find national laws governing transport of waste, you might start with Thomas H. Reynolds & Arturo A. Flores, *Foreign Law Guide.*[5] National laws relating to waste are listed under "Environmental Protection."

> **Example**: To find relevant soft law on internally displaced persons, one effective approach is to search Westlaw or LexisNexis databases of law review articles, putting the phrase "soft law" in the same paragraph as "internally displaced persons" – *"soft law" w/p "internally displaced persons."* This search retrieves articles referring to the Guiding Principles on Internal Displacement, among other instruments.

> **Example**: To find national case law on international criminal law, one approach is to browse the subscription database International Law in Domestic Courts.[6] Browsing the topic of international criminal law uncovers several cases, including a 2011 decision on the Netherlands' responsibility for the conduct of one of its battalions acting as part of a UN peacekeeping force.[7]

5. *Locate relevant practice materials, such as forms, commentary on procedures, etc.* The topical chapters (Part VI) outline some of these materials. You can also search library catalogs using subject terms for your topic combined with keywords such as *procedure* or *practice*.

> **Example**: The subject *international business enterprises,* combined with the keyword *practice,* retrieves sources such as *Negotiating and Structuring International Commercial Transactions* (Mark R. Sandstrom & David N. Goldsweig eds., 2d ed. 2003) and *International Corporate Practice: A Practitioner's Guide to Global Success* (Practising Law Institute, 2008–).

> **Example**: The subject *maritime law,* combined with the keywords *practice or procedure,* retrieves sources such as Colin M. De la Rue & Charles B. Anderson, *Shipping and the Environment: Law and Practice* (1998) and Damien J. Cremean, *Admiralty Jurisdiction: Law and Practice in Australia, New Zealand, Singapore and Hong Kong* (2008).

6. *Locate relevant IGO and NGO documentation.* See Part V on international organizations and this chapter on international topics. Or, once you have

---

[5] http://www.foreignlawguide.com.
[6] http://www.oxfordlawreports.com.
[7] Nuhanović v Netherlands, Appeal judgment, LJN:BR5388; ILDC 1742 (NL 2011).

identified a relevant international organization, search its website or your library catalog to find documents that address your topic.

> **Example**: You probably already know that the UN Security Council makes international law on the use of force. By going to the Security Council's web site, you can review various types of documentation, such as Security Council Resolutions, Mission Reports, Letters to the President of the Security Council, etc. If you're looking for documents on a particular topic, searching the Press Releases helps you identify relevant documents back to 1995. For example, you can search "Libya" in the Press Releases search box. Press releases provide citations (and sometimes links) to key documents on this topic.

> **Example**: If you're researching space law, you might start at the EISIL site. After the section on primary documents, the EISIL page on Space Law has a list of websites, including the United Nations Office for Outer Space Affairs. You can click the link to that site and begin reviewing key instruments in the law of space.

7. *Consider books and articles from other disciplines.* Consult periodical indexes and databases from other disciplines to locate journal articles, working papers, chapters in books, reports from think tanks, and much more. Many of these tools are highlighted in this chapter and in Part II.

> **Example**: For a human rights project, you are researching the law relating to grave desecration. To understand the burial practices and beliefs of various cultures, you should consult anthropology and sociology literature. Most college and university libraries subscribe to indexes such as Anthropology Plus and CSA Sociological Abstracts. In CSA Sociological Abstracts, an initial keyword search for *burial practices* pulls up some relevant documents and also shows that the best index terms are probably *death rituals* and *burials*. Searching again using these index terms brings up more useful abstracts, with links to full-text articles.

> **Example**: While researching international copyright law, you may want to look at policy arguments about what kind of regulation promotes innovation. Searching the terms *international copyright* in the EconLIT[8] database pulls up an abstract of a relevant article by a law professor, looking at protection of software.[9] Because the article appeared in an economics journal, it would not be indexed in legal periodical indexes, nor would it be available in LexisNexis or Westlaw's databases of law reviews.

C. *Specific Topics*

The chapters that follow focus on researching a few of the many topics available: human rights, international criminal law, intellectual property,

---

[8]   http://www.aeaweb.org/econlit/index.php.
[9]   Robert Merges, *Review*, 45 J. ECON. LIT. 451 (2007).

international environmental law, international trade law, private international law, international business transactions, family law, dispute resolution, international arbitration, and international courts and tribunals. As you review these chapters, some similar strategies and sources should emerge and be applicable when researching other international topics.

Chapter Fifteen

Human Rights

I. *Introduction*

International human rights law is part of public international law. It deals with the protection of individuals and groups against violations of their rights under international law. Generally, it excludes "humanitarian law"—that is, the law of human rights during war—though the two fields are obviously related. It also excludes international criminal law, though, again, the two fields overlap somewhat. (See Chapter 16 for information on researching international criminal law.)

The main sources of human rights law are international treaties. These treaties may be universal, such as the International Convention on the Rights of the Child, or they may be regional, such as the African Charter on Human and Peoples' Rights. Some treaties focus on a relatively narrow topic, such as torture (Convention against Torture); others cover a broad spectrum of rights (e.g., International Covenant on Civil and Political Rights (ICCPR)).

In addition to treaties, however, sources of international human rights law include many types of "soft law"—UN resolutions, decisions of human rights bodies, national laws and court decisions, etc. Some of these instruments have risen to the status of customary international law. For example, the Universal Declaration of Human Rights, though not an international agreement, is considered to be a part of customary international law.

The variety of sources used in human rights law can make this a tough area to research. Moreover, you will find a lack of commercial publications (case reporters, digests) of the type you have used for US research. Language barriers and the lack of documentation on human rights violations in some areas can present other problems for the researcher.

II. *Starting Points: Secondary Sources*

Before starting your human rights research, you should carefully define your topic, country or region, time period, and group of interest (e.g., children or a particular ethnic group). Because it can be so hard to identify primary sources of law, you should start with secondary sources.

A. *Library Catalogs*

Among secondary sources, a good treatise on your topic will be the best resource. Publishers like Oxford University Press, Cambridge University Press, and Brill/Nijhoff, among others, have published hundreds of monographs on human rights, ranging from surveys to in-depth treatments of narrow issues. For example, if you need to research the legality of detention at Guantanamo Bay, you might start with Sir Nigel Rodley's book, *The Treatment of Prisoners under International Law* (3d ed. 2009). Of course, you probably won't know of a useful book at the outset. Start by checking your library catalog. Use keywords for your initial search until you find a relevant item. Then, look at the item's Library of Congress subject headings. Most catalogs will let you click on these headings to locate similar materials.

For example, starting with the keywords *child carpet India* retrieves books on children working in the carpet industry in India. Looking at the subject headings assigned to the book, you can see the heading: *Child Labor—India.* Clicking on this heading will retrieve other titles on your topic.

Sometimes you may want to start by searching Library of Congress subject headings, rather than keywords. For general or comparative books on human rights, use the subject headings:

>   *human rights*
>   *civil rights*
>   *civil rights (international law)*

(Some books on human rights cataloged before 1987 may be found under the subject heading *civil rights.*)

You can add a geographic limitation to the subject headings above if you need information on human rights in a particular country or region:

>   *human rights – france*
>   *human rights – indonesia – timor*

You can also search by topic or by group:

>   *asylum, right of*
>   *women's rights*
>   *indians of south america – brazil – civil rights*

As you can see, however, it is not always easy to guess what Library of Congress subject headings are used; that's why starting with keywords may work better for you. If your library doesn't have any items on your topic, you may want to search other libraries' catalogs. One efficient way to search many library catalogs at the same time is to use WorldCat.[1] This database combines the records of over 17,000 libraries, including some law firm, government, and foreign libraries. If you find a useful book at another library, your own library should be able to borrow it for you. For more information on using library catalogs, see Chapter 5, Section II.

Here is an example of how you might use a book to start your human rights research. Suppose you want to research women's right to be protected from domestic violence, and your country of interest is Mexico. You enter a keyword search in your library catalog: *human rights women violence*.

Among the first items you see is this book: Sally Engle Merry, *Human Rights and Gender Violence: Translating International Law into Local Justice* (2006). The book identifies the main treaty on protection of women's human rights: The Convention on the Elimination of All Forms of Discrimination against Women (CEDAW). Having found the most relevant treaty, you now need to know whether Mexico is a party to it. Checking *Multilateral Treaties Deposited with the Secretary-General* (1982–),[2] you find that Mexico signed the treaty in 1980 and became a party in 1981.

Moreover, this source shows that although some states parties attached reservations, understandings, or declarations to their ratification, Mexico did not. Your next step might be to determine what body enforces CEDAW. You could learn more about CEDAW enforcement from the book you already found, or you could also look at a research guide to CEDAW.

B. *Research Guides*

Research guides are another good tool to use at the beginning of human rights research. You can often find a useful research guide by searching the web with terms like "research" or "guide," combined with your topic of interest (e.g., torture, women's rights, children's rights). A quick web search turns up this useful guide: Bora Laskin Law Library, International Women's Human Rights and Humanitarian Law.[3] The guide tells you what body enforces CEDAW, and what documents that body produces. In addition, the

---

[1] http://www.worldcat.org/ (free version); http://firstsearch.oclc.org/ (subscription version).

[2] http://treaties.un.org/pages/ParticipationStatus.aspx.

[3] http://www.law-lib.utoronto.ca/resguide/women2.htm.

guide lists some Inter-American conventions on women's rights that might be helpful.

Research guides on human rights range from comprehensive surveys (e.g., American Society of International Law, Electronic Resources Guide)[4] to narrow topical approaches (e.g., the right to food and water).[5] Some, like the Electronic Resources *Guide*, include only those resources available electronically; others cover both paper and electronic sources. Some guides contain a lot of textual explanations, while others provide only a list of links. Thus, the usefulness of research guides can vary, but finding one will usually save you time and effort.

C. *Periodical Databases and Indexes*

You may find yourself researching a human rights issue that isn't covered by a book or research guide. In many cases, you can find a journal article discussing your topic. As noted in Chapter 5, Section III, journal articles will usually point to relevant sources of law, key concepts, and legal developments. When researching human rights, journal indexes can be of particular use.

Useful indexes include:

- *Current Law Index.* Also available on LexisNexis and on Westlaw in the LRI database; and as the Legaltrac[6] database, available at many law libraries.
- *Index to Foreign Legal Periodicals.* This index adds English-language index terms to articles in foreign languages (and some English-language articles published in foreign law journals).
- *Index to Legal Periodicals.*[7]
- *PAIS International.*[8] This database is available at many college and university libraries and includes articles on international, legal, and political issues.
- *Social Science Index.*[9] The index is available at many college and university libraries.
- Max Planck Institute for Public International Law also has an index that includes some human rights topics.[10]

---

[4] http://www.asil.org/erg/?page=ihr.
[5] http://www.hrea.org/index.php?base_id=145.
[6] http://www.gale.cengage.com/pdf/facts/legal.pdf (LRI on Westlaw; Find a Source > Legal Resource Index on LexisNexis).
[7] http://www.ebscohost.com/academic/index-to-legal-periodicals-books.
[8] http://www.csa.com/factsheets/pais-set-c.php.
[9] http://www.ebscohost.com/wilson.
[10] http://www.mpil.de/ww/en/pub/library/catalogues_databases/doc_of_articles/pil.cfm.

Another approach is to start by finding a relevant journal. You can find numerous periodicals on international human rights law. To find the titles of these periodicals, search your library catalog with subject headings such as:

> *minorities – legal status, laws, etc. – periodicals*
> *human rights – periodicals*
> *civil rights – periodicals*
> *human rights – [region or country] – periodicals*
> *civil rights – [region or country] – periodicals*
> *women's rights – periodicals*

Once you identify a relevant periodical, look for an index either specific to the publication, such as an annual end-of-the-year index, or a broader periodical index that covers the periodical you need. Your library catalog does not contain article titles.

You may also need to search non-legal periodical indexes. For example, a human rights researcher looking for information on grave desecration might look at sociological or anthropological literature to make a case for the severity of such an offense in particular cultures.

For more information about searching periodical indexes, see Chapter 5, Section III.

D. *Nongovernmental Organization Websites*

Another starting point for research might be the website of a nongovernmental organization (NGO) that works on your topic. For example, if you are asked to represent a woman seeking asylum on the grounds of domestic violence, a good starting point would be the Center for Gender & Refugee Studies at UC-Hastings.[11] This site provides well-organized information about relevant laws, country conditions, asylum decisions, and other useful topics.

To find an NGO on your topic, use web searches with combinations of the terms *human rights, advocates, NGO,* or *nongovernmental organization,* along with terms related to your topic. Or check the Minnesota Human Rights Library's list of human rights organizations.[12] You can also use the HuriSearch search engine[13] to search over 5,000 human rights websites, including non-governmental organizations, national human rights institutions, and intergovernmental organizations.

---

[11] http://cgrs.uchastings.edu.
[12] http://www1.umn.edu/humanrts/links/ngolinks.html.
[13] http://www.hurisearch.org.

Most NGOs, however, have websites designed to inform and mobilize the general public. Unlike the Center for Gender & Refugee Studies, for example, they are not intended mainly for lawyers. Thus, an NGO site is not usually as efficient as a good book, article, or research guide.

III. *Treaties and other Human Rights Instruments*

If you know the name of a treaty, you can usually find a copy on the web with a simple search. If you are not sure, and want to look at collections of human rights treaties, there are several good websites.

A. *Compilations of Human Rights Instruments*

UN human rights treaties are located at the Office of the High Commissioner of Human Rights (OHCHR) website.[14] For a list that links to full-text versions, click on "International Law" from the OHCHR homepage. This list does not include regional human rights instruments. If you think that your country of interest belongs to a regional organization, such as the Council of Europe (COE) or the Organization of American States (OAS), check those organizations' websites for human rights treaties.[15] (Of course, you should also check whether your country of interest is currently a member of the organization.)

The United Nations Treaty Database[16] is among the most comprehensive database for treaties, but its coverage lags behind alternative web sources. Other useful collections of human rights treaties include the University of Minnesota Human Rights Library,[17] the Multilaterals Project at Tufts University,[18] and the Netherlands Institute of Human Rights (SIM), Human Rights Treaties.[19] The EISIL database[20] also links to selected human rights treaties, and provides citations and other useful information.

Other treaty databases require a subscription and may be available at your law school. Lexis-Nexis has a database of international treaties,[21] as does

---

[14] http://www.ohchr.org/EN/Pages/WelcomePage.aspx.

[15] For Council of Europe treaties, see http://conventions.coe.int; for OAS treaties, see http://www.oas.org/dil/treaties.htm.

[16] http://treaties.un.org.

[17] http://www1.umn.edu/humanrts.

[18] http://fletcher.tufts.edu/multilaterals.

[19] http://sim.law.uu.nl/SIM/Library/HRinstruments.nsf/%28organization%29?OpenView.

[20] http://www.eisil.org/index.php?t=sub_pages&cat=185.

[21] International Law > Treaties & International Agreements > U.S. Treaties on LexisNexis.

Westlaw.[22] Westlaw and LexisNexis also have *International Legal Materials* (I.L.M.) as a database; I.L.M. contains selected treaties. HeinOnline[23] offers a Treaties and Agreements Library containing US treaties, and also offers I.L.M.

Paper collections of human rights instruments have become less important because of web access. For example, the United Nations publishes a collection called *Human Rights: A Compilation of International Instruments* (2002–), but you can find these instruments on the web.[24] Course books on human rights often include a supplement containing selected human rights instruments.

For more information on searching for treaties, see Chapter 6, Sections I through III.

B. *Status Information*

Before you can argue that a country has treaty obligations to protect or promote human rights, you must ascertain that the country is a party to the treaty in question. For major human rights treaties, the best free source is the OHCHR website. When you click on the name of a treaty (on the Human Rights Instruments page), you will see a page devoted to that treaty. For most treaties, the left-hand side of the page has a link to "Status of ratification." This link takes you to the UN treaties status information. Links from a country name, if any, lead to the text of reservations, declarations, and understandings (RUDs). Note, however, that RUDs added during the ratification process do not always appear in this table. For example, the United States attached significant RUDs to the International Covenant on Civil and Political Rights when the Senate gave its advice and consent to the treaties.[25]

Regional human rights bodies' websites usually contain status information as well. For example, on the OAS site, each treaty contains a link to "Signatories and Ratifications" at the end of the treaty text. To update this information, however, you should also check the page entitled "Recent actions regarding multilateral treaties."[26]

The African Commission on Human and People's Rights has a separate section for "Ratifications," available from the home page as a link under "Documentation."[27] Unfortunately, this information is not always current;

---

[22] CMB-TREATIES database.
[23] http://heinonline.org.
[24] http://www2.ohchr.org/english/law.
[25] http://www1.umn.edu/humanrts/usdocs/civilres.html.
[26] http://www.oas.org/DIL/recentactionstreaties.htm.
[27] http://www.achpr.org/english/_info/index_ratifications_en.html.

for example, in late 2011, the information was current through 2007. You may need to look at a country's own website, or search news sources, to learn whether it has become a party.

For more information on researching treaty status information, see Chapter 6, Sections II.F and III.D.

C. *Reservations, Declarations, and Understandings*

As mentioned above, countries may employ RUDs that affect, or purport to affect, their treaty obligations. Often, information about these provisions appears along with status information. For example, many of them appear in the UN Treaties Collection, in "Status of Multilateral Treaties Deposited with the Secretary-General."[28] Secondary sources will often mention significant reservations; for example, you can find several law review articles discussing the US reservations to the ICCPR.[29] For complete information on reservations, you may also need to check with the embassy or foreign ministry for your country of interest.

IV. *Jurisprudence*

In the human rights context, decisions of international and national tribunals can be used as persuasive authority. International tribunals range from court-like bodies, such as the International Court of Justice (ICJ) and the European Court of Human Rights (ECHR), to international bodies responsible for enforcing treaty rights, such as the Human Rights Committee (HRC), which responds to complaints under the ICCPR, and the Inter-American Human Rights Commission, one of the bodies that responds to complaints under OAS human rights instruments such as the American Declaration of the Rights and Duties of Man. National court decisions, including lower court and administrative decisions, may also be used.

A. *Jurisprudence of International Bodies*

In a perfect world, there would be one database combining all human rights decisions, and that database would be updated daily. Unfortunately, no such database exists. Often, the most current sources for decisions, such as the individual complaints committees at the UN, do not offer keyword-searchable

---

[28] http://treaties.un.org/pages/ParticipationStatus.aspx.
[29] E.g., William A. Schabas, *Invalid Reservations to the International Covenant on Civil and Political Rights: Is the United States Still a Party?*, 21 Brook. J. Int'l L. 277 (1995).

databases. Several websites attempt to provide ways to search a lot of human rights jurisprudence at once; however, these sites are often incomplete or not updated or both. We will cover a few of them here because it is impossible to predict which of them will be current at any given time.

First, there is REFWORLD,[30] which contains documents from various human rights courts and tribunals, and allows Google-style searching. By selecting "Advanced Search," you get a screen that permits you to specify the sources to search (e.g., African Commission on Human and Peoples' Rights, UN Committee against Torture) and the type of document (use "Case Law"). Unfortunately, the REFWORLD site does not provide information on the currentness of its database. In late 2011, the most recent Committee against Torture jurisprudence was from 2009. Your search results will be returned ranked by relevance, but by switching the ranking option to date (after you search), you can quickly see the date of the latest decision.

Another option is the Minnesota Human Rights Library,[31] but in recent years this site has not been updated consistently. In late 2011, its coverage of CEDAW decisions extended only to 2007, while coverage of Committee against Torture jurisprudence was current through 2009. Like REFWORLD, the site offers a Google-powered search page.[32]

As of late 2011, the closest thing to one-stop searching is at World-LII, which offers combined searching of several human rights courts and tribunals. From the main WorldLII page, select the link to "International Decisions."[33] From the "International Courts & Tribunals Collection," you can either use the upper drop-down menu to search the "All Human Rights Courts and Tribunals Databases," or select various individual bodies from the lower drop-down menu. (Note that as of late 2011, the "All Human Rights Courts and Tribunals Databases" option does not include CEDAW decisions or African Commission on Human and Peoples' Rights decisions, though CEDAW decisions are searchable separately.) One outstanding feature of this site is its page informing the researcher of the currentness of the individual databases.[34] Unfortunately, this site does not have the most recent decisions of several of the courts and tribunals included in the site. For example, in late 2011 its coverage of Committee against Torture jurisprudence was a year behind. The best approach is probably to use the most

---

[30] http://www.unhcr.org/cgi-bin/texis/vtx/refworld/rwmain.
[31] http://www1.umn.edu/humanrts/google/localsearch.html.
[32] http://www1.umn.edu/humanrts/google/localsearch.html.
[33] http://www.worldlii.org/int/cases.
[34] http://www.worldlii.org/cgi-bin/cases_status.cgi?mask_path=int/cases.

current site, such as WorldLII, and then use the tribunals' or courts' own sites to see the most recent decisions.

So, for example, if you are making an asylum claim for a Peruvian man based on the Convention against Torture, try one of the sites above, and then look at the jurisprudence of the Committee against Torture on the OHCHR website for any recent decisions. From the OCHCR homepage, click on the link to Human Rights Bodies. Next, click on the link "Search the Treaty Body Database."[35] Using the drop-down menus, you can then specify that you want [Type] "Jurisprudence" relating to [Convention] CAT. You can also select "Peru" from the drop-down menu. Unfortunately, there is no option to add keywords to your search.

Two new subscription databases on international human rights law are part of the Oxford Reports on International Law: Oxford Reports on International Human Rights Law and Oxford Reports on International Criminal Law. These databases include selected decisions from both international and national tribunals.

Starting by searching case law databases, however, is not always the most efficient strategy. Again, secondary sources can point you to key decisions. Start with them if possible. For example, if you need to look at the jurisprudence of the Human Rights Committee (HRC), try Sarah Joseph et al., *The International Covenant on Civil and Political Rights: Cases, Materials, and Commentary* (2d ed. 2004). This book arranges references to selected HRC decisions under the various rights to which they pertain. Similarly, the book *Laurence Burgorgue-Larsen & Amaya Ubeda de Torres, The Inter-American Court of Human Rights: Case-Law and Commentary* (2011) identifies and describes key cases organized by various rights.

Case reporters that cover international bodies, as well as some regional bodies, include the following:

- *International Human Rights Reports* (I.H.R.R.) (1994–).[36] This reporter reproduces cases from the UN Human Rights Committee, the UN Committee against Torture, the Committee on the Elimination of Racial Discrimination (CERD), the Inter-American Commission on Human Rights, the Inter-American Court of Human Rights, the African Commission on Human and Peoples' Rights, the former Yugoslavia and Rwanda War Crimes Tribunals, and the Bosnian Human Rights Chamber.

---

[35] http://tb.ohchr.org/default.aspx.
[36] Also available online by subscription: http://www.nottingham.ac.uk/hrlc/publications/internationalhumanrightsreports.aspx.

- *International Legal Materials* (I.L.M.) (1962–). This is also available on HeinOnline,[37] LexisNexis and Westlaw. It reprints a few selected cases from international courts and tribunals.
- *Human Rights Law Journal* (H.R.L.J.) (1980–2008). This journal reprinted selected cases from various international human rights courts and bodies.
- *International Law Reports* (I.L.R.) (1919–).[38] This reprints, in English, selected decisions from the highest national courts as well as international courts and tribunals. Useful websites include:
  - International Court of Justice (ICJ).[39]
  - World Court Digest, a compendium of the jurisprudence of the ICJ.[40]
  - International Criminal Tribunal for the former Yugoslavia.[41] (International criminal tribunals are treated more fully in chapter 16.)
  - Genocide, War Crimes, and Crimes against Humanity: Topical Digest of the Case Law (Human Rights Watch).[42]
  - International Criminal Tribunal for Rwanda.[43]
  - International Criminal Court.[44]
  - Special Court for Sierra Leone.[45]
  - Commonwealth and International Human Rights Case Law Databases (Interights) (contains summaries only).[46]
  - Netherlands Institute of Human Rights (SIM) Case Law Database.[47]
  - The United Nations Human Rights Treaties.[48]

B. *Jurisprudence of Regional Bodies*

1. *African System*

You may have trouble getting documents from the African Commission on Human and Peoples' Rights in paper or online. The Commission's website is not yet stable; it is often unavailable, and its contents are limited. Some materials are located under "Activity Reports," under the "Documentation"

---

[37] http://heinonline.org.

[38] Now available online, by subscription, from Justis.

[39] http://www.icj-cij.org/homepage/index.php.

[40] http://www.mpil.de/ww/en/pub/research/details/publications/institute/wcd.cfm.

[41] http://www.icty.org.

[42] http://www.hrw.org/sites/default/files/reports/ictr0110webwcover.pdf.

[43] http://www.unictr.org.

[44] http://www.icc-cpi.int/Menus/ICC.

[45] http://www.sc-sl.org.

[46] http://www.interights.org/commonwealth-and-international-law-database/index.html.

[47] http://sim.law.uu.nl/SIM/Dochome.nsf?Open.

[48] http://www.bayefsky.com/docs.php/area/jurisprudence/node/2.

link. If you cannot find what you need there, try the African Human Rights Case Law Database from the University of Pretoria's Centre for Human Rights.[49] That site has various Commission documents, and it has Commission decisions (as well as other decisions) by country and by subject. As with the databases like REFWORLD and WORLDLII noted above, however, the site does not have the most recent decisions. Again, it may work best to start with this site, because it lets you find cases by subject, but you will then have to go to the official site and glance through more recent cases to update your search.

The University of Minnesota Human Rights Library also has some of the Commission's decisions.[50] But as of late 2011, the site was less up-to-date than the Centre for Human Rights site described in the previous paragraph.

To look for other Commission materials, try searching your library catalog using "African Commission on Human and People's Rights" as author, keyword, or subject. Dr. Rachel Murray has also written extensively on human rights in the African system; search by author to find her works. Periodical articles may also refer to or even reprint key documents.

The African Court on Human and Peoples' Rights is still very new, and its website does not offer a way to search cases, but it does offer decisions in .pdf format. In 2008, the African Court on Human and Peoples' Rights merged with the Court of Justice of the African Union to create the African Court of Justice and Human Rights. It is not yet clear if the newly-merged court will get a new website; the current website still has the name African Court on Human and Peoples' Rights.

One of the better sources for jurisprudence is the *African Human Rights Law Reports* (2000–). These reports contain selected national decisions as well as decisions from the African Commission on Human and Peoples' Rights and the UN treaty bodies, dealing with African countries. The reports from 2000 to 2009 are available on the web.[51] These are the same decisions made accessible by the University of Pretoria's Centre for Human Rights, described above.

2. European System
The jurisprudence of the European system is extensive and well documented. Decisions of the European Court of Human Rights (ECHR), and selected

---

[49] http://www.chr.up.ac.za/index.php/documents/african-human-rights-case-law-database.html.

[50] http://www1.umn.edu/humanrts/africa/comcases/comcases.html.

[51] http://www.chr.up.ac.za/index.php/ahrlr-english-editions.html.

decisions from the now-defunct European Commission on Human Rights, are available on Westlaw[52] and on LexisNexis.[53]

Author searches and subject searches are useful for finding decisions and information issued by the European Commission, the European Court, and the Council of Europe.

Paper reports of European human rights jurisprudence include:

- European Commission of Human Rights, *Decisions and Reports* (1975–1998).
- *European Human Rights Reports* (1979–). This is also available on Lexis-Nexis[54] and Westlaw.[55]
- *Human Rights Case Digest* (1990–2008).
- Council of Europe, *Yearbook of the European Convention on Human Rights* (1960–).
- European Court of Human Rights, *Publications of the European Court of Human Rights*. Series A (1961–1996), Series B (1960–1995). Series A contains the official judgments and decisions and Series B contains pleadings, oral arguments, and documents. It was continued by European Court of Human Rights, *Recueil des arrêts et décisions—Reports of Judgments and Decisions* (1996–2006). For decisions after 2006, use the HUDOC website.[56]

For most researchers, it is more convenient to access the ECHR jurisprudence through its website, HUDOC. The HUDOC database provides access to ECHR decisions as well as decisions from the former European Commission on Human Rights. You can search by keyword, title, date, article of the European Convention on Human Rights, and type of document (e.g., decisions on admissibility of complaints, judgments, etc.).

European Union. Some of the decisions of the European Union's Court of Justice (the ECJ) involve human rights issues. With the entry into force of the Treaty of Lisbon, the ECJ has competence to enforce the Charter of Fundamental Rights of the European Union, which incorporates the rights protected by the European Convention on Human Rights. Thus, although the Council of Europe human rights system, described above, is separate from the European Union system, the ECJ will increasingly rule on human rights issues within the EU.

---

[52] EHR-RPTS database.
[53] International Law > Cases > Human Rights Cases (only a handful of Commission cases are included).
[54] International Law > Cases > Human Rights Cases (only a handful of Commission cases are included).
[55] EHR-RPTS database.
[56] http://cmiskp.echr.coe.int/tkp197/search.asp?skin=hudoc-en.

- Court of Justice of the European Communities, *Reports of Cases before the Court of Justice and the Court of the First Instance* (1954–). Decisions are also available on the Court's website,[57] and in EUR-LEX.[58] Westlaw (EU-CS) and LexisNexis (Legal > Global Legal > European Union > Case Law > EUR-Lex European Union Cases) also have databases of these cases.

3. *Inter-American System*
Materials from the Organization of American States (OAS) can be difficult to find online or on paper. Furthermore, decisions are often available in Spanish before they are available in English. To find materials in your library, search *Inter-American Commission* and the *Inter-American Court* as authors and as keywords and subjects.

Inter-American Court on Human Rights

- The Court's decisions are available on its website,[59] and on the University of Minnesota Human Rights website[60] (not usually current, however). Paper versions are published in *Inter-American Court of Human Rights, Series A: Judgments and Opinions, Series B: Pleadings, Oral Arguments and Documents*, and *Series C: Decisions and Judgments*. Unfortunately, publication is irregular and delayed. You will usually have to get cases from the Court's website.
- For summaries of the Court's activity, see *Inter-American Court of Human Rights, Annual Report* (1981–). Annual reports from 1998 onwards are available on the Court's website.
- The Inter-American Human Rights Digest Project at American University offers an index to the Court's jurisprudence from 1980–1997, but this index is in Spanish only.[61]

Inter-American Commission on Human Rights

- *Annual Report* (1977–). Many annual reports are available on the Commission's website.[62] The annual reports contain reports of decisions of the Commission. Documents from the annual reports are also available on

---

[57] http://curia.europa.eu/jurisp/cgi-bin/form.pl?lang=en.
[58] http://eur-lex.europa.eu/RECH_menu.do.
[59] http://www.corteidh.or.cr/index.cfm?&CFID=1407196&CFTOKEN=45059938.
[60] http://www1.umn.edu/humanrts/iachr/iachr.html.
[61] https://www.wcl.american.edu/humright/repertorio/indice.cfm.
[62] http://www.cidh.oas.org/DefaultE.htm.

Westlaw[63] and, usually less up-to-date, on the University of Minnesota Human Rights Library website.[64]

- The Inter-American Human Rights Database at American University provides online access to Commission documents from its inception, but has not been updated since 1998.[65]

The Inter-American System Generally

- *Inter-American Yearbook on Human Rights* (1968–). The *Yearbook* provides background information, key instruments, documents, and a discussion of human rights practices in selected OAS countries.

C. *National Jurisprudence*

Some reporters include both international and national cases.

- *Butterworths Human Rights Cases* (1997–).[66] This covers selected decisions from international, European, and English courts and tribunals.
- *Commonwealth Human Rights Law Digest* (1996–). The Commonwealth and International Human Rights Case Law Databases are available on the Interights website.[67] It includes over 2,000 summaries of significant human rights decisions, from both domestic Commonwealth courts and from tribunals applying international human rights law, such as the African Commission on Human and Peoples' Rights and the European Court of Human Rights.
- *International Law Reports* (I.L.R.) (1919–).[68] This publication reprints, in English, selected decisions from the highest national courts as well as international courts and tribunals.
- Oxford Reports on International Law: Oxford Reports on International Human Rights Law and Oxford Reports on International Criminal Law. These online databases are available through a small number of law libraries. They include selected national court decisions that address international law; some of the cases involve human rights or international criminal law issues.

---

[63] IACHR-OAS.
[64] http://www1.umn.edu/humanrts/cases/commissn.htm.
[65] http://www.wcl.american.edu/pub/humright/digest/Inter-American.
[66] Also on LexisNexis, 1996 to present, International Law > Cases.
[67] http://www.interights.org/commonwealth-and-international-law-database/index.html.
[68] Now available by subscription from Justis.

- University of Michigan Law School, Refugee Caselaw Site.[69] This site contains selected asylum decisions from national courts.

Finally, many journals reprint cases from various jurisdictions as well as international tribunals. Using a periodical index, or a full-text periodicals database, can sometimes help you identify reprinted cases.

V. *Country Reports*

In human rights work, "country reports" is a term of art. It refers to documents produced by governmental, intergovernmental, and nongovernmental organizations, describing the human rights situation in a particular country. Human rights lawyers use these reports in proceedings such as asylum hearings. For example, if an asylum claimant fears persecution if she is returned to her country of origin, her lawyer may introduce various country reports on that country to document that her fear is well-founded.

Some country reports focus only on one issue. For instance, the US Department of State prepares a report each year called the *Annual Report to Congress on International Religious Freedom*.[70] This report describes protection of and threats to religious freedom in countries around the world.

Other country reports summarize a whole range of human rights issues. The US Department of State produces country reports on human rights practices, which address the state of human rights in various countries. US administrative law judges use the Department of State country reports as their starting point for asylum claims. However, attorneys for asylum-seekers often introduce country reports from major human rights organizations such as Amnesty International (AI)[71] and Human Rights Watch (HRW).[72]

Some websites are designed specifically for researching country conditions in the refugee/asylum context. One such site is the Canadian Immigration and Refugee Board.[73] Under "National Documentation Packages," you will find links to the most current major country conditions reports (e.g., HRW, AI) and to many other useful documents.

---

[69] http://www.refugeecaselaw.org/Home.aspx.
[70] http://www.state.gov/g/drl/irf/rpt.
[71] http://www.amnesty.org/en. The most current country report is usually linked from the site's home page.
[72] http://www.hrw.org/publications.
[73] http://www.irb-cisr.gc.ca/eng/resrec/ndpcnd/Pages/index.aspx.

Other useful sites for researching country conditions include:

- Asylumlaw.org.[74] The "Case support" section has a drop-down menu with country names. After choosing a country, you'll see available documents (e.g., UNHCR information on rates of recognition). If you register (without charge) at the site, you can obtain names of experts and even documents (some legal briefs). Unfortunately, as of late 2011 this site has not been updated consistently; much of the information is stale.
- Center for Gender and Refugee Studies.[75] Use the drop-down menu to search by nationality (country) and get free information, such as experts' names. You must fill out an online form to get some of the information. You can also search by issue.
- United Kingdom Border Agency, Country of Origin Information Service.[76] This site has an alphabetical list of country information for the UK's top asylum countries (22 countries as of late 2011).

Many of the research guides noted above include sections on locating country reports.

VI. *News Sources*

Human rights research often requires searching news stories. While you may want to start by searching US newspaper databases such as the *New York Times*, you may also need to search foreign newspapers.

Both LexisNexis and Westlaw offer databases focused on specific countries or regions. In LexisNexis, choose the News & Business tab. Scroll down and select Country & Region (excluding US). Next, select a region. You can also select a country from the list below the list of regions; however, for some countries (e.g., Kenya), LexisNexis does not offer a separate database.

For news stories, the best search approach is usually one that uses "proximity connectors"—connectors that specify your search terms must be within a certain number of words from each other. It is also helpful to specify that your terms must appear in the "headline/lead" segment of the database (i.e., within the headline or the lead paragraph).

Example: *hlead(kenya*) & kenya* w/15 hiv OR aids.*

---

[74] http://www.asylumlaw.org/countries.
[75] http://cgrs.uchastings.edu/country/memos.php.
[76] http://www.ukba.homeoffice.gov.uk/policyandlaw/guidance/coi.

In Westlaw, choose the Business & News tab, then "Global News." The next screen shows a list of databases by region and a search screen. As in Lexis-Nexis, the best search approach is to use "proximity connectors."

> **Example**: *kenya* w/15 aids hiv w/15 discriminat! prejudic! stigma! persecut!*

If you lack access to Westlaw or LexisNexis, general web searching may retrieve relevant news items. You may need to search newspaper archives, however, which regular search engines cannot always access. The web offers a couple of sources for such archives:

- International News Archives on the Web.[77] This site includes an alphabetical list of countries, with links to foreign newspapers and archives (where available).
- Onlinenewspapers.com.[78] This site collects links to foreign newspapers, first by region, then with grids for individual countries.

VII. *Blogs*

Particularly if you work with human rights issues, you may want to subscribe to blogs that focus on human rights. Chapter 3 describes blogs and how to find them, but some useful blogs on human rights topics include the ones listed below.

- The US office of Amnesty International (AI)[79] has a searchable blog on human rights news and AI's work.
- Human Rights Education Associates (HREA) offers several different blogs, including a general human rights news blog, and several topical ones (e.g., prisoners' rights, women's rights).[80]
- Human Rights Watch.[81] HRW also offers human rights news blogs on a wide range of topics.
- Jurist World Legal News.[82] This covers many human rights and international criminal law developments.

---

[77] http://www.ibiblio.org/slanews/internet/intarchives.htm.
[78] http://www.onlinenewspapers.com.
[79] http://blog.amnestyusa.org.
[80] http://www.hrea.org/index.php?base_id=88.
[81] http://www.hrw.org/rss.
[82] http://jurist.law.pitt.edu/worldlatest.

Chapter Sixteen

International Criminal Law

I. *Introduction*

While human rights law focuses on state obligations to protect human rights, international criminal law focuses on individual obligations to respect human rights. Since World War II, the international community has created various mechanisms to deter individuals, as well as states, from violating human rights, and to punish violations of those rights. This section addresses some of those mechanisms. For the most part, it does not deal with "transnational" criminal law issues, such as extradition to face national criminal charges, trafficking, or bilateral treaties on cooperation in criminal matters. Note that international criminal law usually arises in the context of armed conflict; thus, the field overlaps to some extent with international humanitarian law, regulating conduct during war.

Most efforts to implement international criminal law have consisted of the creation of ad hoc tribunals; e.g., the Nuremberg tribunals following World War II, the International Criminal Tribunal for the former Yugoslavia (ICTY),[1] the International Criminal Tribunal for Rwanda (ICTR),[2] and the Special Court for Sierra Leone (SCSL).[3] The International Criminal Court (ICC)[4] is the only court with general jurisdiction over international criminal law. (The International Court of Justice has jurisdiction only over disputes between states.)

The sources of international criminal law include international treaties and the statutes creating the international tribunals; principles of customary international law, such as international humanitarian law, also play a role. The international tribunals do not adhere to "stare decisis"—that is, they are not bound to follow their own decisions. Nonetheless, prosecutors and defendants

---

[1] http://www.icty.org.
[2] http://www.unictr.org.
[3] http://www.sc-sl.org/.
[4] http://www.icc-cpi.int/Menus/ICC.

cite previous judgments extensively in their written and oral presentations to tribunals. They also cite judgments from other international criminal tribunals (including Nuremberg judgments). The United Nations is the founding organization for some of the international criminal tribunals, but hybrid tribunals have also been created. An example is the Extraordinary Chambers in the Courts of Cambodia (ECCC),[5] created by a joint agreement between the Government of Cambodia and the United Nations. The ECCC has tried persons for violations of both international and national law.

Because international criminal tribunals are a relatively recent phenomenon, a lot of research can be done on the web. The various tribunals have websites that include key documents, including founding statutes or treaties, rules of evidence and procedure, judgments, and news. However, keep in mind that the most efficient way to research international criminal law (as opposed to just finding a copy of a decision, for example), is to take advantage of the many books and articles published on this topic.

Useful Library of Congress subject headings include the following:

> *rome statute of the international criminal court (1998)*
> *international criminal law*
> *international crimes*
> *crimes against humanity*
> *war crimes*
> *criminal procedure (international law)*
> *international criminal courts*
> *war crime trials – yugoslavia*
> *international tribunal for the prosecution of persons responsible for serious violations of international humanitarian law committed in the territory of the former yugoslavia since 1991*
> *war crime trials – former yugoslav republics*
> *crimes against humanity – former yugoslav republics*
> *international criminal tribunal for rwanda*
> *special court for sierra leone*
> [name of whatever tribunal you need to research]

Many excellent books on international criminal law have been published. Some of the most-recognized experts in this field include M. Cherif Bassiouni, Antonio Cassese, William Schabas, Leila Sadat, Kevin Jon Heller, and Michael Scharf; search your library catalog to find works by these authors.

A few particularly useful works include:

- *Commentary on the Rome Statute of the International Criminal Court: Observers' Notes, Article by Article* (2d ed. Otto Triffterer ed., 2008).

---

[5] http://www.eccc.gov.kh/en.

- *The Rome Statute of the International Criminal Court: A Commentary* (Antonio Cassese et al. eds., 2002).
- *International Criminal Law* (3d ed., M. Cherif Bassiouni ed., 2008).
- *The Oxford Companion to International Criminal Justice* (Antonio Cassese ed., 2009).
- *Research Handbook on International Criminal Law* (Bartram S. Brown ed., 2011).
- *Routledge Handbook of International Criminal Law* (William Schabas & Nadia Bernaz eds., 2011).
- William A. Schabas, *The UN International Criminal Tribunals: The Former Yugoslavia, Rwanda, and Sierra Leone* (2006).

Keep in mind, however, that a few hundred books exist on the subject; you may want to search for ones that focus on a particular topic within the general subject. For example, if you are researching rape as a war crime, your search would turn up books like Donja de Ruiter, *Sexual Offenses in International Criminal Law* (2011).

Because of the flood of books on international criminal law, your library may not have the best ones for your particular research task. Therefore, you may want to search other libraries' catalogs. One efficient way to search many library catalogs at the same time is to use WorldCat.[6] If you find a useful book at another library, your own library should be able to borrow it for you. For more information on using library catalogs, see Chapter 5, Section II.

> **Example**: One of the more recent developments in the area of international criminal law is victims' rights in these courts and tribunals. The most useful way to explore this area is to look for books and articles on this topic. A keyword search on WorldCat yields a book by T. Markus Funk called *Victims' Rights and Advocacy at the International Criminal Court* (2011). A chapter within this book traces the development of these rights under international law. The legal journal literature contains articles that are more narrow, such as Tom Welch et al., 'Witness Anonymity at the International Criminal Court: Due Process for Defendants, Witnesses or Both?,' 2011 *Denning L.J.* 29. This article examines how the ICC has sought to balance the defendant's due process rights with the physical or psychological well-being of witnesses and victims through its witness protection measures.

A. Research Guides

One of the most useful guides is Amy Burchfield's Update: International Criminal Courts for the Former Yugoslavia, Rwanda and Sierra Leone: A

---

[6] http://www.worldcat.org (free version); http://firstsearch.oclc.org (subscription version).

Guide to Online and Print Resources (2011).[7] Note, however, that this guide does not cover the International Criminal Court. Another excellent guide, focusing primarily on online research, is Gail Partin, International Criminal Law.[8] (Partin's guide covers transnational criminal law as well as international criminal law.) Consider looking for research guides on war crimes and crimes against humanity on the web.

B. *Treaties and Founding Statutes*

Some rules of international criminal law are found in multilateral treaties such as the Genocide Convention,[9] the Convention against Torture,[10] and the humanitarian law conventions referred to as the Geneva Conventions.[11] For information on how to research treaties, including how to find status information, see Chapter 6.

The individual tribunals all provide their founding documents on their website; for example, the ICTY's is within the site's Legal Library.[12] Look under "Legal," "Documents," and similar headings. Status information for the ad hoc tribunals is not relevant as all necessary parties will have signed on to create the tribunal.

C. *Cases*

While the tribunals all provide copies of decisions on their websites, these decisions are generally not searchable there. It is easier to use other sources. Westlaw has decisions of the ICTY[13] and the ICTR,[14] but not others; Lexis-Nexis has none. Selected decisions appear in the *Oxford Reports on International Criminal Law*[15] and *International Law Reports*,[16] both available by subscription at some libraries. WorldLII[17] offers free searching of decisions

---

[7] http://www.nyulawglobal.org/globalex/International_Criminal_Courts1.htm.

[8] http://www.asil.org/erg/?page=icl.

[9] Convention on the Prevention and Punishment of the Crime of Genocide, Dec. 9, 1948, 78 U.N.T.S. 277, 102 Stat. 3045.

[10] Convention against Torture and Other Cruel, Inhuman or Degrading Treatment or Punishment, Dec. 10, 1984, 1465 U.N.T.S. 85, 11.

[11] Including, for example, Geneva Convention Relative to the Protection of Civilian Persons in Time of War (Fourth Geneva Convention), Aug. 12, 1949, 75 U.N.T.S. 287. For a complete collection of treaties on humanitarian law, see the International Committee of the Red Cross website, http://www.icrc.org/ihl.nsf/TOPICS?OpenView.

[12] http://www.icty.org/sections/LegalLibrary/StatuteoftheTribunal.

[13] INT-ICTY database.

[14] INT-ICTR database.

[15] http://www.oxfordlawreports.com.

[16] http://www.justis.com/data-coverage/international-law-reports.aspx.

[17] http://www.worldlii.org/int/cases.

from several tribunals (ICC, ICTY, ICTR, Sierra Leone, Timor Leste), but recent cases may not be available at that site. You may want to do some of your research by searching WorldLII and then look at the tribunal sites themselves for recent decisions.

Selected national cases addressing international humanitarian law are available at the ICRC website.[18]

Currently, there is no citator for international criminal law cases.

Paper versions of decisions are available from several sources, and lag far behind the websites:

- *Annotated Leading Cases of International Criminal Tribunals* (André Klip & Göran Sluiter eds., 1999–).[19] Includes ICTY, ICTR, and Sierra Leone.
- *Basic Documents and Jurisprudence of International/ized Criminal Courts and Tribunals* (2007–).[20] This database covers the following: ECCC, ICC, ICTR, ICTY, SCSL, East Timor, and Indonesia.
- *Global War Crimes Tribunal Collection* (J. Oppenheim & W. van der Wolf eds., 1997–). Covers ICTY, ICTR, ICC, and Sierra Leone.
- *Judicial Reports / International Criminal Tribunal for the Former Yugoslavia = Recueils Judiciaires / Tribunal Pénal pour l'ex-Yougoslavie* (1999–).
- *International Criminal Law Reports* (Helen Malcolm & Rodney Dixon eds., 2000-). Includes ICTY, ICTR, ICC, and domestic proceedings.
- Netherlands Institute of Human Rights, Tribunals Database,[21] includes the jurisprudence of the ICTY and ICTR.
- *The Sierra Leone Special Court Collection* (Claudia Tofan ed., 2008–).
- *Digest of Jurisprudence of the Special Court for Sierra Leone, 2003–2005* (2007) (summaries only).
- *Tribunal Pénal International pour le Rwanda: Recueil des Ordonnances, Décisions et Arrêts, 1995–1997 = International Criminal Tribunal for Rwanda Reports of Orders, Decisions and Judgements, 1995–1997* (Eric David ed., 2000).

D. Useful Websites

In addition to the tribunal sites already mentioned above, there is the Special Tribunal for Lebanon.[22] Generally, if a new tribunal such as the proposed international tribunal for Timor-Leste is created, its website will have basic documents and decisions.

---

[18] http://www.icrc.org/ihl-nat.
[19] Also available online by subscription, http://www.annotatedleadingcases.com.
[20] Available by subscription, http://www.wcl.american.edu/warcrimes/wcro_docs/index.cfm.
[21] http://sim.law.uu.nl/sim/caselaw/tribunalen.nsf/%28Accused_All%29?OpenView.
[22] http://www.stl-tsl.org.

In addition to the national court decisions in its National Implementation Database, the ICRC's website offers a lot of useful tools for researching humanitarian law. For example, you can read the full text of the Commentaries on the four Geneva Conventions and their two Additional Protocols of 1977.[23] The ICRC also provides access to the text of a major study of customary humanitarian law.[24]

Many NGOs are active in monitoring the activities of international criminal tribunals. Some of these organizations issue useful reports and documents for locating relevant caselaw. For example, Human Rights Watch issued two useful digests: one on the caselaw of the International Criminal Tribunal for the Former Yugoslavia (2006)[25] and the other of the caselaw of the International Criminal Tribunal for Rwanda (2010).[26] Both digests are handy tools for accessing the cases by topic.

The Coalition for the International Criminal Court is another organization whose website provides lots of documents and information for researching the ICC. The site has official documents, academic papers and reports, national implementing legislation, UN documents, and so much more. Many of the documents go back to 1996.

There are far too many websites to mention for this topic, but here are some of the most useful:

- ICC Legal Tools Database[27] contains ICC documents, national cases involving international crimes, ICC preparatory works, international criminal judgments, and other related materials. You can browse the collection or search.
- War Crimes Studies Center of UC Berkeley.[28] One of the main activities of this organization is trail monitoring and research. The site provides access to the reports and documents from the monitoring teams for the following courts: Sierra Leone, East Timor, Indonesia, Cambodia, and also covers World War II.
- International Justice Tribune.[29] Part of Radio Netherlands Worldwide, the IJT is a good source for news on international courts and tribunals as well as proceedings from domestic courts.
- War Crimes Research Portal (Frederick K. Cox International Law Center).[30] Contains almost 200 research memoranda on issues pending before the

---

[23] http://www.icrc.org/ihl.nsf/CONVPRES?OpenView.
[24] http://www.icrc.org/eng/war-and-law/treaties-customary-law/customary-law.
[25] http://www.hrw.org/node/11277.
[26] http://www.hrw.org/en/reports/2010/01/12/genocide-war-crimes-and-crimes-against-humanity.
[27] http://www.legal-tools.org/en/what-are-the-icc-legal-tools.
[28] http://socrates.berkeley.edu/~warcrime/index.html.
[29] http://www.rnw.nl/international-justice.
[30] http://law.case.edu/war-crimes-research-portal.

International Criminal Tribunal for the Former Yugoslavia, the International Criminal Tribunal for Rwanda, links to other resources arranged by topic, a research guide and bibliography of sources.

> **Example**: You want to locate the cases from the Rwandan Tribunal that define incitement to commit genocide. The ICTR website does have a search mechanism but it's not particularly effective for this kind of research. Westlaw's ICTR database is more useful for this kind of search since you can use this kind of search: *defin! /s incit! /s genocide.* An even more efficient tool is to use the Human Rights Watch Digest; by reviewing the table of contents, you can find a section called "direct and public incitement to commit genocide, defined/ actus reus." This section provides summaries of the relevant cases from both the trial and the appeals chambers. Since this digest was updated in 2010, you don't have to do much updating. Of course, another approach would be to look for an article on the subject, such as Susan Benesch, 'Vile Crime or Inalienable Right: Defining Incitement to Genocide,' 48 *Va. J. Int'l. L.* 485 (2008).

II. *Historical Research*

Researching war crimes tribunals from World War II has been made easier due to several web projects and many print collections. Of course, books and journal articles abound in this area. Be sure to go beyond the legal literature since historians have done valuable research in this area.

- *Law Reports of Trials of War Criminals* (Selected and prepared by the United Nations War Crimes Commission) (15 vols., 1947–1949).[31]
- *Trial of the Major War Criminals before the International Military Tribunal, Nuremberg, 14 November 1945–1 October 1946* (42 vols., 1947–1949).[32]
- *Trials of War Criminals before the Nuernberg Military Tribunals under Control Council Law No. 10: Nuernberg, October 1946–April, 1949* (15 vols., [1949–53]).[33]
- *The Tokyo Major War Crimes Trial: The Transcripts of the Court Proceedings of the International Military Tribunal for the Far East* (more than 124 vols., 1998–).
- Nazi Crimes on Trial: E-Judgments.[34]
- Nuremberg Trials Project,[35] documents, transcripts, and other resources.

---

[31] Also available on HeinOnline, World Trials Library.
[32] Also available on HeinOnline, World Trials Library.
[33] Also available on HeinOnline, World Trials Library.
[34] http://www1.jur.uva.nl/junsv.
[35] http://nuremberg.law.harvard.edu/php/docs_swi.php?DI=1&text=overview.

More web collections are available for the Nuremberg trials as well as others courts and tribunals.[36]

> **Example:** There is plenty of legal analysis on the Nuremberg Military Tribunals and the impact of these trials on the development of international criminal law. To locate this analysis, you should look to books and articles. Some of these sources can be found by using "history" as a keyword or using the following subject heading in a catalog search: war crime trials—*germany*—*nuremberg*—*history*—*20th century* or *international criminal law*—*history*. An excellent example of this is Kevin Jon Heller's book, *The Nuremberg Military Tribunals and the Origins of International Criminal Law* (2011). Journal indexes will be particularly useful for this kind of research since they provide broader coverage of journal literature than do the full-text law review databases. By searching the *Index to Foreign Legal Periodicals*, you can locate journal literature from a broad range of non-US sources, such as 'La justice Face à la Guerre: de Nuremberg à la Haye,' 13 *Eur. J. Int'l L.* 1261 (2002). This review of Pierre Hazan's *La justice Face à la Guerre: de Nuremberg à la Haye* (2000) provides an interesting review of this particular book as well as several other useful books on the same topic. In fact, this is more than a book review; it's an article on the history of this topic and highlights many useful sources for those researching this area of law.

---

[36] http://www.nesl.edu/research/warcrim.cfm.

Chapter Seventeen

Intellectual Property

I. *Introduction*

The traditional areas of intellectual property (IP) law are patents (separated into "design" and "utility" patents), copyright, trade secrets, and trademark. Technological advances have added issues such as domain names, trademarks as web site "meta-tags," and digital rights management; biotechnology has added another dimension to patent law. Globalization has greatly increased the number of companies selling products and services in other countries, which makes protection of IP rights more financially significant than ever. The number of firms and lawyers practicing IP law, including foreign work, has greatly increased over the last 20 years. You will probably find yourself researching this area at some point.

Due partly to the amount of money at stake, tools for international IP research are fairly good. Also, you will find that this is the area of international and foreign law most integrated into US legal materials. For example, major IP treatises such as *Nimmer on Copyright* (1963–) cover international issues. LexisNexis and Westlaw offer useful foreign and international IP databases, which will be discussed throughout the chapter.

This section will explore the main areas of IP law, with emphasis on useful tools and search strategies.

A. *Legal Framework and Basic Sources*

For the most part, IP law is still "national"—although international treaties affect the content of national laws, the researcher ordinarily looks first to those national laws. The main intergovernmental organization in this area, WIPO (World Intellectual Property Organization), has no tribunal or other body empowered to enforce IP rights. (Although WIPO now offers arbitration, its arbitration procedures are voluntary.) Enforcement of IP rights occurs at the national level, except for a few cases at the World Trade Organization.

1. *National Laws*

Most countries have enacted laws or codes dealing separately with copyright, trademark, and patent law. The same changes that have sparked legal interest in these areas have also prompted amendments to these laws. For example, many countries have amended old laws or added new ones to comply with the TRIPs Agreement.[1] To achieve TRIPs compliance, China amended almost 150 laws.[2] Many countries have also enacted separate laws in response to new technologies; for example, laws regulating the patenting of genetically modified organisms. Because IP is a volatile area, you should pay special attention to the dates of laws, searching news stories and government websites for references to new legislation. For example, to check whether a particular Chinese IP law has been amended, you should check the Chinese patent office site;[3] news sources on Chinese law, such as the databases of Chinese newspapers and wire services on Westlaw and LexisNexis; and miscellaneous web sources via some general searches.

With that caveat in mind, researchers can find the text of IP laws relatively easily. Many countries make these laws available on the websites of their patent office, copyright office, or department of trade. A web search for *patent office [country name]* usually retrieves the correct site; for example, entering *patent office japan* into Google retrieves the Japanese Patent Office as the first search result. If not, check the WIPO Directory of National and Regional Industrial Property Offices.[4]

WIPO also offers a large database of national IP legislation, called WIPO Lex (formerly CLEA).[5] WIPO Lex's "Legislative Texts" system is arranged by country. By selecting a country name through the drop-down box, you can see a list of the laws. You can get a narrower list by adding a topic restriction from the lower drop-down box. For some entries, WIPO Lex has only a citation for the law. But in most cases, WIPO Lex offers the text of the law in English. Often WIPO Lex includes more than one "consolidation"—that is, a document that integrates amendments to the laws. In those cases, make sure to choose the latest available consolidation. Then, check the dates of other laws to see whether they affect that consolidation (i.e., whether they came later). WIPO Lex's information about each law attempts to describe

---

[1] Agreement on Trade-Related Aspects of Intellectual Property Rights, Apr. 15, 1994, Marrakesh Agreement Establishing the World Trade Organization, Annex 1C, 1869 U.N.T.S. 299, *reprinted in* 33 I.L.M. 1197 (1994).

[2] Ruth Taplin, Managing Intellectual Property in the Far East: China, KNOWLEDGELINK NEWSLETTER, Apr. 2005, http://science.thomsonreuters.com/news/2005-04/8272848.

[3] http://www.sipo.gov.cn/sipo_English2008.

[4] http://www.wipo.int/directory/en/urls.jsp.

[5] http://www.wipo.int/wipolex/en.

its relationship to other laws, but you will probably need to work it out for yourself.

If you cannot find the law you need in WIPO Lex, several other sources may help. UNESCO maintains its own smaller database of copyright laws,[6] which sometimes has laws that WIPO Lex doesn't have. For some countries, it occasionally has more up-to-date laws than does WIPO Lex. UNESCO's collection, unlike WIPO Lex, is not searchable; you can only select the country name to see what UNESCO has.

UNESCO's collection is divided by region. Laws from Asian, Western European, and Eastern European countries usually appear in English. Laws from French-speaking African countries and Spanish-speaking Latin American countries often appear only in the vernacular. When using copyright laws from UNESCO, always compare its coverage with that of WIPO Lex. As noted above, UNESCO is sometimes more current; however, usually WIPO Lex has more recent laws. For example, in late 2011, WIPO Lex had the French text of Djibouti's 2006 copyright law, while UNESCO had only a citation to that law.

Another useful web source is WorldLII,[7] which has a subject collection of national laws on IP. At this site, you can look for IP laws by country, find national and regional IP offices, and find links to a small number of major IP treaties.

Major subject collections of IP laws are also available in print and include a few laws unavailable on the web. First, WIPO published print collections of copyright and patent laws until 2001. These collections appear under various titles: *Intellectual Property Laws and Treaties; Copyright and Related Rights Laws and Treaties; Industrial Property Laws and Treaties.* Not all of the laws in these paper collections appear in the WIPO Lex database.

- *World Intellectual Property Rights and Remedies* (Dennis Campbell ed., 2011–) contains laws and some commentary.
- Patent laws are reprinted in *World Patent Law and Practice* (1968–).
- Trademark laws appear in Ethan Horwitz, *World Trademark Law and Practice* (1982–).
- *Intellectual Property: Eastern Europe & Commonwealth of Independent States* (David L. Garrison comp. & ed., 1995–) has laws for Eastern European countries and the Commonwealth of Independent States (CIS). It

---

[6] http://portal.unesco.org/culture/en/ev.php-URL_ID=14076&URL_DO=DO_TOPIC& URL_SECTION=201.html.

[7] http://www.worldlii.org/catalog/315.html.

contains fewer laws than WIPO Lex, but has some laws not included in that database (for example, Lithuania Law on Firm Names).

National IP laws are sometimes available on the WTO site. Start at the WTO TRIPs gateway.[8] Scrolling down, you will see the heading "TRIPS Work in the WTO." Below this heading, choose the link called "Review of Members' Implementing Legislation." This link leads to a page with a specialized search function. The page allows you to specify the country and the type of IP (e.g., copyright) in which you are interested. You will retrieve a list of relevant documents. Usually, documents entitled "Review of Legislation—[Name of country]" contain summaries and explanations of the subject country's IP laws. These Reviews of Legislation often quote sections of laws, though not the full text, and provide the name of the law and relevant dates.

Finding foreign IP cases, as opposed to foreign IP laws, is difficult. European Patent Office (EPO) decisions are published in *European Patent Office Reports* (available on Westlaw),[9] on the EPO website,[10] and in *European Patent Decisions*. *European Trade Mark Reports* (also on Westlaw)[11] include selected trademark cases from the European Court of Justice and various European countries. *Fleet Street Reports* (also on Westlaw)[12] also picks up a few IP cases from European countries. If money is no object, search in the combined Westlaw database IP-RPTS-ALL, which combines selected United Kingdom and European decisions from Sweet & Maxwell's *Entertainment and Media Law Reports, European Trade Mark Reports, Fleet Street Reports, Reports of Patent Cases,* and *European Patent Office Reports.*[13]

2. International Treaties

International agreements on IP fall into three or four groups. The first is the intellectual property protection treaties, which define internationally agreed-upon basic standards of IP protection in each country. Examples include the Berne Convention for the Protection of Literary and Artistic Works[14] and the

---

[8] http://www.wto.org/english/tratop_e/trips_e/trips_e.htm.

[9] EPO-RPTS.

[10] http://www.epo.org.

[11] ETR-RPTS.

[12] FLEET-RPTS.

[13] Although Westlaw gives this database the name UK Intellectual Property Law Reports All, it does include selected non-UK cases.

[14] Berne Convention for the Protection of Literary and Artistic Works, Sept. 9, 1886, as revised at Stockholm on July 14, 1967, 828 U.N.T.S. 222.

Paris Convention for the Protection of Industrial Property[15] (both requiring national treatment).

The second general group is the global protection system treaties. These treaties ensure that one international registration or filing will have effect in any of the relevant signatory states. The Patent Cooperation Treaty,[16] which allows inventors to get protection in over 100 countries with a single filing, exemplifies this type of treaty.

The third general group is the classification treaties. These treaties establish classification systems that organize information about inventions, trademarks, and industrial designs into standard patterns for easy retrieval. One example is the Nice Agreement,[17] which classifies goods and services for the purposes of registering trademarks and service marks. This system makes it much easier to identify and avoid conflicting or confusing marks.

A fourth type of treaty has become important in international IP work. Trade agreements, such as the Agreement on Trade-Related Aspects of Intellectual Property Rights (TRIPs) (see Chapter 19), now require parties to meet certain standards of IP protection. The TRIPs agreement incorporates all of the Paris Convention and Berne Convention provisions, except for the Berne's "moral rights" clause. If member countries do not comply with those provisions, other countries can invoke the World Trade Organization's dispute resolution procedures. The Anti-Counterfeiting Trade Agreement (ACTA), signed in October 2011, is labeled a trade treaty, and establishes standards for IP enforcement.

The United States and the European Union have also incorporated IP provisions into several bilateral free trade agreements. These agreements often require signatory countries to meet a higher standard of IP protection than that required by TRIPs (a standard sometimes referred to as "TRIPS-plus"). As with other IP treaties, implementation is by national legislation and regulation.

Finding multilateral IP treaties on the web is easy. Useful sites include the collections of treaties at the WIPO[18] website. Bilateral treaties can be more difficult. Try IPRsonline,[19] under the "Legal Instruments" tab. While this collection has not been updated recently, it is still a good source of bilateral

---

[15] Paris Convention for the Protection of Industrial Property, as last revised at the Stockholm Revision Conference, July 14, 1967, 21 U.S.T. 1583, 828 U.N.T.S. 303.

[16] Patent Cooperation Treaty, June 19, 1970, 28 U.S.T. 7645, 1160 U.N.T.S. 231, *reprinted in* 9 I.L.M. 978 (1970).

[17] Nice Agreement Concerning the International Classification of Goods and Services for the Purposes of the Registration of Marks, June 15, 1957, 23 U.S.T. 1336, 550 U.N.T.S. 45.

[18] http://www.wipo.int/treaties/en.

[19] http://www.iprsonline.org/index.htm.

free-trade agreements that contain provisions on intellectual property rights. (For more help finding treaties, see Chapter 6.)

B. *Commentary and Guides*

General works on international intellectual property can be retrieved by using the following Library of Congress subject headings in library catalogs:

> *industrial property (international law)*
> *intellectual property (international law)*

More specific subject headings are listed below.

Useful guides to international and foreign IP research include ASIL's Electronic Resource Guide for International Laws, Intellectual Property Law,[20] by Jonathan Franklin; and Stefanie Weigman's Update to Researching Intellectual Property Law in an International Context,[21] which is dated, but very thorough.

Periodical articles can also fill in gaps left by general works on intellectual property. You can find useful articles in the main legal periodical indexes— LegalTrac,[22] *Index to Legal Periodicals*,[23] and *Index to Foreign Legal Periodicals*.[24] (For more information on searching periodicals, see Chapter 5, Section III.)

Key periodicals on international IP law include:

- IIC, *International Review of Industrial Property and Copyright Law* (1970– 2003).
- IIC, *International Review of Intellectual Property and Competition Law* (2004–).
- *World Intellectual Property Report* (1987–). Available as part of BNA's Intellectual Property Library,[25] a subscription-based service.
- *WIPO Magazine* (1998–).[26] Short articles with an international focus.
- WIPO electronic newsletters. WIPO provides free news updates on various IP topics.[27]

---

[20] http://www.asil.org/erg/?page=iipl.

[21] http://www.llrx.com/features/iplaw2.htm.

[22] http://www.gale.cengage.com/pdf/facts/legal.pdf (LRI on Westlaw; Find a Source > Legal Resource Index on LexisNexis).

[23] http://www.ebscohost.com/academic/index-to-legal-periodicals-books.

[24] http://www.law.berkeley.edu/library/iflp.

[25] http://www.bna.com/intellectual-property-law-resource-center-p6594.

[26] http://www.wipo.int/wipo_magazine/en.

[27] http://www.wipo.int/tools/en/mailing-lists.

Other sources for articles on international IP law include the Global IP Network (GIN) collection[28] of the Franklin IP Mall. Working papers such as those posted on the Social Science Research Network (SSRN)[29] are also worth checking. For more information about searching these resources, see Chapter 5.

II. *Major Areas of IP Law*

A. *Trademark*

Formerly nation-by-nation, now trademark law is more international. The Madrid Agreement[30] was the first important international trademark agreement. It was followed by the Madrid Protocol,[31] its successor agreement—but both treaties are still in force. Signatories to either instrument belong to the Madrid Union. This organization enables "one-stop" registration of marks within these countries. However, the scope of protection achieved this way is limited to what the filer's "home" country provides, so for some countries where filing is cheap and protection is broad, a trademark holder might still want to file a separate national application. The Madrid system doesn't include an enforcement system; enforcement is still national.

1. *Researching International Trademark Law*

Generally, US researchers should start with treatises like J. Thomas McCarthy, *McCarthy on Trademarks and Unfair Competition* (1996–) (also on Westlaw)[32] which addresses international protection (see chapter 29 in particular). Useful overviews also appear at the WIPO site, and many individual country sites (patent and trademark offices) also provide explanations of national systems. Depending on the research scenario, you may want to look at foreign laws next. As noted earlier in this chapter, many laws are available in English in WIPO's WIPO Lex.[33] Many of them also appear in Ethan Horwitz, *World Trademark Law and Practice* (1982–) (also on LexisNexis).[34]

---

[28] http://ipmall.info/hosted_resources/gin_index.asp.
[29] http://www.ssrn.com.
[30] 175 Parry 57 (Apr. 14, 1891).
[31] S. Treaty Doc. No. 106–41 (June 27, 1989).
[32] MCCARTHY database.
[33] http://www.wipo.int/wipolex/en.
[34] Legal > Area of Law -By Topic > Trademarks > Treatises & Analytical Materials > Matthew Bender(R) > World Trademark Law and Practice.

Another useful source is *World Intellectual Property Rights and Remedies* (1999–). This source summarizes patent, trademark, copyright and other IP law in over 100 countries and the European Union, though coverage of patent and trademark law is better than for copyright. It also includes the full translated text of many foreign IP laws. For more commentary, though not translated legislation, check *International Encyclopaedia of Laws: Intellectual Property* (1997–).[35]

Use Library of Congress subject headings to find other books and electronic resources in your library:

> *trade-marks*
> *trade-marks (international law)*
> *intellectual property (international law)*
> *competition, unfair*
> *trademarks – law and legislation – [jurisdiction]*
> *trademark infringement – [jurisdiction]*
> *madrid agreement concerning the international registration of marks (1891)*

2. Internet Domain Names

Internet domain names have become an important legal issue, and one that is often covered in trademark treatises. A domain name is the alphanumeric address of a group of computers run by a separate entity, like a business or a university. For example, the Microsoft web servers, together, have the domain name "microsoft.com." An organization called ICANN (Internet Corporation for Assigned Names and Numbers) controls assignment of names in the United States and to some extent, beyond the United States.

Trademark lawyers generally recommend that all businesses, including their international subsidiaries, should register as a domain name any company name, mark, or product name that might be useful for marketing now or in the future.

Internet domain names present new challenges for trademark law because many similar trademarks exist for the same word or acronym. Trademark law has traditionally allowed similar trademarks within different trademark classes or for different types of businesses (e.g., United Airlines, United Van Lines). This system worked well when use of the trademark was unambiguous, but disputes have erupted over trademarks as domain names (e.g., who gets "united.com"?).

Similarly, trademark protection has historically been within defined (mostly national) boundaries. Obviously, the web breaks down national

---

[35] Also available at http://www.ielaws.com, by subscription.

boundaries; a web domain can be "visited" from nearly every country. The lack of national territories for domain names means more conflicts between trademark holders.

a. *Researching Domain Name Issues*
Again, starting with US trademark sources, especially treatises, is probably best for US researchers. For background, WIPO's domain names page[36] can be quite helpful, particularly the FAQ and the Overview of WIPO Panel Views on Selected UDRP Questions.[37] Depending on your research scenario, you may want to look at foreign laws next. Most countries treat domain names under their trademark or unfair competition laws. As such, they are included in WIPO Lex.[38] You may also want to consult the treatise *Domain Names—Global Practice and Procedure* (John R. Olsen et al. eds., 2000–), which covers over 200 jurisdictions' rules on this topic.[39]

WIPO handles many domain name disputes and makes its decisions available on the WIPO web site. WIPO offers full-text searching of its decisions,[40] but you may also want to use the well-organized Index of WIPO UDRP Panel Decisions.[41] Westlaw also has a database of "selected" domain name disputes from 1999–present.[42]

In addition to *Domain Names—Global Practice and Procedure*, above, useful treatises include Ethan Horwitz, *World Trademark Law and Practice* (1982–) (also on LexisNexis),[43] which covers trademark and domain law for a large number of countries. Also look for treatises on "cyberlaw," "Internet law," and "e-commerce"—many titles on these topics address domain names.

Find additional treatises and other sources with Library of Congress subject headings such as:

> *internet domain names*
> *internet domain names – law and legislation – [jurisdiction]*
> *internet – law and legislation.*

---

[36] http://www.wipo.int/amc/en/index.html.

[37] WIPO Overview of WIPO Panel Views on Selected UDRP Questions, Second Edition ("WIPO Overview 2.0") (2011), http://www.wipo.int/amc/en/domains/search/overview2.0/index.html.

[38] http://www.wipo.int/wipolex/en.

[39] On Westlaw as DOMAIN-GPP.

[40] http://www.wipo.int/amc/en/domains/search/index.html.

[41] http://www.wipo.int/amc/en/domains/search/legalindex.jsp.

[42] UDRP-ARB database.

[43] Legal > Area of Law -By Topic > Trademarks > Treatises & Analytical Materials > Matthew Bender(R) > World Trademark Law and Practice.

> *internet domain names – law and legislation*
> *trademarks – law and legislation – [jurisdiction]*
> *trademark infringement*
> *trademark infringement – [jurisdiction]*
> *trademark infringement – cases*

Remember, because this topic is relatively new, you should make a special effort to try keyword searches (e.g., *cyber-squatting* and *cybersquatting, internet regulation, e-commerce,* and *ecommerce*) in addition to subject heading searches. Your searches may pick up titles that the subject searches miss.

3. Geographical Indications

Another sub-species of trademark law that continues to present legal problems is "geographical indications" (GIs). Essentially, a geographical indication is a label used on a product to indicate that the product has a specific geographic origin, which may be a town, country, or region. Examples include Vidalia onion, Champagne, and Swiss watches. Usually, these labels imply that products have certain characteristics or a certain level of quality. Thus, like traditional trademarks, they can have enormous economic value.

While the Lisbon Agreement on the Protection of Appellations of Origin and their Registration[44] attempted to create international rules on GIs, most countries failed to adopt that treaty. The TRIPs Agreement requires WTO members to provide protection for geographical indications, with greater protection for GIs regarding wine and spirits. As with other IP issues, GI disputes are litigated primarily at the national level, although the WTO dispute system has resolved one GI dispute.[45]

a. Researching Geographical Indications

WIPO Lex[46] includes legislation and regulations on GIs for many countries, and the WIPO site has some useful information on GIs.[47] You can find a couple of monographs devoted to GIs, such as Bernard O'Connor, *The Law of Geographical Indications* (2004), and Marsha A. Echols, *Geographical Indications for Food Products: International Legal and Regulatory Perspectives* (2008). Some treatises on trademarks also cover geographical indications;

---

[44] Lisbon Agreement for the Protection of Appellations of Origin and their International Registration, Oct. 31, 1958, 923 U.N.T.S. 205.

[45] Panel Report, European Communities—Protection of Trademarks and Geographical Indications for Agricultural Products and Foodstuffs, WT/DS174/R (Mar. 15, 2005) (disputing the "Budweiser" trademark).

[46] http://www.wipo.int/wipolex/en ("geographical indications" is one of the topics on the drop-down menu).

[47] http://www.wipo.int/geo_indications/en/about.html.

see, for example, Tobias Cohen Jehoram et al., *European Trademark Law: Community Trademark Law and Harmonized National Trademark Law* (2010); J. Thomas McCarthy, *McCarthy on Trademarks and Unfair Competition* (1996–) (see chapter 14).

The most relevant Library of Congress subject heading is *marks of origin*. But you may get better results using keyword searches (*geographical indications*) or relying on trademark subject headings (see section B.1.a, above).

B. *Copyright*

At the international level, basic protection starts with the Berne Convention for the Protection of Literary and Artistic Works ("Berne Convention").[48] This convention, which was first adopted in 1886, has been revised several times to reflect the impact of new technology on the level of protection that it provides.

WIPO administers the treaty, but there is no international copyright registration system. Works are considered protected by copyright as soon as they are created. Generally, the Berne Convention provides protection to copyright-holders by mandating "national treatment" among parties to the Convention. In other words, a state must offer the same protection for works by citizens of parties to the Convention as it provides for the works of its own citizens.

Two more recent treaties, sometimes called the "WIPO Internet treaties," are intended to bring copyright law into the digital age. These two treaties are the WIPO Copyright Treaty (WCT)[49] and WIPO Performances and Phonograms Treaty (WPPT).[50]

Foreign copyright law can be quite different from US law. The most notable difference is the European doctrine of "moral rights." This doctrine creates somewhat indefinite, vague, perpetual rights that are "human rights" rather than the "property rights" of US law. These rights may mean, for example, that no one can present a version of *Waiting for Godot* with a female cast, or that no one can make or show a colorized version of a black and white movie within countries that recognize these rights. Civil law systems also tend to separate copyright from "neighboring rights"—rights of publishers, broadcasters, or producers, as opposed to the "moral rights" of a work's creator.

---

[48] Berne Convention for the Protection of Literary and Artistic Works, Sept. 9, 1886, as revised at Paris on July 24, 1971, and amended in 1979, S. Treaty Doc. No. 99–27 (1986).

[49] WIPO Copyright Treaty, Dec. 20, 1996, S. Treaty Doc. No. 105–17 (1997), *reprinted in* 36 I.L.M. 65 (1997).

[50] WIPO Performances and Phonograms Treaty, Dec. 20, 1996, S. Treaty Doc. No. 105–17 (1997), *reprinted in* 36 I.L.M. 76 (1997).

1. *Researching Foreign/International Copyright*

You may want to start with US secondary sources, such as *Nimmer on Copyright* (1963–). Volume 4, chapter 17 contains an introduction to foreign and international copyright law for the American practitioner. Other US sources such as CCH's *Copyright Law Reporter* (1978–) also address international copyright issues. One readily available source that explains copyright laws of several countries (mostly European or Westernized ones) is *International Copyright Law and Practice* (Melville B. Nimmer & Paul Geller eds., 1988–) (also available on LexisNexis as *International Copyright Law and Practice*).[51]

The WIPO Lex database[52] is an excellent source for the text of foreign copyright laws. Many countries have regulations implementing their copyright laws. WIPO Lex includes some of these regulations; they also appear on national patent and copyright office websites, though they may not be translated into English.

Useful Library of Congress subject headings will help you find books and other materials:

> *berne convention for the protection of literary and artistic works*
> *(1886)*
> *copyright [jurisdiction]*
> *copyright – computer programs*
> *copyright and electronic data processing [jurisdiction]*
> *copyright, international*
> *copyright – neighboring rights*
> *data protection – law and legislation*
> *databases – law and legislation*
> *internet – law and legislation*
> *piracy (copyright)*
> *world intellectual property organization copyright treaty (1996)*
> *world intellectual property organization performances and phonograms treaty*
> *(1996)*

Again, rapid technology changes in this area make keyword searches particularly important. Concepts such as peer-to-peer file-sharing, open-source software, and digital rights management have not become subject headings, but may appear as keywords in book titles or descriptions. Searching by the type of technology in question, such as satellite radio, dvd, mobile apps, or webcasting, may also retrieve useful materials.

---

[51] Legal > Area of Law -By Topic > Copyright Law > Treatises & Analytical Materials > Matthew Bender(R) > International Copyright Law and Practice.

[52] http://www.wipo.int/wipolex/en.

C. Patent

The Paris Convention for the Protection of Industrial Property[53] was the first major international agreement on patent protection. Like the Berne Convention on copyright, the Paris Convention provides for "national treatment" (i.e., countries must give foreigners' inventions the same protection as those of their own citizens).

The Patent Cooperation Treaty,[54] which entered into force in 1987, promotes parallel procedures for patent filings. Applicants can receive protection in many countries by filing one application.

1. Researching International/Foreign Patent Law

As with other IP topics, most researchers should start with secondary sources. US treatises such as *Moy's Walker on Patents* (2003–) (especially chapter 8) and *Chisum on Patents: A Treatise on the Law of Patentability, Validity, and Infringement* (1978–) (especially chapter 14) cover some foreign patent issues. Perhaps the most common issue in foreign patent law is licensing; you can find several treatises dealing with the licensing of intellectual property and of patents in particular. John P. Sinnott, *World Patent Law and Practice* (2001–) includes licensing forms. Another source for forms and commentary is Leslie William Melville et al., *Forms and Agreements on Intellectual Property and International Licensing* (3d ed. 1989–). William F. Fox, *International Commercial Agreements: A Primer on Drafting, Negotiating, and Resolving Disputes* (4th ed. 2009) has a useful chapter on IP licensing agreements. In Larry A. DiMatteo, *Law of International Contracting* (2d ed. 2009), see chapter 10 for discussion of intellectual property licensing.

The Practising Law Institute (PLI)[55] publishes several excellent works that cover foreign and international patent law and licensing; many of these can be found either on Westlaw or in practice-oriented law libraries. Foreign and international patent litigation is covered in the BNA looseleaf *International Patent Litigation: A Country-By-Country Analysis* (Michael N. Meller ed., 1983–).

Collections of patent laws include WIPO Lex; John P. Sinnott & William Joseph Cotreau, *World Patent Law and Practice* (1974–); and regional titles such as *Intellectual Property: Eastern Europe & Commonwealth of Independent*

---

[53] Paris Convention for the Protection of Industrial Property, as last revised at the Stockholm Revision Conference, July 14, 1967, 21 U.S.T. 1583, 828 U.N.T.S. 303.

[54] Patent Cooperation Treaty, June 19, 1970, 28 U.S.T. 7645, 1160 U.N.T.S. 231, *reprinted in* 9 I.L.M. 978 (1970).

[55] http://www.pli.edu.

States (David L Garrison ed., 1995–). Checking national patent office sites, however, is more likely to get you the current laws and regulations.

Library of Congress subject headings include:

computer programs – patents
conflict of laws – patents
foreign licensing agreements
industrial property [jurisdiction]
patent laws and legislation [jurisdiction]
patent licenses
patent practice
patents
patents (international law)
plant varieties – protection

Chapter Eighteen

International Environmental Law

I. *Introduction*

International environmental law (IEL) is a part of public international law. The origin of IEL is relatively recent; most experts date its birth to 1972, with the Stockholm Conference on the Human Environment. The field has grown to encompass subjects such as climate change, biodiversity and endangered species, nuclear and other hazardous materials, and sustainable development.

The transboundary nature of many kinds of environmental issues has forced states to address these problems through international agreements. While IEL is largely treaty-based, some principles of customary international law have also emerged.

II. *Sources of Law*

A. *Treaties*

1. *Introduction*

Despite the short life of international environmental law, states have become parties to more than 300 multilateral treaties.[1] These treaties constitute the major source of law in IEL. A table showing key treaties by subject matter appears in Heidi F. Kuehl, Update: A Basic Guide to International Environmental Legal Research (2006) (see the section entitled "Sub-topics for International Environmental Law").[2]

---

[1] Steve Charnovitz, 'A World Environment Organization,' 27 *Colum. J. Envtl. L.* 323, 331 (2002) (referring to "300-plus" multilateral environmental agreements).

[2] http://www.nyulawglobal.org/globalex/International_Environmental_Legal_Research1.htm.

In some ways, IEL treaties reflect the underlying subject matter. Generally, the uncertain and changing state of scientific information requires more flexibility than the typical treaty regime permits. Thus, drafters of IEL treaties have tended to create general "framework" treaties, with more specific protocols dictating the implementation of the treaties, and highly technical Annexes listing information that may change rapidly.

To better understand this drafting practice, here is an example: The Vienna Convention for the Protection of the Ozone Layer (1985)[3] commits signatories to work towards protection of the ozone layer. It sets forth general goals such as cooperation, research, and centralized information-sharing. By its terms, it contemplates the addition of protocols to flesh out the agreement. Two years after the Convention was signed, the parties concluded the Montreal Protocol on Substances that Deplete the Ozone Layer.[4] The Protocol includes two annexes listing chemical compounds that the parties have pledged to phase out. Unlike a treaty, the annexes can be amended quickly, to reflect current scientific information.

Another example of this approach to treaty-drafting is the Convention on International Trade in Endangered Species of Wild Flora and Fauna (CITES).[5] This treaty has three appendices, each of which lists plant and animal species. The treaty provides for differing treatment of species depending on the appendix in which they are listed.

Thus, to learn what actions are prohibited or required under IEL, you must examine treaty protocols and annexes carefully. Fortunately, most IEL treaties establish a secretariat to administer the treaty, and the secretariat usually creates a website containing the text of key instruments.[6] Once you have identified a relevant treaty, look for a corresponding website. Generally, you will also find treaty status information, along with reservations, understandings, and declarations, if any, at the site.

Another excellent source for treaty status information is the United Nation Environment Program's ECOLEX database.[7] Choose the "Treaties" section and enter the title of the treaty you need. You will retrieve a short record about the treaty, including a "Parties" section with status information.

---

[3] 513 U.N.T.S. 323, *reprinted in* 26 I.L.M. 1529 (1987).

[4] TIAS No. 11,097, 1513 U.N.T.S. 323, *reprinted in* 26 I.L.M. 1529 (1987).

[5] 27 U.S.T. 1087, TIAS 8249, 993 U.N.T.S. 243.

[6] If you search the web for the name of the treaty, such as the International Convention for the Conservation of Atlantic Tunas, your first results usually include a copy of the treaty and the secretariat's website.

[7] http://www.ecolex.org/start.php.

2. *Treaty Collections*

- CIESIN (Center for International Earth Science Information Network).[8] A project of Columbia University, CIESIN offers the full text of over 400 IEL treaties in its ENTRI (Environmental Treaties and Resource Indicators) database.[9] ENTRI offers two ways to search its treaties database. The first, under Treaty Locator, offers much more sophisticated full-text searching than the typical free site. Check the "Search Tips" section for options such as grammatical connectors and wildcards. For example, instead of searching only for *pollution*, you can enter the term *pollut%* and retrieve various forms of the word, such as "polluting" or "polluter."

  The second ENTRI search option, using the box labeled "Search Treaty Texts," allows you to search the full text of treaties using a Google-based search.

  The ENTRI system also contains treaty status information; you can either link to it from the text of a treaty, or retrieve records by country (showing which treaties the country is a party to).

- EISIL (Electronic Information System for International Law, from the American Society of International Law).[10] The International Environmental Law[11] section of the EISIL database offers annotated links to major environmental law treaties. While the full text of the treaties is not searchable through EISIL, you can search the annotations, treaty titles, popular names (e.g., CITES), and other information.

- Treaties/Soft Law Agreements.[12] Wildlife Committee, American Branch of the International Law Association (ABILA). This site has a smaller collection of treaties, organized by topic (e.g., Animal Welfare, Biological Diversity, Fisheries, etc.).

3. *Paper Collections*

- *Basic Documents on International Law and the Environment* (P.W. Birnie & A.E. Boyle eds., 1995).
- *International Protection of the Environment: Treaties and Related Documents* (Bernd Ruster & Bruno Simma, comps. & eds., 1975–1983).

---

[8] http://www.ciesin.org.

[9] http://sedac.ciesin.columbia.edu/entri.

[10] http://www.eisil.org.

[11] http://www.eisil.org/index.php?sid=204626444&t=sub_pages&cat=18.

[12] http://www.internationalwildlifelaw.org/treaties.shtml.

- *International Protection of the Environment: Treaties and Related Documents, Second Series* (Bernd Ruster & Bruno Simma, comps. & eds., 1990–1995).
- *Documents in International Environment Law* (Philippe Sands et al. eds., 1994).
- *Documents in International Environment Law* (Philippe Sands & Paolo Galizzi eds., 2004).
- *International, EC, and US Environmental Law: A Comprehensive Selection of Basic Documents* (Kurt Deketelaere & Jan Gekiere eds., 2002).
- *International Environmental Law: Multilateral Treaties* (9 vols., W.E. Burhenne ed.; Robert Muecke comp., 1974–).

4. *Other Sources*

Of course, IEL treaties also appear in general treaty collections, such as the United Nations Treaty Collection database,[13] and the *United Nations Treaty Series* (1946–) in paper. For more information on treaty research, see Chapter 6, Section III.

B. *Customary International Law*

In addition to finding relevant treaties, your IEL research may include a search for applicable principles of customary international law. While Chapter 7 gives more in-depth advice on researching customary international law, this section provides some guidance specific to international environmental law.

1. *Secondary Sources*

As with other searches for customary international law, you will find it easiest to start with secondary sources. To find general treatises and books on IEL, use the Library of Congress subject heading *environmental law, international*. These general works can be helpful if you need to identify an overarching principle of environmental law. Works by a few individual or institutional authors, moreover, may qualify as the writings of the "most highly qualified publicists" in IEL and may be used as evidence of a customary international principle.

Often, in IEL research, your topic will be relatively narrow. Rather than search for international environmental law generally, use keywords such as *hazardous, ozone,* or *biodiversity,* depending on your topic, coupled with the terms *international* and *law,* to find relevant works in your library catalog. Then check the subject headings assigned to those items, and run

---

[13] http://treaties.un.org.

new searches using those subject headings. Examples of specific subject headings include:

> *climatic changes – law and legislation*
> *hazardous substances – law and legislation*
> *waste disposal in the ocean – law and legislation*
> *sustainable development – law and legislation*
> *biological diversity conservation – international cooperation*

One environmental law concept that some scholars claim as customary international law is the "precautionary principle," which is also a Library of Congress subject heading.

Periodical articles can also provide useful descriptions of the state of customary IEL. They often address recent topics in IEL before treatises and other books. Chapter 5 discusses periodicals and periodical indexes in more detail, but this section will focus on their use in IEL research.

One hazard of periodical research in IEL is that your searches often retrieve materials relating only (or primarily) to US law. For example, searching Lexis Nexis or Westlaw's database of law review articles for topics such as "hazardous waste," "endangered species," or "radioactive materials" will retrieve many articles relating to US state and federal regulation of these topics. Add terms that capture the international nature of your search, such as *international, transnational, transboundary, global*, etc.

If you retrieve too many irrelevant results searching full-text databases, try a periodicals index. Useful periodical indexes include the usual legal periodicals indexes: LegalTrac,[14] *Index to Legal Periodicals*,[15] *Index to Foreign Legal Periodicals*.[16] You may also want to look at:

- *PAIS International*.[17] Available at many college and university libraries, this database includes articles on international, legal, and political issues.
- The Max Planck Institute for Public International Law also has an index[18] that includes some IEL topics (e.g., Environmental Protection and Neighborship, Transboundary Cooperation, Protection of Plants and Animals, Biodiversity, Rio Declaration).

---

[14] On Lexis as Legal > Secondary Legal > Annotations & Indexes > Legal Resource Index; on Westlaw as the LRI database.

[15] http://www.ebscohost.com/academic/index-to-legal-periodicals-books.

[16] http://www.law.berkeley.edu/library/iflp.

[17] http://www.csa.com/factsheets/pais-set-c.php.

[18] http://www.mpil.de/ww/en/pub/library/catalogues_databases/doc_of_articles/pil.cfm.

A long list of environmental law periodicals appears in Heidi F. Kuehl's IEL research guide;[19] however, the list is not limited to international environmental law. To locate periodicals in your library, use the Library of Congress subject heading *environmental law, international—periodicals*.

2. Primary Sources

If you're lucky, secondary sources will provide citations to primary sources that you can use to show the existence of a principle of customary international law. Likely sources include treaties; resolutions, declarations, voting records, and other documents from intergovernmental organizations; decisions of international tribunals; national laws; national court decisions; diplomatic correspondence; and other documents showing state practice. Other ways to find these sources are discussed in the following sections.

3. Treaties

Some strategies for finding treaties are covered in Section A, Treaties, above. When trying to document a principle of customary international law, however, you may need to search for specific terms within treaties. For researchers with access to Westlaw or LexisNexis, the most effective way to do that is to search those services' full-text treaty databases. While these treaty databases are limited to those signed by the United States[20] and the European Union,[21] the United States and European Union have become parties to many IEL treaties.

For example, if you need support for the proposition that the "polluter pays" principle has risen to the level of customary international law, you can use the sophisticated search capabilities of LexisNexis or Westlaw to find treaties that embody this principle: *"polluter pays" OR (polluter OR polluting w/s cost)*. If you do not have access to Westlaw and LexisNexis, your best source for searching environmental law treaties is the ENTRI database,[22] discussed above.

4. IGO Documents

The field of international environmental law lacks a centralized authority, but the United Nations and its related bodies have issued many resolutions,

---

[19] http://www.nyulawglobal.org/globalex/International_Environmental_Legal_Research1 .htm.
[20] Westlaw (CMB-TREATIES database); Lexis (International Law > Treaties & International Agreements > U.S. Treaties on LEXIS).
[21] Westlaw EU-TREATIES); Lexis (Legal > Global Legal > European Union > Treaties & International Agreements > EUR-Lex EU Law Database: Treaties).
[22] http://sedac.ciesin.org/entri.

declarations, and other documents that may express general environmental law principles. While these instruments do not require states to sign and ratify, records of states' votes on these documents can indicate the strength of a principle as well as the commitment of the organization. To search for relevant UN documents, use UNBISnet.[23] You can limit your search to types of documents, such as resolutions.

If you find relevant resolutions, you can retrieve their voting records by using the resolution's document symbol as a search term in UNBISnet's Voting Records database. Just remember to remove all the slashes and other punctuation from the document symbol, as instructed at the site.

A new, useful technique for finding "soft law" documents is available through ENTRI. The ENTRI website has added a new Conference of Parties (COP) decision search tool[24] allowing researchers to search decisions produced by the Parties to several major environmental agreements, including the Convention on Biological Diversity, the Kyoto Protocol, the Ramsar Convention on Wetlands of International Importance (Ramsar), and several others.

Another approach to finding relevant IGO documents is to check the website of the entity that administers treaties in your area of interest. For example, if you need to research evolving international standards for transboundary shipment of discarded electronic equipment such as computers, you might identify the Basel Convention on the Control of Transboundary Movements of Hazardous Wastes and Their Disposal[25] as a relevant treaty. By going to the website of the Secretariat for the Basel Convention,[26] and searching for information on "electronic waste," you can retrieve documents regarding the activities of Basel parties regarding this kind of waste.

Other tools for identifying useful sources include a collection of documents—*International Environmental Soft Law: Collection of Relevant Instruments* (W.E. Burhenne ed. & Marlene Jahnke comp., 1993–), although this set hasn't been updated since 2003.

Another useful source is the *Yearbook of International Environmental Law* (1991–). Like other international law yearbooks, this one identifies significant annual developments and instruments, with attention to emerging principles of customary international law.

---

[23] http://unbisnet.un.org.

[24] http://sedac.ciesin.org/entri.

[25] Basel Convention on the Control of Transboundary Movements of Hazardous Wastes and Their Disposal, Mar. 22, 1989, 1673 U.N.T.S. 125, *reprinted in* 28 I.L.M. 657 (1989).

[26] http://www.basel.int.

5. *Decisions of International Tribunals*

No specific body currently exists for resolving international environmental disputes. The most influential tribunal in IEL is the International Court of Justice (ICJ). Its decisions are available on Westlaw[27] and LexisNexis.[28] Decisions are printed in *Recueil des Arrets, Avis Consultatifs et Ordonnances = Reports of Judgments, Advisory Opinions and Orders* (1947–), and most of them are also available on the ICJ website.[29] The International Tribunal for the Law of the Sea (ITLOS), established under the United Nations Convention of the Law of the Sea (UNCLOS), has dealt with only 19 cases since its inception. Documents relating to those cases are available on the ITLOS website.[30]

Other international tribunals whose decisions deal with IEL include the World Trade Organization's (WTO) panels and appellate body, North American Free Trade Agreement (NAFTA) arbitration bodies, and the European Court of Justice (ECJ). WTO "case law" is available at the WTO website,[31] on LexisNexis[32] and Westlaw,[33] and in print sources. Similarly, NAFTA decisions appear on the website of the NAFTA Secretariat,[34] and on LexisNexis[35] and Westlaw.[36] More information on WTO and NAFTA research is available in Chapter 22.

The ECJ makes its jurisprudence available on the CURIA website.[37] If you have access to Westlaw and LexisNexis, you may find it easier to research ECJ cases on those services.[38] In addition, the EU's environment website[39] has a 2005 document[40] entitled "List of the Leading Cases and Judgements of the ECJ on Environment" with summaries and links to full text.

---

[27] INT-ICJ database.

[28] International Law > Cases > International Court of Justice Decisions, Combined.

[29] http://www.icj-cij.org/homepage/index.php?lang=en.

[30] http://www.itlos.org/index.php?id=10.

[31] http://www.wto.org.

[32] International Trade > Cases > Interpreting Treaties > World Trade Organization Dispute Settlement.

[33] WTO-DEC.

[34] http://www.nafta-sec-alena.org/en/view.aspx.

[35] International Trade > Cases > Interpreting U.S. Law > NAFTA Panel Review Decisions.

[36] NAFTA-AWARDS and NAFTA-BIP.

[37] http://curia.europa.eu/jurisp/cgi-bin/form.pl?lang=en.

[38] LexisNexis (International Law > Find Cases > EUR-Lex European Union Cases); Westlaw (EU-CS).

[39] http://ec.europa.eu/environment/index_en.htm.

[40] http://ec.europa.eu/environment/legal/law/pdf/leading_cases_en.pdf.

6. Decisions of National Courts

Researchers who need to find national court decisions on environmental law should consult *International Environmental Law Reports* (Cairo A.R. Robb ed., 1999–2004). Although the series includes only four volumes, it offers a look at representative and ground-breaking decisions around the world. The full text of decisions is not always included, but key sections are translated into English.

The subscription database International Law in Domestic Courts[41] has about 20 decisions on environmental law as of 2011, but the editors plan to add many decisions each year. Researchers should check whether their library offers access to the database, or to International Law Reports.[42]

The Bureau of National Affairs publishes the *International Environment Reporter* (1978–).[43] Many law libraries offer electronic access to this publication. *International Environment Reporter*, along with its daily update, *International Environment Daily*, summarizes foreign litigation on environmental issues. The Environmental Law Institute's *Environmental Law Reporter* (E.L.R.),[44] while it deals mostly with US and state law, also follows IEL developments such as some foreign litigation.

The UNEP's ECOLEX database[45] contains short summaries of a few hundred national court decisions, though not the full text. In some cases, links to the full text of decisions are provided.

7. National Legislation

Principles of customary international law can also be expressed in national laws. While you can research these laws using the same techniques you use to research any foreign laws (see Chapter 8), you should also know some specialized tools.

Westlaw has a database[46] comprising foreign environmental laws and regulations from several jurisdictions, in English: Brazil, Canada, the European Union, France, Indonesia, Italy, Mexico, Spain, and the United Kingdom. You can also search a separate database for each jurisdiction (e.g., for France, search ENFLEX-FR).

The UNEP's ECOLEX[47] database contains the full text of thousands of foreign environmental laws. Although you can search by English-language

---

[41] http://www.oxfordlawreports.com.
[42] http://www.justis.com/data-coverage/international-law-reports.aspx.
[43] http://www.bna.com/international-environment-reporter-p4897.
[44] http://www.elr.info/index.cfm.
[45] http://www.ecolex.org.
[46] ENFLEX-INT.
[47] http://www.ecolex.org.

topics and keywords, the actual text of the laws is in the vernacular, and it is not searchable.

FAOLEX,[48] from the Food and Agricultural Organization of the United Nations, works much like ECOLEX. You can search using English-language topics and keywords, but the full text of laws is in the vernacular, and it is not searchable. For better results, select the "Advanced Search" function and explore the dropdown menus, including topics such as fisheries, air and atmosphere, and wild species and ecosystems.

Similarly, the Library of Congress's GLIN (Global Legal Information Network)[49] database enables English-language searching of abstracts and citations for foreign laws of over 50 countries. You can retrieve full-text versions of some of these laws from GLIN (availability varies by country). Use the Subject Term Index to identify the best search terms; for example, the term "hazardous waste" is not used; instead, use "hazardous substances." If you spend a few minutes checking this index, you can save yourself time by conducting fewer useless searches.

The Sturm College of Law, University of Denver, has a "Countries" page[50] with a drop-down country list. For each country, the site links to available online sources of environmental laws. (Some links are to ECOLEX or FAOLEX documents.)

The Bureau of National Affairs' *International Environment Reporter*, along with its daily update, *International Environment Daily*, monitors foreign legislation on environmental issues. However, full-text laws are not included.

C. *Other Resources*

1. *Nongovernment Organizations*
Many non-government organizations (NGOs) have a long history of action on IEL. While these NGOs are too numerous to list here, you should keep them in mind as potentially useful information sources. This section will identify a few of the major NGOs active in IEL.

- CIEL (Center for International Environmental Law).[51] This organization, unlike many NGOs working on environmental issues, focuses on international legal regimes. For various topics, such as persistent organic

---

[48] http://faolex.fao.org.
[49] http://www.glin.gov/search.action.
[50] http://law.du.edu/forms/enrgp/weblinks/index2.cfm.
[51] http://www.ciel.org.

pollutants (POPs), the CIEL site identifies relevant treaties and monitors developments.

- EarthJustice.[52] While mostly an advocacy organization, EarthJustice produces useful papers and reports on IEL issues.
- Environmental Law Alliance Worldwide.[53] This NGO's "Resources" section has international and national environmental law instruments by topic or region, though coverage is spotty and not current.
- International Union for Conservation of Nature (IUCN).[54] This major NGO has a section of its extensive website dedicated to its "Environmental Law Programme."[55] This section includes news, policy papers, and other information.

To find other NGOs, particularly those that focus on a specific topic within environmental law, check EnviroLink.[56] The homepage has a list of subjects; after clicking on one, look for the link to "Organizations."

2. Research Guides

- Anne Burnett, International Environmental Law, in ASIL Guide to Electronic Resources for International Law.[57] Although limited to online sources, this guide presents a thorough, carefully documented guide to IEL research.
- David Hunter et al., International Environmental Law & Policy: A Comprehensive Reference Source (2d ed., undated).[58] This source provides an outline of key concepts in IEL, with links to relevant online sources. Topics include IEL history, root causes of environmental problems, IEL lawmaking, specific issues such as air and oceanic pollution, and the relationship of IEL to other legal regimes (e.g., trade, human rights).
- Heidi F. Kuehl, Update: A Basic Guide to International Environmental Legal Research (2006).[59] This guide is noteworthy in part because of its long lists of sources (e.g., listings of LexisNexis and Westlaw databases). It also contains a useful list of acronyms used in IEL.

---

[52] http://earthjustice.org.
[53] http://www.elaw.org.
[54] http://www.iucn.org.
[55] http://www.iucn.org/about/work/programmes/environmental_law.
[56] http://www.envirolink.org.
[57] http://www.asil.org/erg/?page=ienvl.
[58] http://www.wcl.american.edu/environment/iel.
[59] http://www.nyulawglobal.org/globalex/International_Environmental_Legal_Research1.htm.

Chapter Nineteen

International Trade Law

I. *Introduction*

A. *What Is International Trade?*

The term "international trade" encompasses a wide range of subjects: imports, exports, foreign investment, the World Trade Organization (WTO), the North American Free Trade Agreement (NAFTA), and many other trade arrangements. Moreover, international trade law can affect domestic law on a variety of subjects, including environmental protection, intellectual property, consumer protection, and labor law.

The general legal framework of international trade includes the WTO, with 153 member states; and a web of regional and bilateral trade agreements, such as NAFTA. Trade agreements generally include dispute resolution mechanisms. Moreover, trade obligations in these agreements may affect or even supplant domestic laws.

B. *Background Research*

Perhaps more than any other area of international law, international trade has a vocabulary of its own. Dumping, antidumping, zeroing, phytosanitary measures, countervailing measures, fast-track, tariff rate quotas, safeguards—once you enter the world of international trade, you will need a way to decipher these terms of art.

Some introductory works on international trade explain these terms and basic concepts you may need to know. Sources include:

- Ralph H. Folsom et al., *International Trade and Economic Relations in a Nutshell* (4th ed. 2009).
- Jan H. Dalhuisen, *Dalhuisen on Transnational Comparative Commercial, Financial, and Trade Law* (4th ed. 2010).

Dictionaries focusing on international trade include:

- Raj Bhala, *Dictionary of International Trade Law* (2008).
- Walter Goode, *Dictionary of Trade Policy Terms* (5th ed. 2007).
- Edward G. Hinkelman, *Dictionary of International Trade: Handbook of the Global Trade Community* (9th ed. 2010).
- Jerry M. Rosenberg, *Dictionary of International Trade* (1994).
- Merritt R. Blakeslee, *The Language of Trade* (3d ed. 2000).[1]

To find trade dictionaries in your library, search your library catalog for the titles above, or try the Library of Congress subject heading *international trade—dictionaries*.

C. International Agreements

Many of the agreements needed for international trade research are noted in other parts of this section. To locate other trade agreements as well as agreements on related topics, like contracts and sales, see the following websites:

- Free Trade Agreements (Foreign Trade Information Center, OAS).[2] This is an excellent collection of trade agreements between countries in the Western Hemisphere (both bilateral and multilateral).
- Juris International.[3] This searchable collection provides the full text of many conventions, model laws, as well as standards and customs of international trade.

D. Other Trade Research Resources

1. Tariff Schedules

One important aspect when researching the international trade regime is each country's tariff system. You may need to determine the extent of tariff, if any, imposed on imports. For the United States, the document that provides this information is the Harmonized Tariff Schedule, readily available on the web.[4] For other countries, see their government's department or ministry of trade, or the USDA's searchable collection.[5]

---

[1] http://usinfo.org/enus/economy/trade/langtrade.html.
[2] http://www.sice.oas.org/agreements_e.asp.
[3] http://www.jurisint.org (site has not been updated recently, but still has useful materials).
[4] http://www.usitc.gov/tata/hts.
[5] http://www.fas.usda.gov/scriptsw/wtopdf/wtopdf_frm.asp.

2. Current Awareness

Some of the more useful periodicals covering trade include the following:

- *Inside U.S. Trade* (1983–). Weekly summaries of trade developments from US perspective. It is also available on the web[6] (by subscription) and on LexisNexis from October 2005.[7]
- *Inside U.S.-China Trade* (2001–). Weekly summaries of US trade policies toward China. It is available on the web[8] (by subscription) and on Lexis-Nexis from February 2006.[9]
- *BRIDGES Weekly Trade News Digest*.[10] Critique of WTO activities from the International Center on Trade and Sustainable Development.
- *International Trade Reporter* (1984–). The "Current Reports" portion of this publication is a weekly trade update.
- *Inter-American Trade Report* (1997–2005). This newsletter reported on new trade law and developments for the countries in the Inter-American system. It is also available on the National Law Center for Inter-American Free Trade website.[11]
- *Focus*, the WTO's newsletter (1995–2007).[12] WTO news is now disseminated through RSS feeds and podcasts. See the "News and Events" tab on the WTO website.[13]
- *WTO Reporter* (2000–). Similar to the *International Trade Reporter*, but focuses on the WTO.
- International Economic Law and Policy Blog.[14]

II. Foreign Investment

Foreign investment raises some different legal issues from those raised in international trade. Generally, foreign investment law is governed by bilateral agreements. These bilateral investment treaties (BITs) usually provide that investors from one state party shall be treated the same as investors from the other state party. The agreements further establish mechanisms to

---

[6] http://insidetrade.com.
[7] News & Business > Individual Publications > I > Inside U.S. Trade.
[8] http://insidetrade.com.
[9] News & Business > Individual Publications > I > Inside U.S.-China Trade.
[10] http://ictsd.org/news/bridgesweekly.
[11] http://natlaw.com/bulletin/report.htm.
[12] http://www.wto.org/english/res_e/focus_e/focus_e.htm.
[13] http://www.wto.org/english/news_e/news_e.htm.
[14] http://worldtradelaw.typepad.com.

resolve disputes between the states parties and between investors and states. Often, the mechanism chosen is arbitration by the International Center for Settlement of Investment Disputes (ICSID). Much of the legal work in this area involves representing parties in arbitration before ICSID or other tribunals. A good introduction to foreign investment law is M. Sornarajah, *The International Law on Foreign Investment* (3d ed. 2010).

A. *Finding Investment Treaties*

To determine whether two states have entered into a bilateral investment treaty, check the ICSID's database of Bilateral Investment Treaties.[15] Unfortunately, ICSID does not provide the text of the listed treaties, and its list includes only those BITs concluded from 1956 to 2007. The UN agency UNCTAD (United Nations Conference on Trade and Development) has another list of BITs, through 1999.[16] UNCTAD offers a collection of BITs at its website.[17] Use the drop-down lists of countries to select the states parties you need. However, not all BITs are available at this site. Another collection of BITS appears on the Foreign Trade Information (SICE—from its Spanish acronym—*Sistema de Información Comercio Exterior*) website.[18] You may also need to check national treaty series (see Chapter 6), check websites for the Trade Ministry or other government offices for the country in question, or the ICSID looseleaf publication, *Investment Promotion and Protection Treaties* (1983–). In addition, keep in mind that you may not be able to find a particular BIT in English.

B. *Finding National Laws on Foreign Investment*

Another piece of researching foreign investment issues is to locate national laws and regulations on foreign investment. Numerous English translations of foreign investment laws are reprinted in the looseleaf set *Investment Laws of the World* (1972–), now published by Oxford University Press. Another useful source for foreign investment laws is the subscription database RIA Checkpoint. Moreover, to encourage foreign investment, many countries make English translations of these laws available on their government websites. For example, to find the foreign investment law of Argentina, you can search the web with the terms *"foreign investment law" argentina*. Your first-ranked results will not include the official Argentine government site; instead,

---

[15] http://icsid.worldbank.org (use the Quick Locator link to locate this database).
[16] http://www.unctad.org/en/docs/poiteiiad2.en.pdf.
[17] http://www.unctadxi.org/templates/docsearch____779.aspx.
[18] http://www.sice.oas.org/Investment/bitindex_e.asp.

you will retrieve commercial sites offering help to investors. Restricting your search to official Argentine government pages will send the best result to the top of your results: *"foreign investment law" argentina site:.gov.ar.* This search retrieves an English translation of Argentina's Foreign Investment Law.[19]

If you need a foreign investment law from Latin America, the National Law Center for Inter-American Free Trade offers translations for a fee.[20] The Center has laws in the vernacular and some English translations. To find laws of other countries, Thomas H. Reynolds & Arturo A. Flores, *Foreign Law Guide* (1987–),[21] is, as usual, another helpful resource.

C. Finding Arbitration Awards

The most difficult task in foreign investment research is finding relevant arbitration awards. With a few exceptions, these awards are not routinely published. (For more on researching arbitration, see Chapter 21.) Selected ICSID arbitration decisions appear on the ICSID website.[22] Unfortunately, the full text of these decisions is not searchable, though you can search by parties and a few other attributes. Some libraries subscribe to *ICSID Reports: Reports of Cases Decided under the Convention on the Settlement of Investment Disputes between States and Nationals of Other States, 1965* (1972–). If your library provides access to the Kluwer Arbitration Database,[23] this will be the most comprehensive source available to you. For ICSID awards in particular, the book Richard Happ & Noah Rubins, *Digest of ICSID Awards and Decisions: 2003-2007* (2009) can be quite helpful, since it allows you to find relevant cases by topic. The Oxford Reports on International Law subscription database include a module on International Investment Claims, which aims to provide "all publicly available awards and decisions arising out of international investment arbitrations, and related enforcement or review decisions from national courts."[24]

Other sources contain some awards pertaining to foreign investment; for a list, see Jean Wenger, *International Commercial Arbitration: Locating the Resources—Revised.*[25] Check your law library catalog using the Library of Congress subject headings:

---

[19] http://www.cnv.gov.ar/LeyesyReg/Leyes/ing/LEY21382.htm.
[20] http://natlaw.com/index.html.
[21] http://www.foreignlawguide.com.
[22] http://icsid.worldbank.org/ICSID/Index.jsp.
[23] http://www.kluwerarbitration.com.
[24] http://www.oxfordlawreports.com/about#aboutiic.
[25] http://www.llrx.com/features/arbitration2.htm.

investments, foreign (international law) – cases
arbitration and award (international) – cases

D. *Other Resources for Foreign Investment Research*

To locate other resources on foreign investment law, use the Library of Congress subject headings:

investments, foreign (international law), foreign trade regulation
investments, foreign – law and legislation [country name]
international business enterprises – law and legislation

A few useful works include:

- Kenneth J. Vandevelde, *Bilateral Investment Treaties: History, Policy, and Interpretation* (2010).
- Lucy Reed et al., *Guide to ICSID Arbitration* (2d ed. 2011).
- Christoph H. Schreuer, *The ICSID Convention: A Commentary: A Commentary on the Convention on the Settlement of Investment Disputes Between States and Nationals of Other States* (2d ed. 2009).
- UNCTAD, *Investor-State Dispute Settlement and Impact on Investment Rulemaking* (2007).[26]
- UNCTAD, *International Investment Arrangements: Trends and Emerging Issues* (2006).[27]
- UNCTAD, *Investor-State Disputes Arising from Investment Treaties: A Review* (2005).[28]
- Rudolf Dolzer & Margrete Stevens, *Bilateral Investment Treaties* (1995).
- Zachary Douglas, *The International Law of Investment Claims* (2009).

III. *GATT/WTO System*

A. *History of the WTO/GATT System*

The current World Trade Organization (WTO) system is built on the General Agreement on Trade and Tariffs (GATT), which came into effect in 1948. GATT was designed to cut tariffs (i.e., fees imposed on the import of goods), thereby making markets more accessible across national borders.[29]

---

[26] http://www.unctad.org/en/docs/iteiia20073_en.pdf.
[27] http://www.unctad.org/en/docs/iteiit200511_en.pdf.
[28] http://www.unctad.org/en/docs/iteiit20054_en.pdf.
[29] World Trade Org., The Multilateral Trading System—Past, Present and Future, http://www.wto.org/english/thewto_e/whatis_e/inbrief_e/inbr01_e.htm.

The GATT system included periodic "rounds" of negotiations to achieve further cuts in tariffs, and it had a system for resolving disputes between members. While often referred to as an international organization, the GATT had only a *de facto* role as an international organization before the creation of the WTO.

The GATT system eventually failed to respond to challenges such as the increasing trade in services and the use of nontariff trade barriers. In 1994, after years of negotiations, the WTO was created. The WTO includes many separate agreements; the following are among the most important:

1. 1994 GATT Agreement,[30] which covers trade in goods. All WTO member States are bound by this agreement.
2. Marrakesh Agreement Establishing the World Trade Organization (Marrakesh or WTO Agreement).[31] All member States are bound by this agreement.
3. General Agreement on Trade in Services (GATS).[32] Not all member states have agreed to be bound by this agreement.
4. Agreement on Trade-Related Aspects of Intellectual Property Rights (TRIPs).[33] All member states are bound, although a few least-developed states have an extended deadline for compliance.
5. Understanding on Rules and Procedures Governing the Settlement of Disputes (DSU).[34] All member states are bound.

The goals of the WTO are to improve the world economic system by converting all trade barriers (e.g., quotas, subsidies) into tariffs and eventually eliminating them. Tariffs are more transparent and are easier to administer than other kinds of protective measures. The WTO system provides "most-favored-nation" treatment to all members; that is, any trade preference must be extended to all members equally.[35] The WTO agreements, however, provide several exceptions to this rule, including allowing member states to set up free trade areas among themselves. The European Union and the European Free Trade Association (EFTA)[36] are examples of such free trade areas,

---

[30] General Agreement on Tariffs and Trade 1994, Apr. 15, 1994, 1867 U.N.T.S. 187, *reprinted in* 33 I.L.M. 1153 (1994).

[31] 1867 U.N.T.S. 154, *reprinted in* 33 I.L.M. 1144 (1994).

[32] 1869 U.N.T.S. 183, *reprinted in* 33 I.L.M. 1167 (1994).

[33] 1869 U.N.T.S. 299, *reprinted in* 33 I.L.M. 1197 (1994).

[34] 1869 U.N.T.S. 401, *reprinted in* 33 I.L.M. 1226 (1994).

[35] World Trade Org., Principles of the Trading System, http://www.wto.org/english/thewto_e/whatis_e/tif_e/fact2_e.htm.

[36] http://www.efta.int.

as is NAFTA. Another key principle of the WTO system is the principle of "national treatment"—that is, that member states should treat other member states' goods the same way they treat their own.[37]

B. *Structure and Workings of the WTO*

The WTO is governed by its General Council, and run by the Secretariat, which comprises the WTO's permanent professional staff. Higher-level direction comes from the Ministerial Body, which meets every two years.

Dispute resolution has become an important aspect of the WTO. A member state initiates the process by filing a request for consultations (roughly analogous to a complaint). If negotiations fail to resolve the conflict, the WTO sets up a panel and appoints panelists. The panel then issues a report, which can be adopted by the Dispute Settlement Body (DSB), or appealed to the DSB.[38] The DSB is the General Council, acting as the DSB. Appeals are heard by three members of a permanent seven-member Appellate Body established by the DSB. Although the DSB can reject the Appellate Body's final judgments, it can do so only with consensus,[39] so such rejection has been rare.

If a complaint is upheld, the state that has violated WTO law must bring its laws and policies into compliance with that law. A state that fails to do so must enter into negotiations with the complaining state to determine compensation (e.g., specific tariff reductions). If the states cannot reach agreement, the complaining state can impose limited trade sanctions on the losing state.[40]

C. *Starting Points for WTO Research*

Although the WTO has an extensive website with voluminous documentation, it is not a good starting point unless you are merely searching for a known document. Instead, start with a secondary source, such as a treatise or law review article. (The WTO also provides explanations of WTO law on its website, but it has an optimistic slant that may not give you the best understanding of its actual workings.)

---

[37] World Trade Org., Principles of the Trading System, http://www.wto.org/english/thewto_e/whatis_e/tif_e/fact2_e.htm.

[38] World Trade Org., *Settling Disputes*, http://www.wto.org/english/thewto_e/whatis_e/tif_e/disp1_e.htm.

[39] Id.

[40] Id.

Useful sources include the following:

- *Corporate Counsel's Guide: Laws of International Trade* (William H. Hancock ed., 1986–2005).
- Ralph H. Folsom et al., *International Trade and Economic Relations in a Nutshell* (4th ed. 2009).
- Hans van Houtte, *The Law of International Trade* (2d ed. 2002).
- Harvey Kaye & Christopher A. Dunn, *International Trade Practice* (rev. ed. 2011–).
- Mitsuo Matsushita et al., *The World Trade Organization: Law, Practice, and Policy* (2d ed. 2006).
- *The WTO's Core Rules and Disciplines* (Kym Anderson & Bernard Hoekman eds., 2006).

To find other sources, use the following Library of Congress subject headings as subject searches:

> *international trade*
> *free trade*
> *foreign trade regulation*
> *tariff – law and legislation*
> *investments, foreign – law and legislation*
> *world trade organization*

Also try the keyword *WTO* in library catalogs.

In both of the major legal periodical indexes, LegalTrac (LRI)[41] and *Index to Legal Periodicals* (ILP),[42] *world trade organization* is a subject heading. For international trade generally, ILP uses the subject heading *international trade*, while LRI uses *international trade regulation*. The indexes also have much more specific subject headings, such as *subsidies, most-favored-nation clause*, and *international trade dispute resolution* in the Index to Legal Periodicals. As usual, experiment with keywords to find relevant articles. Once you have found them, use their subject headings to lead you to additional useful articles.

If you prefer to start with an online research guide, one of the best is Jeanne Rehberg, *WTO and GATT Research*[43] (New York University). Another excellent guide is Jean Wenger, *International Economic Law*[44] (American Society

---

[41] http://www.gale.cengage.com/pdf/facts/legal.pdf (LRI on Westlaw; Find a Source > Legal Resource Index on LexisNexis).

[42] http://www.ebscohost.com/academic/index-to-legal-periodicals-books.

[43] http://nyulaw.libguides.com/wto_gatt.

[44] http://www.asil.org/erg/?page=iel.

for International Law). Both of these guides identify key sources for WTO research, including sources for agreements, dispute resolution documents, and commentary.

D. Sources for Dispute Resolution Documents

1. Reports
Selected WTO and GATT panel reports are available on LexisNexis.[45] (Generally, GATT reports are from 1948–1994, with WTO decisions from 1995–present.) Westlaw also has selected WTO and GATT panel decisions.[46]

Free online sources include the WTO website[47] and WorldTradeLaw.net,[48] a site that contains some free components and some fee-based ones. Generally, it is easier to download dispute resolution documents from WorldTradeLaw .net rather than from the WTO site. Another excellent though fee-based source is TradeLawGuide,[49] which offers full-text searching and a citator.

The WTO Dispute Settlement page[50] provides access to WTO dispute resolution documents including panel reports, Appellate Body reports, and adopted panel reports. It also includes Adopted Panel Reports Within the Framework of GATT 1947.[51] (For more information about searching the WTO website, see below.)

For published reports, researchers have a variety of sources:

- *Dispute Settlement Reports* (1996–). This set is not annotated, and is considered the "official" WTO version.
- *WTO Basic Instruments and Selected Documents* (BISD) (2003–). Note, however, that this series publishes only selected reports, generally long after they are issued.
- *International Legal Materials* (I.L.M.) (1962–). This periodical publishes selected, important WTO decisions. You can search the I.L.M. on Westlaw,[52] HeinOnline,[53] and LexisNexis.[54]

---

[45] International Trade > WTO > Gatt Panel and World Trade Decisions.
[46] WTO-DEC.
[47] http://www.wto.org.
[48] http://www.worldtradelaw.net.
[49] http://www.tradelawguide.com.
[50] http://www.wto.org/english/tratop_e/dispu_e/dispu_e.htm.
[51] http://www.wto.org/english/tratop_e/dispu_e/gt47ds_e.htm.
[52] ILM database.
[53] http://www.heinonline.org.
[54] International Law > Treaties & International Agreements > International Legal Materials.

- *International Trade Law Reports* (1996–). This series publishes only selected WTO decisions. There is no cumulative index. The best way to search them is to look at the colored tabs that separate documents. These have the name of the matter and the type of document (e.g., *Shrimp/ Turtle—Appellate Body Report*).
- *WTO Appellate Body Repertory of Reports and Awards, 1995–2010* (2011) (compiled by the Appellate Body Secretariat; fairly well-indexed).
- *Law & Practice of the World Trade Organization* (1995–). This contains three binders of selected WTO decisions.
- *World Trade Organization Dispute Settlement Decisions: Bernan's Annotated Reporter* (1997–). *Bernan's Annotated Reporter* is much more comprehensive than the publications noted above. Coverage starts with 1996 decisions. A comprehensive subject index tells you what volume contains the decision you're looking for. Subjects correspond to the titles *or* subjects of the WTO documents (e.g., Measures Affecting Textiles is indexed under "Measures Affecting Textiles," rather than "Textiles." "Regime for the Importation, Sale and Distribution of Bananas," however, is indexed under Bananas.) The index does not provide a page number—just a volume number. However, each volume has only a few decisions in it, and they're listed in the table of contents at the front of each volume.

2. Indexes and Digests

To locate relevant WTO decisions, one useful source is the online WTO Analytical Index—Guide to WTO Law and Practice.[55] This webpage offers an extremely detailed index to WTO law, with citations and links to Appellate Body decisions. It is considered the authoritative guide to the interpretation and application of findings and decisions of WTO panels, the WTO Appellate Body, and other WTO bodies.

One of the two indexes within this page is a topical index. When you click a link within the index, you retrieve an entry containing excerpts from relevant decisions. The other index is keyed to provisions to the various treaties involved in the WTO framework.

> **Example:** You are asked to research the meaning of a provision in Article III of the Dispute Settlement Agreement, which states that the dispute settlement system serves to "clarify the existing provisions" of the WTO agreements "in accordance with customary rules of interpretation of public international law."[56]

---

[55] http://www.wto.org/english/res_e/booksp_e/analytic_index_e/analytic_index_e.htm (also available in print, but only updated to 2007).
[56] Dispute Settlement Understanding art. III, 1869 U.N.T.S. 401, *reprinted in* 33 I.L.M. 1226 (1994).

You need to find out how the WTO has defined "the customary rules of inter-pretation of public international law."

Starting at the main Analytical Index page,[57] you would click on the abbre-viation "DSU" in the Agreement/Article index. This action retrieves a Table of Contents to the DSU[58] which links to entries for individual articles.

The Analytical Index offers several subpoints under this heading, such as "(v) Principle of effective treaty interpretation." Clicking on that entry retrieves excerpts of relevant decisions, along with citations.

There are several alternatives to the Analytical Index.

- WorldTradeLaw.net's WTO Case Law Index[59] indicates the relevant WTO panel reports, Appellate Body reports, or arbitrations that have interpreted each WTO legal provision or legal term/concept. You can also browse by index term or by agreement. Subject or article-by-article indexes accompany the *World Trade Organization Dispute Settlement Decisions: Bernan's Annotated Reporter.*
- TradeLawGuide,[60] available through some law libraries, is similar to WorldTradeLaw.net in that it permits full-text searching of WTO deci-sions, and offers an index to decisions by topic. TradeLawGuide also offers a citator function that enables you to see if later WTO decisions have cited to a paragraph in an earlier decision.
- Pierre Pescatore et al., *Handbook of WTO/GATT Dispute Settlement* (1991–). This three-volume looseleaf publication provides summaries of all GATT and WTO dispute settlement decisions. The decisions are indexed by keyword, WTO/GATT Agreement article numbers, participants, and other criteria. The set is supposed to be updated semi-annually, but the latest update in 2011 is from 2009.

Using Westlaw, LexisNexis, TradeLawGuide, or WorldTradeLaw.net, you can use keywords to search GATT and WTO decisions. Keep in mind that these decisions are often extremely long; you may find it more efficient to start with an index or digest rather than a full-text search. The text of the decisions can be confusing, too, because they recite all the parties' arguments before giving the panel's or Appellate Body's opinions. Be careful not to mis-take the parties' arguments for the actual holdings.

Finally, you may sometimes want to find parties' submissions in WTO disputes. While these are confidential, the parties have the option of making

---

[57] http://www.wto.org/english/res_e/booksp_e/analytic_index_e/analytic_index_e.htm.
[58] http://www.wto.org/english/res_e/booksp_e/analytic_index_e/dsu_e.htm.
[59] http://www.worldtradelaw.net/dsc/wtoindex.htm.
[60] http://www.tradelawguide.com/index.asp?toc=content&id=88.

their submissions public, and some choose to do so, usually after the matter is concluded. Many briefs filed by the United States in WTO proceedings are available online.[61] The EU also makes its filings available online.[62] Moreover, WorldTradeLaw.net also collects links to various countries' submissions in WTO and NAFTA disputes.[63]

E. *Finding Other WTO Documents*

Along with WTO dispute resolution documents, you can find most WTO documents on the WTO's website.[64] The site has two main components: the general section, with reports, news, and statistics; and the Documents Online[65] section, which provides access to official WTO documents from 1995. In 2006, the General Council decided to make all official GATT documents available from Documents Online.[66] This collection is not yet complete, so another source for older documents is the GATT Digital Archive: 1947–1994.[67] The Documents Online database is accessible from the WTO homepage, but it is also linked to various topics throughout the website. So, for example, if you select "Intellectual Property" from the list of Trade Topics on the homepage, the TRIPS Gateway you'll retrieve has a link to TRIPS: Disputes Concerning the TRIPS Agreement.

The Trade Topics are a convenient way to locate relevant documents without trying to navigate through the Documents Online database. Each Trade Topic page or gateway has specialized document search forms at the end of the main page. These pages are also very helpful when researching an unfamiliar topic.

The Documents Online database lets you browse or search for documents. Most of the time, you will probably be searching. You can choose between Simple or Advanced Search options; both of them allow you to search the full text of documents using keywords.

The Advanced Search has several advantages over the Simple Search. First, you can search by products, which lets you avoid documents that mention a product but do not really concern that product. You can also search by GATT/WTO treaty article. If you use this feature, you must click

---

[61] http://www.ustr.gov/trade-topics/enforcement/dispute-settlement-proceedings/wto-dispute-settlement.
[62] http://trade.ec.europa.eu/wtodispute/search.cfm.
[63] http://www.worldtradelaw.net/submissions.htm.
[64] http://www.wto.org.
[65] http://docsonline.wto.org/gen_home.asp?language=1&_=1.
[66] http://www.wto.org/english/docs_e/gattdocs_e.htm.
[67] http://gatt.stanford.edu/page/home.

on the question mark to the right of the search box to get the list of treaty abbreviations. For example, the General Agreement on Trade in Services is abbreviated as GATS. Clicking on the entry for GATS in the list of abbreviations makes it expand to a list of articles, and by clicking on an entry, you can add it to the search form.

The Documents Online Advanced Search also lets you search by an established list of subjects (click on the question mark to the right of the search box to retrieve the list). In addition to these limitations, the Advanced Search offers several other options for narrowing your results. You should take advantage of these options, because looking at your search results in the database is cumbersome. Usually, the document title displayed in the search results does not give you enough information to know whether you want to read the document. You can get an idea of a document's contents by looking at its catalog record; click on the link to the left of the document title. Often, however, this is not enough information. Thus, you will have to open many documents in a typical search.

Like other IGO documentation discussed elsewhere in this book, WTO documents have their own unique numbering system. To understand the symbols used, click on the question mark to the right of the document symbol search box. For example, "WT/DSB/M/" means WTO Dispute Settlement Body, Minutes. The "Help" section of the Documents Online homepage[68] has extensive information on WTO document symbols and numbering; look under "Document nomenclature" in the list of Help Contents.

IV. *North American Free Trade Agreement*

A. *Introduction*

The North American Free Trade Agreement (NAFTA) built on an earlier trade agreement between the United States and Canada.[69] NAFTA's purpose is to create a free trade area comprising Canada, Mexico, and the United States. NAFTA entered into force on January 1, 1994. Liberalization of trade rules between the countries has greatly increased the volume of trade[70] and created business for lawyers.

---

[68] http://docsonline.wto.org/gen_home.asp?language=1&_=1.

[69] United States-Canada Free Trade Agreement, 27 I.L.M. 293 (1988).

[70] Two-thirds of US exports go to Canada and Mexico. U.S. Chamber of Commerce, Steps to a 21st Century U.S.-Mexico Border (2011), http://www.uschamber.com/sites/default/files/reports/mexicoreportfullbook.pdf.

If you have not yet become familiar with the NAFTA regime, you may want to start with a book that gives an overview. You can find general works on NAFTA in your library catalog using Library of Congress subject headings such as:

free trade – north america
foreign trade regulation – north america
north america – economic integration
north america – commercial treaties
canada. treaties, etc. 1992 Oct. 7

Also try the keyword *nafta*.

The two major legal periodical indexes, LegalTrac[71] and *Index to Legal Periodicals* (ILP),[72] each have a specific subject heading for NAFTA. In Legal-Trac, use *free trade agreement, 1992, united states-canada-mexico*; in ILP, use *north american free trade agreement*. As always, you can combine a subject heading with more specific terms to focus on your topic (e.g., agriculture, lumber, taxation, etc.).

A useful research guide to NAFTA is Francisco Avalos & Maureen Garmon, Update: Basic Info and Online Sources for NAFTA and CAFTA Research (2010).[73] (As its title indicates, that guide also provides sources for researching the Central American Free Trade Agreement (CAFTA).) Another way to get some basic information on NAFTA is to check Ralph H. Folsom, *NAFTA and Free Trade in the Americas in a Nutshell* (3d ed. 2008).

B. *Agreements*

NAFTA and the two main "side agreements" can be found easily on the web.[74] The side agreements concern environmental[75] and labor[76] issues.

Another side agreement concerns "emergency action."[77] You may also need to consult the US implementing legislation, the North American Free

---

[71] http://www.gale.cengage.com/pdf/facts/legal.pdf (LRI on Westlaw; Find a Source > Legal Resource Index on LexisNexis).

[72] http://www.ebscohost.com/academic/index-to-legal-periodicals-books.

[73] http://www.nyulawglobal.org/globalex/NAFTA_CAFTA_Research1.htm.

[74] http://www.nafta-sec-alena.org/en/view.aspx?x=343.

[75] North American Agreement on Environmental Cooperation, Sept. 13, 1993, 32 I.L.M. 1480, http://www.cec.org/Page.asp?PageID=1226&ContentID=&SiteNodeID=567&BL_ExpandID=154.

[76] North American Agreement on Labor Cooperation, Sept.14, 1993, 32 I.L.M. 1499, http://www.naalc.org/naalc/naalc-full-text.htm.

[77] Understanding between the Parties to the North American Free Trade Agreement Concerning Chapter Eight-Emergency Action, Sept. 14, 1993, 32 I.L.M. 1519, http://infousa.state.gov/economy/trade/nafta/surgestm.htm.

Trade Agreement Implementation Act, Pub. L. No. 103–182, 107 Stat. 2057 (1993), 19 U.S.C §§ 3301 et seq.[78] (The legislative history of this law—not the negotiating history of the NAFTA agreement—is available on Westlaw in NAFTA-LH.) Finally, the United States and Mexico entered into a separate agreement relating to abatement of environmental problems along the US-Mexico border. This agreement, the US-Mexico Agreement Concerning the Establishment of a Border Environment Cooperation Commission and a North American Development Bank,[79] is much harder to find on the web, but a replica of the International Legal Materials version can be found at FAOLEX.[80]

One of the best sites on which to find the NAFTA Agreements is the website of the Foreign Trade Information System (SICE—from its Spanish acronym—*Sistema de Información al Comercio Exterior*).[81] SICE is maintained under the aegis of the Organization of American States. The site provides extensive information on trade in the western hemisphere. SICE includes the text of free trade and investment agreements; updates on the progress of treaty negotiations; dispute resolution documents (e.g., panel reports under NAFTA); national laws on trade-related issues, such as intellectual property; articles; reports; and other trade-related materials.

NAFTA created a Free Trade Commission to deal with policy matters related to NAFTA, but this entity does not have a permanent bureaucratic establishment. It is composed of the trade ministers from each country, and they operate from their own country's trade departments. NAFTA also created a Secretariat[82] to administer the dispute resolution portions of the main NAFTA Agreement. As is typical of intergovernmental organizations, the Secretariat's website offers a lot of useful information on the organization.

C. *Dispute Resolution*

NAFTA has spawned a lot of dispute resolution activity, both formal and informal. The NAFTA Agreement provides several dispute resolution mechanisms, with the default provisions laid out under Chapter 20; it also has special provisions for certain types of disputes (e.g., Chapter 11 of the Agreement provides for the resolution of investment disputes). Moreover,

---

[78] The analogous Canadian legislation is North American Free Trade Implementation Act of June 23, 1993, 1993 S.C. ch. 44. Mexico assigns implementation to the Executive Branch, rather than to its Legislative Branch, so there is no analogous Mexican law.

[79] Nov. 18, 1993, 32 I.L.M. 1545.

[80] http://faolex.fao.org/docs/pdf/mul15756.pdf.

[81] http://www.sice.oas.org.

[82] http://www.nafta-sec-alena.org.

the two side agreements on labor and environment provide their own dispute resolution procedures.

The NAFTA framework encourages informal dispute resolution. One of the functions of the Free Trade Commission is to facilitate informal resolution; it provides technical advice, mediators, and other support. The Free Trade Commission can also set up arbitration proceedings if the parties request it.

Westlaw[83] and LexisNexis[84] provide good coverage of NAFTA binational panel decisions, and they are most easily searchable through those services. Decisions are also online for free at the NAFTA Secretariat's website, although they are not searchable.[85] These are also published in *NAFTA Arbitration Reports* (2002–). Another useful source available at some law libraries is *North American Free Trade Agreements* (James R. Holbein & Donald J. Musch eds., 1992–).

In addition, the US Department of State provides extensive information about investor-state arbitrations, including parties' submissions, orders, and other key documents, at a section of its website.[86] The Canadian website on Foreign Affairs and International Trade also provides information about past and current arbitrations, including parties' documents relating to arbitrations to which Canada is a party.[87] The Mexican Ministry of the Economy has documentation also, but it is primarily in Spanish.[88]

The best source for NAFTA disputes regarding investor-state dispute settlement is NAFTAClaims.com (a.k.a. NAFTALaw.org), operated by Todd Grierson Weiler.[89] The disputes are organized by country and include many of the documents filed and issued in a dispute. There is also a collection of legal documents, including NAFTA negotiating texts and other documents. All of the documents are available in PDF.

WorldTradeLaw.net, a subscription-based website,[90] also provides NAFTA decisions in PDF format. The site offers a search engine specifically for searching the text of NAFTA decisions, but does not include decisions under Chapter 11.

---

[83] NAFTA-BIP for panel decisions; NAFTA-AWARDS for arbitration awards.

[84] International Trade > Cases > Interpreting U.S. Law > NAFTA Panel Review Decisions.

[85] http://www.nafta-sec-alena.org/en/DecisionsAndReports.aspx?x=312.

[86] http://www.state.gov/s/l/c3439.htm.

[87] http://www.international.gc.ca/trade-agreements-accords-commerciaux/disp-diff/nafta .aspx?lang=en&view=d.

[88] http://www.economia.gob.mx/comunidad-negocios/comercio-exterior/tlc-acuerdos.

[89] http://naftaclaims.com.

[90] http://www.worldtradelaw.net.

D. *Additional Research Resources*

The scope of BNA's *International Trade Reporter* (*I.T.R.*) (1994–) extends beyond NAFTA to encompass WTO and other international trade issues, but it provides good coverage of NAFTA disputes and negotiations related to NAFTA (e.g., expansion of NAFTA's coverage). The *I.T.R.* is updated weekly. Your library may have this title in paper or online, or both.[91] In print or online, check the index under "North American Free Trade Agreement," or see specific topics such as "Wood" or "Rules of Origin." The *I.T.R.*'s online version is also fully searchable. Although the *I.T.R.* summarizes actions in pending arbitrations, it does not provide the full text for most decisions.

Another source for developments in international trade generally, but including NAFTA, is the weekly publication *Inside U.S. Trade* (1983–), available electronically[92] or in a paper version. *Inside U.S. Trade* is also available on LexisNexis.[93] This source has very short news stories about legal and political developments in international trade. It sometimes reprints the text of letters from US officials on trade issues. You may also want to look at a blog on international trade: International Economic Law and Policy Blog,[94] which offers contributions from leading experts.

---

[91] Also available on LexisNexis and Westlaw under some subscription plans.
[92] http://www.insidetrade.com.
[93] International Trade > General News & Information > Inside U.S. Trade.
[94] http://worldtradelaw.typepad.com.

Chapter Twenty

Private International Law

I. *Introduction*

A. *What Is Private International Law?*

One effect of globalization is that family and commercial situations often cross national borders. Of course, different countries apply different legal rules to these situations, so the question arises: What law should apply? The answer can affect the parties' rights and duties as well as the sources of law you should consider. National laws are the primary sources of private international law. However, private international law is also embodied in treaties and conventions (e.g., the Hague Conventions on Private International Law), model laws, legal guides, and other instruments that regulate transactions.

To resolve differences between legal systems, states have adopted rules called "private international law." This body of law includes procedural rules for deciding whether to apply the law of one country or another. Those rules are often called "choice-of-law" or "conflict of law" rules, particularly in common law systems. In civil law systems, the term "private international law" is used for these rules. But private international law also includes *substantive* rules on which countries have agreed.

Several international organizations work to establish uniform rules. Their work covers many areas, including banking, contracts, and other commercial law; and family law issues such as child protection, marriage, divorce, and spousal support. Another major area involves aspects of international dispute resolution, from service of process to enforcement of judgments and arbitral awards.

B. *Codification of Private International Law*

During the last century, a few groups tried to codify certain customary norms of private international law. Organizations such as the United Nations Commission on International Trade Law (UNCITRAL) have drafted several multilateral treaties and model laws. For example, the UNCITRAL Model Law on International Commercial Arbitration has formed the basis of arbitration laws in over 60 jurisdictions.[1] The Hague Conference on Private International Law, another organization, focuses on treaties; it has completed 39 of them to date.[2] While not all of these organizations' initiatives have been widely adopted, their efforts have increased uniformity and predictability in many areas of law.

C. *General Research Strategies and Sources*

Does Any Treaty Apply?

One of the first questions you'll need to answer is whether an existing treaty addresses your topic. For example, if you need to enforce a US court judgment in another country, you should look for a treaty on the uniform recognition of court judgments. Using secondary sources, such as books or articles on transnational litigation, you can determine that while many European countries have signed the multilateral Brussels and Lugano Conventions, which cover enforcement of foreign judgments, the United States has not. Another way you might find this information is by looking at the US Department of State's webpage on this topic.[3] You could retrieve this page by a web search like *state department enforcement foreign judgments.*

Knowing that no treaty controls this area, you would next look at the foreign state's law on enforcement of foreign judgments. The sources you use would depend, as always, on what you have available. One widely used tool is *Enforcement of Foreign Judgments* (Louis Garb & Julian Lew eds., 1994–). This publication provides information on the enforceability of foreign judgments in many jurisdictions. Alternatively, you might use sources for foreign law research such as codes, treatises, periodical articles, or web sites. For more assistance researching the national law of other countries, see Part IV of this book.

What if a treaty does apply to your question? Let's say you need to know how to enforce an arbitral award in a foreign country. Again, start by looking for a treaty. Another way to find out whether the United States is a party to any relevant treaty is to look in *Treaties in Force.*[4] You can open the current version as a PDF document, and search for the word "award."

---

[1] http://www.uncitral.org/uncitral/en/uncitral_texts/arbitration/1985Model_arbitration_status.html.
[2] http://www.hcch.net/index_en.php?act=conventions.listing.
[3] http://travel.state.gov/law/judicial/judicial_691.html.
[4] http://www.state.gov/s/l/treaty/tif/index.htm.

This search leads you to the entry for the Convention on the Recognition and Enforcement of Foreign Arbitral Awards. You can quickly find the text of this treaty online through a variety of sources. After reviewing the treaty text, you would follow up on any unanswered questions by using secondary sources, checking national legislation, calling foreign authorities, or any other necessary approach.

What If No Treaty Applies?

If your search of treaty and secondary sources tells you that no treaty applies, you will need to find out what other law applies. "In civil law countries, private international law rules are generally set forth as preliminary provisions to the basic codes."[5] For example, Article 3 of the French Civil Code[6] sets forth some of these rules:

> Statutes relating to public policy and safety are binding on all those living on the territory. Immovables are governed by French law even when owned by aliens. Statutes relating to the status and capacity of persons govern French persons, even those residing in foreign countries.

Thomas H. Reynolds & Arturo A. Flores, *Foreign Law Guide*, identifies the applicable foreign laws for many jurisdictions.[7] Look under the heading "Conflict of Laws and Private International Law." Thus, by using a combination of primary and secondary sources, you would determine the conflict of law rules of the foreign jurisdiction involved.

Another part of your research involves looking at the US rules, but that topic is mostly beyond the scope of this book. You will find useful information in the *Restatement of the Law, Second, Conflict of Laws* (1971–).[8] Treatises on US civil and criminal procedure, such as Charles Alan Wright et al., *Federal Practice & Procedure* (1969–), cover some aspects of procedure involving foreign jurisdictions. For example, 4B Fed. Prac. & Proc. Civ. 3d § 1133 et seq. is entitled Service in a Foreign Country.

D. *Other International Organizations*

Two other international organizations are involved in private international law issues: UNCITRAL and UNIDROIT. The United Nations Commission

---

[5] Detlev Vagts & Louis F. Del Duca, *Book Review*, 83 Am.J. Int'l L. 444, 444 (1989) (reviewing *Problemi di Riforma del Diritto Internazionale Privato Italiano* (1986)).

[6] C. Civ. art. 3 (Georges Rouhette & Anne Rouhette-Berton trans.), Legifrance, at http://195.83.177.9/code/liste.phtml?lang=uk&c=22&r=209.

[7] Subscription database, http://www.foreignlawguide.com.

[8] The Restatements are also available on LexisNexis (Legal > Secondary Legal > Restatements > Conflict of Laws) and Westlaw (REST-CONFL).

for International Trade Law (UNCITRAL)[9] works on the progressive harmonization of private international law, especially in the areas of the CISG and arbitration (see Chapter 21 for more information). The International Institute for the Unification of Private Law (UNIDROIT)[10] is active in "modernising, harmonising and co-ordinating private and in particular commercial law as between states and groups of states and to formulate uniform law instruments, principles and rules to achieve those objectives."[11] The websites for both organizations contain the text of the conventions, model laws, rules, and other relevant documentation.

II. *International Business Transactions*

Researching international business transactions involves locating national law from various jurisdictions, both legislation and case law; obtaining commentary on how to conduct a particular kind of transaction; locating sample forms or language needed for contracts and agreements; and locating international law sources, including treaties, model rules from international organizations, and case law from international courts and tribunals.

When faced with a particular business transaction, you may not always start your research the same way. There are some standard methods for beginning a project focusing on locating and interpreting national law of another jurisdiction.

First, locate some information about the legal system in question. This is done by consulting both research guides and sources that describe the legal system and even the climate for doing business. Let's look at Mexico as an example. There are several print and electronic sources worth consulting.

Using a library catalog, search the subject *law—Mexico* and you will retrieve records for books about the legal system; for example, Stephen Zamora's *Mexican Law* (2004). The catalog record indicates that the table of contents contains the following:

> The history of Mexican law—Legal education and the legal profession—Sources of law—Federalism and centrism—Executive and legislative powers—The judicial system—Constitutional guarantees of individual rights—Judicial procedures of enforce the constitution—Administrative law—Civil procedure—Criminal law and procedure—Regulation of the economy and environmental regulation—Labour law, agrarian reform, and social welfare—The civil and commercial codes—Family law and the law of persons—Property law and

---

[9] http://www.uncitral.org.
[10] http://www.unidroit.org.
[11] See Overview, http://www.unidroit.org/dynasite.cfm?dsmid=103284.

inheritance law—Contracts and other obligations—Commercial law—Business organizations—Financial institutions—Intellectual property law—Conflicts of law.

Other worthwhile sources include Jorge A. Vargas, *Mexican Legal Dictionary* (2009). By searching the web, you can find a guide called An Electronic Guide to Mexican Law, by Francisco A. Avalos and Elisa Donnadieu (2011).[12] All of these sources will describe the legal system, provide citations to relevant codes and laws, and set a framework for continuing your research.

Typical questions about doing business in a foreign country include: What types of entities can do business there (e.g., corporations, partnerships, limited liability companies)? What are the advantages and disadvantages of using each entity? What requirements must an entity fulfill before doing business (e.g., registration, capitalization, designation of an agent)? For Mexico, the chapter on "Business Organizations" in the Zamora book cited above would be an excellent starting point. Good secondary sources provide citations to applicable laws and regulations; for instance, this chapter refers to specific sections of the Civil Code, identifies leading treatises on Mexican corporate law, and provides an overview of business entities.

If you had questions about the applicability of a Mexican Civil Code provision, you might next look for an English translation of that Code. Searching a library catalog with the subject *mexico* and the title keywords *civil code* will retrieve your local library's translations. You may also want to check WorldCat[13] for more recent translations. One such translation is a 2009 version from West, *Mexican Civil Code Annotated*.

You may have more specific questions depending on the type of business involved. For example, will the business need to trademark its name, acquire a license, or meet health and safety requirements? After checking the more general sources such as the Zamora book, you may want to check the *Foreign Law Guide*[14] to identify Mexican legislation on narrower topics. Periodical articles can also provide more specialized information; see Chapter 5.

As another example, consider a project to locate Japanese banking laws. Again, a good source to consult is the *Foreign Law Guide*. The section on Japan from this database indicates that there are several relevant laws, and it also points to a few sources for English-language translations, including the *EHS Law Bulletin Series* (1958–) and *Doing Business in Japan* (1980–). Both of these print sources translate the laws, and *Doing Business in Japan* provides some commentary and explanation. *Foreign Law Guide* also notes

---

[12] http://www.nyulawglobal.org/globalex/Mexico1.htm.
[13] http://www.worldcat.org/ (free version); http://firstsearch.oclc.org/ (subscription version).
[14] http://www.foreignlawguide.com.

that there are a few websites worth consulting. Other sources do something similar to *Foreign Law Guide*, but they provide much less detail. See Chapter 8 for more details.

Free web sources also have a role in locating national law. A good way to locate collections of laws is to consult the "countries" catalog on WorldLII. Countries are arranged alphabetically. Looking at Singapore, the sites are further divided into categories:

- Courts & Case-Law
- Education
- Government
- Inter-Government Organisations
- Law Journals
- Law Reform
- Lawyers
- Legislation
- Other Indexes
- Parliament
- Treaties & International Agreements.

By selecting the "legislation" category, you will get a fairly long list of potential sites. One that stands out is Singapore Statutes Online, a free resource provided by the Singapore Attorney General's Chambers. This site provides access to laws by chapter number or alphabetically. A search mechanism and a subject index are also available. A "last updated" date is listed on the homepage. All of this makes this a good site for accessing needed legislation.

The same people who work on the WorldLII site are also busy creating "Legal Information Institutes"—these sites provide access to freely available public legal information. Some of the best include AustLII, BAILII, and PacLII, but there are several more.[15]

There are other important websites that are freely available, and they also contain the full-text of laws, sometimes in English, or a good abstract and citation to the relevant laws. These sites are often provided by intergovernmental organizations, nongovernmental organizations, academic institutions, learned societies, and even law firms. Many of these are organized by

---

[15] Australasia (AustLII), UK & Ireland (BAILII), Canada (CanLII), The Commonwealth (CommonLII), Cyprus (CyLaw), Droit Francophone, Hong Kong (HKLII), JuriBurkina, New Zealand (NZLII), Pacific Islands (PacLII), Southern Africa (SAFLII), and USA (LII(Cornell)), and others. Links to these sites are available at http://www.worldlii.org; see bottom of the homepage.

topic. A good example is the database of national labor, social security, and related human rights legislation called NATLEX, produced by the International Labour Organization.[16] NATLEX provides abstracts of legislation and citation information and even provides links to the complete text of the law, if possible. Access is by country or subject, and a search engine is available as well. The World Bank has a website worth noting, the Doing Business Law Library, containing a collection of business laws and regulations, and it includes translations, where possible.[17] The topics include banking, bankruptcy, civil codes, commercial and company laws, securities law, and other areas of law. For example, if you are interested in foreign investment in Albania, you can start with this library by selecting the country of interest and then selecting "Commercial and Company Laws (Starting a Business, Protecting Investors, Closing a Business)"—this search will link you to Albanian law on foreign investment.

Other such websites include WIPO Lex for intellectual property laws;[18] FAOLEX for laws related to food and agriculture;[19] and UNCTAD's collection of national competition laws.[20] To locate more of these valuable websites, see WorldLII subject categories[21] or Mary Rumsey, Update: Basic Guide to Researching Foreign Law.[22]

To supplement the laws, you will also want some commentary that explains how these laws work and how to conduct or structure certain transactions. Some of these sources will contain citations to laws, and some may even provide the text of the legislation (or portions of it). Many of these sources are referenced in *Foreign Law Guide*. There are some standard tools that make good starting points and reference works too. Some of these tools focus on specific countries and some on specific regions. One category of such tools are the many *Doing Business in...* titles; for example, *Doing Business in Japan* (1980–), *Doing Business in Mexico* (1980–), or *Doing Business in Asia* (1991–). While many of these titles are in looseleaf format, the scope and depth of these sources varies; some contain translated legislation or sample forms; others are more of an outline. Some are even available on subscription databases, as is the case with *China Laws for Foreign Business*, and some are

---

[16] http://www.ilo.org/dyn/natlex/natlex_browse.home.
[17] http://www.doingbusiness.org/law-library.
[18] http://www.wipo.int/wipolex/en.
[19] http://faolex.fao.org.
[20] http://www.unctad.org/Templates/Page.asp?intItemID=4169&lang=1.
[21] http://www.worldlii.org/catalog/272.html.
[22] http://www.nyulawglobal.org/Globalex/Foreign_Law_Research1.htm.

available on LexisNexis.[23] Other standards include *Business Operations in…*[24] and *Legal Aspects of Doing Business in….*[25]

Other similar tools are available by topic, like the websites by topic noted above. In the area of international business, there are many books and loose-leaf services that provide valuable guidance about transactional work. Some of these sources provide sample forms, phone numbers for necessary governmental departments, and other practical information. The topics vary from arbitration to trademarks. For example: *Securing and Enforcing Judgments in Latin America* (2011–), a practical guide on how to enforce a foreign money judgment and attach assets in many countries in this region; *Trade Marks, Trade Names and Unfair Competition: World Law and Practice* (1999–), detailed information on regulations and enforcement for many countries; and *Transnational Contracts* (2011–) covering conflicts of laws and applicable contractual language.

III. *Family Law*

The area of law known as "domestic relations" has increasingly included transnational twists. Thus, lawyers who practice in the area of marriage dissolution, adoption, and child custody sometimes need to extend their research across national boundaries. Trusts and estates lawyers, too, have seen their practice expand to address foreign law questions. Unfortunately, the availability of good research sources in this area lags behind that of other legal topics, so research requires extra persistence and flexibility.

The Hague Conference on Private International Law has completed numerous conventions in these areas of law.[26] Topics include child abduction, child support, adoption, marriage and divorce, spousal maintenance, forms of wills, estate administration and succession, and trusts. Thus, when faced with a family law or estate question that involves a foreign party or asset, make sure to check whether a treaty may apply.

As usual, the most efficient way to check for treaties is to consult secondary sources. The US State Department website[27] can sometimes offer enough information to get you started. Another overview appears in the *International*

---

[23] On LexisNexis, follow this path: Lexis (Legal > Find Laws by Country or Region > Foreign Laws & Legal Sources > International Analysis & Commentary).

[24] These titles are part of the *Tax Management Portfolios* in print and online from BNA.

[25] See *Legal Aspects of Doing Business in Asia,…in Africa,* and *… in Latin America,* all published by Juris.

[26] http://www.hcch.net/index_en.php?act=conventions.listing.

[27] http://travel.state.gov/law/family_issues/family_issues_601.html.

Lawyer's Deskbook (L. Law et al. eds., 2d ed. 2003), which has chapters on wills, trusts, estates, and on family law. Law review articles and treatises on international family or succession law will highlight relevant international instruments (some of these are noted below).

Family and succession law questions, however, will usually require you to research foreign law as well as treaties. Some of the more readily available sources include the *Martindale-Hubbell International Law Digest*, the *International Encyclopaedia of Laws: Family & Succession* (Walter Pintens ed., 1997–); Louis Garb, *International Succession* (3d ed. 2010); and *The International Survey of Family Law* (Andrew Bainham ed., 1994–). Unfortunately, these sources often highlight just a few countries. To identify relevant laws from other countries, check Thomas H. Reynolds & Arturo A. Flores, *Foreign Law Guide* under headings such as Adoption, Family, Guardian and Ward, Marriage, Inheritance and Succession, Trusts and Trustees, and Wills.

> **Example:** A US client, divorced from her child's father in Germany, has brought the child to the United States without the father's consent. The father files a Request for Return of Child under the Hague Convention on Civil Aspects of Child Abduction with the Central Authority of Germany. In this scenario, you already know that the Hague Convention applies. The Hague Convention lets a petitioning parent recover a child where, among other conditions, the removal was in breach of the parent's custody rights under the law of his or her home country. Thus, to determine each parent's rights, you would have to look at the child custody laws of Germany. One possible source of information is the treatise *Family Law in Europe* (Carolyn Hamilton & Alison Perry eds., 2d ed. 2002). *Foreign Law Guide* also notes the International Family Law Procedure Act; available (in English) from the Federal Ministry of Justice updated through May 2011.[28]

When researching family law issues, consider using sources that focus on human rights issues (like the rights of women and the rights of children, in particular). For example, for information on Egyptian family law, see Jasmine Moussa, *Competing Fundamentalisms and Egyptian Women's Family Rights: International Law and the Reform of Shari'a-derived Legislation* (2011).

Family law research also requires you to know about the history of the legal system. In some jurisdictions, common law and customary law are important factors. More often than not, you won't find any relevant legislation, so secondary sources are very important for this kind of research.

> **Example:** You are working with a client in your clinic and you need to know the impact of customary or common law marriages in Nigeria. Before jumping straight into this research, you should consult Charles Mwalimu's book called *The Nigerian Legal System* (2005). This will give you needed background for this

---

[28] http://www.gesetze-im-internet.de/englisch_intfamrvg/index.html.

research. Next, take a look at Jude Oseloka Ezeanokwasa, *The Legal Inequality of Muslim and Christian Marriages in Nigeria: Constitutionally Established Judicial Discrimination* (2011). Articles on customary marriage in Africa would also be useful; for instance, John Y. Luluaki, 'Customary Marriage Laws in the Commonwealth: A Comparison between Papua New Guinea and Anglophonic Africa,' 11 *Int'l J.L. Pol. & Fam.* 1 (1997).

Here's another research tidbit. If the country you are interested in researching is a party to one of the major UN human rights treaties, check out the State party reports because they may yield some useful information on family law, marriage, inheritance and succession. State parties (countries who have ratified the treaty) are required to issue a regular report containing information on how that country has implemented the treaty, including information on law and policy. The UN High Commissioner for Human Rights website provides information on ratification and also access to these reports.[29]

Along the same lines, look at websites on women's human rights or gender. The World Bank's Gender Law Library is a collection of national legal provisions affecting women's economic status in 183 economies.[30] See also, the "Legal and Other Resources" section of the Avon Global Center for Women and Justice at Cornell Law School. This site links to domestic cases, reports, articles, and other resources.[31]

To find materials at your library, use the following Library of Congress subject headings:

> *conflict of laws – inheritance and succession conflict of laws – wills*
> *conflict of laws – domestic relations*
> *intercountry adoption*
> *convention on protection of children and co-operation in respect of intercountry adoption (1993) [or any other treaty that you think is relevant]*
> *domestic relations – [country name]*
> *marriage law – [country name]*
> *inheritance and succession – [country name]*

Also try International Academy of Estate and Trust Law (as author or keyword).

While not extensive, both the *Elgar Encyclopedia of Comparative Law* (2006) and *The Oxford Handbook of Comparative Law* (2006) have chapters on family law and other related areas. These sources provide a solid framework for your research and reference other books and articles for further exploration.

---

[29] http://www.ohchr.org/EN/Countries/Pages/HumanRightsintheWorld.aspx.
[30] http://wbl.worldbank.org/WBLLibrary/elibrary.aspx?libid=17.
[31] http://ww2.lawschool.cornell.edu/womenandjustice/legalresources/index.cfm.

IV. *International Litigation*

Increasingly, lawyers represent clients whose interests cross national borders, and often those interests lead the client to some form of dispute resolution. Businesses often prefer to arbitrate transnational disputes (see Chapter 21), because arbitration provides a faster, more confidential outcome, from a neutral arbiter. Thus, international business contracts often contain provisions indicating that disputes will be settled through arbitration.

Nonetheless, many individuals and other entities find themselves embroiled in transnational litigation.

A. *Stages of Litigation*

1. *Service of Process*

A Los Angeles lawyer commented that service on foreign defendants is "inherently complicated without being very interesting."[32] Generally, when researching this topic, you will be looking for information such as whether you can effect service by mail and whether you must provide translations of all the documents.

The State Department tries to help lawyers figure out the correct procedure, and its website on Judicial Assistance is a good starting point.[33] One part of the site (Service of Process Abroad)[34] provides general information and will help you become familiar with key treaties and terms (e.g., letters rogatory). Another section of the site, entitled "Country-Specific Information,"[35] gives you information tailored to particular countries; unfortunately, many countries are not covered in this section.

> **Example:** A Seventh Circuit case confirmed that a US corporation couldn't serve a Canadian corporation by sending an express package containing a copy of the complaint.[36] So, rather than try service by FedEx, you could check the State Department site for information about how to accomplish effective service. The country-specific page[37] has detailed information on service in Canada, including contact information for the government offices that handle service in each province.

---

[32] Arin Greenwood, *Idea from the Front: Serving Them Right*, ABA J., June 2005, at 24, 24 (quoting Dan Swanson).

[33] http://travel.state.gov/law/judicial/judicial_702.html.

[34] http://travel.state.gov/law/judicial/judicial_2513.html.

[35] http://travel.state.gov/law/judicial/judicial_2510.html.

[36] Audio Enterprises, Inc. v. B & W Loudspeakers, 957 F.2d 406, 408 (7th Cir. 1992).

[37] http://travel.state.gov/law/judicial/judicial_682.html.

For countries not covered at the State Department's site, or for additional information, consult the *Martindale-Hubbell International Law Digest*.[38] An EU website[39] also provides some guidance on this topic, as well as other matters related to civil and commercial matters. For example, if you need to serve documents in Germany, there is an English-language page that outlines the process and cites to relevant German law.

From the State Department site, you also learn about the treaties on service. One is the Hague Convention of the Service Abroad of Judicial and Extra-Judicial Documents in Civil and Commercial Matters.[40] The Conference also has a website devoted to Service[41] which includes contact details and practical information for national authorities, and the model form annexed to the convention. With the pages on practical information, you can supplement the information from the State Department's website on service in Germany, including information on any bilateral treaties on judicial cooperation.

If you need to dig even more deeply, the following sources may be useful.

- *International Encyclopaedia of Laws: Civil Procedure* (Paul Lemmens ed., 1994–).
- Anthony Colman, *Encyclopedia of International Commercial Litigation* (1991–).
- *International Civil Procedure* (2d ed. Christian Campbell ed., 2010–).
- David Epstein et al., *International Litigation: A Guide to Jurisdiction, Practice, and Strategy* (4th rev. ed. 2010).
- Stephen C. McCaffrey & Thomas O. Main, *Transnational Litigation in Comparative Perspective: Theory and Application* (2010).
- Lawrence W. Newman & Michael Burrows, *The Practice of International Litigation* (2d ed. 1998–).
- *Transnational Litigation: A Practitioner's Guide* (Richard Kreindler ed., 1997–).
- National continuing legal education materials, such as those published by the Practising Law Institute (PLI) or the American Law Institute-American Bar Association (ALI-ABA), cover aspects of transnational

---

[38] Available on LexisNexis; see International Law > Treatises & Analytical Materials > Martindale-Hubbell(R) International Law Digest.

[39] European Judicial Network (EJN), http://ec.europa.eu/civiljustice/index_en.htm.

[40] http://www.hcch.net/index_en.php?act=conventions.text&cid=17.

[41] http://www.hcch.net/index_en.php?act=text.display&tid=44.

litigation. Many of these publications are available on LexisNexis[42] and Westlaw,[43] or on paper in law school or law firm libraries.

- Major treatises on civil procedure, such as Charles Alan Wright et al., _Federal Practice & Procedure_ (1969–), have some discussion of transnational litigation issues (e.g., 4B Fed. Prac. & Proc. Civ. 3d § 1133, Service in a Foreign Country).

See also Radu D. Popa & Mirela Roznovschi, Update: Comparative Civil Procedure: A Guide to Primary and Secondary Sources,[44] for more information on both general works and specific jurisdictions.

To find additional materials, use the following Library of Congress subject headings:

> _civil procedure (international law)_
> _jurisdiction (international law) – cases_
> _judgments, foreign_
> _conflict of laws_
> _judicial assistance_
> _letters rogatory_
> _commercial treaties_
> _foreign law pleading and proof of – united states_
> _discovery (law)_
> _executions (law)_
> _foreign law (pleading and proof)_
> _jurisdiction (international law)_

2. _Discovery_

Discovery in transnational litigation presents its own set of problems. Generally, foreign jurisdictions have much less liberal discovery rules than does the United States. One source of rules for transnational discovery is the Hague Convention on the Taking of Evidence Abroad in Civil or Commercial Matters;[45] you will often start your research by finding out whether the foreign country in question has become a party to that treaty.

Once again, the State Department's Judicial Assistance webpage provides a useful starting point. The State Department circular _Obtaining Evidence Abroad_[46] offers an overview of the topic. You should also check the "Country

---

[42] Legal > Secondary Legal > CLE Materials > Combined ALI-ABA Course of Study Materials. Lexis does not have the PLI publications.

[43] PLI and ALI-ABA databases.

[44] http://www.nyulawglobal.org/Globalex/Comparative_Civil_Procedure1.htm.

[45] http://www.hcch.net/index_en.php?act=conventions.text&cid=82.

[46] http://travel.state.gov/law/judicial/judicial_2514.html.

Specific Information" page[47] to see whether the State Department has created a page specific to your country of interest. In addition, some countries, such as Australia, have created their own webpages providing information for foreign attorneys.[48] It is worth checking for such pages from whatever country you're researching.

For more in-depth research, check the secondary sources listed above (Section II.1.), Service of Process.

3. *Enforcement of Judgments*

Currently, no multilateral or bilateral treaty between the United States and other countries allows for the reciprocal enforcement of foreign judgments. Thus, you will have to look closely at the domestic law of the foreign state to determine the enforceability of a US judgment in that jurisdiction. The State Department's circular on *Enforcement of Judgments*[49] is once again a good starting point; also check for country-specific information.[50] *Martindale-Hubbell's International Law Digest* also addresses this topic for about 80 countries.

For more in-depth research, check the secondary sources listed above (Section II.1.) as well as the following:

- *Attachments of Assets* (Lawrence W. Newman ed., 1999–).
- *Enforcement of Money Judgments* (Lawrence W. Newman ed., 1988–).
- *International Execution against Judgment Debtors* (Dennis Campbell ed., 2011–).

In addition, Thomas H. Reynolds & Arturo A. Flores, *Foreign Law Guide*[51] identifies relevant legislation under the subject heading "Judgments (Including Foreign Judgments)."

---

[47] http://travel.state.gov/law/judicial/judicial_2510.html.
[48] https://www.ag.gov.au/www/agd/agd.nsf/Page/Internationalcivilprocedure_TakingofEvidenceinAustraliaforForeignCourtProceedings.
[49] http://travel.state.gov/law/judicial/judicial_691.html.
[50] http://travel.state.gov/law/judicial/judicial_2510.html.
[51] http://www.foreignlawguide.com.

Chapter Twenty-One

International Commercial Arbitration

I. *Introduction*

The widespread adoption of the New York Convention on the Recognition and Enforcement of Foreign Arbitral Awards (1958),[1] which limits the grounds upon which arbitral awards may be attacked, has made international arbitration a preferred option for many businesses and organizations.

International arbitration is usually controlled much more by contractual arrangement than by foreign legislation. Parties can specify the forum, rules, and governing law that will apply to any arbitration. If the parties designate an existing arbitral institution to handle any ensuing disputes, this is known as "institutional arbitration." If they set up rules for arbitration outside of an existing organization, this is referred to as *ad hoc* arbitration.

In addition to the distinction between institutional and *ad hoc* arbitration, transnational arbitration is often separated into disputes that involve a state as a party and those that do not. Organizations that handle disputes involving states include the Permanent Court of Arbitration,[2] the International Center for the Settlement of Investment Disputes (ICSID),[3] and the London Court of International Arbitration (LCIA).[4]

Some international organizations specialize in only one type of dispute. For example, WIPO's Arbitration and Mediation Center[5] handles intellectual property issues, with an overwhelming focus on domain name disputes. The Court of Arbitration for Sport[6] handles commercial and disciplinary matters related to sports. Others, like the London Court of International Arbitration

---

[1] http://www.uncitral.org/uncitral/uncitral_texts/arbitration/NYConvention.html.
[2] http://www.pca-cpa.org/showpage.asp?pag_id=363.
[3] http://icsid.worldbank.org/ICSID/Index.jsp.
[4] http://www.lcia.org.
[5] http://www.wipo.int/amc/en/index.html.
[6] http://www.tas-cas.org.

(LCIA), provide international arbitration services for any kind of international commercial dispute.

Another important institution in arbitration is the United Nations Commission on International Trade Law (UNCITRAL).[7] Although it does not handle arbitration disputes, it created a set of arbitration rules and a model law that have been widely adopted. Its website has useful resources for arbitration researchers, including reports, bibliographies, links to arbitral organizations, and a database of arbitration abstracts (CLOUT), discussed below.

For researchers, the most frustrating aspect of arbitration is that awards and proceedings are usually confidential. In contrast to the transparency of litigation, documents relating to arbitration are not routinely published electronically or in paper. Because some arbitration awards *do* get published, however, you can't assume these decisions are always unavailable. Unfortunately, researching this area of law can also be time-consuming and frustrating because there is no centralized source for obtaining all of the legal authorities needed.

Types of legal authority used in international commercial arbitration:[8]

- International treaties (both bilateral and multilateral)
  For example:
  ◦ Convention on the Recognition and Enforcement of Foreign Arbitral Awards ("New York Convention")
  ◦ Convention on the Settlement of Investment Disputes between States and Nationals of Other States ("ICSID Convention")
  ◦ Bilateral Investment Treaties (BITs)
- National laws
  For example:
  ◦ National arbitration statute in effect in the arbitral forum
  ◦ UNCITRAL Model Law on International Commercial Arbitration
  ◦ National case law (persuasive authority)
- Arbitral rules (international and regional arbitral institutions)
  For example:
  ◦ UNCITRAL Arbitration Rules
  ◦ Commercial Arbitration and Mediation Center for the Americas (CAMCA) Rules

---

[7] http://www.uncitral.org.
[8] Compiled from S.I. Strong, *Research in International Commercial Arbitration: Special Skills, Special Sources*, 29 AM. REV. INT'L ARB. 119 (2009), available at http://www.cisg.law.pace .edu/cisg/moot/Strong.pdf.

- Law of the dispute
  For example:
  - ° Arbitration agreement
  - ° Rules and orders of the arbitration tribunal
- Arbitral awards (no precedential value and are not binding; persuasive authority)
- Expert commentary (books and articles)

II. *Getting Started*

A. *Research Guides*

As with any topic, a research guide is a good place to begin your research. In fact, research guides are particularly useful places to start when you are new to this topic.

- Hernando Otero and Omar García-Bolívar, International Arbitration between Foreign Investors and Host States (2011).[9]
- Gloria Miccioli, ASIL Guide to Electronic Resources for International Law: International Commercial Arbitration.[10]
- Caroline Osborne, *Pathfinder on International Investment Law and Alternative Dispute Resolution Web Based Resources* (2010).[11]
- Stacie Strong, 'Research in International Commercial Arbitration: Special Skills, Special Sources,' 29 *Am. Rev. Int'l Arb.* 119 (2009).[12]
- *Stacie Strong, Research and Practice in International Commercial Arbitration: Sources and Strategies* (2009).
- Jean Wenger, Update to International Commercial Arbitration: Locating the Resources.[13] A bit dated but provides useful information on print sources.

III. *Treaties, Agreements, Model Laws & Rules*

The materials noted in this section will cover arbitration treaties and agreements as well as other documents, such as arbitration rules and model clauses.

---

[9] http://www.nyulawglobal.org/Globalex/International_Arbitration_Foreign_Investors_Host_States.htm.

[10] http://www.asil.org/arb1.cfm.

[11] http://papers.ssrn.com/sol3/papers.cfm?abstract_id=1625763.

[12] Also available at http://www.cisg.law.pace.edu/cisg/moot/Strong.pdf.

[13] http://www.llrx.com/features/arbitration2.htm.

Generally, treaties are easy to locate by using one of the sources below. If you know you want a specific treaty, like the Inter-American Convention on International Commercial Arbitration (Panama Convention), you can start by going to the OAS website or run a search on the web using the name of the convention. If you want to look at a collection of treaties, you can go to one of the sources noted below that aggregates documents, like the Lex Mercatoria website or *International Arbitration Treaties.*

The international, regional, and national arbitral institutions all have websites providing the arbitral rules (detailed information on procedures) as well as subject-specific guidelines, like the SCC Arbitrator's Guidelines. If you are looking for model arbitration clauses, you should also check the institution's website. While most of these sites are not listed in this section, you can simply search the name of the arbitral body using Google or another search engine.

A. *Web Collections*

- ICC Rules and Clauses.[14]
- ICSID Conventions, Regulations, Rules.[15]
  - ○ Official Documents and Model Clauses.[16]
  - ○ Bilateral Investment Treaties.[17]
- Investment Treaty Arbitration (treaties, model BITs, free trade agreements with investment protections).[18]
- International Council for Commercial Arbitration (conventions and rules).[19]
- Juris International (conventions and rules).[20]
- Kluwer Arbitration (BITs, conventions, rules).[21]
- Lex Mercatoria (a large collection of treaties and rules).[22]

---

[14] http://www.iccwbo.org/court/arbitration/id4424/index.html.

[15] http://icsid.worldbank.org/ICSID/ICSID/RulesMain.jsp.

[16] http://icsid.worldbank.org/ICSID.
FrontServlet?requestType=CasesRH&actionVal=ShowHome&pageName=Documents_
Home.

[17] http://icsid.worldbank.org/ICSID/FrontServlet (see "Bilateral Investment Treaties" in Quick Locators box).

[18] http://italaw.com/investmenttreaties.htm.

[19] http://www.arbitration-icca.org/related-links.html.

[20] http://www.jurisint.org.

[21] http://www.kluwerarbitration.com.

[22] http://www.jus.uio.no/lm/arbitration/toc.html.

- Permanent Court of Arbitration, Basic Documents (conventions, rules, model clauses).[23]
- UNCITRAL Texts and Status (including the New York Convention, UNCITRAL rules, and model laws).[24]
- UNCTAD
  - Investment Instruments Online, International Investment Instruments: A Compendium.[25]
  - Bilateral Investment Treaties.[26]
- U.S., Trade Compliance Center, Bilateral Investment Treaties (US and other countries).[27]

B. *Print Resources*

- *Arbitration Rules—International Institutions: Guides to International Arbitration* (3d ed., Loukas Mistelis et al. eds., 2010–). Contains institutional rules and commentary.
- *Arbitration Rules—National Institutions: Guides to International Arbitration* (2d ed., Loukas Mistelis et al. eds., 2010–). Provides the text of more than 50 national arbitration institution's rules, as well as background information, model clause, and other information.
- *International Arbitration Treaties* (3d ed., Loukas Mistelis et al. eds., 2010–). Contains major multilateral treaties, treaties with arbitration dispute settlement mechanisms, and some bilateral investment treaties.
- *Investment Promotion and Protection Treaties* (International Centre for the Settlement of Investment Disputes, comp., 1983–). Covers bilateral investment treaties for over 130 countries.
- *World Arbitration Reporter: International Encyclopaedia of Arbitration Law and Practice* (2d ed., Loukas Mistelis et al. eds., 2010–). Detailed commentary and analysis, rules of procedure, treaties and agreements.

IV. *National Law*

You will need the international commercial arbitration statute in effect in the arbitral forum, as well as any cases interpreting the statute. Many national

---

[23] http://www.pca-cpa.org/showpage.asp?pag_id=1067.
[24] http://www.uncitral.org/uncitral/en/uncitral_texts.html.
[25] http://www.unctadxi.org/templates/DocSearch____780.aspx. Also available in print.
[26] http://www.unctad.org/Templates/Page.asp?intItemID=2344&lang=1.
[27] http://tcc.export.gov/Trade_Agreements/Bilateral_Investment_Treaties/index.asp.

arbitration statutes are based on the UNCITRAL Model Law. The websites, databases and print sources help identify relevant national laws and, in some cases, provide access to the text of the laws.

A handy way to locate national arbitration statutes is to use the ASIL Guide to Electronic Resources for International Law: International Commercial Arbitration (noted above in section II.A.), which provides links to many of these laws. For example, if you want Argentina's domestic legislation, there is a link on the ASIL Guide. However, it links to a source in Spanish only. If you want to locate an English translation or verify that this is the correct law, check Foreign Law Guide. The entry for Argentina notes the dates of the laws, the relevant sections of the Commercial and Civil Procedure codes, and also identifies the print sources for the English translations (there are three, all of which are noted below: *International Handbook on Commercial Arbitration, World Arbitration Reporter*, and *National Arbitration Laws*).

For more assistance locating national legislation, see Chapter 8.

- *Foreign Law Guide*[28] (See subject heading "arbitration, domestic and international (civil)").
- International Council for Commercial Arbitration, *National Arbitration Laws.*[29]
- *International Commercial Arbitration* (2d. enl. ed., Eric E. Bergsten ed., 1979–). Provides national laws for 112 jurisdictions.
- *International Handbook on Commercial Arbitration* (Jan Paulsson ed., 1984–). Each national report provides commentary and the full text of some national laws.
- *Investment Laws of the World* (1972–). Contains investments laws and regulations for more than 150 countries.
- Kluwer Arbitration.[30]
- *National Arbitration Laws* (2d ed., Loukas Mistelis et al. eds., 2010–). Each national report covers information on arbitration for the countries covered with citations to and excerpts of national laws.
- *World Arbitration Reporter: International Encyclopaedia of Arbitration Law and Practice* (2010–). The national reports contain detailed commentary and analysis on legislation from more than 100 countries.

---

[28] http://www.foreignlawguide.com.
[29] http://www.arbitration-icca.org/related-links.html#03.
[30] http://www.kluwerarbitration.com.

V. *Awards and Decisions*

While there are a variety of print and electronic sources for awards, not all awards are published due to confidentiality issues. To complicate matters even further, there is no one source for locating all awards and decisions.

If you have a citation, go to the source for the citation. Or, if you know the arbitral body, you can try the body's website or a collection of awards. For example, M.C.I. Power Group L.C. et al. v. Ecuador, ICSID Case No. ARB/03/6, Decision on Annulment (Oct. 19, 2009). Since this is an ICSID case, start with the ICSID website. Using the advanced search engine in the section called "Search ICSID Cases," you can search by claimant, respondent, or case number; the above citation provides all of the necessary pieces of information for the advanced search.

If you don't have a citation, use the databases below to search by name of the award. If you know the name of the arbitral body (UNCITRAL, NAFTA, etc.), try searching the websites of these bodies. Several of the websites listed below are pretty good when you don't have a citation; try searching Kluwer Arbitration, Investment Treaty Arbitration, and TransLex. Also try searching full-text journal articles on Lexis or Westlaw to see if someone else cited the case and provides a useable citation or source. If you have the following citation: S.D. Myers, Inc. v. Canada, Partial Award on the Merits (NAFTA Ch. 11 Arb. Trib. Nov. 13, 2000), you should start with a site that provides access to NAFTA Chapter 11 arbitration decisions, like NAFTA Claims. This site doesn't have a search engine, but it's easy to locate cases since there are only three countries involved in the disputes (Canada, Mexico, and the United States). In contrast, if you have this citation: Himpurna California Energy Ltd. v. PT. (Persero) Persusahaan Listruik Negara (Indonesia), Final Award (May 4, 1999), you should start with one of the databases or websites that allow for searching by claimant or defendant.

- CISG Database (large collection of national cases and arbitral awards related to CISG).[31]
- ICC DRL (Dispute Resolution Library) (a subscription database containing summaries of cases, with citations to sources, from ICC arbitral awards).[32]

---

[31] http://www.cisg.law.pace.edu/cisg/text/caseschedule.html.
[32] http://www.iccdrl.com.

- ICSID Cases (browse the list or search the publically available cases and awards; if the text is not available, there is a citation to the source).[33]
- International Arbitration Case Law (IACL) (a small collection of summaries from arbitral tribunals, international tribunals and national courts in matters of international arbitration).[34]
- Investment Claims (fully searchable collection of publically available awards and decisions from international investment arbitrations, and related enforcement or review decisions from national courts; subscription database).[35]
- Investment Treaty Arbitration (a large collection of full-text awards that can be located chronologically, alphabetically by claimant or respondent, and there is a search engine).[36]
- Investor-State LawGuide (good for NAFTA and ICSID cases as well as ad hoc tribunal decisions; subscription database).[37]
- JURIS International Arbitration (a large but rather hit-or-miss collection of information on commercial arbitration, mediation, conciliation, alternative dispute resolution centers or services, including some rules and model clauses; subscription database).[38]
- KluwerArbitration (searchable collection of New York Convention decisions from national courts and awards; subscription database).[39]
- NAFTAClaims (documents and decisions related to NAFTA investor-state dispute settlement).[40]
- Permanent Court of Arbitration (PCA) (contains pending and past cases).[41]
- TradeLawGuide (WTO jurisprudence; subscription database).[42]
- Trans-Lex (search or browse by the Trans-Lex Principles; links to arbitral awards but these may not be the entire award).[43]

---

[33] http://icsid.worldbank.org/ICSID/FrontServlet?requestType=CasesRH&actionVal=ShowHome&pageName=Cases_Home.

[34] http://www.internationalarbitrationcaselaw.com.

[35] http://investmentclaims.com.

[36] http://italaw.com.

[37] http://www.investorstatelawguide.com.

[38] http://www.jurispub.com/cart.php?m=content&page=12.

[39] http://www.kluwerarbitration.com.

[40] http://www.naftaclaims.com.

[41] http://www.pca-cpa.org/showpage.asp?pag_id=1029.

[42] http://www.tradelawguide.com.

[43] http://trans-lex.org.

- UNCITRAL, CLOUT (Case Law on UNICTRAL Texts) (provides summaries of court decisions and arbitral awards involving the UNCITRAL Model Law, with citations or links to full-text sources, if available).[44]
- UNCTAD Database of Treaty-Based Investor-State Dispute Settlement Cases (browse list or use the filter to search).[45]
- UNILEX on CISG & UNIDROIT Principles: International Case Law & Bibliography (cases on the CISG and UNIDROIT Principles of International Commercial Contracts; search by country, date, instrument article, or issue).[46]
- Worldtradelaw.net (great source for commentaries on WTO panel reports and arbitrations).[47]

Several of the tools noted above (CISG database, CLOUT, UNILEX), report on cases involving the United Nations Convention on the International Sale of Goods (CISG). The UNCITRAL Digest of Case Law on the United Nations Convention on the International Sale of Goods (CISG)[48] is one of the better tools for researching international commercial arbitration issues. Most disputes involving the sale of goods under the CISG involve Article 35, non-conformity of goods.

Example: Suppose you are researching whether a company is liable for shipping food packed for resale in containers that lack adequate labeling under the destination country's regulations. The contract requires the food to be shipped "ready for resale." The buyer claims the goods are non-conforming.

You can pull up the entire UNCITRAL Digest of Case Law and use the table of contents to navigate to the section on Article 35, or use the control-F "find" function to look for the term *label*. In its treatment of Article 35, the Digest refers to several cases involving non-conforming packaging. One of the cases deals with non-compliance with food labeling requirements. The Digest, in the footnote to this case reference, indicates that the case

---

[44] http://www.uncitral.org/uncitral/en/case_law.html. See also Index to 'CLOUT' case abstracts which relate to Model Arbitration Law (MAL) cases, http://interarb.com/clout (updated October 2003).

[45] http://www.unctad.org/iia-dbcases/index.html.

[46] http://www.unilex.info. Also available in print, *UNILEX: International Case Law & Bibliography on the UN Convention on Contracts for the International Sale of Goods* (1996–, not updated since 2008).

[47] http://www.worldtradelaw.net.

[48] http://www.uncitral.org/pdf/english/clout/08-51939_Ebook.pdf.

is "CLOUT case No. 202 [Cour d'appel, Grenoble, France, 13 September 1995]."

Using the CLOUT case search page,[49] you enter "202" in the box for "Case number," and retrieve the CLOUT entry for the case, which includes a link to the abstract and the full text, and also gives a citation to two published commentaries on the decision.

Since the UNCITRAL Digest was last updated in 2008, you can use the CISG Database, Cases on the CISG, to update your research. You can search the database by article or keyword or browse the list of cases by organized by CISG article. If you use the list of cases, you can then use the control-F "find" function to search for cases involving *packaging* and focus on those cases issued after 2008. Most of the cases have a notation indicating the goods involved; for example Switzerland 27 November 2008 Kantonsgericht [District Court] Zug (Packaging foils case).

Many libraries and law firms subscribe to the Kluwer Arbitration database. As noted above, this resource contains BITs, treaties, statutes, awards and decisions, and commentary (books and articles). There are some nice features on the Kluwer database. By going to the "jurisdiction" category, you can select a specific country. If you select Argentina, for example, you will be able to get the arbitration rules, many of the BITs, commentary, awards, legislation, model clauses, and relevant conventions. If you want all of the awards issued related to a specific article of the NY Convention, go to the "NY Convention Decisions" section of the site and click on the article and get a list of the awards. If you only have the name of a party in an award or decision, for example, Société Van Hopplynus, search using the "advanced search" page and put the name into the "party" field and tick the boxes for awards and decisions in the "text type" field. This search yields two court decisions—one is the English translation of excerpts from the decision, which was published in the *Yearbook, Commercial Arbitration*, and the other is the French version of the decision from *Revue de l'Arbitrage*.

LexisNexis and Westlaw (not WestlawNext) provide some international arbitration decisions and awards. On LexisNexis, go to Legal > Area of Law— By Topic > International Arbitration. From here, you can access *Mealey's Litigation Report*. On Westlaw, follow this path: All Databases > Topical Materials by Area of Practice > Alternative Dispute Resolution > Case Law.

Here is a list of the most prominent print publications. It's impossible to provide a comprehensive list of these sources. To locate the print version of some of the awards, try subject searching:

---

49 http://www.cnudmi.org/clout/showSearchDocument.do.

arbitration and award, international – periodicals
arbitration and award, international – cases

- *ASA Bulletin* (1983–).[50]
- *Collection of ICC Arbitral Awards* (covers 1974–2007) (1990–).
- *ICC International Court of Arbitration Bulletin* (1990–).
- *ICSID Reports* (1993–).
- *International Arbitration Court Decisions* (3d ed., Stephen Bond and Frédéric Bachand eds., 2011).
- *Iran-United States Claims Tribunal Reports* (1983–).[51]
- *Journal de Droit International* (1915–).
- *Lloyd's Arbitration Reports* (1988–).
- *Mealey's International Arbitration Report* (1986–).[52]
- *Reports of International Arbitral Awards* (1948–).[53]
- *Stockholm International Arbitration Review* (previous title *Stockholm Arbitration Report*) (2005–).
- *SCC Arbitral Awards, 2004–2009* (2011).
- *World Arbitration Reporter: International Encyclopaedia of Arbitration Law and Practice* (2d ed., Loukas Mistelis et al. eds., 2010–).
- *World Trade and Arbitration Materials* (1989–).[54]
- *Yearbook, Commercial Arbitration* (1976–).[55]

VI. *Commentary*

There are many books on various aspects of arbitration, such as practice and procedure, materials that focus on arbitration in a specific region, or books on specialized topics such as arbitration clauses for international contracts. The relevant subject headings are:

arbitration and award, international
arbitration and award – [name of country or region]
contracts (international law)

---

[50] Available on KluwerArbitration and HeinOnline.
[51] See also, Iran-United States Claims Tribunal, http://www.iusct.org and the Iran-United States Claims Tribunal, IUSCT Public Database, http://www.iusct.com (must register for access). Also available on Westlaw.
[52] Available on LexisNexis.
[53] Available at http://www.un.org/law/riaa and on HeinOnline.
[54] Available on HeinOnline.
[55] Also available on KluwerArbitration.

- *Arbitration Procedures in Asia* (Ben Beaumont ed. 1999–).
- Nigel Blackaby et al., *Redfern and Hunter on International Arbitration* (5th ed. 2009).[56]
- Gary Born, *International Commercial Arbitration* (2009).[57]
- Gary Born, *International Arbitration and Forum Selection Agreements: Drafting and Enforcing* (3d ed. 2010).
- Michael Bühler & Thomas H. Webster, *Handbook of ICC Arbitration: Commentary, Precedents, Materials* (2d ed. 2008).[58]
- *Fouchard, Gaillard, Goldman on International Commercial Arbitration* (Philippe Fouchard et al. eds., 1999).
- Paul D. Friedland, *Arbitration Clauses for International Contracts* (2d ed. 2007).
- *Enforcement of Arbitration Agreements and International Arbitral Awards: The New York Convention in Practice* (Emmanuel Gaillard et al., eds., 2008).
- *Handbook on International Arbitration and ADR* (Thomas E. Carbonneau et al., eds., 2006).
- *International Handbook on Commercial Arbitration* (Jan Paulsson ed., 1984–).
- John J. Kerr, *Comparison of International Arbitration Rules* (3d ed. 2008).
- Herbert Kronke, *Recognition and Enforcement of Foreign Arbitral Award: A Global Commentary on the New York Convention* (2010).
- Julian D.M. Lew et al., *Comparative International Commercial Arbitration* (2003).
- Vesna Lazic, *Insolvency Proceedings and Commercial Arbitration* (1998).
- Campbell McLachlan et al., *International Investment Arbitration: Substantive Principles* (2007).
- *World Arbitration Reporter: International Encyclopaedia of Arbitration Law and Practice* (2d ed. Loukas A. Mistelis et al., 2010).
- William W. Park, *Arbitration of International Business Disputes* (2006).
- Thomas Webster, *Handbook of UNCITRAL Arbitration: Commentary, Precedents & Models for UNCITRAL Based Arbitration Rules* (2010).

Journal literature is a valuable source for commentary as well as information about new awards, citations to laws and cases, and practice-oriented

---

[56] Also available on Kluwer Arbitration.
[57] Also available on Kluwer Arbitration.
[58] Also available on Westlaw.

information. There are specialized arbitration and dispute resolution journals, arbitration yearbooks, and regional arbitration journals. Many of these sources are indexed in the legal journal indexes reviewed in Chapter 5 of this book. These periodicals can also be located in an online catalog using the following subject headings:

> arbitration and award, international – periodicals.
> dispute resolution (law) – periodicals.
> mediation, international – periodicals.
> arbitration agreements, commercial – periodicals.

For example, if you are interested in doing a review of arbitration seats in Asia, and Singapore in particular, you can search an online catalog or the journal indexes using keywords (*international & commercial & arbitration & Singapore or Asia*—or some variation). By doing these searches, you may locate these sources: Simon Greenberg et al., *International Commercial Arbitration: An Asia-Pacific Perspective* (2011); Gordon Smith & Andrew Cook, 'International Commercial Arbitration in Asia-Pacific: A Comparison of the Australian and Singapore Systems,' 77 *Arb.* 108 (2011); and Chong Yee Leong & Qin Zhiqian, 'Comparative Arbitration Law in Asia,' 6 *Global Arb. Rev.* 5 (2011).

Of course, if you don't have access to these articles and books, you may want to try some freely available collections of international arbitration articles. A keyword search on Google retrieves some potentially useful materials; such as Michael Hwang, *Why is There Still Resistance to Arbitration in Asia?*, a lecture delivered at The International Arbitration Club, Table Talk (Autumn 2007)[59] as well as several Singapore Law Reform Publications on arbitration.[60] A couple of major differences between the materials located using Google and those located using catalogs and indexes are the currency of the materials and the depth of the analysis.

VII. *Other Resources*

Because international arbitration is a big business, there are other resources that are useful to the researcher.

---

[59] http://www.arbitration-icca.org/articles.html.
[60] http://www.agc.gov.sg/publications/Law_Reform_Publications_by_subject.htm#arbitration.

- Digest of International Investment Jurisprudence.[61]
- Digest of Investment Treaty Awards and Decisions (this Digest annotates publicly available final decisions rendered on or before July 30, 2008 in investor-State arbitrations conducted pursuant to investment treaties).[62]
- Investment Arbitration Reporter (IA Reporter, a subscription database, is a news and analysis service focusing on investor-state arbitrations, including some confidential information—a very good current awareness tool).[63]
- Kluwer Arbitration Blog (the blog contributors include well-known professors and practitioners—you don't need to subscribe to the database to access the blog).[64]
- Transnational Dispute Management (TDM) (contains commentary as well as selected national laws, decisions and awards; subscription database).[65]

---

[61] http://www.investment-law-digest.com/default.aspx.
[62] http://www.arbitration-icca.org/media/0/12404936822530/investment_treaty_decisions_consolidated_2006_2008_as.pdf.
[63] http://www.iareporter.com.
[64] http://kluwerarbitrationblog.com.
[65] http://www.transnational-dispute-management.com/welcome.asp.

Chapter Twenty-Two

International Courts and Tribunals

I. *Introduction*

Over the past twenty years or so, international courts and tribunals have proliferated. Many of these courts have been established by treaties and UN resolutions. (Sometimes these treaties are called statutes; e.g., the Rome Statute of the International Criminal Court.) The founding treaties describe the courts' jurisdiction, authorize the promulgation of rules of procedure and evidence, and set other ground rules, such as the type of relief that the courts can provide. Thus, they are an important source of law. However, you may find that a secondary source explains the courts' powers and procedures more clearly than the treaty language, and therefore provides a better starting point for research. Several useful sources are listed in the next section ("Practice and Procedure"). The entries in the *Max Planck Encyclopedia of Public International Law*[1] are also useful for giving overviews of various courts and tribunals.

II. *Researching Decisions*

Decisions of the international courts are generally accessible on the courts' own websites. Some, like decisions of WTO and NAFTA panels, or ICJ decisions, are also available from several commercial sources. More information on specific courts is available from other chapters in this book; check the index or Table of Contents.

---

[1] Subscription database, http://www.mpepil.com. Also available in print, but the print has not yet been updated.

A. *Digests*

There are print and online digests available for a few of the international courts, but not all. For example, there are digests of International Court of Justice opinions, including the free online World Court Digest.[2] Another excellent source is Shabtai Rosenne, *The Law and Practice of the International Court, 1920–2005* (2006).

For the ICC, there is *The Annotated Digest of the International Criminal Court* (2007–). See also Karin N. Calvo-Goller, *The Trial Proceedings of the International Criminal Court: ICTY and ICTR Precedents* (2006).

The WTO Analytical Index: Guide to WTO Law and Practice (2007) functions as a digest of WTO caselaw, as do the topical indexes in the World TradeLaw.net and TradeLawGuide databases.

B. *Citators*

Generally, no citators exist for international court decisions.[3] This lack of citators reflects, in part, the practice of such courts in not requiring adherence to precedent. Nonetheless, you may want to check whether a decision has been cited by another court. Lacking a citator, your best bet is to run the name of the case, or other information commonly used in its citation, as a terms and connectors search in a database of the courts' decisions.[4]

For example, perhaps you want to learn if the ICTY's Tadic Decision on the Prosecution's Motion Requesting Protective Measures for Victims and Witnesses has been cited by the ICTY since it was decided in 1995. Searching Westlaw's INT-ICTY database for *tadic /s "motion requesting protective measures"* retrieves 25 documents. While this method is less reliable than using citators due to variation in the ways courts refer to judgments, it will usually retrieve most of the relevant documents. Experiment with searching alternative terms (e.g., case name and then document number) to ensure the widest retrieval.

III. *Practice and Procedure*

Many of these courts have specific rules, codes of conduct, practice directions and other procedures and these documents are often available on the court or tribunal's website. For example, perhaps you need to file a request for interim measures under Rule 39 of the European Court of Human Rights.

---

[2] http://www.mpil.de/ww/en/pub/research/details/publications/institute/wcd.cfm.
[3] The WTO jurisprudence citator offered by TradeLawGuide.com, by subscription, is a rare exception.
[4] This maneuver is sometimes referred to as the "poor man's citator."

If you start with the court's website, select "applicants" and then "interim measures" you will see a section on practical information indicating the information needed in the application and practice directions.[5]

The following section lists various works about international courts and tribunals. You can find other items in your library by using the name of the court as a subject or title search. Some works focus on a specific procedure or remedy; for example, Constantine Antonopoulos, *Counterclaims before the International Court of Justice* (2011). You may want to include such terms (e.g., *counterclaim? international court justice*) in your catalog search, particularly if your law library has a large international law collection.

Other useful subject headings, in addition to the names of the courts, include

> *international criminal courts*
> *international criminal courts – rules and practice*
> *jurisdiction (international law)*
> *pacific settlement of international disputes*
> *international courts*
> *rome statute of the international criminal court (1998)*

Don't forget journal literature as a source for more information on practice and procedure in international courts and tribunals. One journal in particular is worth mentioning—*The Law and Practice of International Courts and Tribunals* (2002–).[6] Each issue contains a section on procedural developments in a particular international court or tribunal. Other topics include dealing with witnesses, evidence, preliminary ruling procedures, and more.

A. *Multiple Courts/Tribunals*

- Ruth Mackenzie et al., *Manual on International Courts and Tribunals* (2010).
- Vladimir Tochilovsky, *Jurisprudence of the International Criminal Courts and the European Court of Human Rights: Procedure and Evidence* (2008).
- J.G. Merrills, *International Dispute Settlement* (5th ed. 2011).

B. *International Court of Justice*

- D.W. Bowett, *The International Court of Justice: Process, Practice and Procedure* (1997).

---

[5] http://www.echr.coe.int/ECHR/EN/Header/Applicants/Interim+measures/Practical +information.
[6] Also available on the publisher's website and HeinOnline.

- Sir Gerald Fitzmaurice, *The Law and Procedure of the International Court of Justice* (1986).
- Anna Riddell & Brendan Plant, *Evidence before the International Court of Justice* (2009).
- Shabtai Rosenne, *The Law and Practice of the International Court, 1920–2005* (2006).
- Shabtai Rosenne, *Procedure in the International Court: A Commentary on the 1978 Rules of the International Court of Justice* (1983).

C. *European Court of Justice*

- Morten Broberg & Niels Fenger, *Preliminary References to the European Court of Justice* (2010).
- Noreen Burrows & Rosa Greaves, *The Advocate General and EC Law* (2007).
- *Administrative Law of the European Union: Judicial Review* (Ronald M. Levin et al. eds., 2008).

D. *European Court of Human Rights*

- *European Court of Human Rights: Remedies and Execution of Judgments* (Theodora A. Christou & Juan Pablo Raymond eds., 2005).
- Philip Leach, *Taking a Case to the European Court of Human Rights* (3d ed. 2011).
- *Theory and Practice of the European Convention on Human Rights* (4th ed. P. van Dijk et al. eds., 2006).

E. *Inter-American Court of Human Rights*

- Laurence Burgorgue-Larsen and Amaya Úbeda de Torres, *The Inter-American Court of Human Rights: Case Law and Commentary* (2011).
- Clara Burbano Herrera, *Provisional Measures in the Case Law of the Inter-American Court of Human Rights* (2010).
- Jo M. Pasqualucci, *The Practice and Procedure of the Inter-American Court of Human Rights* (2003).

F. *International Criminal Courts Generally*

- Basic Documents and Jurisprudence of International/ized Criminal Courts and Tribunals (American University, Washington College of Law).[7] Contains some of the rules, practice directions, etc. for various international criminal courts and tribunals: Cambodia, ICJ, ICC, ICTR, ICTY,

---

[7] https://www.wcl.american.edu/warcrimes/wcro_docs/index.cfm.

Nuremberg and Far East Tribunals, Sierra Leone, and State Court of Bosnia and Herzegovina; subscription database.

- *International Criminal Justice: Law and Practice from the Rome Statute to Its Review* (Roberto Bellelli ed., 2010).
- John R.W.D. Jones & Steven Powles, *International Criminal Practice: The International Criminal Tribunal for the Former Yugoslavia, the International Criminal Tribunal for Rwanda, the International Criminal Court, the Special Court for Sierra Leone, the East Timor Special Panel for Serious Crimes, War Crimes Prosecutions in Kosovo* (3d ed. 2003).
- Karim A.A. Khan et al., *Archbold: International Criminal Courts Practice, Procedure and Evidence* (3rd ed. 2009).
- Christine Schuon, *International Criminal Procedure: A Clash of Legal Cultures* (2010).
- Vladimir Tochilovsky, *Jurisprudence of the International Criminal Courts and the European Court of Human Rights: Procedure and Evidence* (2008).
- Note that the War Crimes Research Office, American University Washington College of Law, has published a series of papers dealing with issues from several courts, and these are available for free online.[8] See, for example, *The Confirmation of Charges Process at the International Criminal Court* (2008).[9]

G. International Criminal Court

- *The Emerging Practice of the International Criminal Court* (Carsten Stahn & Goran Sluiter eds., 2009).
- Georghios M. Pikis, *The Rome Statute for the International Criminal Court: Analysis of the Statute, the Rules of Procedure and Evidence, the Regulations of the Court and Supplementary Instruments* (2010).

H. ICTY and ICTR

- John Ackerman, *Practice and Procedure of the International Criminal Tribunal for the Former Yugoslavia: With Selected Materials from the International Criminal Tribunal for Rwanda* (2000).

---

[8] http://www.wcl.american.edu/warcrimes.

[9] http://www.wcl.american.edu/warcrimes/icc/documents/WCROReportonConfirmation-ofCharges.pdf?rd=1.

I. *International Tribunal for the Law of the Sea*

- *The Rules of the International Tribunal for the Law of the Sea: A Commentary* (P. Chandrasekhara Rao & Ph. Gautier eds., 2006).

J. *WTO*

- Michelle T. Grando, *Evidence, Proof, and Fact-Finding in WTO Dispute Settlement* (2009).
- Mitsuo Matsushita, et al., *The World Trade Organization: Law, Practice, and Policy* (2d ed. 2006) (a useful section on "Dispute Settlement" begins on p. 103).
- David Palmeter & Petros C. Mavroidis, *Dispute Settlement in the World Trade Organization: Practice and Procedure* (2d ed. 2004).
- WTO, *A Handbook on the WTO Dispute Settlement System* (2004).
- Peter Gallagher, *Guide to Dispute Settlement* (2002) (though it's not apparent from the title, this work covers the WTO dispute settlement process).

K. *NAFTA*

- Ralph H. Folsom et al., *Handbook of NAFTA Dispute Settlement* (1998–2000).

IV. *Parties' Submissions*

Researchers are sometimes interested in seeing the parties' filings before various international courts and tribunals. In many cases, these filings are confidential and will not be available during (and sometimes after) the proceedings. The following section provides information on the availability of parties' submissions. Keep in mind that you can always try contacting the parties themselves; in some cases, they may be permitted and willing to share the documents.

A. *International Court of Justice*

The pleadings are confidential until final judgment. Parties may choose to make their pleadings public. For example, Australia has made public its Application against Japan in the whaling case before the ICJ.

Pleadings, Oral Arguments, Documents

Volumes in this series are published after the termination of each case and contain the documentation relating to the case in the original language, i.e. English or French. This comprises the document instituting proceedings, the written pleadings and (selected) annexes, the verbatim record of the oral proceedings, any documents submitted to the Court after the closure of the written proceedings, and selected correspondence.

You can usually find the pleadings on the ICJ website after the judgment, including transcripts of oral proceedings. For example, in the matter of the Arrest Warrant of 11 April 2000 (Democratic Republic of the Congo v. Belgium), oral arguments and proceedings are available in .pdf from the website.[10]

B. *African Court on Human and Peoples' Rights/African Court of Justice and Human Rights*

No information available. The Court does not have the resources to respond to requests, even if it would allow visitors to view filings.

C. *African Commission on Human and Peoples' Rights*

No information available. The Commission does not have the resources to respond to requests, even if it would allow visitors to view filings.

D. *European Court of Human Rights*

The ECHR no longer publishes briefs, but will send them upon request. Initial petitions may not be available (some are confidential).

E. *Inter-American Court of Human Rights*

The Court makes a number of parties' filings available in the virtual folders of cases on its website. See Files under the Jurisprudence link.

F. *Inter-American Commission on Human Rights*

The parties' submissions are not disclosed by the IACHR, even after the final report is published, as they are part of a confidential file. The only public part is what appears summarized or quoted in the approved IACHR report.

However, each party is free to publish its own submissions, but not the other party's. Parties may sometimes choose to make their submissions available online, see, e.g., Gonzalez [Lenahan] v. United States.[11]

---

[10] http://www.icj-cij.org/docket/index.php?p1=3&p2=3&k=36&case=121&code=cobe&p3=2.
[11] http://www.law.columbia.edu/center_program/human_rights/InterAmer/GonzalesvUS/ CaseDocs.

G. *European Court of Justice*

The ECJ ruled in September 2010 that pleadings filed by the European Commission will be confidential until after the Court issues its final decision in a matter.

Parties' submissions to the ECJ are treated as confidential and are not made available to persons or bodies who are not parties to the case. This is so even after judgment has been handed down.

The European Commission, if a specific request is made, sometimes makes available the submissions it has lodged, provided that the judgment has been handed down.

H. *International Criminal Court*

Warrants of arrests are unavailable until they are unsealed, at which point they are available from the ICC website.

No additional filings are available through the court.

I. *International Criminal Tribunal for the former Yugoslavia*

Indictments are usually released before trial proceedings begin, and if so, will be available at the ICTY website.

J. *International Criminal Tribunal for Rwanda*

Indictments are usually released before trial proceedings begin, and if so, will be available under the "Cases" link on the ICTR website.

K. *World Trade Organization (panels and Appellate Body)*

Countries need not disclose their own submissions but may choose to do so. WTO will not provide them. The best source is WorldTradeLaw.net. US submissions are usually on the Office of the Trade Representative, under the Pending WTO Disputes section of the website.

L. *NAFTA*

The website has only orders.

The most comprehensive collection of documents is at the NAFTA Claims website.

M. *International Tribunal for the Law of the Sea*

Copies of special agreements and written applications submitting disputes to the Tribunal, as well as written pleadings in cases before the Tribunal, may be obtained from the Press Office:

Press Office
International Tribunal for the Law of the Sea
Am Internationalen Seegerichtshof 1
22609 Hamburg
Germany
Tel.: (49) 40 35607–227
Fax: (49) 40 35607–245
press@itlos.org

V. *Research Guides*

Many of the courts mentioned in this chapter are covered in the other topical chapters in Part VI of this book, so you may want to consult those chapters for more help with researching courts and tribunals.

- Germain's International Court of Justice Research Guide (Cornell Law Library).[12]
- International Court of Justice Research Guide (UC Hastings Law Library).[13]
- International Courts and Tribunals (Harvard Law Library).[14]
- UN Documentation: Research Guide—International Law: Courts and Tribunals.[15]
- Amy Burchfield, Update: International Criminal Courts for the Former Yugoslavia, Rwanda and Sierra Leone: A Guide to Online and Print Resources.[16]

---

[12] http://library.lawschool.cornell.edu/WhatWeDo/ResearchGuides/ICJ.cfm#bib.
[13] http://library.uchastings.edu/library/foreign-and-international-research/icj.html.
[14] http://libguides.law.harvard.edu/intlcourtstribunals.
[15] http://www.un.org/depts/dhl/resguide/specil.htm#trib.
[16] http://www.nyulawglobal.org/Globalex/International_Criminal_Courts1.htm.

VI. *Other Resources*

- International Courts Data.[17] Site provides access to datasets and includes data on compliance, judicial dissents, biographical information on judges, case-law citations, background information on judgments, sentencing by criminal courts, reservations made by states to the jurisdiction of courts, and more. Covers the following: ECHR, ECJ, GATT/WTO, ICJ, criminal tribunals, Andean Tribunal, IACHR, and arbitration.
- International Courts & Tribunals Collection (WORLDLII). Provides the ability to search for cases across courts and tribunals.[18] Coverage varies for each court and tribunal included.
- Gender Jurisprudence and International Criminal Law Project (American University, War Crimes Office and Women and International Law Program),[19] contain judgments, decisions, orders, and other documents issued by any of these twelve international/ized courts and tribunals contained in the WCRO Jurisprudence Collections (see above).
- Oxford Reports on International Law.[20] A subscription database of decisions on public international law from international law courts, domestic courts, and ad hoc tribunals.

---

[17] http://www9.georgetown.edu/faculty/ev42/ICdata.htm.
[18] http://www.worldlii.org/int/cases.
[19] http://www.wcl.american.edu/gender/wilp/gicl.
[20] http://www.oxfordlawreports.com.

Appendix

This is a cumulative bibliography of all of the sources cited in all chapters and includes information on print sources, subscription databases, and freely available websites. All sources are arranged alphabetically by author or title of the resource. Where possible, the abbreviation or acronym of a source is provided in [brackets] following the title. As with any printed list, website locations are bound to change or disappear. *Note: All LexisNexis and Westlaw references are to the regular versions of these databases and not to Lexis Advance or WestlawNext.*

Abbreviations of Legal Publications (Monash University), http://www.lib.monash.edu.au/legal-abbreviations.

ABGHARI, ADINEH, INTRODUCTION TO THE IRANIAN LEGAL SYSTEM AND THE PROTECTION OF HUMAN RIGHTS IN IRAN (London: British Institute of International and Comparative Law, 2008).

Access to Legislation in Europe: Guide to the Legal Gazettes and Other Information Sources in the European Union and the European Free Trade Association, http://circa.europa.eu/irc/opoce/ojf/info/data/prod/data/pdf/AccessToLegislationInEuropeGUIDE2009.pdf.

AccessUN, subscription database, http://infoweb.newsbank.com.

ACCIDENTAL TOURIST ON THE NEW FRONTIER: AN INTRODUCTORY GUIDE TO GLOBAL LEGAL RESEARCH (Jeanne Rehberg & Radu D. Popa eds., Littleton, CO: F.B. Rothman, 1998).

ACKERMAN, JOHN, PRACTICE AND PROCEDURE OF THE INTERNATIONAL CRIMINAL TRIBUNAL FOR THE FORMER YUGOSLAVIA: WITH SELECTED MATERIALS FROM THE INTERNATIONAL CRIMINAL TRIBUNAL FOR RWANDA (The Hague; Boston: Kluwer Law International, 2000).

ACRONYMS AND ABBREVIATIONS COVERING THE UNITED NATIONS SYSTEMS AND OTHER INTERNATIONAL ORGANIZATIONS (New York: United Nations, 1981).

ACTUALITÉ LÉGISLATIVE DALLOZ (Paris: Jurisprudence Genérale Dalloz, 1983–).

ADELEYE, GABRIEL, WORLD DICTIONARY OF FOREIGN EXPRESSIONS: A RESOURCE FOR READERS AND WRITERS (Wauconda, IL: Bolchazy-Carducci Publishers, 1999).

ADMINISTRATIVE LAW OF THE EUROPEAN UNION: JUDICIAL REVIEW (Ronald M. Levin et al. eds., Chicago, Ill.: ABA Section of Administrative Law and Regulatory Practice, 2008).

African Court of Justice, http://www.africa-union.org/root/au/organs/court_of_justice_en.htm.

African Human Rights Case Law Analyser, http://caselaw.ihrda.org.

African Human Rights Case Law Database (Centre for Human Rights, University of Pretoria), http://www.chr.up.ac.za/index.php/documents/african-human-rights-case-law-database.html.

AFRICAN HUMAN RIGHTS LAW REPORTS (Lansdowne, South Africa: Juta Law, 2000–). The reports from 2000–2009 are available at http://www.chr.up.ac.za/index.php/ahrlr-english-editions.html.

African Union [AU], http://www.au.int/en.

African Union, African Court of Justice, http://www.africa-union.org/root/au/organs/court_of_justice_en.htm.

AFRICAN YEARBOOK ON INTERNATIONAL HUMANITARIAN LAW (Lansdowne, South Africa: Juta, 2006–).

AFRICAN YEARBOOK OF INTERNATIONAL LAW = ANNUAIRE AFRICAIN DE DROIT INTERNATIONAL (Dordrecht; Boston: M. Nijhoff; Norwell, MA, U.S.A.: Sold and distributed in the U.S.A. and Canada by Kluwer Academic Publishers, 1994–). Available on HeinOnline.

AGIM, EMMANUEL AKOMAYE, THE GAMBIAN LEGAL SYSTEM (Tallinding, The Gambia: Artwoods Production, 2009).

AHMED, SHARIFAH SUHANA, MALAYSIAN LEGAL SYSTEM (2d ed., Selangor Darul Ehsan: Malayan Law Journal Sdn. Bhd.; Dayton, Ohio: LexisNexis, 2007).

Alford, Duncan, Update: European Union Legal Materials: An Infrequent User's Guide (2011), http://www.nyulawglobal.org/globalex/European_Union1.htm.

allAfrica.com, http://allafrica.com.

ALL ENGLAND LAW REPORTS (London: The Law Journal, [1948]–).

ALVAREZ, JOSÉ, INTERNATIONAL ORGANIZATIONS AS LAW-MAKERS (Oxford; New York: Oxford University Press, 2005).

Alvarez, José, International Organizations: Then and Now, 100 AM.J. INT'L. L. 324 (2006).

AMERASINGHE, CHITTHARANJAN F., PRINCIPLES OF THE INSTITUTIONAL LAW OF INTERNATIONAL ORGANIZATIONS (2d rev. ed., Cambridge, UK; New York: Cambridge University Press, 2005).

AMERICAN FOREIGN POLICY: BASIC DOCUMENTS 1977–1980 (Washington, DC: Dept. of State: For sale by the Supt. of Docs., U.S. G.P.O., 1983).

AMERICAN FOREIGN POLICY: CURRENT DOCUMENTS (Washington, DC: Historical Division, Bureau of Public Affairs: For sale by the Supt. of Docs., U.S. G.P.O., 1959–1969).

AMERICAN FOREIGN POLICY: CURRENT DOCUMENTS (Washington, DC: Dept. of State: For sale by the Supt. of Docs., U.S. G.P.O., 1984–1991).

AMERICAN JOURNAL OF COMPARATIVE LAW (Berkeley: American Association for the Comparative Study of Law, 1952–). Available on HeinOnline and JSTOR.

AMERICAN JOURNAL OF INTERNATIONAL LAW ([Washington, etc.] American Society of International Law [etc.], 1907–). Available on HeinOnline and JSTOR.

AMERICAN LAW REPORTS INTERNATIONAL [ALR Int.] ([Eagan, MN]: West, 2010–).

American Law Sources Online, http://www.lawsource.com/also.

American Society of International Law [ASIL], http://www.asil.org.

American Society of International Law, ASIL Guide to Electronic Resources for International Law, http://www.asil.org/erg.

American Society of International Law, ASIL Insights, http://www.asil.org/insights.cfm.

American Society of International Law, International Law in Brief, http://www.asil.org/ilibmenu.cfm.

AMERICAN STATE PAPERS: DOCUMENTS, LEGISLATIVE AND EXECUTIVE, OF THE CONGRESS OF THE UNITED STATES (reprint, Buffalo, NY: W.S. Hein, 1998). Available on the Library of Congress, A Century of Lawmaking for a New Nation, http://memory.loc.gov/ammem/amlaw/lwsp.html and by subscription, http://infoweb.newsbank.com.

American University, Inter-American Human Rights Digest Project, http://www.wcl.american.edu/humright/repertorio.

AMNESTY INTERNATIONAL, COUNTRY REPORTS (London: Amnesty International Publications, 1962–), http://www.amnesty.org/en.

Amnesty International (US Office), http://blog.amnestyusa.org.

ANDENAES, MADS, & FRANK WOOLDRIDGE, EUROPEAN COMPARATIVE COMPANY LAW (Cambridge, UK; New York: Cambridge University Press, 2009).

Andersen, Maureen Ratynski, Where to Begin... When You Don't Know How to Start: Tips for Researching UN Legal Materials, 31 INT'L J. LEGAL INFO. 264 (2003).

THE ANNOTATED DIGEST OF THE INTERNATIONAL CRIMINAL COURT (Cyril Laucci comp., Leiden: Nijhoff Publishers, 2007–).

ANNOTATED LEADING CASES OF INTERNATIONAL CRIMINAL TRIBUNALS (André Klip & Göran Sluiter eds., Antwerpen: Intersentia, 1999–). Also available by subscription, http://www.annotatedleadingcases.com.

ANTONOPOULOS, CONSTANTINE, COUNTERCLAIMS BEFORE THE INTERNATIONAL COURT OF JUSTICE (The Hague, Netherlands: T.M.C. Asser Press, 2011).

ANNUAIRE DE L'INSTITUT DE DROIT INTERNATIONAL (Gand: Bureau de la Revue de Droit International, 1877–).

ANNUAIRE EUROPÉEN = EUROPEAN YEARBOOK (The Hague: Nijhoff, 1955–).

ANNUAIRE FRANÇAIS DE DROIT INTERNATIONAL (Paris: Centre National de la Recherche Scientifique, 1955–).

Annual Review of Population Law (Medford, MA: Law and Population Programme, Fletcher School of Law and Diplomacy, 1975–2000). Available on HeinOnline and http://cyber.law.harvard.edu/population.

Annual Review of United Nations Affairs (New York: New York University Press; Dobbs Ferry, NY: Oceana Publications, 1949–).

Annual Survey of International & Comparative Law (San Francisco, CA: Golden Gate University School of Law, [1994]–). Available on HeinOnline.

Antoine, Rose-Marie Belle, Commonwealth Caribbean Law and Legal System (2d ed., New York: Routledge-Cavendish, 2008).

Anuario Iberoamericano de Justicia Constitucional (Madrid: Centro de Estudios Constitucionales, 1997–).

Anuario Juridico Interamericano = Inter-American Juridical Yearbook (Washington, DC: Pan American Union, 1948–).

Anuario Mexicano de Derecho Internacional (Mexico, D.F.: Instituto de Investigaciones Jurídicas, Universidad Nacional Autónoma de México, 2001–).

Apple, James G., & Robert P. Deyling, *A Primer on the Civil-Law System* ([1995]), http://www.fjc.gov/public/pdf.nsf/lookup/CivilLaw.pdf/$file/CivilLaw.pdf.

Arbitration Procedures in Asia (Ben Beaumont ed., Hong Kong: Sweet & Maxwell Asia, 1999–).

Arbitration Rules—International Institutions: Guides to International Arbitration (3d ed., Loukas Mistelis et al. eds., Huntington, N.Y.: Juris, 2010–).

Arbitration Rules—National Institutions: Guides to International Arbitration (2d ed., Loukas Mistelis et al. eds., Huntington, N.Y.: Juris, 2010–).

Arizona Journal of International and Comparative Law (Tucson, Ariz.: College of Law of the University of Arizona, 1982–). Available on HeinOnline.

ASA Bulletin (Dordrecht: Kluwer Academic Publishers, 1983–). Also available by subscription on KluwerArbitration and HeinOnline.

Asian Yearbook of International Law (Dordrecht; Boston: M. Nijhoff; Norwell, MA, U.S.A.: Sold and distributed in the U.S.A. and Canada by Kluwer Academic Publishers, 1993–). Available on HeinOnline.

Association of Legal Writing Directors and Darby Dickerson, ALWD Citation Manual: A Professional System of Citation (4th ed., Gaithersburg, MD: Aspen Law & Business, 2010).

Asylum Law.org, http://www.asylumlaw.org/countries.

Attachment of Assets (Lawrence W. Newman ed., Yonkers, NY: Juris Pub., 1999–).

Australia Department of Foreign Affairs and Trade, http://www.dfat.gov.au.

Australian Government Attorney-General, Department, Private international Law, Taking of Evidence in Australia for Foreign Court Proceedings, https://www.ag.gov.au/www/agd/agd.nsf/Page/Internationalcivilprocedure_TakingofEvidenceinAustraliaforForeignCourt Proceedings.

Australian Guide to Legal Citation (3d ed., Melbourne: Melbourne University Law, Review Association, 2010). Available online, http://mulr.law.unimelb.edu.au/go/AGLC3.

Australian Treaties Library, http://www.austlii.edu.au/au/other/dfat.

Australian Year Book of International Law (Sydney: Butterworths, 1966–). Available on HeinOnline.

Avalon Project: Alphabetical Title List, http://avalon.law.yale.edu/default.asp.

Avalos, Francisco A., & Elisa Donnadieu, An Electronic Guide to Mexican Law (2011), http://www.nyulawglobal.org/globalex/Mexico1.htm.

Avalos, Francisco A., & Maureen Garmon, Update: Basic Info and Online Sources for NAFTA and CAFTA Research (2010), http://www.nyulawglobal.org/globalex/NAFTA_CAFTA_Research1.htm.

Avon Global Center for Women and Justice at Cornell Law School, http://ww2.lawschool.cornell.edu/womenandjustice/legalresources/index.cfm.

Babel Fish, http://world.altavista.com.

Baer, George W., International Organizations, 1918–1945: A Guide to Research and Research Materials (rev. ed., Wilmington, DE: Scholarly Resources Inc., 1991).

Baltic Yearbook of International Law (The Hague: Kluwer Law International, 2002–). Available on HeinOnline.

Basel Convention Secretariat website, http://www.basel.int.

Base Pacte, http://basedoc.diplomatie.gouv.fr/Traites/Accords_Traites.php.

Basic Documents and Jurisprudence of International/ized Criminal Courts and Tribunals (Washington, DC: Washington College of Law, 2007), subscription database, https://www.wcl.american.edu/warcrimes/wcro_docs/index.cfm.

BASIC DOCUMENTS ON INTERNATIONAL LAW AND THE ENVIRONMENT (P.W. Birnie & A.E. Boyle eds., Oxford: Clarendon Press, 1995).

BASIC FACTS ABOUT THE UNITED NATIONS (New York: United Nations, 1983–).

BAXTER, J.W., & JOHN P. SINNOTT, WORLD PATENT LAW AND PRACTICE (New York: M. Bender, 1968–).

Beck-Online, subscription database, http://beck-online.beck.de/default.aspx.

BEDERMAN, DAVID J., CUSTOM AS A SOURCE OF LAW (Cambridge; New York: Cambridge University Press, 2010).

BELL, JOHN, ET AL., PRINCIPLES OF FRENCH LAW (2d ed., Oxford, UK; New York: Oxford University Press, 2008).

Benesch, Susan, *Vile Crime or Inalienable Right: Defining Incitement to Genocide*, 48 VA. J. INT'L. L. 485 (2008).

BENNETT, A. LEROY, HISTORICAL DICTIONARY OF THE UNITED NATIONS (Lanham, MD: Scarecrow Press, 1995).

bepress Legal Repository, http://law.bepress.com/repository.

Berring, Robert C., *Legal Information and the Search for Cognitive Authority*, 88 CAL. L. REVIEW 1673 (2000).

Berring, Robert C., A Tinkerbell in Buffalo, http://www.slaw.ca/2011/04/19/a-tinkerbell-in-buffalo.

BHALA, RAJ, DICTIONARY OF INTERNATIONAL TRADE LAW (Newark, NJ: LexisNexis, 2008).

Bilateral Agreements (Federal Aviation Administration), http://www.faa.gov/aircraft/air_cert/international/bilateral_agreements.

Bilateral Investment Treaties and Related Agreements (U.S. Dept. of State), http://www.state.gov/e/eb/ifd/bit/index.htm.

BIRYUKOV, ALEXANDER, & INNA SHYROKOVA, THE LAW AND LEGAL SYSTEM OF UKRAINE (Huntington, N.Y.: Juris Pub., Inc., 2005).

BLACKABY, NIGEL, ET AL., REDFERN AND HUNTER ON INTERNATIONAL ARBITRATION (5th ed., Oxford; New York: Oxford University Press, 2009). Also available on KluwerArbitration.

BLACK'S LAW DICTIONARY (9th ed., St. Paul, MN: Thomson/West, 2009).

BLAKESLEE, MERRITT R., & CARLOS A. GARCIA, THE LANGUAGE OF TRADE (3d ed., [Washington, DC]: Office of International Information Programs, U.S. Dept. of State, 2000). Also available at http://usinfo.org/enus/economy/trade/langtrade.html.

Blawg, http://www.blawg.org.

BLEDSOE, ROBERT L., & BOLESLAW A. BOCZEK, THE INTERNATIONAL LAW DICTIONARY (Santa Barbara, CA: ABC-CLIO, 1987).

THE BLUEBOOK: A UNIFORM SYSTEM OF CITATION (19th ed., Cambridge, MA: Harvard Law Review Association, 2010). Also available by subscription, http://www.legalbluebook.com.

BOCZEK, BOLESLAW A., INTERNATIONAL LAW: A DICTIONARY (Lanham, MD: Scarecrow Press, 2005).

Bora Laskin Law Library, International Women's Human Rights and Humanitarian Law, http://www.law-lib.utoronto.ca/resguide/women2.htm.

BORN, GARY, INTERNATIONAL ARBITRATION AND FORUM SELECTION AGREEMENTS: DRAFTING AND ENFORCING (3d ed., Austin [Tex.]: Walter Kluwer Law & Business; Alphen aan den Rijn, The Netherlands: Kluwer Law International; Frederick, MD: Sold and distributed in North, Central and South America by Aspen Publishers, 2010).

BORN, GARY, INTERNATIONAL COMMERCIAL ARBITRATION (Austin, Tex.: Wolters Kluwer; Alphen Aan Den Rijn: Kluwer Law International, 2009). Also available on Kluwer-Arbitration.

BOSTON COLLEGE INTERNATIONAL AND COMPARATIVE LAW REVIEW (Newton Centre: Boston College School of Law, 1979–). Available on HeinOnline.

THE BOUNDARIES OF STRICT LIABILITY IN EUROPEAN TORT LAW (Franz Werro & Vernon Valentine Palmer eds., Durham, NC: Carolina Academic Press, 2004).

Bowett, D.W., The International Court of Justice: Process, Practice and Procedure (London: B.I.I.C.L., 1997).

Bradford, William, *International Legal Compliance: Surveying the Field*, 36 Geo.J. Int'l L. 495 (2005).

BRIDGES Weekly Trade News Digest (Geneva: International Centre for Trade and Sustainable Development, 1997–), http://ictsd.org/news/bridgesweekly.

Brierly, J.L., Law of Nations: An Introduction to the International Law of Peace (6th ed., Oxford: Clarendon Press, 1963).

Brimmer, Brenda, et al., A Guide to the Use of United Nations Documents (Dobbs Ferry, NY: Oceana Publications, 1962).

British Digest of International Law (Clive Parry ed., Sir Gerald Fitzmaurice consulting ed., London: Stevens, 1965–).

British International Law Cases (Prepared under the auspices of the International Law Fund and the British Institute of International and Comparative Law, London: Stevens, 1964–1973).

British Year Book of International Law (London: Oxford University Press, 1920–). Available on HeinOnline.

Broberg, Morten, & Niels Fenger, Preliminary References to the European Court of Justice (Oxford; New York: Oxford University Press, 2010).

Brownlie, Ian, Principles of Public International Law (7th ed., Oxford; New York: Oxford University Press, 2008).

Brüggemeier, Gert, Modernising Civil Liability Law in Europe, China, Brazil and Russia: Texts and Commentaries (Cambridge; New York: Cambridge University Press, 2011).

Bühler, Michael, & Thomas H. Webster, Handbook of ICC Arbitration: Commentary, Precedents, Materials (2d ed., London: Thomson/Sweet & Maxwell, 2008). Also available on Westlaw.

Buergenthal, Thomas, & Sean D. Murphy, Public International Law in a Nutshell (4th ed., St. Paul, MN: West, 2007).

Bulletin on Constitutional Case Law (Strasbourg: Secretariat of the Venice Commission, Council of Europe, 1993–). See also CODICES, the Infobase on Constitutional Case-Law of the Venice Commission, http://codices.coe.int/NXT/gateway.dll?f=templates&fn=default.htm.

Bundesgesetzblatt (Bonn: Bundesministerium der Justiz, 1949–), available at http://www.bundesgesetzblatt.de.

Burbano Herrera, Clara, Provisional Measures in the Case Law of the Inter-American Court of Human Rights (Antwerp; Portland: Intersentia; Portland, OR: International Specialized Book Services [distributor for the U.S.A. and Canada], 2010).

Burchfield, Amy, International Sports Law (2011), http://www.nyulawglobal.org/Globalex/International_Sports_Law1.htm.

Burchfield Amy, Update: International Criminal Courts for the Former Yugoslavia, Rwanda and Sierra Leone: A Guide to Online and Print Resources (2011), http://www.nyulawglobal.org/globalex/International_Criminal_Courts1.htm.

Burgorgue-Larsen, Laurence, & Amaya Ubeda de Torres, The Inter-American Court of Human Rights: Case-Law and Commentary (Oxford; New York: Oxford University Press, 2011).

Burnett, Anne, Guide to Researching the Council of Europe (2000), http://www.llrx.com/features/coe.htm.

Burnett, Anne, ASIL Guide to Electronic Resources for International Law: International Environmental Law, http://www.asil.org/erg/?page=ienvl.

Burnham, William, et al., Law and Legal System of the Russian Federation (4th ed., Huntington, N.Y.: Juris Publishing, 2009).

Burrows, Noreen, & Rosa Greaves, Advocate General and EC Law (Oxford; New York: Oxford University Press, 2007).

Business Operations in…(Arlington, VA: Tax Management, dates vary). Also available by subscription on BNA, Tax and Accounting Center, http://taxandaccounting.bna.com.

Butler, William E., Russian Law (3d ed., New York, Oxford: Oxford University Press, 2009).

Butterworth's Human Rights Cases (London: Butterworths, 1907–). Available on LexisNexis.

Cadwalader, John L., Digest of Published Opinions of the Attorneys-General and of the Leading Decisions of the Federal Courts, with Reference to International Law, Treaties, and Kindred Subjects (rev. ed., Washington, DC: U.S. G.P.O., 1877). Available on HeinOnline.

Les Cahiers du Conseil Constitutionnel (Paris: Dalloz, 1996–).

Calvo-Goller, Karin N., The Trial Proceedings of the International Criminal Court: ICTY and ICTR Precedents (Leiden; Boston: Martinus Nijhoff Publishers, 2006).

Canada, Foreign Affairs and International Trade, Dispute Settlement: NAFTA–Chapter 11–Investment, http://www.dfait-maeci.gc.ca/tna-nac/gov-en.asp.

Canada, Treaty Series (Ottawa: J.O. Patenaude, Printer to the King's Most Excellent Majesty, 1928–).

Canadian Encyclopedic Digest (4th ed., [Toronto]: Carswell Co., 2012–). Also available on Westlaw Canada.

Canadian Immigration and Refugee Board, http://www.irb-cisr.gc.ca/eng/resrec/ndpcnd/Pages/index.aspx.

The Canadian Guide to Uniform Legal Citation (7th ed., Scarborough, Ont.: Carswell, 2010).

Canadian Yearbook of International Law = Annuaire Canadien de Droit International (Vancouver: University of British Columbia Press etc., 1963–). Available on HeinOnline.

Capela, John J., & Stephen W. Hartman, Dictionary of International Business Terms (3d ed., Hauppauge, NY: Barron's, 2004).

Cardiff Index to Legal Abbreviations, http://www.legalabbrevs.cardiff.ac.uk.

Cardozo Journal of International and Comparative Law (New York: Benjamin N. Cardozo School of Law, Yeshiva University, 1995–). Available on HeinOnline.

Case Law on UNCITRAL Texts (CLOUT), http://www.uncitral.org/uncitral/en/case_law.html.

Cavadino, Michael, & James Dignan, Penal Systems: A Comparative Approach (London: Sage, 2006).

Center for Gender and Refugee Studies (UC hastings), http://cgrs.uchastings.edu.

Central & Eastern European Legal Materials ([Ardsley-on-Hudson, NY]: Transnational Juris Publications; [London]: Graham & Trotman/Martinus Nijhoff, 1990–).

Charnovitz, Steve, *Nongovernmental Organizations and International Law*, 100 Am.J. Int'l L. 348 (2006).

Charnovitz, Steve, *A World Environment Organization*, 27 Colum. J. Envtl. L. 323, 331 (2002).

Charter of the United Nations: A Commentary (2d ed., Bruno Simma ed., Oxford; New York: Oxford University Press, 2002).

Chemical Weapons Convention Secretariat, http://www.opcw.org.

Cheng, Bin, General Principles of Law, as Applied by International Courts and Tribunals (London: Stevens, 1953).

Chesterman, Simon et al., Law and Practice of the United Nations: Documents and Commentary (New York: Oxford University Press, 2008).

The Chicago Manual of Style (16th ed., Chicago: University of Chicago Press, 2010).

China Law and Practice (Hong Kong: China Law and Practice Ltd., 1987–). Available by subscription, http://www.chinalawandpractice.com.

ChinaLawInfo, subscription database, http://www.pkulaw.cn/.

China Laws for Foreign Business ([North Ryde, N.S.W.]: CCH Australia Ltd., 1985–). Available by subscription, http://business.cch.com/primesrc/bin/login.asp.

Chinese Yearbook of International Law and Affairs ([Baltimore, MD]: Published by Occasional Paper/Reprints Series in Contemporary Asian Studies, Inc. for the Chinese Society of International Law–Chinese (Taiwan) Branch of International Law Association, 1982–2000). Continued by Chinese (Taiwan) Yearbook of International Law and Affairs ([Baltimore, MD]: Published by the Chinese Society of International Law–Chinese (Taiwan) Branch of the International Law Association, 2001–).

Chinkin, Christine M., *The Challenge of Soft Law: Development and Change in International Law*, 38 INT'L COMP. L.Q. 850 (1989).

CHISHOLM, RICHARD, & GARTH NETTHEIM, UNDERSTANDING LAW: AN INTRODUCTION TO AUSTRALIA'S LEGAL SYSTEM (8th ed., Chatswood, N.S.W.: LexisNexis Butterworths, 2012).

CHISUM, DONALD S., CHISUM ON PATENTS: A TREATISE ON THE LAW OF PATENTABILITY, VALIDITY, AND INFRINGEMENT (New York: LEXIS Pub., 1978–).

CIEL (Center for International Environmental Law), http://www.ciel.org.

CIESIN (Center for International Earth Science Information Network), http://www.ciesin.org.

CISG Database (UN Convention on Contracts for the International Sale of Goods), http://www.cisg.law.pace.edu.

CISG Database, Cases on the CISG, http://www.cisg.law.pace.edu/cisg/text/caseschedule.html.

CISG-online.ch, http://www.globalsaleslaw.org/index.cfm?pageID=28.

CIS INDEX TO PUBLICATIONS OF THE UNITED STATES CONGRESS [and microfiche] (Washington, DC: Congressional Information Service, 1970–). See also Proquest Congressional, subscription database, http://web.lexis-nexis.com/congcomp.

LES CODES LARCIER (Bruxelles: Larcier, 1995–).

CODICES, Constitutional Case Law from Europe (Council of Europe, Venice Commission), http://codices.coe.int/NXT/gateway.dll?f=templates&fn=default.htm.

CODICES, Laws on the Courts (Council of Europe, Venice Commission), http://codices.coe.int/NXT/gateway.dll?f=templates&fn=default.htm.

COHEN, JEHORAM T. ET AL., EUROPEAN TRADEMARK LAW: COMMUNITY TRADEMARK LAW AND HARMONIZED NATIONAL TRADEMARK LAW (lphen aan den Rijn, The Netherlands: Kluwer Law International; Frederick, MD: Sold and distributed in North, Central, and South America by Aspen Publishers, 2010).

COHEN, MORRIS, ET AL., HOW TO FIND THE LAW 565 (9th ed., St. Paul, MN: West Pub. Co., 1995).

COLLECTION OF ICC ARBITRAL AWARDS (Paris; New York: ICC Pub.; Deventer; Boston: Kluwer Law and Taxation Publishers, 1990).

Collection of Foreign Databases by Jurisdiction (New York University), http://www.law.nyu.edu/library/foreignintl/country.html.

COLMAN, ANTHONY, ENCYCLOPEDIA OF INTERNATIONAL COMMERCIAL LITIGATION (London: Graham & Trotman; Norwell, MA: Kluwer Academic Publishers, 1991–).

COLUMBIA GAZETTEER OF THE WORLD (New York: Columbia University Press, 2008). Available by subscription, http://www.columbiagazetteer.org.

Columbia Law Library, A Selective List of Guides to Foreign Legal Research, http://www.law.columbia.edu/library/Research Guides/foreign law/foreignguide.

Columbia Law Library, Research Guide: The United Nations, http://library.law.columbia.edu/guides/United_Nations.

Columbia Law Library, Researching Public International Law, http://www.law.columbia.edu/library/ResearchGuides/internat law/pubint.

COMMENTARY ON THE ROME STATUTE OF THE INTERNATIONAL CRIMINAL COURT: OBSERVERS' NOTES, ARTICLE BY ARTICLE (2d ed., Otto Triffterer ed., München, Germany: Beck; Portland, Or.: Hart, 2008).

COMMERCIAL LAWS OF EUROPE (London: European Law Centre, 1978–).

COMMERCIAL LAWS OF THE WORLD (Ormond Beach, FL: Foreign Tax Law, Inc., dates vary). Available by subscription, http://checkpoint.riag.com.

Commonwealth and International Human Rights Case Law Databases (London: Interights, 1996–), http://www.interights.org/commonwealth-and-international-law-database/index.html.

COMMON LAW, CIVIL LAW AND THE FUTURE OF CATEGORIES (Janet Walker & Oscar G. Chase eds., Markham, Ont.: LexisNexis, 2010).

COMMON MARKET LAW REPORTS [C.M.L.R.] (London: Common Law Reports Ltd., 1962–).

COMMONWEALTH HUMAN RIGHTS LAW DIGEST (London: Interights 1996–). The Commonwealth and International Human Rights Case Law Databases are available on the Interights

website, http://www.interights.org/commonwealth-and-international-law-database/index
.html.

COMPARATIVE CONSTITUTIONAL LAW (Tom Ginsburg & Rosalind Dixon eds., Cheltenham,
UK; Northampton, MA: Edward Elgar, 2011).

COMPARATIVE ENVIRONMENTAL LAW AND REGULATION (Dobbs Ferry, NY: Oceana Publications, 1996–).

COMPARATIVE LAW: AN INTRODUCTION (Vivian Grosswald Curran ed., Durham, NC:
Carolina Academic Press, 2002).

COMPARATIVE LAW IN THE 21ST CENTURY (Andrew Harding & Esin Örücü eds., London;
New York: Kluwer Academic Publishers, 2002).

A CONCISE ENCYCLOPEDIA OF THE UNITED NATIONS (2d rev. ed., Helmut Volger ed., Leiden
[The Netherlands]; Boston: Martinus Nijhoff, 2010).

CONFORTI, BENEDETTO, THE LAW AND PRACTICE OF THE UNITED NATIONS (4th rev. ed., Leiden;
Boston: Martinus Nijhoff Publishers, 2010).

CONGRESSIONAL INDEX (Chicago: Commerce Clearing House, 1938–).

CONGRESSIONAL RECORD (Washington: Govt. Print. Off., 1874–). Available on HeinOnline,
http://thomas.loc.gov/home/LegislativeData.php?&n=Record,   and   http://www.gpo.gov/
fdsys/browse/collection.action?collectionCode=CREC.

CONGRESSIONAL RECORD INDEX (Washington, DC: U.S. G.P.O., 1873–).

CONSOLIDATED TREATIES AND INTERNATIONAL AGREEMENTS (Dobbs Ferry, NY: Oceana
Publications, 1990–). Available by subscription as part of Treaties and International Agreements Online.

CONSOLIDATED TREATY SERIES [C.T.S.] (Clive Perry ed., Dobbs Ferry, NY: Oceana Publications [1969]–1981).

CONSTITUTIONAL LAW & POLICY REVIEW (St. Leonard's, NSW: Prospect Media Pty., 1998–).

The Constitution Finder (University of Richmond), http://confinder.richmond.edu.

CONSTITUTIONS OF DEPENDENCIES AND TERRITORIES (Philip Raworth ed., New York, NY:
Oxford University Press, 2012–). Available by subscription, http://www.oxfordonline.com.
This source was published by Oceana and is currently still available on http://www.oceanalaw
.com.

Constitutions of the Americas, http://pdba.georgetown.edu.

CONSTITUTIONS OF THE COUNTRIES OF THE WORLD (Philip Raworth & G. Alan Tarr eds.,
New York, NY: Oxford University Press, 2012–). Available by subscription, http://www
.oxfordonline.com. This source was published by Oceana and is currently still available on
http://www.oceanalaw.com.

CONSTITUTIONS OF THE WORLD FROM THE LATE 18TH CENTURY TO THE MIDDLE OF THE
19TH CENTURY (München: K.G. Sauer, 2005–).

CONSTITUTIONS OF THE WORLD: 1850 TO THE PRESENT [microform] ([München]: K.G. Saur,
[2002]–).

CONTEMPORARY PRACTICE OF PUBLIC INTERNATIONAL LAW (Ellen G. Schaffer & Randall J.
Snyder eds., Dobbs Ferry, NY: Oceana Publications, 1997).

Contemporary Women's Issues, subscription database, http://www.gale.com.

COOPER, ANDREW FENTON, & THOMAS F. LEGLER, INTERVENTION WITHOUT INTERVEN-
ING?: THE OAS DEFENSE AND PROMOTION OF DEMOCRACY IN THE AMERICAS (New York:
Palgrave Macmillan, 2006).

COPYRIGHT LAW REPORTER (Chicago: Commerce Clearing House, 1978–).

CORPORATE COUNSEL'S GUIDE: LAWS OF INTERNATIONAL TRADE (William H. Hancock ed.,
Chesterland, Ohio: Business Laws, Inc., 1986–2005).

CORRIN, JENNIFER, & DON PATERSON, INTRODUCTION TO SOUTH PACIFIC LAW (2d ed.,
London; New York; Routledge-Cavendish, 2007).

Council of Europe [COE], http://www.coe.int.

Council of Europe, A–Z Index, http://www.coe.int/t/dc/General/indexAZ/default_en.asp.

Council of Europe, Committee of Ministers, http://www.coe.int/t/cm/home_en.asp.

Council of Europe, Treaties, http://conventions.coe.int.

COUNCIL OF EUROPE, EUROPEAN TREATY SERIES [E.T.S.] (Strasbourg: The Council, 1949–).
Also available at http://conventions.coe.int.

Council of Europe, full catalogue of its publications, http://book.coe.int/EN (look for a link
to "Publications").

Council of Europe, http://www.coe.int/DefaultEN.asp.

Council of Europe, HUDOC, http://cmiskp.echr.coe.int/tkp197/search.asp?skin=hudoc-en.

Council of Europe, Online Bookshop, http://book.coe.int/EN.

Council of Europe, Parliamentary Assembly, http://assembly.coe.int/defaultE.asp.

COUNCIL OF EUROPE TREATY SERIES [C.E.T.S.] (2004–).

COUNCIL OF EUROPE, YEARBOOK OF THE EUROPEAN CONVENTION ON HUMAN RIGHTS (The Hague: Martinus Nijhoff, 1960–).

Country Studies (Library of Congress), http://lcweb2.loc.gov/frd/cs/profiles.html.

Court of Arbitration for Sport, http://www.tas-cas.org.

COURT OF JUSTICE OF THE EUROPEAN UNION, REPORTS OF CASES BEFORE THE COURT (Luxembourg: Court of Justice of the European Communities, [1993?–]). Available at http://curia.europa.eu; Westlaw (EU-CS) and LexisNexis (Legal > Global Legal > European Union > Case Law > EUR-Lex European Union Cases) also have databases of these cases.

CREMEAN, DAMIEN J., ADMIRALTY JURISDICTION: LAW AND PRACTICE IN AUSTRALIA, NEW ZEALAND, SINGAPORE AND HONG KONG (3d ed., Annandale, N.S.W.: Federation Press, 2008).

CROOK, TIM, COMPARATIVE MEDIA LAW AND ETHICS (London; New York: Routledge, 2010).

CUMULATIVE DIGEST OF UNITED STATES PRACTICE IN INTERNATIONAL LAW (Washington, DC: Office of the Legal Adviser, Dept. of State: For sale by U.S. G.P.O., Supt. of Docs., 1993–).

Current Index to Legal Periodicals [CILP] (University of Washington Law School Library), subscription database, http://lib.law.washington.edu/cilp/cilp.html. Also available on Westlaw.

CURRENT LAW INDEX ([Los Altos, Calif.] Information Access Corp, 1980–). Available on LexisNexis, Westlaw, and on the web as LegalTrac.

Current Law Journal Content (Washington & Lee Law School), http://lawlib.wlu.edu/cljc. Updating of CLJC ceased on May 13, 2011. Existing indexing (approximately 2000—April 2011) will remain searchable from this site.

CURRENT TREATY INDEX (Igor I. Kavass and Adolf Sprudzs, eds., Buffalo, NY: W.S. Hein, 1991–). Available on HeinOnline from 1982 .

CUSTOMARY INTERNATIONAL HUMANITARIAN LAW (Jean-Marie Henckaerts & Louise Doswald-Beck eds., Cambridge, UK; New York: Cambridge University Press, 2005). Also available from the Customary IHL website by the ICRC, http://www.icrc.org/customary-ihl/eng/docs/home.

CUSTOMARY INTERNATIONAL LAW ON THE USE OF FORCE: A METHODOLOGICAL APPROACH (Enzo Cannizzaro & Paolo Palchetti eds., Leiden; Boston: M. Nijhoff, 2005).

CZECH YEARBOOK OF INTERNATIONAL LAW (New York, N.Y.: Juris Publishing, 2010–).

CZECH YEARBOOK OF INTERNATIONAL LAW (Prague: Czech Society of International Law, 2010–), http://www.cyil.eu. This publication is also called CZECH YEARBOOK OF PUBLIC & PRIVATE INTERNATIONAL LAW.

DABBAH, MAHER M., INTERNATIONAL AND COMPARATIVE COMPETITION LAW (Cambridge; New York: Cambridge University Press, 2010).

DAHL, HENRY SAINT, DAHL'S LAW DICTIONARY: FRENCH TO ENGLISH/ENGLISH TO FRENCH:AN ANNOTATED LEGAL DICTIONARY, INCLUDING DEFINITIONS FROM CODES, CASE LAW, STATUTES, AND LEGAL WRITING = DICTIONNAIRE JURIDIQUE DAHL (3d ed., Buffalo, NY: W.S. Hein, 2007).

DAHL, HENRY SAINT, DAHL'S LAW DICTIONARY: SPANISH-ENGLISH/ENGLISH-SPANISH: AN ANNOTATED LEGAL DICTIONARY, INCLUDING AUTHORITATIVE DEFINITIONS FROM CODES, CASE LAW, STATUTES, AND LEGAL WRITING = DICCIONARIO JURÍDICO DAHL (5th ed., Buffalo, NY: W.S. Hein, 2010).

DALHUISEN, JAN H., DALHUISEN ON TRANSNATIONAL AND COMPARATIVE COMMERCIAL, FINANCIAL, AND TRADE LAW (4th ed. Oxford; Portland, OR: Hart Pub., 2010).

Dalton, Robert E., *National Treaty Law and Practice: United States, in* NATIONAL TREATY LAW AND PRACTICE: DEDICATED TO THE MEMORY OF MONROE LEIGH (Duncan B. Hollis et al. eds., Leiden; Boston: M. Nijhoff, 2005). The first edition of this chapter is available on the web; 'National Treaty Law and Practice: United States,' *in* NATIONAL TREATY LAW AND PRACTICE: AUSTRIA, CHILE, COLOMBIA, JAPAN, THE NETHERLANDS, UNITED STATES

(Washington, DC: American Society of International Law, 1999), www.asil.org/files/dalton
.pdf.
DASHWOOD, ALAN, & DERRICK WYATT, WYATT AND DASHWOOD'S EUROPEAN UNION LAW
(6th ed., Oxford; Portland, OR: Hart Pub., 2011).
DataCenta, http://www.datacenta.com.
DAVID, RENÉ, & JOHN E.C. BRIERLY, MAJOR LEGAL SYSTEMS IN THE WORLD TODAY: AN
INTRODUCTION TO THE COMPARATIVE STUDY OF LAW (3d ed., London: Stevens, 1985).
DAVIS, URI, CITIZENSHIP AND THE STATE: A COMPARATIVE STUDY OF CITIZENSHIP LEGISLA-
TION IN ISRAEL, JORDAN, PALESTINE, SYRIA AND LEBANON EDITION (Reading, Berkshire,
UK: Ithaca Press, 1997).
A DECADE OF AMERICAN FOREIGN POLICY: BASIC DOCUMENTS, 1941–1949 (rev. ed., Washing-
ton, DC: Dept. of State, 1985).
DE CRUZ, PETER, COMPARATIVE LAW IN A CHANGING WORLD (3d ed., London: Cavendish
Pub., 2008).
DeJure, subscription database, http://dejure.giuffre.it.
DE LA RUE, COLIN M., & CHARLES B. ANDERSON, SHIPPING AND THE ENVIRONMENT: LAW
AND PRACTICE (London: LLP, 1998).
DEGAN, VLADIMIR DJURO, SOURCES OF INTERNATIONAL LAW (The Hague; Boston: Martinus
Nijhoff Publishers, 1997).
Delegation of the European Commission to the United States, http://www.eurunion.org.
THE DEVELOPMENT OF PRODUCT LIABILITY (Simon Whittaker ed., Cambridge; New York:
Cambridge University Press, 2010).
DIGEST OF COMMERCIAL LAWS OF THE WORLD ([Dobbs Ferry] NY: Oceana Publications,
[1998]–).
DIGEST OF INTERNATIONAL CASES ON THE LAW OF THE SEA (New York: United Nations,
2007). Also available on HeinOnline.
Digest of International Investment Jurisprudence (International Investment Law Centre
Cologne), http://www.investment-law-digest.com.
Digest of Investment Treaty Awards and Decisions, http://www.arbitration-icca.org/media/0/
12404936822530/investment_treaty_decisions_consolidated_2006_2008_as.pdf.
DIGEST OF JURISPRUDENCE OF SPECIAL COURT FOR SIERRA LEONE, 2003–2005 (Leiden;
Boston: M. Nijhoff, 2007).
DIGEST OF UNITED STATES PRACTICE IN INTERNATIONAL LAW (Washington, DC: U.S. G.P.O.,
1973–1980; Washington, DC: International Law Institute, 2001–). Documents referenced in
the Digest are available at http://www.state.gov/s/l/c8183.htm.
DIGEST OF UNITED STATES PRACTICE IN INTERNATIONAL LAW (Washington, DC: Office of
the Legal Adviser, Dept. of State: For sale by the Supt. of Docs., U.S. G.P.O., 1974–). Avail-
able on HeinOnline.
DiMATTEO, LARRY A., LAW OF INTERNATIONAL CONTRACTING (2d ed., Austin [Tex.]: Wolt-
ers Kluwer Law & Business; Alphen aan den Rijn, The Netherlands: Kluwer Law Interna-
tional; Frederick, MD: Sold and distributed in North, Central and South America by Aspen
Publishers, 2009).
Dinwoodie, Graeme B., *Private Ordering and the Creation of International Copyright Norms:
The Role of Public Structuring*, 160 J. INST. & THEOR. ECON. 161 (2004).
Diplomatische Dokumente der Schweiz, Swiss National Commission for the Publication of
Diplomatic Documents, http://www.dodis.ch/e/home.asp.
DISPATCH (Washington, DC: Office of Public Communication, Bureau of Public Affairs,
1990–1999).
DISPUTE SETTLEMENT REPORTS (Cambridge, UK; New York: Cambridge University Press,
1996–).
DOCUMENTS IN INTERNATIONAL ENVIRONMENT LAW (Philippe Sands et al. eds., Cambridge,
UK; New York: Cambridge University Press, 1994).
DOCUMENTS IN INTERNATIONAL ENVIRONMENTAL LAW (2d ed., Philippe Sands & Paolo
Galizzi eds., Cambridge, UK; New York: Cambridge University Press, 2004).
DOCUMENTOS OFICIALES DE LA OEA [Proceedings] (Washington, DC: OAS, 1959–).
DocuTicker, http://www.docuticker.com.

Doebbler, F.J., *A Complex Ambiguity: The Relationship between the African Commission on Human and Peoples' Rights and Other African Union Initiatives Affecting Respect for Human Rights*, 13 TRANSNAT'L L. & CONTEMP. PROBS. 7 (2003).

DOING BUSINESS IN ASIA (Singapore: CCH Asia Ltd., 1991–).

DOING BUSINESS IN JAPAN (New York, N.Y.: M. Bender, 1980–).

DOING BUSINESS IN MEXICO (S. Theodore Reiner & Anne E. Reiner eds., New York: M. Bender, 1980–).

Doing Business, Law Library (World Bank), http://www.doingbusiness.org/law-library.

DOLZER, RUDOLF, & MARGRETE STEVENS, BILATERAL INVESTMENT TREATIES (The Hague; Boston: M. Nijhoff, 1995).

DomCLIC Project, http://www.haguejusticeportal.net/eCache/DEF/6/579.html.

DOMAIN NAMES—GLOBAL PRACTICE AND PROCEDURE (John R. Olsen et al. eds., London: Sweet and Maxwell, 2000–). Also available on Westlaw, DOMAIN-GPP.

Dotan, Yoav, *The Spillover Effect of Bills of Rights: A Comparative Assessment of the Impact of Bills of Rights in Canada and Israel*, 53 AM. J. COMP. LAW 293 (2005).

DUKE JOURNAL OF COMPARATIVE & INTERNATIONAL LAW (Durham, NC: Duke University School of Law, 1991–). Available on HeinOnline and http://www.law.duke.edu/journals/djcil.

Dupuy, Pierre-Marie, *Soft Law and the International Law of the Environment*, 12 MICH. J. INT'L L. 420, 434 (1991).

EarthJustice, http://www.earthjustice.org.

ECHOLS, MARSHA A., GEOGRAPHICAL INDICATIONS FOR FOOD PRODUCTS: INTERNATIONAL LEGAL AND REGULATORY PERSPECTIVES (Austin: Wolters Kluwer Law & Business; Alphen aan den Rijn, The Netherlands: Kluwer Law International, 2008).

ECOLEX, http://www.ecolex.org/start.php.

EconLit (American Economic Association), subscription database, http://www.aeaweb.org/econlit/index.php.

Editions Dalloz, subscription database, http://www.dalloz.fr.

EDMONDSON, LARRY E., DOMKE ON COMMERCIAL ARBITRATION: THE LAW AND PRACTICE OF COMMERCIAL ARBITRATION (3d ed., St. Paul, MN: Thomson/West, 2003–).

EGGERMONT, FREDERIC, & STEFAAN SMIS, RESEARCH GUIDE TO INSTRUMENTS OF EUROPEAN REGIONAL ORGANIZATIONS (Antwerp; Portland, OR: Intersentia, 2010).

EHS LAW BULLETIN (Tokyo: Eibun-Horei-Sha, 1958–).

Eko, Lyombe, *American Exceptionalism, the French Exception, Intellectual Property Law, and Peer-to-Peer File Sharing on the Web*, 10 J. MARSHALL REV. INTELL. PROP. L. 95 (2010).

Electronic Information System for International Law [EISIL], http://www.eisil.org.

Electoral Knowledge Network (Ace Project), http://aceproject.org/regions-en.

ELECTRONIC JOURNAL OF COMPARATIVE LAW (1997–), http://www.ejcl.org.

ELGAR ENCYCLOPEDIA OF COMPARATIVE LAW (Jan M. Smits ed., Cheltenham, UK; Northampton, MA: Edward Elgar Pub., 2006).

THE EMERGING PRACTICE OF THE INTERNATIONAL CRIMINAL COURT (Carsten Stahn & Goran Sluiter eds., Leiden; Boston: Martinus Nijhoff Publishers, 2009).

ENCYCLOPEDIA OF ASSOCIATIONS: INTERNATIONAL ORGANIZATIONS (Detroit: Gale Research Co., 1989–). Available by subscription, http://galenet.galegroup.com.

ENCYCLOPEDIA OF EUROPEAN UNION LAW (Neville March Hunnings ed., London: Sweet & Maxwell, 1996–).

ENCYCLOPEDIA OF HUMAN RIGHTS (David P. Forsythe ed., Oxford; New York: Oxford University Press, 2009). Also available by subscription from publisher.

ENCYCLOPÉDIE JURIDIQUE (Paris: Dalloz, date varies). Edition and publication dates vary depending on topic.

ENDESHAW, ASSAFA, INTELLECTUAL PROPERTY IN ASIAN EMERGING ECONOMIES: LAW AND POLICY IN THE POST-TRIPS ERA (Farnham, Surrey, England; Burlington, VT: Ashgate Pub., 2010).

ENFORCEMENT OF ARBITRATION AGREEMENTS AND INTERNATIONAL ARBITRAL AWARDS: THE NEW YORK CONVENTION IN PRACTICE (Emmanuel Gaillard et al., eds., London: Cameron May, 2008).

ENFORCEMENT OF FOREIGN JUDGMENTS (Louis Garb & Julian Lew eds., Deventer; Boston: Kluwer Law and Taxation Publishers, 1994–).

ENFORCEMENT OF MONEY JUDGMENTS (Lawrence W. Newman ed., Yonkers, N.Y.: Juris, 1988–).

ENGLISH-FRENCH-SPANISH-RUSSIAN MANUAL OF THE TERMINOLOGY OF PUBLIC INTERNATIONAL LAW (LAW OF PEACE) AND INTERNATIONAL ORGANIZATIONS (Brussels: Published for the Graduate Institute of International Studies, 1983).

ENTERTAINMENT AND MEDIA LAW REPORTS (Richard Parkes & Godwin Busuttil eds., Oxford: Sweet & Maxwell, 1993–).

ENTRI (Environmental Treaties and Resource Indicators) database, http://sedac.ciesin.columbia.edu/entri.

EnviroLink, http://www.envirolink.org.

Environmental & Natural Resources Law Links (Sturm College of Law, University of Denver), http://law.du.edu/forms/enrgp/weblinks/index2.cfm.Environmental Law Alliance Worldwide, http://www.elaw.org.

ENVIRONMENTAL LAW INSTITUTE, ENVIRONMENTAL LAW REPORTER [E.L.R.] (Washington, DC: The Institute, 1971–), subscription database, http://www.elr.info/index.cfm.

Environmental Treaties and Resource Indicators (ENTRI), http://sedac.ciesin.org/entri/treatySearch.jsp.

EPSTEIN, DAVID, ET AL., INTERNATIONAL LITIGATION: A GUIDE TO JURISDICTION, PRACTICE, AND STRATEGY (4th ed., Ardsley, NY: Transnational Publishers, 2010).

Erickson, R.J., *The Making of Executive Agreements by the United States Department of Defense: An Agenda for Progress*, 13 B.U. INT'L L.J. 45 (1995).

Essien, Victor, Researching Ghanaian Law, http://www.nyulawglobal.org/globalex/ghana1.htm.

Ethnic NewsWatch, subscription database (date of coverage varies by publication indexed), http://www.proquest.com/en-US/catalogs/databases/detail/ethnic_newswatch.shtml.

EUR-Lex, http://eur-lex.europa.eu/RECH_menu.do?ihmlang=en.

EURO-LEX list, http://www.listserv.dfn.de/cgi-bin/wa?SUBED1=euro-lex&A=1.

Europa, http://europa.eu/index.htm.

THE EUROPA DIRECTORY OF INTERNATIONAL ORGANIZATIONS (London: Europa Publications, 1999–). Available by subscription, http://www.europaworld.com.

THE EUROPA WORLD YEAR BOOK (London, England: Europa Publications Limited, 1989–). Available by subscription, http://www.europaworld.com.

EUROPEAN COMMISSION OF HUMAN RIGHTS, DECISIONS AND REPORTS [D & R] (Strasbourg: The Commission, 1975–1998).

EUROPEAN COURT OF HUMAN RIGHTS, PUBLICATIONS DE LA COUR EUROPÉENNE DES DROITS DE L'HOMME. SÉRIE A, ARRÊTS ET DÉCISIONS = PUBLICATIONS OF THE EUROPEAN COURT OF HUMAN RIGHTS. SERIES A, JUDGMENTS AND DECISIONS (Strasbourg: Greffe de la Cour, Conseil de l'Europe, 1961–1996).

EUROPEAN COURT OF HUMAN RIGHTS, PUBLICATIONS DE LA COUR EUROPÉENNE DES DROITS DE L'HOMME. SÉRIE B, MÉMOIRES, PLAIDOIRIES ET DOCUMENTS = PUBLICATIONS OF THE EUROPEAN COURT OF HUMAN RIGHTS. SERIES B, PLEADINGS, ORAL ARGUMENTS, AND DOCUMENTS (Strasbourg: Greffe de la Cour, Conseil de l'Europe, 1962–1995).

EUROPEAN COURT OF HUMAN RIGHTS, RECUEIL DES ARRÊTS ET DÉCISIONS = REPORTS OF JUDGMENTS AND DECISIONS (Köln: Carl Heymanns Verlag, 1996–).

EUROPEAN COURT OF HUMAN RIGHTS: REMEDIES AND EXECUTION OF JUDGMENTS (Theodora A. Christou & Juan Pablo Raymond eds., London: British Institute of International and Comparative Law, 2005).

European Court of Justice, http://curia.europa.eu.

European Court of Justice, Leading Cases of the European Court of Justice, EC Environmental Law (2005), http://ec.europa.eu/environment/legal/law/pdf/leading_cases_en.pdf.

European Free Trade Association (EFTA), http://www.efta.int.

EUROPEAN HUMAN RIGHTS REPORTS [E.H.R.R.] (London: European Law Centre Ltd., 1979–). Available on LexisNexis and Westlaw.

EUROPEAN JOURNAL OF INTERNATIONAL LAW ([Munich]: Law Books in Europe, 1990–). Available by subscription, http://ejil.oxfordjournals.org, http://www.ingentaconnect.com/content/oup/ejilaw, and HeinOnline.

European Judicial Network [EJN], http://ec.europa.eu/civiljustice/index_en.htm.

European Library, http://search.theeuropeanlibrary.org/portal/en/index.html.

European Patent Decisions: A Compendium of the More Important Decisions of the Boards of Appeal of the European Patent Office (London: Sweet & Maxwell, 1992–).

European Patent Office, http://www.epo.org.

European Patent Office Reports (Oxford: ESC Pub., 1986–). Also available on Westlaw, ENP-RPTS database.

European Trade Mark Reports (London: Sweet & Maxwell, 1996–). Also available on Westlaw, ETR-RPTS database.

European Treaty Series [E.T.S.] (Strasbourg: Council of Europe, 1949–2003). New series is Council of Europe Treaty Series.

European Communities, Official Journal [O.J.] ([Luxembourg: Office for Official Publications of the European Communities], 1952–).

European Union [EU], Accession Treaties, http://eur-lex.europa.eu/en/treaties/index.htm#accession.

European Union, Council of the European Union, http://www.consilium.europa.eu/homepage.aspx?lang=en.

European Union, Delegation to the USA, http://www.eurunion.org/eu.

European Union, Directorates-General and Services, http://ec.europa.eu/about/ds_en.htm.

European Union, Directory of European Union Consolidated Legislation, http://eur-lex.europa.eu/en/consleg/latest/index.htm.

European Union, EUR-Lex, http://eur-lex.europa.eu/RECH_menu.do?ihmlang=en.

European Union, Europa Gateway, http://europa.eu/index_en.htm.

European Union, European Commission, http://ec.europa.eu/index_en.htm.

European Union, European Commission, Alphabetical Index, http://ec.europa.eu/atoz_en.htm.

European Union, European Commission, Codecision, http://ec.europa.eu/codecision/index_en.htm.

European Union, European Parliament, http://www.europarl.europa.eu/portal/en.

European Union, EuroVoc (EU's multilingual thesaurus), http://eurovoc.europa.eu/drupal.

European Union, Founding Treaties, http://eur-lex.europa.eu/en/treaties/index.htm#accession.

European Union, N-Lex: A Common Gateway to National Law, http://eur-lex.europa.eu/n-lex/pri/pri_en.htm.

European Union, Other Treaties and Protocols, http://eur-lex.europa.eu/en/treaties/index.htm#other.

European Union, PreLex, http://ec.europa.eu/prelex/apcnet.cfm?CL=en.

European Union Law Reporter (London: Sweet & Maxwell, 2000–).

European Union, Summaries of EU Legislation, http://europa.eu/legislation_summaries/index_en.htm. Formerly known as "SCADPLUS." European Union, Treaties, http://europa.eu.int/eur-lex/lex/en/treaties/treatiesother.htm.

European Yearbook (The Hague: Nijhoff, 1955–).

European Yearbook of Disability Law (Antwerp [Belgium]; Portland [Or.]: Intersentia, 2009–).

European Yearbook of Minority Issues (The Hague; New York: Kluwer Law International, 2003–). Also available on HeinOnline.

EuroVoc (EU's multilingual thesaurus), http://eurovoc.europa.eu/drupal.

Everyone's United Nations (New York: United Nations, Dept. of Public Information, 1979–).

Exalead, http://www.exalead.com/search.

Executive Agreement Series [E.A.S.] (Washington, DC: U.S. G.P.O, 1929–1946).

Extradition Laws and Treaties (Buffalo, NY: Hein, 1980–).

Extraordinary Chambers in the Courts of Cambodia [ECCC], http://www.eccc.gov.kh/en.

Ezeanokwasa, Oseloka, The Legal Inequality of Muslim and Christian Marriages in Nigeria: Constitutionally Established Judicial Discrimination (Lewiston, NY: Edwin Mellen Press, 2011).

FAMILY LAW IN EUROPE (2d ed., Carolyn Hamilton & Alison Perry eds., London: LexisNexis Butterworths Tolley; Dayton, OH: LexisNexis, 2002).

FAOLEX (FAO), http://faolex.fao.org.

FEDERAL CIVIL CODE OF MEXICO (trans. and updated Jorge A. Vargas, St. Paul, MN: Thomson/ West, 2009).

FINNISH YEARBOOK OF INTERNATIONAL LAW (Helsinki: Ius Gentium Association, 1990–). Available on HeinOnline.

First Search (OCLC), subscription database, http://www.oclc.org/home.

THE FIRST TEN YEARS OF THE KOREAN CONSTITUTIONAL COURT: 1988–1998 ([SEOUL]: THE CONSTITUTIONAL COURT OF KOREA, 2001). Also available at http://www.ccourt.go.kr/ home/english/decision10year.htm.

Fishlex (FAO), http://faolex.fao.org/fishery/index.htm.

FITZMAURICE, GERALD, THE LAW AND PROCEDURE OF THE INTERNATIONAL COURT OF JUSTICE (Cambridge [Cambridgeshire]: Grotius, 1986).

Flare Index to Treaties, http://193.62.18.232/dbtw-wpd/textbase/treatysearch.htm.

FLEET STREET REPORTS (London: The European Law Centre at Sweet & Maxwell, 1992–). Also available on Westlaw, FLEET-RPTS.

Focus, the WTO's newsletter (Geneva: Information and Media Relations Division, World Trade Organization, 1995–2007), http://www.wto.org/english/res_e/focus_e/focus_e.htm. WTO news is now available on the WTO website, http://www.wto.org/english/news_e/ news_e.htm.

FOLSOM, RALPH H., EUROPEAN UNION LAW IN A NUTSHELL (7th ed., St. Paul, MN: Thomson/ West, 2011).

FOLSOM, RALPH H., ET AL., HANDBOOK OF NAFTA DISPUTE SETTLEMENT (Ardsley, N.Y.: Transnational Publishers, 1998–2000).

FOLSOM, RALPH H., ET AL., INTERNATIONAL TRADE AND ECONOMIC RELATIONS IN A NUT-SHELL (4th ed., St. Paul, MN: Thomson/West, 2009).

FOLSOM, RALPH H., NAFTA AND FREE TRADE IN THE AMERICAS IN A NUTSHELL (4th ed., St. Paul, MN: Thomson/West, 2012).

FOLSOM, RALPH H., PRINCIPLES OF EUROPEAN UNION LAW (3d ed., St. Paul, MN: Thomson/ West, 2011).

Food and Agriculture Organization [FAO], Conventions and Agreements, http://www.fao .org/Legal/TREATIES/Treaty-e.htm.

Foreign and International Law Resources: An Annotated Guide to Web Sites Around the World, http://www.law.harvard.edu/library/research/guides/int_foreign/web-resources/index .html.

Foreign Governments (Northwestern University), http://www.library.northwestern.edu/ libraries-collections/evanston-campus/government-information/international-documents/ foreign.

FOREIGN RELATIONS OF THE UNITED STATES (Washington, DC: U.S. G.P.O., 1861–). Available at http://history.state.gov/historicaldocuments and http://uwdc.library.wisc.edu/ collections/FRUS.

Foreign Trade Information Center (OAS), http://www.sice.oas.org/disciplines-e.asp. See also SICE.

FOSTER, NIGEL, & SATISH SULE, GERMAN LEGAL SYSTEM & LAWS (4th ed., Oxford; New York: Oxford University Press, 2010).

FOUCHARD, GAILLARD, GOLDMAN ON INTERNATIONAL COMMERCIAL ARBITRATION (Philippe Fouchard et al. eds., The Hague; Boston : Kluwer Law International, 1999).

FOUNDATIONS OF COMPARATIVE LAW: METHODS AND TYPOLOGIES (William E. Butler ed., London: Wildy, Simmonds & Hill, 2011).

FOX, JAMES R., DICTIONARY OF INTERNATIONAL AND COMPARATIVE LAW (3d ed., Dobbs Ferry, NY: Oceana Publications, 2003).

FOX, WILLIAM F., INTERNATIONAL COMMERCIAL AGREEMENTS: A PRIMER ON DRAFTING, NEGOTIATING, AND RESOLVING DISPUTES (4th ed., Cambridge, MA: Kluwer Law International, 2009).

Franklin, Jonathan, ASIL Guide to Electronic Resources for International Law: International Intellectual Property Law, http://www.asil.org/erg/?page=iipl.

FRIEDLAND, PAUL D., ARBITRATION CLAUSES FOR INTERNATIONAL CONTRACTS (2d ed., Huntington, NY: Juris, 2007).

Frequently-Cited Treaties and Other International Instruments (University of Minnesota), http://www.law.umn.edu/library/tools/pathfinders/most-cited.html.

THE FUNDAMENTAL RULES OF THE INTERNATIONAL LEGAL ORDER: JUS COGENS AND OBLIGATIONS ERGA OMNES (Christian Tomuschat & Jean Marc Thouvenin eds., Leiden; Boston: Martinus Nijhoff Publishers, 2006).

FUNK, T. MARKUS, VICTIMS' RIGHTS AND ADVOCACY AT THE INTERNATIONAL CRIMINAL COURT (Oxford; New York, N.Y.: Oxford University Press, 2011).

GACETA CONSTITUCIONAL (Sucre, Bolivia: Editorial Judicial, [1998?]–).

GALLAGHER, PETER, GUIDE TO DISPUTE SETTLEMENT (London; Boston: Kluwer Law International, 2002).

GARB, LOUIS, INTERNATIONAL SUCCESSION (3d ed., The Hague; New York: Kluwer Law International, 2010).

GAREAU, FREDERICK H., THE UNITED NATIONS AND OTHER INTERNATIONAL INSTITUTIONS: A CRITICAL ANALYSIS (Chicago: Burnham, 2002).

GATT Digital Library: 1947–1994, http://gatt.stanford.edu/page/home.

GATT documents, http://www.wto.org/english/docs-e/gattdocs-e.htm.

Gender Jurisprudence and International Criminal Law Project (American University, War Crimes Office and Women and International Law Program), http://www.wcl.american.edu/gender/wilp/gicl.

Gender Law Library (World Bank), http://wbl.worldbank.org/WBLLibrary/elibrary.aspx?libid=17.

GenderWatch, subscription database, http://www.proquest.com/products-pq/descriptions/genderwatch.shtml.

Genocide, War Crimes and Crimes Against Humanity: Topical Digests of the Case Law of the International Tribunal for the Former Yugoslavia (2006, http://www.hrw.org/node/11277.

Genocide, War Crimes and Crimes Against Humanity: Topical Digests of the Case Law of the International Tribunal for Rwanda (2010), http://www.hrw.org/reports/2010/01/12/genocide-war-crimes-and-crimes-against-humanity.

GEORGIA JOURNAL OF INTERNATIONAL AND COMPARATIVE LAW (1970–). Available on Hein Online.

Geraghty, Anne H., *Universal Jurisdiction and Drug Trafficking: A Tool for Fighting One of the World's Most Pervasive Problems*, 16 FLA.J.INT'L L. 371, 391 (2004).

GERMAIN, CLAIRE M., GERMAIN'S TRANSNATIONAL LAW RESEARCH (Ardsley-on-Hudson, NY: Transnational Juris Publications, 1991). The chapter on French Law is available at http://library.lawschool.cornell.edu/encyclopedia/countries/france.

Germain, Claire M., Germain's International Court Research Guide, http://library.lawschool.cornell.edu/WhatWeDo/ResearchGuides/ICJ.cfm#bib.

GERMAN COMMERCIAL CODE & CODE OF CIVIL PROCEDURE IN ENGLISH (Dobbs Ferry, NY: Oceana Publications, 2001).

German Law Archive, http://www.iuscomp.org/gla.

GERMAN YEARBOOK OF INTERNATIONAL LAW = JAHRBUCH FÜR INTERNATIONALES RECHT (Berlin: Duncker & Humblot, 1948–).

Germany, Auswärtiges Amt, http://www.auswaertiges-amt.de.

GLENDON, MARY ANN, ET AL., COMPARATIVE LEGAL TRADITIONS IN A NUTSHELL (3d ed., St. Paul, MN: West Group, 2008).

GLENN, PATRICK H., LEGAL TRADITIONS OF THE WORLD (4th ed., Oxford; New York: Oxford University Press, 2010).

GLOBAL COMMUNITY: YEARBOOK OF INTERNATIONAL LAW AND JURISPRUDENCE (Dobbs Ferry, NY: Oceana Publications, Inc., 2001–).

GLOBAL CONSTITUTIONAL LAW COLLECTION (Boxtel, Netherlands: Global Law Association & Wolf Legal Publishers, 1996–).

Global Courts: Supreme Court Decisions from Around the World, http://www.globalcourts.com.

THE GLOBAL ENCYCLOPAEDIA OF DATA PROTECTION REGULATION (The Hague; Boston: Kluwer Law International, 1999–).

Global IP Network (GIN) collection, Franklin IP Mall, http://ipmall.info/hosted_resources/gin_index.asp.

Global Law Working Papers, Human Rights and Global Justice Working Papers, Jean Monnet Working Papers, and Institute for International Law and Justice Working Papers (New York University), http://www.law.nyu.edu/global/index.htm.

Global Legal Information Catalog (Law Library of Congress), http://www.loc.gov/lawweb/servlet/Glic?home.

Global Legal Information Network [GLIN] (Law Library of Congress), http://www.glin.gov/.search.action. Access to summaries is free, access to full-text documents by subscription.

Global Legal Monitor (Law Library of Congress), http://www.loc.gov/lawweb/servlet/lloc_news.

GLOBAL WAR CRIMES TRIBUNAL COLLECTION (J. Oppenheim & W. van der Wolf eds., Nijmegen, the Netherlands: Global Law Association; Holmes Beach, FL: Gaunt, 1997–).

Globalex, http://www.nyulawglobal.org/globalex/index.html.

GODINHO, JORGE A.F., MACAU BUSINESS LAW AND LEGAL SYSTEM (HONG KONG: LEXISNEXIS, 2007).

Goldman, Eric, *Wikipedia's Labor Squeeze and Its Consequences*, 8 J. TELECOMM. & HIGH TECH. L. 157, 164–65 (2010).

Gomes, Lee, *Google Translate Tangles With Computer Learning*, FORBES, July 22, 2010.

GOODE, WALTER, DICTIONARY OF TRADE POLICY TERMS (5th ed., Cambridge, UK: New York: Cambridge University Press, 2007).

Google Books, http://books.google.com.

Google Translate, http://translate.google.com.

GORDLEY, JAMES, FOUNDATIONS OF PRIVATE LAW: PROPERTY, TORT, CONTRACT, UNJUST ENRICHMENT (Oxford; New York: Oxford University Press, 2006).

Government Gazettes Online (University of Michigan), http://www-personal.umich.edu/~graceyor/doctemp/gazettes/index.htm.

GOVERNMENT INFORMATION QUARTERLY (Greenwich, CT: JAI Press, 1984–). Available by subscription, http://www.sciencedirect.com.

GPO's Federal Digital System (FDsys), http://www.gpo.gov/fdsys.

GRANDO, MICHELLE T., EVIDENCE, PROOF, AND FACT-FINDING IN WTO DISPUTE SETTLEMENT (Oxford; New York: Oxford University Press, 2009).

GREENBERG, SIMON, ET AL., INTERNATIONAL COMMERCIAL ARBITRATION: AN ASIA-PACIFIC PERSPECTIVE (Cambridge; New York: Cambridge University Press, 2011).

Greenleaf, Graham, *Free Access to Legal Information, LIIs, and the Free Access to Law Movement, in* THE IALL INTERNATIONAL HANDBOOK OF LEGAL INFORMATION MANAGEMENT HANDBOOK 201 (Richard A. Danner & Jules Winterton eds., Farnham, Surrey; Burlington, VT: Ashgate Pub., 2011).

GUIDE TO FOREIGN AND INTERNATIONAL LEGAL CITATIONS (2d ed., New York, NY: Aspen Publishers, 2009).

Guide to Foreign and International Legal Databases (New York University), http://www.law.nyu.edu/library/foreign-intl.

GUIDE TO INTERNATIONAL LEGAL RESEARCH (Newark, NJ: LexisNexis, 2002–).

GUIDE TO THE UNITED STATES TREATIES IN FORCE (Igor I. Kavass & Adolf Sprudzs eds., Buffalo, NY: W.S. Hein, 1982–). Available on HeinOnline. Supplemented by *Guide to the United States Treaties in Force: Current Treaty Action Supplement.*

Guzman, Andrew T., *Saving Customary International Law*, 27 MICH. J. INT'L L. 115, 125 (2005).

HACKWORTH, GREEN HAYWOOD, DIGEST OF INTERNATIONAL LAW (Washington, DC: U.S. G.P.O., 1940–44). Available on HeinOnline.

HAGUE ACADEMY OF INTERNATIONAL LAW, RECUEIL DES COURS (Paris: Libraire Hachette, 1925–). Topical and author database available. You can search this collection at http://www.peacepalacelibrary.nl/collection/e-resources/recueil-des-cours/, but access to the full text is limited to those with subscriptions. Also available on HeinOnline and Martinus Nijhoff Online, http://www.nijhoffonline.nl/public_home.

Hague Conference on Private International Law, http://www.hcch.net/index_en.php?act=home.splash.

Hague Conventions, http://www.hcch.net/index_en.php?act=conventions.listing.

Hague Justice Portal, http://www.haguejusticeportal.net.

Hague Peace Palace Library, http://www.ppl.nl.

HAGUE YEARBOOK OF INTERNATIONAL LAW = ANNUAIRE DE LA HAYE DE DROIT INTERNATIONAL (Dordrecht: M. Nijhoff, 1988–).

HAJNAL, PETER I., GUIDE TO UNITED NATIONS ORGANIZATION, DOCUMENTATION AND PUBLISHING FOR STUDENTS, RESEARCHERS, LIBRARIANS (Dobbs Ferry, NY: Oceana, 1978).

Halley, Janet, & Rittich, Kerry, *Critical Directions in Comparative Family Law: Genealogies and Contemporary Studies of Family Law Exceptionalism*, 58 AM. J. COMP. L. 753 (2010).

HALSBURY'S STATUTORY INSTRUMENTS (London: Butterworths; St. Paul, MN: Butterworth Legal Publishers, 1986–).

HALSBURY'S LAWS OF ENGLAND (4th ed., London; Butterworths, 1973–).

HAMZAH, WAN ARFAH, & RAMY BULAN, AN INTRODUCTION TO THE MALAYSIAN LEGAL SYSTEM (Shah Alam, Selangor Darul Ehsan: Fajar Bakti, 2003).

HANDBOOK ON INTERNATIONAL ARBITRATION AND ADR (Thomas E. Carbonneau et al., Huntington, N.Y.: JurisNet, 2006).

HAPP, RICHARD, & NOAH RUBINS, DIGEST OF ICSID AWARDS AND DECISIONS: 2003–2007 (Oxford: Oxford University Press 2009).

HASTINGS INTERNATIONAL AND COMPARATIVE LAW REVIEW (San Francisco: University of California, Hastings College of the Law, 1978–). Available on HeinOnline.

HEIDENHAIN, MARTIN, ET AL., GERMAN ANTITRUST LAW: AN INTRODUCTION TO THE GERMAN ANTITRUST LAW WITH GERMAN TEXT AND SYNOPTIC ENGLISH TRANSLATION OF THE ACT AGAINST RESTRAINTS OF COMPETITION (5th ed., Frankfurt am Main: F. Knapp, 1999).

HeinOnline, subscription database, http://home.heinonline.org.

HeinOnline's Foreign and International Law Resources Database, http://heinonline.org/HOL/Index?collection=intyb.

HELLER, KEVIN JON, & MARKUS DIRK DUBBER, THE HANDBOOK OF COMPARATIVE CRIMINAL LAW (Stanford, Calif.: Stanford Law Books, 2011).

HELSINKI MONITOR, see SECURITY AND HUMAN RIGHTS.

HENKIN, LOUIS, INTERNATIONAL LAW: CASES AND MATERIALS (3d ed., St. Paul, MN: West Pub. Co., 1993).

HERBST, ROBERT, DICTIONARY OF COMMERCIAL, FINANCIAL AND LEGAL TERMS (6th ed., rev. and enl., Thun, Switzerland: Translegal, 1998–2003).

HERZ, MÔNICA, THE ORGANIZATION OF AMERICAN STATES (OAS): GLOBAL GOVERNANCE AWAY FROM THE MEDIA (Abingdon, Oxon; New York: Routledge, 2011).

HINKELMAN, EDWARD G., DICTIONARY OF INTERNATIONAL TRADE: HANDBOOK OF THE GLOBAL TRADE COMMUNITY (9th ed., Novato, CA: World Trade Press, 2010).

HODGES, CHRISTOPHER J.S., THE REFORM OF CLASS AND REPRESENTATIVE ACTIONS IN EUROPEAN LEGAL SYSTEMS: A NEW FRAMEWORK FOR COLLECTIVE REDRESS IN EUROPE (Oxford: Hart Publishing, 2008).

Hoffman, Marci, Researching U.S. Treaties and Agreements, http://www.llrx.com/features/ustreaty.htm.

HOLTZMANN, HOWARD M., & JOSEPH E. NEUHAUS, A GUIDE TO THE UNCITRAL MODEL LAW ON INTERNATIONAL COMMERCIAL ARBITRATION: LEGISLATIVE HISTORY AND COMMENTARY (Deventer; Boston: Kluwer Law and Taxation Publishers, 1989).

HORWITZ, BETTY, THE TRANSFORMATION OF THE ORGANIZATION OF AMERICAN STATES: A MULTILATERAL FRAMEWORK FOR REGIONAL GOVERNANCE (London; New York: Anthem Press, 2010).

HORWITZ, ETHAN, WORLD TRADEMARK LAW AND PRACTICE (New York: M. Bender, 1982–). Also available on LexisNexis, Legal >Area of Law -By Topic >Trademarks >Treatises & Analytical Materials >Matthew Bender(R) >World Trademark Law and Practice.

HOUTTE, HANS VAN, THE LAW OF INTERNATIONAL TRADE (2d ed., London: Sweet & Maxwell, 2002).

HUDOC, http://cmiskp.echr.coe.int/tkp197/search.asp?skin=hudoc-en.

HUMAN RIGHTS: A COMPILATION OF INTERNATIONAL INSTRUMENTS (New York: United Nations, 2002–).

HUMAN RIGHTS CASE DIGEST (London: British Institute of Human Rights, 1990—2008). Also available on HeinOnline and Ingenta.
Human Rights Education Associates [HREA], Blogs, http://www.hrea.org/index.php?base_id=88.
Human Rights Education Associates, Study Guides, Food & Water, http://www.hrea.org/index.php?base_id=145.
HUMAN RIGHTS LAW JOURNAL [H.R.L.J.] (Kehl am Rhein; Arlington [Va.]: N.P. Engel, 1980–).
Human Rights Watch [HRW], Country Reports, http://www.hrw.org/publications.
Human Rights Watch, Blogs, http://www.hrw.org/rss.
HUNGARIAN RULES OF LAW IN FORCE (Budapest: Ötlet Ltd. and UNIO Ltd., 1990–).
Hunter, David, et al., International Environmental Law & Policy: A Comprehensive Reference Source (2d ed., undated), http://www.wcl.american.edu/environment/iel.
HuriSearch, http://www.hurisearch.org.
Husa, Jaakko, *Classification of Legal Families Today: Is it Time for a Memorial Hymn?*, 66 R.I.D.C. 11 (2004).
HYDE, CHARLES C., INTERNATIONAL LAW CHIEFLY AS INTERPRETED AND APPLIED BY THE UNITED STATES (2d rev. ed., Boston: Little, Brown and Company, 1945). First edition (1922) is available on HeinOnline.
IALL INTERNATIONAL HANDBOOK OF LEGAL INFORMATION (Richard A. Danner & Jules Winterton eds., Farnham, Surrey; Burlington, VT: Ashgate Pub., 2011).
ICC Legal Tools Database, http://www.legal-tools.org/en/what-are-the-icc-legal-tools.
ICC INTERNATIONAL COURT OF ARBITRATION BULLETIN (Paris, France: ICC International Court of Arbitration, 1990–).
ICSID Convention, http://icsid.worldbank.org/ICSID/ICSID/RulesMain.jsp.
ICSID REPORTS: REPORTS OF CASES DECIDED UNDER THE CONVENTION ON THE SETTLEMENT OF INVESTMENT DISPUTES BETWEEN STATES AND NATIONALS OF OTHER STATES (Cambridge, UK: Grotius Publications, 1993–).
IIC: INTERNATIONAL REVIEW OF INDUSTRIAL PROPERTY AND COPYRIGHT LAW (Weinheim/Bergstr.,VCH Verlagsgesellschaft mbH [etc.], 1970–2003).
IIC: INTERNATIONAL REVIEW OF INTELLECTUAL PROPERTY AND COMPETITION LAW (Verlag C.H. Beck; Oxford: Hart Pub., 2004–).
ILSA JOURNAL OF INTERNATIONAL & COMPARATIVE LAW (Ft. Lauderdale, FL: Nova Southeastern University, Shepard Broad Law Center, 1995–). Available on HeinOnline.
Income Tax Treaties (Internal Revenue Service), http://www.irs.gov/businesses/international/article/0,,id=96739,00.html.
INDEX TO FOREIGN LEGAL PERIODICALS [IFLP] (London: Institute of Advanced Legal Studies; Chicago: American Association of Law Libraries, 1960–). Available by subscription on HeinOnline; 1985 onwards is fully searchable with links to full-text articles (where available); 1960–1984 available to browse and search in digital form.
INDEX TO LEGAL PERIODICALS AND BOOKS [ILP] (Bronx, NY: H.W. Wilson Co., 1994–). Also by subscription, http://www.ebscohost.com/academic/index-to-legal-periodicals-books.
Indian Affairs: Laws and Treaties (Electronic version of the treatise compiled and edited by Charles J. Kappler), http://digital.library.okstate.edu/kappler.
INDIANA INTERNATIONAL & COMPARATIVE LAW REVIEW (Indianapolis, IN: Indiana University School of Law–Indianapolis, 1991–). Available on HeinOnline.
INDIGENOUS PEOPLES AND THE LAW: COMPARATIVE AND CRITICAL PERSPECTIVES (Benjamin J. Richardson et al. eds., Oxford; Portland, Or.: Hart, 2009).
INDLAW, subscription database, http://www.indlaw.com.
Infolegis, http://www.infolegis.com.br.
Infomine Scholarly Internet Resource Collections, http://infomine.ucr.edu.
INFORMATION SOURCES IN LAW (2d ed., Jules Winterton & Elizabeth M. Moys eds., London; New Providence, NJ: Bowker-Saur, 1997).
International Justice Tribune, http://www.rnw.nl/international-justice.
INSIDE U.S.-CHINA TRADE (Washington, DC: Inside Washington Publishers, 2001–). Also available by subscription on the web and on LexisNexis from Februrary 2006; News & Business >Individual Publications >I >Inside U.S.-China Trade.

INSIDE U.S. TRADE (Washington, DC: Inside Washington Publishers, 1983–). Also available by subscription on the web and on LexisNexis from October 2005; News & Business >Individual Publications >I >Inside U.S. Trade.

Institute of Global Law, http://www.ucl.ac.uk/laws/global_law/.

INTELLECTUAL PROPERTY: EASTERN EUROPE & COMMONWEALTH OF INDEPENDENT STATES (David L. Garrison comp. & ed., New York: Oceana Publications, 1995–).

INTELLECTUAL PROPERTY LAWS AND TREATIES (Geneva: WIPO, 1998–2001).

INTER-AMERICAN COMMISSION ON HUMAN RIGHTS ANNUAL REPORT (Washington, DC: General Secretariat, Organization of American States, 1977–). Also available on the Commission's website, http://www.cidh.oas.org/publi.eng.htm. See also Westlaw (IACHR-OAS database) and the University of Minnesota Human Rights Library, http://www1.umn.edu/humanrts/cases/commissn.htm.

Inter-American Commission on Human Rights Documents, University of Minnesota Human Rights Library, http://www1.umn.edu/humanrts/cases/commissn.htm.

INTER-AMERICAN COURT OF HUMAN RIGHTS, ANNUAL REPORT (Washington, DC: The Court, 1981–). Also available on the Court's website from 1980 on, http://www.corteidh.or.cr/informes.cfm.

Inter-American Court of Human Rights, Decisions, http://www.corteidh.or.cr/index.cfm?&CFID=1492519&CFTOKEN=79392452.

Inter-American Court of Human Rights, Decisions, http://www1.umn.edu/humanrts/iachr/series_A.html.

INTER-AMERICAN COURT OF HUMAN RIGHTS, SERIES A: JUDGMENTS AND OPINIONS (San Jose, Costa Rica: Secretaría de la Corte, 1982–).

INTER-AMERICAN COURT OF HUMAN RIGHTS, SERIES B: PLEADINGS, ARGUMENTS AND DOCUMENTS (San Jose, Costa Rica: Secretaría de la Corte, 1983–).

INTER-AMERICAN COURT OF HUMAN RIGHTS, SERIES C: DECISIONS AND JUDGMENTS (San Jose', Costa Rica: Secretaría de la Corte, 1987–). Note: none have been published since 2006.

Inter-American Human Rights Digest Project at American University, http://www.wcl.american.edu/humright/repertorio/indice.cfm.

THE INTER-AMERICAN SYSTEM OF HUMAN RIGHTS (David J. Harris & Stephen Livingstone eds., Oxford: Clarendon Press; New York: Oxford University Press, 1998).

INTER-AMERICAN TRADE REPORT (Tucson, AZ: National Law Center for Inter-American Free Trade, 1997–2005). Also available on the National Law Center for Inter-American Trade website, http://www.natlaw.com/bulletin/report.htm.

INTER-AMERICAN TREATIES AND CONVENTIONS: SIGNATURES, RATIFICATIONS, AND DEPOSITS WITH EXPLANATORY NOTES (Washington, DC: General Secretariat, Organization of American States, 1954–).

INTER-AMERICAN YEARBOOK ON HUMAN RIGHTS (Dordrecht; Boston: Nijhoff, 1987–). Prior to 1974, this was published by the General Secretariat of the Organization of American States (1968–[1970]?).

InterEnvironment, http://www.interenvironment.org/wd.

INTERNATIONAL AND COMPARATIVE LAW QUARTERLY [I.C.L.Q.] (London: Society of Comparative Legislation, 1952–). Available by subscription: HeinOnline, JSTOR, Ingenta Select, Oxford University Press.

International Antitrust and Consumer Protection Cooperation Agreements (Federal Trade Commission), http://www.ftc.gov/oia/agreements.shtm.

International Arbitration Case Law (School of Arbitration), http://www.internationalarbitrationcaselaw.com.

INTERNATIONAL ARBITRATION TREATIES (3d ed., Loukas Mistelis et al. eds., Huntington, NY: Juris, 2010–).

INTERNATIONAL ARBITRATION COURT DECISIONS (3d ed., Stephen Bond & Frédéric Bachand eds., Huntington, N.Y.: Juris, 2011).

International Bureau of Fiscal Documentation [IBFD], subscription database, http://www.org.

International Centre for Settlement of Investment Disputes [ICSID], http://icsid.worldbank.org/ICSID/Index.jsp.

International Centre for Settlement of Investment Dispute], ICSID Cases, http://icsid
.worldbank.org/ICSID/FrontServlet?requestType=CasesRH&actionVal=ShowHome&page
Name=Documents_Home.

International Centre for Settlement of Investment Disputes, Bilateral Investment Treaties,
http://icsid.worldbank.org/ICSID/FrontServlet.

International Child Abduction Database (Hague Conference on Private International Law),
http://www.incadat.com.

International Chamber of Commerce, Dispute Resolution Library [ICC DRL], subscription
database, http://www.iccdrl.com.

INTERNATIONAL CIVIL PROCEDURE (2d ed. Christian Campbell ed., Huntington, N.Y.: Juris
Publishing, 2010–).

INTERNATIONAL COMMERCIAL ARBITRATION (2d. enl. ed., Eric E. Bergsten ed., Dobbs Ferry,
NY, Oceana Publications, 1979–).

International Committee for the Red Cross [ICRC], International Humanitarian Law—
Treaties and Documents, http://www.icrc.org/ihl.nsf/CONVPRES?OpenView.

International Committee of the Red Cross, National Implementation Database, http://www
.icrc.org/ihl-nat.

International Constitutional Law, http://www.servat.unibe.ch/law/icl/index.html.

International Constitutional Law Project, http://www.oefre.unibe.ch/law/icl.

INTERNATIONAL COPYRIGHT LAW AND PRACTICE (Melville B. Nimmer & Paul Geller eds.,
New York: Matthew Bender, 1988–). Also available on LexisNexis, Legal >Area of Law—
By Topic >Copyright Law >Treatises & Analytical Materials >Matthew Bender(R) >Inter-
national Copyright Law and Practices [sic].

INTERNATIONAL CORPORATE PRACTICE: A PRACTITIONER'S GUIDE TO GLOBAL SUCCESS (New
York City: Practising Law Institute, 2008–).

International Council for Commercial Arbitration [ICCA], http://www.arbitration-icca.org/
related-links.html.

International Council for Commercial Arbitration, National Arbitration Laws, http://www
.arbitration-icca.org/related-links.html#03.

International Court of Arbitration, http://www.iccwbo.org/court/arbitration/id4424/index
.html.

International Court of Justice [ICJ], http://www.icj-cij.org.

INTERNATIONAL COURT OF JUSTICE, MEMOIRES, PLAIDOIRIES ET DOCUMENTS = PLEADINGS,
ORAL ARGUMENTS AND DOCUMENTS (The Hague: The Court, 1947–).

INTERNATIONAL COURT OF JUSTICE, RECUEIL DES ARRETS, AVIS CONSULTATIFS ET ORDON-
NANCES = REPORTS OF JUDGMENTS, ADVISORY OPINIONS AND ORDERS (Leyden: A.W.
Sijthoff, 1947–).

INTERNATIONAL COURT OF JUSTICE, RÉPERTOIRE DE LA JURISPRUDENCE DE LA COUR INTER-
NATIONALE DE JUSTICE (1947–1992) (Dordrecht; Boston: M. Nijhoff; Norwell, MA: Sold
and distributed in the U.S.A. and Canada by Kluwer Academic Publishers, 1995).

International Court of Justice Research Guide (UC Hastings Law Library), http://library
.uchastings.edu/library/foreign-and-international-research/icj.html.

INTERNATIONAL COURT OF JUSTICE, YEARBOOK (The Hague: The Court, 1947–). Available
on HeinOnline.

International Courts and Tribunals Research Guide (Harvard Law Library), http://libguides
.law.harvard.edu/intlcourtstribunals.

International Courts Data, http://www9.georgetown.edu/faculty/ev42/ICdata.htm.

International Criminal Court [ICC], http://www.icc-cpi.int.

International Criminal Court Legal Tools Database, http://www.legal-tools.org/en/what-are-
the-icc-legal-tools.

INTERNATIONAL CRIMINAL JUSTICE: LAW AND PRACTICE FROM THE ROME STATUTE TO ITS
REVIEW (Roberto Bellelli ed., Farnham, Surrey, England; Burlington, VT: Ashgate Pub.,
2010).

INTERNATIONAL CRIMINAL LAW (3d ed., M. Cherif Bassiouni ed., Leiden, Netherlands: Martinus Nijhoff Pub., 2008).

THE INTERNATIONAL CRIMINAL LAW REPORTS (Helen Malcolm & Rodney Dixon eds., London: Cameron May, 2000–).

International Criminal Tribunal for Rwanda [ICTR], http://www.ictr.org.

International Criminal Tribunal for the Former Yugoslavia [ICTY], http://www.icty.org.

INTERNATIONAL DOCUMENTS ON CHILDREN (2d rev. ed., Geraldine Van Bueren ed., The Hague; Boston: M. Nijhoff, 1998).

INTERNATIONAL, EC, AND US ENVIRONMENTAL LAW: A COMPARATIVE SELECTION OF BASIC DOCUMENTS (Kurt Deketelaere & Jan Gekiere eds., The Hague: Kluwer Law International; Frederick, MD: Sold and distributed in North, Central, and South America by Aspen Publishers, 2002).

International Economic Law and Policy Blog, http://worldtradelaw.typepad.com.

INTERNATIONAL ECONOMIC LAW: BASIC DOCUMENTS (Philip Kunig, et al. eds., 2d enl. ed., Berlin; New York: W. de Gruyter, 1993).

INTERNATIONAL ENCYCLOPAEDIA FOR LABOUR LAW AND INDUSTRIAL RELATIONS (Roger Blanpain ed., Deventer: Kluwer, 1977–).

INTERNATIONAL ENCYCLOPAEDIA OF LAWS (The Hague; Cambridge, MA: Kluwer Law International, date varies). Topics include: civil procedure, commercial and economic law, constitutional law, contracts, corporations and partnerships, criminal law, cyber law, energy law, environmental law, family and succession law, insurance law, intellectual property, intergovernmental organizations, medical law, private international law, property and trust law, social security law, sports law, tort law, and transport law. Available by subscription, http://www.kluwerlawonline.com/index.php?area=Looseleafs.

INTERNATIONAL ENCYCLOPEDIA OF COMPARATIVE LAW (Tubingen: J.C.B. Mohr Paul Siebeck; New York: Oceana, 1973–).

INTERNATIONAL ENFORCEMENT LAW REPORTER (Washington, DC: International Law Enforcement Reporter, 1985–).

INTERNATIONAL ENVIRONMENT DAILY (Washington, DC: Bureau of National Affairs, Inc., 2001–). Available by subscription, http://www.bna.com.

INTERNATIONAL ENVIRONMENT REPORTER (Washington, DC: Bureau of National Affairs, Inc., 1978–). Available by subscription, http://www.bna.com.

INTERNATIONAL ENVIRONMENTAL LAW: MULTILATERAL TREATIES (W.E. Burhenne ed.; Robert Muecke comp., Berlin: E. Schmidt, 1974–).

INTERNATIONAL ENVIRONMENTAL LAW REPORTS (Cairo A.R. Robb ed., Cambridge, UK: Cambridge University Press, 1999–2004).

INTERNATIONAL ENVIRONMENTAL SOFT LAW: COLLECTION OF RELEVANT INSTRUMENTS (W.E. Burhenne ed. & Marlene Jahnke comp., The Hague; Boston: Martinus Nijhoff, 1993–). This collection has not been updated since 2003.

INTERNATIONAL EXECUTION AGAINST JUDGMENT DEBTORS (Dennis Campbell ed., [Eagan, MN]: Thomson Reuters/West, 2011–).

INTERNATIONAL FRANCHISING (2d ed., Dennis Campbell ed., Huntington, NY: Juris Pub., 2011–).

INTERNATIONAL IMMIGRATION AND NATIONALITY LAW (2d ed., Dennis Campbell ed., Huntington, NY: Juris Pub., 2011–).

INTERNATIONAL INFORMATION: DOCUMENTS, PUBLICATIONS, AND INFORMATION SYSTEMS OF INTERNATIONAL GOVERNMENTAL ORGANIZATIONS (Peter I. Hajnal ed., 2d ed., Englewood, CO: Libraries Unlimited, 1997).

INTERNATIONAL HANDBOOK ON COMMERCIAL ARBITRATION (Jan Paulsson ed., Deventer, The Netherlands; Boston: Kluwer Law and Taxation Pub., 1984–).

INTERNATIONAL HUMAN RIGHTS REPORTS [I.H.R.R.] (Nottingham, United Kingdom: Human Rights Law Centre, Department of Law, University of Nottingham, 1994–). Also available online by subscription: http://www.nottingham.ac.uk/hrlc/publications/international humanrightsreports.aspx.

International Humanitarian Law [IHL], http://www.icrc.org/ihl.

International Institute for the Unification of Private Law (UNIDROIT), http://www.unidroit.org.

INTERNATIONAL JOURNAL OF CONSTITUTIONAL LAW: I-CON (Oxford, UK: Oxford University Press, 2003–). Available on HeinOnline, Ingenta Connect, and publisher's website.

INTERNATIONAL JOURNAL OF LEGAL INFORMATION ([Nashville]: Institute for International Legal Information, 1982–). Available on HeinOnline.

International Labour Law Reports (Alphen aan de Rijn: Sijthoff & Noordhoff, 1978–). Also available on HeinOnline.

International Labour Organization [ILO], NATLEX, http://www.ilo.org/dyn/natlex/natlex_browse.home.

ILOLEX (International Labour Organization), http://www.ilo.org/ilolex/english.

International Law Association, Report of the Conference (London: W. Clowes, 1873–). Also available on HeinOnline.

International Law & World Order: Basic Documents (Burns H. Weston ed., Irvington-on-Hudson, NY: Transnational Publishers, 1994–).

International Law, Chiefly as Interpreted and Applied in Canada (Hugh M. Kindred et al., eds., 7th ed., Toronto: Emond Montgomery Publications, 2006). See website for links to treaties and cases, http://www.emp.ca/index.php/international-law-chiefly-as-interpreted-and-applied-in-canada.

International Law in Domestic Courts [I.L.D.C.] (Oxford University Press), subscription database, http://ildc.oxfordlawreports.com.

International Law Reports [I.L.R.] (Cambridge, UK: Grotius, 1919–). Available by subscription, http://www.justis.com.

The International Lawyer ([Chicago]: Section of International Law, American Bar Association, 1966–). Also available on HeinOnline.

The International Lawyer's Deskbook (Lucinda A. Low et al. eds., 2d ed., Chicago: Section of International Law and Practice, American Bar Association, 2002).

International Legal Materials [I.L.M.] (Washington: American Society of International Law, 1962–). Available on HeinOnline, LexisNexis, and Westlaw.

International Maritime and Commercial Law Yearbook (London: LLP, 2002–).

International Maritime Organization [IMO], http://www.imo.org/blast/mainframemenu.asp?topic_id=1488.

International Organization (Boston, Mass.: World Peace Foundation, 1947–). Available by subscription, http://journals.cambridge.org/, JSTOR, and Westlaw.

International Organizations: A Dictionary and Directory (7th ed., Houndmills, Basingstoke, Hampshire, UK; New York: Palgrave, 2008).

International Organizations (University of Colorado), http://ucblibraries.colorado.edu/govpubs/int/internat.htm.

International Organizations (Northwestern University), http://libguides.northwestern.edu/IGO.

International Organizations Law Review (Leiden, Netherlands: M. Nijhoff, 2004–). Available by subscription, http://www.ingentaconnect.com.

International Patent Litigation: A Country-By-Country Analysis (Michael N. Meller ed., Washington, DC: Bureau of National Affairs, 1983–).

International Protection of the Environment: Agenda 21 and the UNCED Proceedings (Nicholas A. Robinson ed., 3d series, Dobbs Ferry, New York: Oceana Publications, 1992–).

International Protection of the Environment: Treaties and Related Documents (Bernd Rüster & Bruno Simma comps. & eds., Dobbs Ferry, NY: Oceana Publications, 1975–1983).

International Protection of the Environment: Treaties and Related Documents, Second Series (Bernd Rüster & Bruno Simma comps. & eds., Dobbs Ferry, NY: Oceana Publications, 1990–1995).

The International Survey of Family Law (Andrew Bainham ed., The Hague; Boston: M. Nijhoff; Cambridge, MA: Sold and distributed in the U.S.A. and Canada by Kluwer Law International, 1994–).

International Trade Reporter (Washington, DC: Bureau of National Affairs, 1984–). Also available on LexisNexis and Westlaw under some subscription plans.

The International Trade Law Reports (London: Cameron May, 1996–).

International Tribunal for the Law of the Sea [ITLOS], http://www.itlos.org.

International Trust Laws and Analysis (William H. Byrnes & Robert J Munro, eds., The Hague; Boston, MA: Kluwer Law International, 1995–).

INTERNATIONAL YEARBOOK OF MINORITY ISSUES (Den Bosch, The Netherlands: BookWorld Publications, 2002–).

INT-LAW list, http://listserver.ciesin.columbia.edu/cgi-bin/wa?A0=Int-Law.

IntLawGrrls, http://intlawgrrls.blogspot.com/index.html.

INTNEWS on Westlaw.

INTRODUCTION TO BRAZILIAN LAW (Fabiano Deffenti & Welber Barral eds., Alphen aan den Rijn, The Netherlands: Wolters Kluwer; Frederick, MD: Sold and distributed in North, Central and South America by Aspen Publishers, 2011).

INTRODUCTION TO CHINESE LAW (Wang Chenguang & Zhang Xianchu eds., Hong Kong: Sweet & Maxwell Asia, 1997).

INTRODUCTION TO DUTCH LAW (4th rev. ed., J.M.J. Chorus et al. eds., Alphen aan den Rijn: Kluwer Law International; Frederick, MD: Sold and Distributed in North, Central, and South America by Aspen Publishers, 2006).

INTRODUCTION TO FOREIGN LEGAL SYSTEMS (Richard A. Danner & Marie-Louise H. Bernal eds., New York: Oceana Publications, 1994).

INTRODUCTION TO GREEK LAW (Konstantinos D. Kerameus & Phaedon J. Kozyris eds., 3d rev. ed., Deventer, Netherlands; Boston: Kluwer Law and Taxation Publishers; Athens: Sakkoulas, 2008).

INTRODUCTION TO INTERNATIONAL ORGANIZATIONS (Lyonette Louis-Jacques & Jeanne S. Korman eds., New York: Oceana Publications, 1996).

INTRODUCTION TO THE LAW OF ISRAEL (Amos Shapira & Keren C. DeWitt-Arar eds., The Hague; Boston: Kluwer Law International, 1995).

INTRODUCTION TO THE LAW OF SOUTH AFRICA (C.G. van der Merwe & Jacques E. du Plessis eds., The Hague: Kluwer Law International, 2004).

INTRODUCTION TO TRANSNATIONAL LEGAL TRANSACTIONS (Marylin J. Raisch & Roberta I. Shaffer eds., New York: Oceana Publications, 1995).

INTRODUCTION TO TURKISH LAW (Tugrul Ansay & Don Wallace, Jr. eds., 5th ed. [New York]: Kluwer Law International, 2005).

INTRODUCTIONS OR DOING BUSINESS IN . . . See, e.g., *Doing Business in Mexico, Introduction to Chinese Law, Introduction to Dutch Law, Doing Business in Asia,* or *Doing Business in Argentina.*

Investment Arbitration Reporter [IA Reporter], subscription database, http://www.iareporter .com.

Investment Claims (Oxford University Press), subscription database, http://investmentclaims .com.

INVESTMENT LAWS OF THE WORLD (Dobbs Ferry, NY: Oceana Publications, 1972–).

INVESTMENT PROMOTION AND PROTECTION TREATIES (International Centre for the Settlement of Investment Disputes comp., London; New York: Oceana Publications, 1983–).

Investment Treaty Arbitration [ITA], http://italaw.com.

Investment Treaty Arbitrations, Investment Treaties, http://italaw.com/investmenttreaties.htm.

Investor-State Law Guide, subscription database, http://www.investorstatelawguide.com.

Ipl2, http://www.ipl.org.

IPRsonline, http://www.iprsonline.org/index.htm.

Iran-United States Claims Tribunal, http://www.iusct.org.

Iran-United States Claims Tribunal, IUSCT Public Database, http://www.iusct.com.

IRAN-UNITED STATES CLAIMS TRIBUNAL REPORTS (Cambridge, [Cambridgeshire]: Grotius Publications, 1983–). Also available on Westlaw.

IRISH YEARBOOK OF INTERNATIONAL LAW (Oxford; Portland, Oregon: Hart Pub., 2008–). Also available on HeinOnline.

ISIL YEAR BOOK OF INTERNATIONAL HUMANITARIAN AND REFUGEE LAW (New Delhi: Indian Society of International Law, 2001–).

iSinolaw, subscription database, http://www.isinolaw.com.

THE ITALIAN YEARBOOK OF INTERNATIONAL LAW (Napoli: Editoriale Scientifica; [Dobbs Ferry, NY: Distributed by Oceana Publications], 1975–).

Iwasaki, Kazuo, Asian Investment Law Database, http://homepage3.nifty.com/Prof_K_ Iwasaki/index-en.html.

JAPANESE ANNUAL OF INTERNATIONAL LAW (Tokyo: Japan Branch of the International Law Association, 1957–).

JAPANESE FAMILY LAW IN COMPARATIVE PERSPECTIVE (Harry N. Scheiber & Laurent Mayali eds., Berkeley, Calif.: Robbins Collection Publications, 2009).

JESSUP, PHILIP C., TRANSNATIONAL LAW (New Haven, CT: Yale University Press, 1956).

JONES, JOHN R.W.D., & STEVEN POWLES, INTERNATIONAL CRIMINAL PRACTICE: THE INTERNATIONAL CRIMINAL TRIBUNAL FOR THE FORMER YUGOSLAVIA, THE INTERNATIONAL CRIMINAL TRIBUNAL FOR RWANDA, THE INTERNATIONAL CRIMINAL COURT, THE SPECIAL COURT FOR SIERRA LEONE, THE EAST TIMOR SPECIAL PANEL FOR SERIOUS CRIMES, WAR CRIMES PROSECUTIONS IN KOSOVO (3d ed., Ardsley, NY: Transnational Publishers; Oxford; [New York]: Oxford Unversity Press, 2003).

JOSEPH, SARAH, ET AL., THE INTERNATIONAL COVENANT ON CIVIL AND POLITICAL RIGHTS: CASES, MATERIALS, AND COMMENTARY (2d ed., Oxford; New York: Oxford University Press, 2004).

JOURNAL DE DROIT INTERNATIONAL (Paris: Marchal et Godde: [puis] Godde: [puis] Ed. Techniques: [puis] Ed. du Juris-Classeu, 1915–).

JOURNAL OF CONSTITUTIONAL LAW IN EASTERN AND CENTRAL EUROPE (Boxtel, Netherlands: TFLR-Institute, 1994–).

JOURNAL OF INTERNATIONAL AFFAIRS (New York: School of International Affairs, Columbia University, 1952–). Available by subscription, http://web.ebscohost.com.

JOURNAL OF INTERNATIONAL ECONOMIC LAW [J.I.E.L.] (Oxford, UK: Oxford University Press, 1998–). Also available by subscription, http://jiel.oxfordjournals.org.

JOURNAL OFFICIEL DE LA RÉPUBLIQUE FRANÇAISE (Paris: [s.n.], 1946–). Available from 1990 to present, http://www.legifrance.gouv.fr.

JOURNAL OF INTERNATIONAL ORGANIZATIONS STUDIES (2010–).

JSTOR: The Scholarly Journal Archive, subscription database, http://www.jstor.org.

JUDICIAL REPORTS / INTERNATIONAL CRIMINAL TRIBUNAL FOR THE FORMER YUGOSLAVIA = RECUEILS JUDICIAIRES / TRIBUNAL PÉNAL POUR L'EX-YOUGOSLAVIE (The Hague: Kluwer Law International, 1999–).

JUDICIARIES IN COMPARATIVE PERSPECTIVE (H.P. Lee ed., Cambridge, UK; New York: Cambridge University Press, 2011).

JuriGlobe World Legal Systems, http://www.juriglobe.ca.

JURIS, subscription database, http://www.gesetzesportal.de/jportal/portal/page/fpgesetze.psml.

JURIS International Arbitration, subscription database, http://www.jurispub.com/cart.php?m=content&page=12.

JurisClasseur Lexis/Nexis, subscription database, http://www.lexisnexis.fr.

Juris International, http://www.jurisint.org/pub.

THE JURISPRUDENCE ON REGIONAL AND INTERNATIONAL TRIBUNALS DIGEST (Nairobi, Kenya; Dar es Salaam, Tanzania; Kampala, Uganda: LawAfrica Pub., 2007).

Jurist World Legal News, http://jurist.law.pitt.edu/worldlatest.

Justis, subscription database, http://www.justis.com.

JUTASTAT, subscription database, http://www.jutalaw.co.za.

Kadir, Rizgar Mohammed, *The Scope and the Nature of Computer Crimes Statutes—A Critical Comparative Study*, 11 GERMAN L.J. 609 (2010), http://www.germanlawjournal.com/pdfs/Vol11-No6/PDF_Vol_11_No_06_609–632_RM_kadir.pdf.

KAYE, HARVEY, & CHRISTOPHER A. DUNN, INTERNATIONAL TRADE PRACTICE (annual, Eagan, MN: West, 2011–).

KERR, JOHN J. COMPARISON OF INTERNATIONAL ARBITRATION RULES (3d ed., Huntington, N.Y.: JurisNet, LLC, 2008).

Khmer Rouge Trials, http://www.unakrt-online.org. Kidane, Won, *Managing Forced Displacement by Law in Africa: The Role of the New African Union IDPS Convention*, 44 VAND. J. TRANSNAT'L L. 1 (2011).

Kim-Prieto, Dennis, *En La Tierra del Ciego, el Tuerco es Rey: Problems with Current English-Spanish Legal Dictionaries, and Notes toward a Critical Comparative Legal Lexicography*, 100 L. LIBR. J. 251 (2008).

Kirchner, Hildebert, Abkürzungsverzeichnis der Rechtssprache (6th ed., Berlin: De Gruyter Recht, 2008).

Kirgis, Frederic, *International Agreements and U.S. Law*, ASIL Insight, No. 10, May 1997, http://www.asil.org/insights/insigh10.htm.

Klabbers, Jan, An Introduction to International Institutional Law (2d ed., Cambridge, UK; New York: Cambridge University Press, 2009).

Klabbers, Jan, International Organizations (Aldershot, UK; Burlington, VT: Ashgate/ Dartmouth, 2005).

KluwerArbitration.com, subscription database, http://www.kluwerarbitration.com.

Kluwer Arbitration Blog, http://kluwerarbitrationblog.com.

Kodeks Law Databases, subscription database, http://kodeks.mosinfo.ru.

Kolber, Adam, *Citing Wikipedia, posted to PrawfsBlawg*, Dec 13, 2006, http://prawfsblawg .blogs.com/prawfsblawg.

Kommers, Donald P., The Constitutional Jurisprudence of the Federal Republic of Germany (2d ed., Durham, NC: Duke University Press, 1997).

Korean Ministry of Government Legislation, http://www.moleg.go.kr/english/korLawEng.

Kost, Ingrid, *Bibliography on the Katanga Case*, 23 Leiden J. Int'l L. 375 (2010).

Krishna, Vern, The Canada-U.S. Tax Treaty: Text and Commentary (Markham, Ont.; Dayton, Ohio: LexisNexis Butterworths, 2004).

Kronke, Herbert, Recognition and Enforcement of Foreign Arbitral Award: A Global Commentary on the New York Convention (Alphen aan den Rijn, The Netherlands: Kluwer Law International; Austin: Wolters Kluwer Law & Business; Frederick, MD: Distributed in North, Central, and South America by Aspen Publishers, 2010).

Kuehl, Heidi F., A Basic Guide to International Environmental Legal Research (2010), http:// www.nyulawglobal.org/globalex/International_Environmental_Legal_Research1.htm.

Landmark Cases in Public International Law (Malgosia Fitzmaurice & Eric Heinze eds., London; Boston: Kluwer Law International, 1998).

Latin American Legal Abbreviations: A Comprehensive Spanish/Portuguese Dictionary with English Translations (Arturo L. Torres & Francisco Avalos comps., New York: Greenwood Press, 1989).

LawAfrica.com, http://lawafrica.com.

Law and Judicial Systems of Nations (4th rev. ed., Charles S. Rhyne ed., Washington, DC: World Jurist Association, 2002).

The Law and Legal System of Uzbekistan (Ilias Bantekas ed., Huntington, NY: Juris Publishing, Inc., 2005).

The Law and Practice of International Courts and Tribunals (The Hague; New York: Kluwer Law International, 2002–). Also available by subscription on the publisher's website and HeinOnline.

Law & Practice of the World Trade Organization (New York: Oceana Publications, 1995–).

Law Reports of the Commonwealth [LRC] (Abingdon, Oxfordshire, UK: Professional Books, 1985–).

Law Reports of Trials of War Criminals (Selected and prepared by the United Nations War Crimes Commission) (London, Pub. for the United Nations War Crimes Commission by H.M. Stationery Off., 1947–1949). Also available on HeinOnline.

Lawson, Frederick H., A Common Lawyer Looks at the Civil Law (Ann Arbor: University of Michigan Law School, 1955).

Lazic, Vesna, Insolvency Proceedings and Commercial Arbitration (The Hague; Boston: Kluwer Law International, 1999).

Leach, Philip, Taking a Case to the European Court of Human Rights (3d ed., Oxford: Oxford University Press, 2011).

League of Nations Treaty Series [L.N.T.S.] (London: Harrison & Sons, 1919–1945). Available at http://treaties.un.org/Pages/LONOnline.aspx.

Legal Aspects of Doing Business in Africa (2d ed., Huntington, N.Y.: Juris, 2011–).

Legal Aspects of Doing Business in Asia (2d ed., Huntington, N.Y.: Juris, 2011–).

Legal Aspects of Doing Business in Latin America (2d ed., Huntington, N.Y.: Juris, 2011–).

LEGAL CULTURE IN THE AGE OF GLOBALIZATION: LATIN AMERICA AND LATIN EUROPE (Lawrence M. Friedman & Rogelio Pérez-Perdomo eds., Stanford, CA: Stanford University Press, 2003).

LEGAL JOURNALS INDEX [LJI], available on Westlaw and through Current Legal Information, http://www.sweetandmaxwell.co.uk/online/cli.html.

LEGAL LOOSELEAFS IN PRINT (New York: Infosources Pub., 1981–).

Legal Research Guide for China, Taiwan, Korea and Japan (University of Washington), http://lib.law.washington.edu/eald/eald.html#Legal%20Research%20Guides.

LEGAL RESOURCE INDEX [LRI], available in print as CURRENT LAW INDEX, on LexisNexis and Westlaw, and as Legaltrac on the web, http://infotrac.galegroup.com.

LEGAL SYSTEMS OF THE WORLD: A POLITICAL, SOCIAL, AND CULTURAL ENCYCLOPEDIA (Herbert M. Kritzer ed., Santa Barbara, CA: ABC-CLIO, 2002).

LegalTrac, subscription database, http://www.gale.cengage.com/pdf/facts/legal.pdf, see also LEGAL RESOURCE INDEX (LRI on Westlaw; Find a Source > Legal Resource Index on Lexis Nexis).

LegiFrance, http://www.legifrance.gouv.fr.

Legislationonline.org (OSCE), http://www.legislationline.org.

THE LEGITIMACY OF INTERNATIONAL ORGANIZATIONS (Jean-Marc Coicaud & Veijo Heiskanen eds., Tokyo; New York: United Nations University Press, 2001).

Leong, Chong Yee, & Qin Zhiqian, *Comparative Arbitration Law in Asia*, 6 GLOBAL ARB. REV. 5 (2011).

LEPARD, BRIAN D., CUSTOMARY INTERNATIONAL LAW: A NEW THEORY WITH PRACTICAL APPLICATIONS (Cambridge U.K.; New York, N.Y: Cambridge University Press, 2010).

Levine, Robert, *The Many Voices of Wikipedia, Heard in One Place*, NY TIMES, Aug. 7, 2006, at C4.

LexisNexis Argentina, subscription database, http://www.lexisnexis.com.ar/Portada/portalln.asp.

LexisNexis Butterworths, subscription database, http://www.lexisnexis.co.uk.

LexisNexis Quicklaw, subscription database, http://www.lexisnexis.com/ca/legal.

LexisNexis, Legal > Area of Law—By Topic > International Law > Find Cases > Human Rights Cases.

LexisNexis, Legal > Area of Law—By Topic > International Law > Find Cases > International Court of Justice Decisions, Combined.LexisNexis, Legal > Area of Law—By Topic > International Law > Find Cases > EUR-Lex European Union Cases.

LexisNexis, Legal > Secondary Legal > CLE Materials > Combined ALI-ABA Course of Study Materials.

LexisNexis, Legal > Area of Law—By Topic > International Law > Search Analysis & CLE Materials > International Law Digests.

LexisNexis, Legal > Area of Law—By Topic > International Law >Find Treaties & International Agreements >U.S. Treaties on LEXIS.

LexisNexis, Legal > Area of Law—By Topic > International Trade > Find Cases > Interpreting U.S. Law > NAFTA Panel Review Decisions.

LexisNexis, Legal > Area of Law—By Topic > International Trade > Find Cases > Interpreting Treaties > World Trade Organization Dispute Settlement.

LexisNexis, Legal > Area of Law—By Topic > International Trade > Interpreting Treaties > GATT Panel and World Trade Decisions.LexisNexis, Legal > Area of Law—By Topic > International Arbitration.

LexisNexis, Legal > Find Laws by Country or Region > Foreign Laws & Legal Sources > European Union > Caselaw.

LexisNexis, Legal > Find Laws by Country or Region > Foreign Laws & Legal Sources > European Union > Legislation & Regulations.

LexisNexis, Legal > Find Laws by Country or Region > Foreign Laws & Legal Sources > European Union > Treaties & Intl Agreements.

LexisNexis, Legal > Legislation & Politics—U.S. & U.K. > U.S. Congress > Legislative Histories.

LexisNexis, News & Business >Individual Publications > I >Inside U.S. China Trade.

LexisNexis, News & Business >Individual Publications > I >Inside U.S. Trade.

LexisNexis, News & Business >Individual Publications > S > South China Morning Post.

LexisNexis, News & Business > Country & Region (excluding U.S.) > Middle East & Africa > News > Global News Wire–Middle East & Africa Stories, or use News & Business > Country & Region (excluding U.S.) > Middle East & Africa > News > Middle East/Africa News Information Sources.

Lex Mercatoria, http://www.jus.uio.no/lm/arbitration/toc.html.

LEW, JULIAN D.M., COMPARATIVE INTERNATIONAL COMMERCIAL ARBITRATION (The Hague; New York: Kluwer Law International; Frederick, MD: Sold and distributed in North, Central and South America by Aspen, 2003).

Library of Congress, http://www.loc.gov/index.html.

Library of Congress Catalog, http://catalog.loc.gov.

LibWeb, http://lists.webjunction.org/libweb.

LINDBERGH, ERNEST, INTERNATIONAL LAW DICTIONARY (London: Blackstone Press Ltd., 1992).

LINDBLOM, ANNA-KARIN, NON-GOVERNMENTAL ORGANISATIONS IN INTERNATIONAL LAW (Cambridge, UK; New York: Cambridge University Press, 2005).

Links to Constitutional Courts and Equivalent Bodies (Venice Commission, Council of Europe), http://www.venice.coe.int/site/dynamics/N_court_links_ef.asp.

LLOYD's ARBITRATION REPORTS (London: Lloyd's Publ. 1919–). Available by subscription on i-law.com, http://www.i-law.com/ilaw/browse_lawreports.htm?name=Lloyd%27s%20Law%20Reports.

LLRX.com, Comparative/Foreign Law, http://www.llrx.com/category/1050.

List of the Leading Cases and Judgements of the ECJ on Environment, http://ec.europa.eu/environment/legal/law/cases_judgements.htm.

Liu, Chenglin, *Chinese Law on Trade, Investment and Intellectual Property Rights: A Bibliography of Selected English-Language Materials*, 32 INT'L. J. LEGAL INFO.1 (2004).

Lobey, Sophie, Update: History, Role, and Activities of the Council of Europe: Facts, Figures and Information Sources, http://www.nyulawglobal.org/globalex/Council_of_Europe1.htm.

London Court of International Arbitration (LCIA), http://www.lcia.org.

LOMIO, J. PAUL, ET AL., LEGAL RESEARCH METHODS IN A MODERN WORLD: A COURSEBOOK (3d ed., Copenhagen: DJØF, 2011). See also the companion website, http://hssph.net/legalrm.

LOYOLA OF LOS ANGELES INTERNATIONAL & COMPARATIVE LAW REVIEW (Los Angeles, Calif.: Loyola Law School, 1999–). Also available on HeinOnline.

LUO, WEI, CHINESE LAW AND LEGAL RESEARCH (Buffalo, NY: W.S. Hein, 2005).

Luluaki, John Y., *Customary Marriage Laws in the Commonwealth: A Comparison between Papua New Guinea and Anglophonic Africa*, 11 INT'L J.L. POL. & FAM. 1 (1997).

MAASTRICHT JOURNAL OF EUROPEAN AND COMPARATIVE LAW (Antwerp: Maklu; Baden-Baden: Nomos, 1994–).

MACKENZIE, RUTH, ET AL., MANUAL ON INTERNATIONAL COURTS AND TRIBUNALS (2d ed., Oxford; New York: Oxford University Press, 2010).

MADHUKU, LOVEMORE, AN INTRODUCTION TO ZIMBABWEAN LAW (Harare [Zimbabwe]: Weaver Press: Friedrich-Ebert Stiftung, 2010).

MALANCZUK, PETER, AKEHURST'S MODERN INTRODUCTION TO INTERNATIONAL LAW (7th rev. ed., London; New York: Routledge, 1997).

Manupatra, subscription database, http://www.manupatra.com.

Margolis, Ellie, *Authority without Borders: The World Wide Web and the Delegalization of Law*, 41 SETON HALL L. REV. 909 (2011).

Martindale Hubbell International Law Digest, http://www.martindale.com/legal-library. Also available on LexisNexis, International Law >Global Legal >Multinational Publications >Law Digests.

Materials on International Governmental Organizations (Michigan State University), http://libguides.lib.msu.edu/internationalgovernmentorganizations.

Mathijsen, P.S.R.F., A GUIDE TO EUROPEAN UNION LAW: AS AMENDED BY THE TREATY OF LISBON (10th ed., London: Sweet & Maxwell, 2010).

MATSUSHITA, MITSUO, ET AL., THE WORLD TRADE ORGANIZATION: LAW, PRACTICE, AND POLICY (2d ed., Oxford; New York: Oxford University Press, 2006).

MAX PLANCK ENCYCLOPEDIA OF PUBLIC INTERNATIONAL LAW (Rüdiger Wolfrum ed., New York, NY: Oxford University Press, 2008–), subscription database, http://www.mpepil.com. New edition is available in print, February 2012.

Max Planck Institute for Comparative Public Law and International Law, Online Public Access Catalog, http://www.mpil.de/ww/en/pub/library/catalogues_databases.cfm.

MAX PLANCK YEARBOOK OF UNITED NATIONS LAW (London; Boston: Kluwer Law International, 1998–). Volumes 1–6 are available at http://www.mpil.de/ww/en/pub/research/details/publications/institute/mpyunl.cfm#volumes, volumes 6–9 are available by subscription, http://www.ingentaconnect.com/content/mnp/mpunyb, and also available from Hein-Online.

MCCAFFREY, STEPHEN C., & THOMAS O. MAIN, TRANSNATIONAL LITIGATION IN COMPARATIVE PERSPECTIVE: THEORY AND APPLICATION (New York: Oxford University Press, 2010).

MCCARTHY, THOMAS, MCCARTHY ON TRADEMARKS AND UNFAIR COMPETITION (Deerfield, IL: Clark Boardman Callaghan, 1996–). Also available on Westlaw, MCCARTHY database.

MCCORQUODALE, ROBERT, INTERNATIONAL LAW BEYOND THE STATE: ESSAYS ON SOVEREIGNTY, NON-STATE ACTORS AND HUMAN RIGHTS (London: Cameron May, 2011).

MCHUGH, JAMES T., COMPARATIVE CONSTITUTIONAL TRADITIONS (New York: P. Lang, 2002).

MCLACHLAN, CAMPBELL, ET AL., INTERNATIONAL INVESTMENT ARBITRATION: SUBSTANTIVE PRINCIPLES (Oxford; New York: Oxford University Press, 2007).

MEALEY'S INTERNATIONAL ARBITRATION REPORTER (Wayne, PA: Mealey Publications, 1986–). Also available on LexisNexis.

MELVILLE, LESLIE WILLIAM, FORMS AND AGREEMENTS ON INTELLECTUAL PROPERTY AND INTERNATIONAL LICENSING (New York: Clark Boardman; London: Sweet & Maxwell, 1989–).

MENSKI, WERNER, COMPARATIVE LAW IN A GLOBAL CONTEXT: THE LEGAL SYSTEMS OF ASIA AND AFRICA (2d ed., Cambridge, UK; New York: Cambridge University Press, 2006).

MERINO-BLANCO, ELENA, SPANISH LAW AND LEGAL SYSTEM (2d ed., London: Sweet & Maxwell, 2006).

MERRILLS, J.G., INTERNATIONAL DISPUTE SETTLEMENT (5th ed., Cambridge, UK; New York: Cambridge University Press, 2011).

MERRY, SALLY ENGLE, HUMAN RIGHTS AND GENDER VIOLENCE: TRANSLATING INTERNATIONAL LAW INTO LOCAL JUSTICE (Chicago: University of Chicago Press, 2006).

MERRYMAN, JOHN HENRY, THE CIVIL LAW TRADITION: AN INTRODUCTION TO THE LEGAL SYSTEMS OF EUROPE AND LATIN AMERICA (3d ed., Stanford, CA: Stanford University Press, 2007).

MERRYMAN, JOHN HENRY, ET AL., THE CIVIL LAW TRADITION: EUROPE, LATIN AMERICA, AND EAST ASIA (Charlottesville, VA: Michie Co., 1994). Successor edition to JOHN HENRY MERRYMAN & CLARK, DAVID S., COMPARATIVE LAW: WESTERN EUROPEAN AND LATIN AMERICAN LEGAL SYSTEMS (Indianapolis: Bobbs-Merrill, 1978).

THE MEXICAN CIVIL CODE (Abraham Eckstein & Enrique Zepeda Trujillo trans., [St. Paul]: West, 1996).

Mexico, Ministry of the Economy, http://www.economia.gob.mx/comunidad-negocios/comercio-exterior/tlc-acuerdos.

Miccioli, Gloria, ASIL Guide to Electronic Resources for International Law: International Commercial Arbitration, http://www.asil.org/arb1.cfm.

Minnesota Human Rights Library, http://www1.umn.edu/humanrts.

Minnesota Human Rights Library, http://www1.umn.edu/humanrts/links/ngolinks.html.

MIXED JURISDICTIONS WORLDWIDE: THE THIRD LEGAL FAMILY (Vernon Valentine Palmer ed., New York, NY: Cambridge University Press, 2001).

MIXED LEGAL SYSTEMS AT NEW FRONTIERS (Esin Örücü ed., London: Wildy, Simmonds & Hill, 2010).

MODERN LEGAL SYSTEMS CYCLOPEDIA (Kenneth R. Redden ed., Buffalo, NY: W.S. Hein, 1984–). Available on HeinOnline.

Moniteur Belge, http://www.ejustice.just.fgov.be/cgi/welcome.pl.

MOORE, JOHN BASSETT, DIGEST OF INTERNATIONAL LAW (Washington, DC: U.S. G.P.O., 1906). Available on HeinOnline.

MOUSSA, JASMINE, COMPETING FUNDAMENTALISMS AND EGYPTIAN WOMEN'S FAMILY RIGHTS: INTERNATIONAL LAW AND THE REFORM OF SHARI'A-DERIVED LEGISLATION (Leiden: Boston: Brill, 2011).

Moy, R. Carl, Moy's Walker on Patents (St. Paul, Minn: Thomson/West, 2003–).

Multilateral Treaties Deposited with the Secretary General (New York: United Nations, 1982–). Available at http://treaties.un.org/pages/ParticipationStatus.aspx.

Multilateral Treaties: Index and Current Status (M.J. Bowman & D.J. Harris eds., London: Butterworths, 1984). Includes a cumulative supplement, 11th ed. (1995).

Multilaterals Project, http://fletcher.tufts.edu/multilaterals.

Murray, Rachel, Human Rights in Africa: From the OAU to the African Union (Cambridge: Cambridge University Press, 2004).

Mwalimu, Charles, The Nigerian Legal System (New York: P. Lang, 2005).

NAFTA Arbitration Reports (London: Cameron May, 2002–).

NAFTA Secretariat, http://www.nafta-sec-alena.org/en/view.aspx.

NAFTA Secretariat, Decisions and Reports, http://www.nafta-sec-alena.org/en/DecisionsAndReports.aspx?x=312.

NAFTAClaims.com (a.k.a. NAFTALaw.org), http://www.naftaclaims.com.

National Arbitration Laws (2d ed., Loukas Mistelis et al. eds., Huntington, N.Y.: Juris, 2010–).

Nationality and International Law in Asian Perspective (Ko Swan Sik ed., Dordrecht; Boston: M. Nijhoff; Norwell, MA, 1990).

National Constitutions, http://www.constitution.org/cons/natlcons.htm. National Journal of Constitutional Law = Revue Nationale de Droit Constitutionnel (Scarborough, Ontario: Carswell, 1991–).

National Law Center for Inter-American Free Trade, subscription database, http://www.natlaw.com.

National Laws and Regulations on the Prevention and Suppression of International Terrorism (New York: United Nations, 2002–).

National Treaty Law and Practice: Austria, Chile, Colombia, Japan, the Netherlands, United States (Monroe Leigh & Merritt R. Blakeslee eds., Washington, DC: American Society of International Law, 1999). Available on HeinOnline.

National Treaty Law and Practice: Canada, Egypt, Israel, Mexico, Russia, South Africa (Monroe Leigh et al. eds., Washington, DC: American Society of International Law 2003). Available on HeinOnline.

National Treaty Law and Practice: Dedicated to the Memory of Monroe Leigh (Duncan B. Hollis ed., Leiden; Boston: M. Nijhoff, 2005).

National Treaty Law and Practice: France, Germany, India, Switzerland, Thailand, United Kingdom (Monroe Leigh & Merritt R. Blakeslee eds., Washington, DC: American Society of International Law, 1995). Available on HeinOnline.

Nations of the World, http://www.loc.gov/law/guide/nations.html.

NATO Basic Texts, http://www.nato.int/ifor/general/home.htm.

Nazi Crimes on Trial: E-Judgments, http://www1.jur.uva.nl/junsv.

Negotiating and Structuring International Commercial Transactions (Mark R. Sandstrom & David N. Goldsweig eds., 2d ed., Chicago: Section of International Law and Practice, American Bar Association, 2003).

Netherlands Helsinki Committee, http://www.nhc.nl.

Netherlands Institute of Human Rights [SIM], Case Law Database, http://sim.law.uu.nl/SIM/Dochome.nsf?Open (scroll down to "Case law").

Netherlands Institute of Human Rights [SIM], Human Rights Treaties, http://sim.law.uu.nl/SIM/Library/HRinstruments.nsf/%28organization%29?OpenView.

Netherlands International Law Review (Leiden: Sijthoff, 1975–). Available by subscription, http://journals.cambridge.org/action/displayJournal?jid=NLR.

Netherlands Yearbook of International Law (Leiden: A.W. Sijthoff, 1971–).

Newman, Lawrence W., & Michael Burrows, The Practice of International Litigation (2d ed., [Irvington-on-Hudson, NY]: Juris Pub., 1998–).

New York University Law Library, European Union Research, http://www.law.nyu.edu/library/research/researchguides/europeanunionresearch/index.htm.

New Zealand Yearbook of International Law ([Christchurch, N.Z.]: International Law Group, School of Law, University of Canterbury, 2004–).

Nimmer, Melville B., Nimmer on Copyright; A Treatise on the Law of Literary, Musical and Artistic Property, and the Protection of Ideas (New York: M. Bender, 1963–).

N-Lex: A Common Gateway to National Law, http://eur-lex.europa.eu/n-lex/pri/pri_en.htm.

Noble's International Guide to the Law Reports (Scott Noble ed., Etobicoke, Ont.: Nicol Island Pub., 2002).

Norman, Paul, Update: Comparative Law, http://www.nyulawglobal.org/globalex/Comparative_Law1.htm.

The North American Free Trade Agreement (NAFTA)—Chapter 11—Investment (Foreign Affairs and International Trade Canada), http://www.international.gc.ca/trade-agreements-accords-commerciaux/disp-diff/nafta.aspx?lang=en&view=d.

Northwestern University, Foreign Governments, http://www.library.nwu.edu/govpub/resource/internat/foreign.html.

Northwestern University, International Organizations Website, http://www.library.nwu.edu/govpub/resource/internat/igo.html.

Northwestern University, Research Guide to League of Nations Documents and Publications, http://digital.library.northwestern.edu/league/background.html.

Novissimo Digesto ([Torino]: Unione Tipografico-Editrice Torinese 1956–).

Nuremberg Trials Project, http://www.nesl.edu/research/warcrim.cfm.

OAU/AU Summit, http://www.au2002.gov.za.

OCLC, http://www.oclc.org/us/en/default.htm.

O'Connor, Bernard, The Law of Geographical Indications (London: Cameron May, 2004).

OECD's Anti-Bribery Convention: National Implementing Legislation, http://www.oecd.org/document/30/0,2340,en_2649_34859_2027102_1_1_1_1,00.html.

Oehmke, Thomas H., Oehmke Commercial Arbitration (3d ed., St. Paul, MN: Thomson/West, 2003–).

Office of the High Commissioner for Human Rights [OHCHR], http://www.ohchr.org/EN/Pages/WelcomePage.aspx.

Office of the High Commissioner for Human Rights, Human Rights by Country, http://www.ohchr.org/EN/Countries/Pages/HumanRightsintheWorld.aspx.

Office of the High Commissioner for Human Rights, International Human Rights Treaties, http://www2.ohchr.org/english/law/index.htm.

Office of the U.S. Trade Representative, U.S. Briefs Filed in WTO Dispute Settlement Proceedings, http://www.ustr.gov/trade-topics/enforcement/dispute-settlement-proceedings/wto-dispute-settlement.

Official Journal of the European Union [formerly Official Journal of the European Communities] [O.J.] (Luxembourg, Office for Official Publications of the European Communities, 1973–) [English edition], http://eur-lex.europa.eu/JOIndex.do.

Olong, Adefi M., The Nigerian Legal System: An Introduction (2d ed., Lagos, Nigeria: Malthouse Press, 2007).

Online Human Rights Documents (IDC/Brill), subscription database, http://hrd.idcpublishers.info/hrd. Also available on microfiche.

Opinio Juris, http://opiniojuris.org.

Oppenheim's International Law (9th ed., Robert Jennings & Arthur Watts eds., Harlow, Essex, UK: Longman, 1992).

Orakhelashvili, Alexander, Peremptory Norms in International Law (Oxford; New York, NY: Oxford University Press, 2006).

Organization for Security and Co-operation in Europe [OSCE], http://www.osce.org.

Organization for Security and Co-operation in Europe, Index of Permanent Council Decisions, http://www.osce.org/pc/documents.

Organization for Security and Co-operation in Europe, Library, http://www.osce.org/library.

Organization of American States [OAS] Charter, http://www.oas.org/en/about/who_we_are.asp.

Organization of American States, Documents, http://www.oas.org/en/, select "Documents" from the home page.

Organization of American State, Document Search, https://www.apps.oas.org/publicsearch/default.asp.

Organization of American States, Department of International Legal Affairs, http://www.oas.org/DIL/international_law.htm.

Organization of American States, Department of Legal Services, http://www.oas.org/legal/intro.htm.

Organization of American States, Summit of the Americas, http://www.summit-americas.org/default_en.htm.

Organization of American States, Treaties and Agreements, http://www.oas.org/DIL/treaties_and_agreements.htm and Recent Actions Regarding Multilateral Treaties, http://www.oas.org/DIL/recentactionstreaties.htm.

Osborne, Caroline, Pathfinder on International Investment Law and Alternative Dispute Resolution Web Based Resources, http://papers.ssrn.com/sol3/papers.cfm?abstract_id=1625763 (2010).

OSCE Documents Library, http://www.osce.org/documents.

OSMANCZYK, EDMUND J., THE ENCYCLOPEDIA OF THE UNITED NATIONS AND INTERNATIONAL AGREEMENTS (3d ed., Anthony Mango ed. & rev., New York: Routledge, 2003). Also available by subscription, Routledge Politics and International Relations Online, http://www.routledgeonline.com/politics/Book.aspx?id=w032.

Otero, Hernando, & Omar García-Bolívar, International Arbitration between Foreign Investors and Host States (2011), http://www.nyulawglobal.org/globalex/International_Arbitration_Foreign_Investors_Host_States.htm.

THE OXFORD COMPANION TO INTERNATIONAL CRIMINAL JUSTICE (Antonio Cassese ed., Oxford; New York: Oxford University Press, 2009).

THE OXFORD HANDBOOK OF COMPARATIVE LAW (Reinhard Zimmermann & Mathias Reimann eds., Oxford; New York: Oxford University Press, 2008).

Oxford Reports on International Law [ORIL], subscription database, http://www.oxfordlawreports.com/ (contains several modules: International Courts of General Jurisdiction, International Criminal Law, International Human Rights Law, International Investment Claims, and International Law in Domestic Courts).

PAIS International ([Bethesda, MD]: Cambridge Scientific Abstracts), subscription database, http://www.csa.com/factsheets/pais-set-c.php.

PALMETER, DAVID, & PETROS C. MAVROIDIS, DISPUTE SETTLEMENT IN THE WORLD TRADE ORGANIZATION: PRACTICE AND PROCEDURE (2d ed., Cambridge, UK; New York: Cambridge University Press, 2004).

PARK, WILLIAM W., ARBITRATION OF INTERNATIONAL BUSINESS DISPUTES (Oxford; New York: Oxford University Press, 2006).

PARRY & GRANT ENCYCLOPAEDIC DICTIONARY OF INTERNATIONAL LAW (3d ed., Craig Barker & John P. Grant eds., New York: Oxford University Press, 2009). Available by subscription, http://www.oxford-internationallaw.com.

Partin, Gail, ASIL Guide to Electronic Resources for International Law: International Criminal Law, http://www.asil.org/erg/?page=icl.

PARTINGTON, MARTIN, AN INTRODUCTION TO THE ENGLISH LEGAL SYSTEM (6th ed., Oxford; New York: Oxford University Press, 2008).

PASQUALUCCI, JO M., THE PRACTICE AND PROCEDURE OF THE INTER-AMERICAN COURT OF HUMAN RIGHTS (Cambridge, UK; New York: Cambridge University Press, 2003).

PASSOS, EDILENICE, DOING LEGAL RESEARCH IN BRAZIL (Den Bosch, The Netherlands: Book World Publications, 2001.). An updated (2008) version of this is available on GlobaLex, http://www.nyulawglobal.org/Globalex/Brazil1.htm.

Paust, Jordan J., *The Importance of Customary International Law during Armed Conflict*, 12 ILSA J. INT'L & COMP. L. 601 (2006).

Peace Agreements Digital Collection (USIP), http://www.usip.org.

Peace Palace Library, http://www.peacepalacelibrary.nl/.

PEERENBOOM, RANDALL, ET AL., HUMAN RIGHTS IN ASIA: A COMPARATIVE LEGAL STUDY OF TWELVE ASIAN JURISDICTIONS, FRANCE, AND THE USA (New York: Routledge, 2006).

PELTZER, MARTIN, ET AL., GERMAN LAW PERTAINING TO COMPANIES WITH LIMITED LIABILITY/GmbHG -GmbH-GESETZ (4th rev. ed., Köln: O. Schmidt, 2000).

Permanent Court of Arbitration [PCA], http://www.pca-cpa.org/showpage.asp?pag_id=363.

Permanent Court of Arbitration, Hague Court Reports (New York: Oxford University Press, American branch; [etc.,], 1916–1932).

Permanent Court of International Justice [PCIJ], Actes et Documents Relatifs aux Arrêts et aux Avis Consultatifs de la Cour = Acts and Documents Relating to Judgments and Advisory Opinions [Series C] (Leyden: A.W. Sijthoff, 1922–1939). Available on HeinOnline.

Permanent Court of International Justice, Case Law of the International Court (Leyden: A.W. Sijthoff, 1952–1976).

Permanent Court of International Justice, Publications de la Cour Permanente de Justice Internationale, Série A/B: Recueil des arrêts, avis consultatifs et ordonnances = Publications of the Permanent Court of International Justice, Series A./B., Judgments, Orders and Advisory Opinions (Leyden: A.W. Sijthoff, 1931–[1940]). Available on HeinOnline.

Permanent Court of International Justice, Publications de la Cour Permanente de Justice Internationale. Serie B, Recueil des avis consultatifs = Publications of the Permanent Court of International Justice. Series B, Collection of advisory opinions (Leyden: A.W. Sijthoff, 1922–1930). Available on HeinOnline.

Permanent Court of International Justice [PCIJ], Recueil des Arrets = Collection of Judgments [Series A] (Leyden: A.W. Sijthoff, 1923–30). Available on HeinOnline.

Permanent Court of International Justice (1922–1946), http://www.icj-cij.org/pcij/index.php?p1=9 or http://www.worldcourts.com.

Pierre Pescatore et al., Handbook of WTO/GATT Dispute Settlement (Ardsleyon-Hudson, N.Y.: Transnational Publications; Hague: Kluwer Law International, 1991–).

Pikis, Georghios M., The Rome Statute for the International Criminal Court: Analysis of the Statute, the Rules of Procedure and Evidence, the Regulations of the Court and Supplementary Instruments (Leiden; Boston: Martinus Nijhoff Publishers, 2010).

The Polish Yearbook of International Law (Wroclaw: Zaklad Narodowy Im. Ossolinskich, 1967–).

Political Database of the Americas, Judicial Institutions of the Americas (Georgetown University), http://pdba.georgetown.edu/Judicial/judicial.html.

Popa, Radu D., & Mirela Roznovschi, Update: Comparative Civil Procedure: A Guide to Primary and Secondary Sources, http://www.nyulawglobal.org/Globalex/Comparative_Civil_Procedure1.htm.

Port, Kenneth L., *Japanese Intellectual Property Law in Translation: Representative Case and Commentary*, 34 Vand. J. Transnat'l. L. 847 (2001).

Practising Law Institute (PLI), http://www.pli.edu.

Pratter, Jonathan, A la Recherche des Travaux Préparatoires: An Approach to Researching the Drafting History of International Agreements, http://www.nyulawglobal.org/globalex/Travaux_Preparatoires.htm.

PreLex, http://ec.europa.eu/prelex/apcnet.cfm?CL=en.

Private International Law (U.S. Dept. of State), http://www.state.gov/s/l/c3452.htm.

Project on International Courts and Tribunals [PICT], http://www.pict-pcti.org.

Proquest Congressional Publications, subscription database, http://cisupa.proquest.com/ws_display.asp?filter=Congressional%20Overview.

Puckett, Jason, Zotero: A Guide for Librarians, teachers and Educators (Chicago: American Library Association, 2011), http://jasonpuckett.net/zotero.

Punitive Damages: Common Law and Civil Law Perspectives (Helmut Koziol, Vanessa Wilcox eds., New York: Springer, 2009).

Public International Law: A Current Bibliography of Articles (Berlin; New York: Springer-Verlag, 1975–). Available online at http://www.mpil.de/ww/en/pub/library/catalogues_databases/doc_of_articles/pil.cfm.

Public Papers of the Presidents of the United States (Washington: Federal Register Division, National Archives and Records Service, General Services Administration: For sale by the Supt. of Docs., U.S. G.P.O.). Available online from 1991 on, http://www.gpoaccess.gov/pubpapers/search.html.

Ragazzi, Maurizio, The Concept of International Obligations Erga Omnes (New York: Clarendon Press, 1997).

Raimondo, Fabián O., General Principles of Law in the Decisions of International Criminal Courts and Tribunals (Leiden; Boston: M. Nijhoff Pub., 2008). There is also an earlier article on this topic by this author, Fabián O. Raimondo, *General Principles of Law as Applied by International Criminal Courts and Tribunals*, 6 L. & Prac. Int'l. Courts & Trib. 393 (2007).

Raisch, Marylin, European Union Law: An Integrated Guide to Electronic and Print Research (2006), http://www.llrx.com/features/eulaw2.htm.

Raistrick, Donald, Index to Legal Citations and Abbreviations (2d ed., London; New Jersey: Bowker-Saur, 1993).

Raybould, D.M., Comparative Law of Monopolies (The Hague; New York: Kluwer Law International, 2004-).

Reed, Lucy, & Nigel Blackaby, Guide to ICSID Arbitration (2d ed., Austin: Wolters Kluwer; Alphen aan den Rijn, The Netherlands: Kluwer Law International; Frederick, MD: Sold and distributed in North, Central and South America by Aspen Publishers, 2011).

Refugee Survey Quarterly (Geneva: Centre for Documentation on Refugees, 1994-). Also available from Oxford University Press.

REFWORLD (UNHCR), http://www.unhcr.org/cgi-bin/texis/vtx/refworld/rwmain.

The Regulation of Genetically Modified Organisms: Comparative Approaches (Luc Bodiguel & Michael Cardwell eds., Oxford; New York, N.Y.: Oxford University Press, 2010).

Rehberg, Jeanne M., *Finding Treaties and Other International Agreements*, in Accidental Tourist on the New Frontier: An Introductory Guide to Global Legal Research 123 (Jeanne M. Rehberg & Radu Popa eds., Littleton, Colo.: F.B. Rothman, 1998).

Rehberg, Jeanne M., WTO and GATT Research (New York University), http://nyulaw.libguides.com/wto_gatt.

Reimann, Mathias, *Codifying Torts Conflicts: The 1999 German Legislation in Comparative Perspective*, 60 La. L.Rev. 1297 (2000).

Repertory of Practice of United Nations Organs (New York: United Nations, 1955). Available at http://www.un.org/law/repertory.

Reports of Cases before the Court of Justice and the Court of First Instance [European Court Reports] (Luxembourg: Court of Justice of the European Communities, 1990-). [Previous title: Court of Justice of the European Communities, Reports of Cases before the Court (Luxembourg: Court of Justice of the European Communities, 1959-1989).]

Research Handbook on International Criminal Law (Bartram S. Brown ed., Cheltenham, UK; Northampton, MA: Edward Elgar, 2011).

Research Handbook on the Law of International Organisations (Jan Klabbers & Åsa Wallendahl eds., Cheltenham, UK; Northampton, MA, USA: Edward Elgar, 2011).

Restatement on the Law, Second, Conflict of Laws (St. Paul: American Law Institute, 1971-). Supplemented annually, available on LexisNexis and Westlaw.

Restatement of the Law, Third, the Foreign Relations Law of the United States (Rev. and enl., St. Paul: American Law Institute Publishers, 1987). Supplemented annually, available on LexisNexis and Westlaw.

Review of Constitutional Studies = Revue d'études Constitutionnelles (Edmonton: Alberta Law Review and Centre for Constitutional Studies, 1993-).

Revista Española de Derecho Constitucional (Madrid: Centro de Estudios Constitucionales, 1981-).

Revue de Droit Africain: Doctrine & Jurisprudence (Bruxelles: Recherches et Documention Juridiques Africaines, 2002-).

Revue Française de Droit Constitutionnel (Paris: Presses universitaires de France, 1990-).

Revue Internationale de Droit Comparé (Paris: Société de Législation Comparée, [1949]-).

Reynolds, Thomas H., & Auturo A. Flores, Foreign Law Guide ([Berkeley, Calif.: University of California?], 2000-), subscription, database, http://www.foreignlawguide.com.

RIA Checkpoint, subscription database, https://checkpoint.riag.com.

RIA Worldwide Tax & Commercial Law (dates vary), subscription database, https://checkpoint.riag.com.

RIDDELL, ANNA, & BRENDAN PLANT, EVIDENCE BEFORE THE INTERNATIONAL COURT OF JUSTICE (London: British Institute of International and Comparative Law, 2009).

Rise of Modern Constitutionalism, 1776–1849, http://www.modern-constitutions.de.

RISTAU, BRUNO A., INTERNATIONAL JUDICIAL ASSISTANCE: CIVIL AND COMMERCIAL (Washington, DC: International Law Institute, 2000–).

Roberts, Anthea E., *Traditional and Modern Approaches to Customary International Law: A Reconciliation*, 95 AM. J. INT'L. L. 757 (2001).

ROBERTS, JOHN E., A GUIDE TO OFFICIAL GAZETTES AND THEIR CONTENTS (rev. ed., Washington, DC: Law Library, Library of Congress, 1985).

RODLEY, NIGEL, THE TREATMENT OF PRISONERS UNDER INTERNATIONAL LAW (3d ed., Oxford; New York: Oxford University Press, 2009).

RODRÍGUEZ-PINZÓN, DIEGO, & CLAUDIA MARTIN, THE PROHIBITION OF TORTURE AND ILL-TREATMENT IN THE INTER-AMERICAN HUMAN RIGHTS SYSTEM: A HANDBOOK FOR VICTIMS AND THEIR ADVOCATES (Geneva: World Organization Against Torture (OMCT), 2006).

THE ROME STATUTE OF THE INTERNATIONAL CRIMINAL COURT: A COMMENTARY (Antonio Cassese et al. eds., Oxford [England]; New York: Oxford University Press, 2002).

ROSENBERG, JERRY M., DICTIONARY OF INTERNATIONAL TRADE (New York: J. Wiley, 1994).

ROSENNE, SHABTAI, THE LAW AND PRACTICE OF THE INTERNATIONAL COURT, 1920–2005 (2006).

ROSENNE, SHABTAI, PRACTICE AND METHODS OF INTERNATIONAL LAW (London; New York: Oceana Publications, 1984).

ROSENNE, SHABTAI, PROCEDURE IN THE INTERNATIONAL COURT: A COMMENTARY ON THE 1978 RULES OF THE INTERNATIONAL COURT OF JUSTICE (The Hague; Boston: M. Nijhoff, 1983).

ROSSI, INGRID, LEGAL STATUS OF NON-GOVERNMENTAL ORGANIZATIONS IN INTERNATIONAL LAW (Antwerp; Portland, OR: Intersentia, 2010).

ROSSIISKII EZHEGODNIK MEZHDUNARODNOGO PRAVA = RUSSIAN YEARBOOK OF INTERNATIONAL LAW (Sankt-Peterburg: Sotsialno-kommercheskaia firma 'Rossiia-Neva', 1994–).

ROUTLEDGE HANDBOOK OF INTERNATIONAL CRIMINAL LAW (William Schabas & Nadia Bernaz eds., London; New York: Routledge, 2011).

Rühl, Giesela, *Common Law, Civil Law, and the Single European Market for Insurances*, 55 INT'L & COMP. L.Q. 879 (2006).

RUITER, DONJA DE, SEXUAL OFFENSES IN INTERNATIONAL CRIMINAL LAW (The Hague: International Courts Association, 2011).

THE RULE OF LAW IN COMPARATIVE PERSPECTIVE (Mortimer Sellers & Tadeusz Tomaskewski eds., Dordrecht: Springer Science+Business Media B.V., 2010).

THE RULES OF THE INTERNATIONAL TRIBUNAL FOR THE LAW OF THE SEA: A COMMENTARY (P. Chandrasekhara Rao & Ph. Gautier eds., Leiden; Boston: Martinus Nijhoff Pub., 2006).

Rumsey, Mary, Update: Basic Guide to Researching Foreign Law (2010), http://www.nyulawglobal.org/Globalex/Foreign_Law_Research1.htm.

RUSSIA AND THE REPUBLICS: LEGAL MATERIALS (Ardsley-on-Hudson, NY: Transnational Juris Publications; U.K.: Graham & Trotman; The Netherlands; Kluwer Academic Publishers, 1992–).

RUSSIA AND THE REPUBLICS: LEGAL MATERIALS [2d ser.] ([Huntington, NY]: Juris Publishing, 2006–).

SANDS, PHILIPPE, PRINCIPLES OF INTERNATIONAL ENVIRONMENTAL LAW (2d ed., Cambridge, U.K.; New York: Cambridge University Press, 2000).

SANDS, PHILIPPE, & PIERRE KLEIN, BOWETT'S LAW OF INTERNATIONAL INSTITUTIONS (6th ed., London: Sweet & Maxwell, 2009).

SCC ARBITRAL AWARDS (Huntington, NY: JurisNet, 2011).

Schabas, William A., *Invalid Reservations to the International Covenant on Civil and Political Rights: Is the United States Still a Party?*, 21 BROOK. J. INT'L L. 277 (1995).

SCHABAS, WILLIAM A., THE UN INTERNATIONAL CRIMINAL TRIBUNALS: THE FORMER YUGOSLAVIA, RWANDA, AND SIERRA LEONE (Cambridge, UK; New York: Cambridge University Press, 2006).

SCHERMERS, HENRY G., & NIELS M. BLOKKER, INTERNATIONAL INSTITUTIONAL LAW: UNITY WITHIN DIVERSITY (5th rev. ed., Boston: Martinus Nijhoff Publishers, 2011).

SCHIAVONE, GIUSEPPE, INTERNATIONAL ORGANIZATIONS: A DICTIONARY AND DIRECTORY (7th ed., Houndmills, Basingstoke, Hampshire, UK; New York: Palgrave Macmillan, 2008).

SCHREUER, CHRISTOPH H., THE ICSID CONVENTION: A COMMENTARY: A COMMENTARY ON THE CONVENTION ON THE SETTLEMENT OF INVESTMENT DISPUTES BETWEEN STATES AND NATIONALS OF OTHER STATES (2d ed., Cambridge; New York: Cambridge University Press, 2009).

SCHLÜTTER, BIRGIT, DEVELOPMENTS IN CUSTOMARY INTERNATIONAL LAW: THEORY AND THE PRACTICE OF THE INTERNATIONAL COURT OF JUSTICE AND THE INTERNATIONAL AD HOC CRIMINAL TRIBUNALS FOR RWANDA AND YUGOSLAVIA (Leiden; Boston: Martinus Nijhoff Publishers, 2010).

SCHREUER, CHRISTOPH H., THE ICSID CONVENTION: A COMMENTARY: A COMMENTARY ON THE CONVENTION ON THE SETTLEMENT OF INVESTMENT DISPUTES BETWEEN STATES AND NATIONALS OF OTHER STATES (2d ed., Cambridge, UK; New York: Cambridge University Press, 2009).

SCHUON, CHRISTINE, INTERNATIONAL CRIMINAL PROCEDURE: A CLASH OF LEGAL CULTURES (The Hague: T.M.C. Asser Press, 2010).

SCHWARZENBERGER, GEORG, A MANUAL OF INTERNATIONAL LAW (6th ed., London: Professional Books Limited, 1976).

SCHWEIZERISCHES JAHRBUCH FUR INTERNATIONALES RECHT = ANNUAIRE SUISSE DE DROIT INTERNATIONAL (Zürich: Polygraphischer Verlag, 1944–1990).

SCHWEIZERISCHE ZEITSCHRIFT FUR INTERNATIONALES UND EUROPAISCHES RECHT = REVUE SUISSE DE DROIT INTERNATIONAL ET DE DROIT EUROPEEN (Zurich: Schulthess Polygraphischer Verlag, 1991–).

SECURING AND ENFORCING JUDGMENTS IN LATIN AMERICA (rev. ed., Lawrence w. Newman ed., Huntington, NY: JurisNet, 2011–).

SECURITY AND HUMAN RIGHTS (formerly HELSINKI MONITOR) (Leiden: Brill Academic Publishers, 1991–) (issues before 2004 published by other publishers). Also available by subscription, http://api.ingentaconnect.com.

SELECTED JUDGMENTS OF THE SUPREME COURT OF ISRAEL (Jerusalem: Ministry of Justice; New York: Oceana Publications, Distributors, 1962–).

A Selective List of Guides to Foreign Legal Research (Columbia Law Library), http://library.law.columbia.edu/guides/A_Selective_List_of_Guides_to_Foreign_Legal_Research.

SENATE EXECUTIVE DOCUMENTS AND REPORTS [and microfiche] ([Washington, DC]: CIS, 1987).

SENATE EXECUTIVE REPORTS (Washington, DC: U.S. G.P.O., n.d.). Available at http://www.gpoaccess.gov/serialset/creports/index.html.

SENATE TREATY DOCUMENTS (Washington, DC: U.S. G.P.O., 1981–).

Serious Crimes Unit, East Timor, http://ist-socrates.berkeley.edu/~warcrime/Serious%20Crimes%20Unit%20Files/default.html.

SHAW, CAROLYN M., COOPERATION, CONFLICT, AND CONSENSUS IN THE ORGANIZATION OF AMERICAN STATES (New York: Palgrave Macmillan, 2004).

SHAW, MALCOLM N., INTERNATIONAL LAW (6th ed., Cambridge, UK; New York: Cambridge University Press, 2008).

SICE (OAS Foreign Trade Information Center), Adopted Panel Reports Within the Framework of GATT 1947, http://www.sice.oas.org/DISPUTE/gatdispe.asp.

SICE, Bilateral Investment Treaties, http://www.sice.oas.org/investment/bitindexe.asp.

SICE Trade Agreements in Force, http://www.sice.oas.org/agreements_e.asp.

THE SIERRA LEONE SPECIAL COURT COLLECTION (Claudia Tofan ed., Oisterwijk, the Netherlands: Wolf Legal Publishers, 2008–).

SINGAPORE YEAR BOOK OF INTERNATIONAL LAW (Sinagpore: Faculty of Law, National University of Singapore, 2004–). Available on HeinOnline.

SMIT & HERZOG ON THE LAW OF THE EUROPEAN UNION (2d ed., Newark, NJ: LexisNexis/Matthew Bender, 2005–).

Smith, Gordon, & Andrew Cook, *International Commercial Arbitration in Asia-Pacific: A Comparison of the Australian and Singapore Systems*, 77 ARB. 108 (2011).

Social Science Index (H.W. Wilson Company, coverage varies by journal indexed), subscription database, http://www.ebscohost.com/wilson.

Social Science Research Network (SSRN), subscription database, http://www.ssrn.com.

Sociological Abstracts (CSA, 1952–), subscription database, http://www.csa.com/factsheets/socioabs-set-c.php.

Sornarajah, M., The International Law on Foreign Investment (3d ed., Cambridge, UK; Cambridge University Press, 2010).

Sources of State Practice in International Law (Ralph Gaebler & Maria Smolka-Day eds., Ardsley, NY: Transnational Publishers, 2001–).

South African Law Reports (Capetown: Juta and Co., 1947–).

South African Studies (Grahamstown, South Africa: National Inquiry Services Centre, [19–]).

South African Yearbook of International Law = Suid-Afrikaanse Jaarboek vir Volkereg (Pretoria: VerLoren Van Themaat Centre for International Law, University of South Africa, 1975–).

South China Morning Post, available on LexisNexis (News & Business >Individual Publications >S >South China Morning Post) and Westlaw (SCHMP).

Sovetskii Ezhegodnik Mezhdunarodnogo Prava = Soviet Year-Book of International Law (Moskva: Izd-vo Akademii nauk SSSR, 1959–1992).

Spanish Yearbook of International Law (Dordrecht; Boston: M. Nijhoff, 1994–). Also available on HeinOnline.

Special Court for Sierra Leone, http://www.sc-sl.org.

Special Tribunal for Lebanon, http://www.stl-tsl.org.

Statement of Treaties and International Agreements Registered or Filed and Recorded with the Secretariat during the Month of (New York: United Nations, [1950?]–). Available at http://treaties.un.org/Pages/Publications.aspx?pathpub=Publication/MS/Page1_en.xml.

State Practice Regarding State Immunities (Council of Europe ed., Leiden, The Netherlands; Boston, MA: Martinus Nijhoff, 2006).

Statutes at Large of the United States (Washington: U.S. G.P.O., 1847–). Available on HeinOnline and some volumes at http://memory.loc.gov/ammem/amlaw/lwsl.html.

Statutes of the Republic of Korea (Seoul: Korea Legislation Research Institute, 1997–).

Stefiszyn, Karen, *The African Union: Challenges and Opportunities for Women*, 5 Afr. Hum. Rts. L.J. 358 (2005).

Steiner, Eva, French Law: A Comparative Approach (Oxford; New York: Oxford University Press, 2010).

Steiner, Jo, & Lorna Woods, EU Law (10th ed., Oxford; New York: Oxford University Press, 2009).

Stockholm International Arbitration Review (previous title Stockholm Arbitration Report) (Huntington, N.Y.: JurisNet, 2005–).

Strong, Stacie, Research and Practice in International Commercial Arbitration: Sources and Strategies (Oxford: Oxford University Press, 2009).

Strong, Stacie, *Research in International Commercial Arbitration: Special Skills, Special Sources*, 29 Am. Rev. Int'l Arb. 119 (2009). Available at http://www.cisg.law.pace.edu/cisg/moot/Strong.pdf.

The Supreme Court Law Review (Toronto: Butterworths, 1980–).

Svensk Författningssamling (Stockholm: tryckt i Kongl. Tryckeriet, 1825–). Available online, http://www.riksdagen.se/Webbnav/index.aspx?nid=3910.

Swiss Diplomatic Documents (DDS), http://www.dodis.ch/en.

Swiss Institute for Comparative Law, http://www.isdc.ch.

SwissLex, subscription database, https://www.swisslex.ch.

Szasz, Paul C., Selected Essays on Understanding International Institutions and the Legislative Process (Ardsley, NY: Transnational Pub., 2001).

Szladits' Bibliography on Foreign and Comparative Law: Books and Articles in English (Dobbs Ferry, NY: Published for the Parker School of Foreign and Comparative Law, Columbia University in the City of New York, by Oceana Publications, 1790–Apr. 1, 1953–1989).

Takdin, subscription database, http://www.takdin.co.il.

TAX LAWS OF THE WORLD (Ormond Beach, FL: Foreign Tax Law, Inc.; Valhalla, NY: Thomson/ RIA, 2005–). Available by subscription, http://checkpoint.riag.com.

TAX MANAGEMENT INTERNATIONAL JOURNAL (Washington: Tax Management Inc., 1973–). See "Current Status of U.S. Tax Treaties and International Tax Agreements" section.

TAX TREATIES (Chicago, Ill.: Commerce Clearing House, 1952–). Also available by subscription, CCH Intelliconnect, http://intelliconnect.cch.com.

THEORY AND PRACTICE OF THE EUROPEAN CONVENTION ON HUMAN RIGHTS (4th ed. Pieter van Dijk et al. eds., Antwerpen: Intersentia; Holmes Beach, Florida Distribution for North America by Gaunt, 2006).

Thomas: Treaties, http://thomas.loc.gov/home/treaties/treaties.html.

THOMAS, CHRISTOPHER R., & JULIANA T. MAGLOIRE, REGIONALISM VERSUS MULTILATERALISM: THE ORGANIZATION OF AMERICAN STATES IN A GLOBAL CHANGING ENVIRONMENT (Boston: Kluwer Academic Publishers, 2000).

Thorpe, Suzanne, *A Guide to International Legal Bibliography, in* CONTEMPORARY PRACTICE OF PUBLIC INTERNATIONAL LAW 17 (Ellen G. Schaffer & Randall J. Snyder eds., 1997).

TJADEN, TED, LEGAL RESEARCH AND WRITING (3d ed., Toronto: Irwin Law, 2010).

TOCHILOVSKY, VLADIMIR, JURISPRUDENCE OF THE INTERNATIONAL CRIMINAL COURTS AND THE EUROPEAN COURT OF HUMAN RIGHTS: PROCEDURE AND EVIDENCE (Leiden; Boston: Martinus Nijhoff Publishers, 2008).

THE TOKYO MAJOR WAR CRIMES TRIAL: THE TRANSCRIPTS OF THE COURT PROCEEDINGS OF THE INTERNATIONAL MILITARY TRIBUNAL FOR THE FAR EAST (Lewiston, N.Y.: Published for the Robert M.W. Kempner Collegium by E. Mellen Press, 1998–).

TORRES, ARTURO L., LATIN AMERICAN LEGAL ABBREVIATIONS: A COMPREHENSIVE SPANISH/ PORTUGUESE DICTIONARY WITH ENGLISH TRANSLATIONS (New York: Greenwood Press, 1989).

Torres, Esther Sánchez, *The Spanish Law on Dependent Self-Employed Workers: A New Evolution in Labor Law*, 31 COMP. LAB. L. & POL'Y J. 231 (2010).

Trade Agreements (U.S. Dept. of Agriculture), http://www.fas.usda.gov/itp/agreements.asp.

Trade Agreements (Office of the United States Trade Representative), http://www.ustr.gov/ trade-agreements.

Trade Agreements (OAS, Foreign Trade Information System), http://www.sice.oas.org/ agreements_e.asp.

Trade and Related Agreements (U.S. Dept. of Commerce, International Trade Administration), http://tcc.export.gov/Trade_Agreements/index.asp.

TradeLawGuide, subscription database, http://www.tradelawguide.com.

TRADE MARKS, TRADE NAMES AND UNFAIR COMPETITION: WORLD LAW & PRACTICE (John R. Olsen & Spyros M. Maniatis eds., London: Sweet & Maxwell, 1999–).

Trans-Lex, http://trans-lex.org.

TRANSNATIONAL CONTRACTS (Lawrence J. Bogard et al., eds., Eagan, MN: West, a Thomson Reuters business, 2011–).

Transnational Dispute Management (TDM), subscription database, http://www.transnational disputemanagement.com.

Transnational Law Database (Center for Transnational Law at the University of Cologne, Germany), http://www.tldb.net.

TRANSNATIONAL LITIGATION: A PRACTITIONER'S GUIDE (Richard Kreindler ed., Dobbs Ferry, N.Y.: Oceana Publications, 1997–).

TREATIES AND ALLIANCES OF THE WORLD (8th ed., London: John Harper; Farmington Hills, Mich.: Distributed in United States and Canada by Gale Group, 2007).

Treaties and International Agreements Online, subscription database, http://www.oceanalaw .com.

TREATIES AND OTHER INTERNATIONAL ACTS OF THE UNITED STATES OF AMERICA (Hunter Miller ed., Washington, DC: U.S. G.P.O., 1931). Available on HeinOnline.

TREATIES AND OTHER INTERNATIONAL ACTS SERIES [T.I.A.S.] (Washington, DC: U.S. G.P.O., 1946–). T.I.A.S. 11060 to T.I.A.S. 12734 available on HeinOnline. The State Department's website provides access to T.I.A.S. from 1996–2008, http://www.state.gov/s/l/treaty/tias/ index.htm.

Treaties and Other International Agreements, Chapter 720, Foreign Affairs Manual [Circular 175] (revised Sept. 25, 2006), http://www.state.gov/s/l/treaty/c175/index.htm.

TREATIES AND OTHER INTERNATIONAL AGREEMENTS OF THE UNITED STATES OF AMERICA, 1776–1949 (Charles I. Bevans ed., Washington, DC: U.S. G.P.O., 19681976). Available on HeinOnline.

TREATIES AND OTHER INTERNATIONAL AGREEMENTS: THE ROLE OF THE UNITED STATES SENATE: A STUDY, prepared for the Committee on Foreign Relations, United States Senate, S. Print 106–71, (Washington: U.S. G.P.O.: [U.S. G.P.O., Supt. of Docs., Congressional Sales Office, distributor], 2001). Available at http://www.gpo.gov/fdsys/pkg/CPRT-106SPRT66922/pdf/CPRT-106SPRT66922.pdf and on HeinOnline.

TREATIES, CONVENTIONS, INTERNATIONAL ACTS, PROTOCOLS, AND AGREEMENTS BETWEEN THE U.S.A. AND OTHER POWERS (William M. Malloy ed., v. 1–2; C.F. Redmond & Edward J. Trenwith eds., v. 3–4, Washington, DC: U.S. G.P.O., 1910–1938). Available on Hein Online.

TREATIES IN FORCE [TIF] (Washington, DC: Office of the Legal Advisor, U.S. Dept. of State, 1950–). The current version is also available at http://www.state.gov/s/l/treaty/tif/index.htm and HeinOnline. Older editions are available HeinOnline, LexisNexis (Legal > Area of Law—By Topic > International Law > Find Treaties & International Agreements > U.S. Treaties in Force), and Westlaw (USTIF).

Treaties/Soft Law Agreements, Wildlife Committee, American Branch of the International Law Association (ABILA), http://www.internationalwildlifelaw.org/treaties.shtml.

TREATY SERIES (Washington, DC: General Secretariat, Organization of American States, 1970–). Also available on the OAS website, http://oas.org/dil/treaties_and_agreements.htm.

TREATY SERIES [T.S.] (Washington, DC: U.S. G.P.O, 1908–1946).

TRIAL OF THE MAJOR WAR CRIMINALS BEFORE THE INTERNATIONAL MILITARY TRIBUNAL, NUREMBERG, 14 NOVEMBER 1945–1 OCTOBER 1946 (Nuremberg, Germany: [s.n.], 1947–1949).

TRIALS OF WAR CRIMINALS BEFORE THE NUERNBERG MILITARY TRIBUNALS UNDER CONTROL COUNCIL LAW NO. 10: NUERNBERG, OCTOBER 1946–APRIL, 1949 (Washington: U. S. Govt. Print. Off., [1949–53]).

TRIBUNAL PÉNAL INTERNATIONAL POUR LE RWANDA: RECUEIL DES ORDONNANCES, DÉCISIONS ET ARRÊTS, 1995–1997 = INTERNATIONAL CRIMINAL TRIBUNAL FOR RWANDA REPORTS OF ORDERS, DECISIONS AND JUDGEMENTS, 1995–1997 (Eric David ed., Bruxelles: Bruylant, 2000).

UNBISnet, the UN Bibliographic Information System, http://unbisnet.un.org.

UN CHRONICLE (New York, NY: United Nations Dept. of Public Information, 1996–). Available at http://www.un.org/Pubs/chronicle/index.html.

UNDEX (New York, NY: United Nations).

UNDOC: CURRENT INDEX (New York, NY: United Nations).

UNESCO, Collection of National Copyright Laws, http://portal.unesco.org/culture/en/ev.php-URL_ID=14076&URL_DO=DO_TOPIC&URL_SECTION=201.html.

UNESCO Legal Instruments, http://portal.unesco.org/en/ev.php-URL_ID=12025&URL_DO=DO_TOPIC&URL_SECTION=-471.html.

UNILEX (CISG and UNIDROIT Principles), http://www.unilex.info.

UNILEX: INTERNATIONAL CASE LAW & BIBLIOGRAPHY ON THE UN CONVENTION ON CONTRACTS FOR THE INTERNATIONAL SALE OF GOODS (Michael Joachim Bonell ed., Irvington, N.Y.: Transnational Publishers, 1996–). Has not been updated since 2008.

United Kingdom Border Agency, Country of Origin Information Service, http://www.ukba.homeoffice.gov.uk/policyandlaw/guidance/coi.

UNITED KINGDOM TREATY SERIES [U.K.T.S.] (London: H.M.S.O., 1892–).

United Kingdom's Foreign and Commonwealth Office, http://www.fco.gov.uk.

UN News Centre, http://www.un.org/News.

UN Pulse, http://unhq-appspub-01.un.org/lib/dhlrefweblog.nsf.

UN Treaty Handbook, http://treaties.un.org/pages/Publications.aspx?pathpub=Publication/TH/Page1_en.xml.

UN Watch, http://www.unwatch.org.

UN Wire, https://www.smartbrief.com/un_wire/index.jsp.

United Nations Administrative Tribunal [UNAT], http://untreaty.un.org/UNAT/main_page.htm.

United Nations Commission on International Trade Law [UNCITRAL], http://www.uncitral.org.

UNCITRAL Digest of Case Law on the United Nations Convention on the International Sale of Goods (CISG) (2008), http://www.uncitral.org/pdf/english/clout/08-51939_Ebook.pdf.

United Nations Conference on Trade and Development [UNCTAD], Bilateral Investment Treaties: 1959-1999, http://www.unctad.org/en/docs/poiteiiad2.en.pdf.

United Nations Conference on Trade and Development, Database of Treaty-Based Investor-State Dispute Settlement Cases, http://www.unctad.org/iia-dbcases/index.html.

United Nations Conference on Trade and Development, Investment Instruments Online: Bilateral Investment Treaties, http://www.unctadxi.org/templates/docsearch____779.aspx.

UNITED NATIONS CONFERENCE ON TRADE AND DEVELOPMENT, INTERNATIONAL INVESTMENT ARRANGEMENTS: TRENDS AND EMERGING ISSUES (New York: United Nations, 2006). Also available on the UNCTAD's website, http://www.unctad.org/en/docs/iteiit200511_en.pdf.

UNITED NATIONS CONFERENCE ON TRADE AND DEVELOPMENT, INVESTOR-STATE DISPUTE SETTLEMENT AND IMPACT ON INVESTMENT RULEMAKING (New York: United Nations, 2007). Also available on UNCTAD's website, http://www.unctad.org/en/docs/iteiia20073_en.pdf.

UNITED NATIONS CONFERENCE ON TRADE AND DEVELOPMENT, INVESTOR-STATE DISPUTES ARISING FROM INVESTMENT TREATIES: A REVIEW (New York: United Nations, 2005). Also available on UNCTAD's website, http://www.unctad.org/en/docs/iteiit20054_en.pdf.

THE UNITED NATIONS CONVENTION ON THE RIGHTS OF THE CHILD: A GUIDE TO THE "TRAVAUX PRÉPARATOIRES" (Sharon Detrick ed. & comp., Dordrecht; Boston: M. Nijhoff Publishers; Norwell, MA, U.S.A.: Sold and distributed in the U.S.A. and Canada by Kluwer Academic Publishers, 1992).

United Nations, *Core Document Forming Part of the Reports of States Parties*, U.N. Doc. HRI/Core/[country abbreviation]/[year], http://www2.ohchr.org/english/bodies/coredocs.htm.

UNITED NATIONS CUMULATIVE TREATY INDEX (Buffalo, NY: William S. Hein, 1999-). Supplemented by CD-ROM.

UNITED NATIONS, DEPT. OF POLITICAL AND SECURITY COUNCIL AFFAIRS, REPERTOIRE OF THE PRACTICE OF THE SECURITY COUNCIL (New York: The Department, 1954-). Available at http://www.un.org/en/sc/repertoire/index.shtml.

United Nations Diplomatic Conferences, http://untreaty.un.org/cod/diplomaticconferences/index.html.

United Nations Documentation: Research Guide, http://www.un.org/Depts/dhl/resguide.

UN Documentation: Research Guide—International Law: Courts and Tribunals, http://www.un.org/depts/dhl/resguide/specil.htm#trib.

UNITED NATIONS DOCUMENTS INDEX [UNDI] (New York, NY: United Nations).

United Nations Environment Programme (UNEP), Environmental Law Instruments, http://www.unep.org/law/Law_instruments/index.asp.

United Nations Framework Convention on Climate Change, http://unfccc.int/2860.php.

UNITED NATIONS, GENERAL ASSEMBLY, RESOLUTIONS AND DECISIONS ADOPTED BY THE GENERAL ASSEMBLY (New York: United Nations, 1976-). Available at http://www.un.org/documents/resga.htm.

UNITED NATIONS HANDBOOK (Wellington, N.Z.: Ministry of Foreign Affairs, 1973-).

United Nations High Commission for Refugees [UNHCR], Legal Information, http://www.unhcr.org.

The United Nations Human Rights Treaties (bayefsky.com), http://www.bayefsky.com.

UNITED NATIONS, INTERNATIONAL INVESTMENT ARRANGEMENTS: TRENDS AND EMERGING ISSUES (New York: United Nations, 2006).

UNITED NATIONS INTERNATIONAL LAW COMMISSION, YEARBOOK OF THE INTERNATIONAL LAW COMMISSION (New York: United Nations, 1949-). Some are available at http://untreaty.un.org/ilc/publications/yearbooks/yearbooks.htm.

UNITED NATIONS, INVESTOR-STATE DISPUTES ARISING FROM INVESTMENT TREATIES: A REVIEW (New York: United Nations, 2005).

UNITED NATIONS JURIDICAL YEARBOOK (New York: United Nations, 1962–). Available on HeinOnline.

UNITED NATIONS LEGISLATIVE SERIES (New York: United Nations, 1951–). Available on HeinOnline.

UNITED NATIONS LIBRARY, BIBLIOGRAPHIE MENSUELLE = MONTHLY BIBLIOGRAPHY (Genève: Bibliothèque des Nations Unies, 1998–).

UNITED NATIONS OFFICE OF LEGAL AFFAIRS, LIST OF TREATY COLLECTIONS (New York: United Nations, 1956).

UNITED NATIONS, OFFICE OF LEGAL AFFAIRS, REPORTS OF INTERNATIONAL ARBITRAL AWARDS [RIAA] ([Lake Success?]: United Nations, 1948–). Also available on the UN website, http://www.un.org/law/riaa, and on HeinOnline.

United Nations Official Documents System (ODS), http://documents.un.org/welcome .asp?language=E.

United Nations System Pathfinder, http://www.un.org/Depts/dhl/pathfind/frame/start.htm.

THE UNITED NATIONS SYSTEM AND ITS PREDECESSORS (Oxford; New York: Oxford University Press, 1997).

United Nations Treaty Database, http://treaties.un.org.

United Nations Treaty Reference Guide and Glossary of Terms Related to Treaty Actions, http://treaties.un.org/Pages/Overview.aspx?path=overview/treatyRef/page1_en.xml.

UNITED NATIONS TREATY SERIES [U.N.T.S.] (New York: United Nations, 1947–), http:// treaties.un.org.

UNITED NATIONS TREATY SERIES INDEX (New York: United Nations, 1946–), http://untreaty .un.org.

UNITED STATES CODE SERVICE (Rochester, NY, Lawyers Co-operative Pub. Co.; San Francisco, Bancroft-Whitney Co., 1972–).

United States Official Harmonized Tariff Schedule, http://www.usitc.gov/tata/hts.

UNITED STATES TREATIES AND OTHER INTERNATIONAL AGREEMENTS [U.S.T.] (Washington, DC: U.S. G.P.O, 1950–). Volumes 1–35 available on HeinOnline.

UNITED STATES TREATIES AND OTHER INTERNATIONAL AGREEMENTS CUMULATIVE INDEX 1776–1949: CUMULATIVE INDEX TO UNITED STATES TREATIES AND OTHER INTERNATIONAL AGREEMENTS 1776–1949 AS PUBLISHED IN STATUTES AT LARGE, MALLOY, MILLER, BEVANS, AND OTHER RELEVANT SOURCES (Igor I. Kavass & Mark A. Michael comps., Buffalo, NY: W.S. Hein, 1975).

UNITED STATES TREATIES AND OTHER INTERNATIONAL AGREEMENTS CURRENT SERVICE [microfiche] (Buffalo, NY: W.S. Hein, 1990–). Part of this service available on HeinOnline.

UNITED STATES TREATY INDEX (Igor I. Kavass ed., Buffalo, NY: W.S. Hein Co., 1991–).

University of Denver, Sturm College of Law, "Countries," http://law.du.edu/forms/enrgp/ weblinks/index.cfm.

University of Michigan Law School, Refugee Caselaw Site, http://www.refugeecaselaw.org/ Home.aspx.

UNIVERSITY OF PENNSYLVANIA JOURNAL OF CONSTITUTIONAL LAW (Philadelphia, PA: University of Pennsylvania Law School, 1998–). Available at http://www.law.upenn.edu/ conlaw/ and HeinOnline.

UNODC, Electronic Legal Resources on International Terrorism, https://www.unodc.org/ tldb/en/index.html.

UNODC Legal Library, http://www.unodc.org/enl/index.html.

UNPERFECTED TREATIES OF THE UNITED STATES OF AMERICA, 1776–1976 (Dobbs Ferry, NY: Oceana Publications, 1976–1994).

US Bureau of Arms Control-Related Treaties and Agreements (US Dept. of State), http:// www.state.gov/t/avc/trty.

US Bureau of Nonproliferation, Treaties and Agreements (U.S. Dept. of State), http://www .state.gov/t/isn/trty/.

US Department of State, Annual Report to Congress on International Religious Freedom, http://www.state.gov/g/drl/irf/rpt.

US Department of State, Country Reports on Human Rights Practices (Washington, DC: U.S. G.P.O., 1977–). Reports from 1993–1999 are available from the archive of the State Department's website, at http://www.state.gov/www/global/human_rights/drl_reports.html and from 1999–2006 are at http://www.state.gov/g/drl/rls/hrrpt.

US Department of State, Country-Specific Information, http://travel.state.gov/law/judicial/judicial_2510.html.

US Department of State, Electronic Reading Room, http://www.state.gov/m/a/ips/c26355.htm.

US Department of State, Department of State Bulletin (Washington, DC: Office of Public Communication, Bureau of Public Affairs, 1939–1989).

US Department of State, Enforcement of Judgments, http://travel.state.gov/law/judicial/judicial_691.html.

US Department of State, Judicial Assistance, http://travel.state.gov/law/judicial/judicial_702.html.

US Department of State, Judicial Assistance—Country-Specific Information, http://travel.state.gov/law/judicial/judicial_2510.html.

US Department of State, Judicial Assistance—Obtaining Evidence Abroad, http://travel.state.gov/law//judicial/judicial_2514.html.

US Department of State, Judicial Assistance—Service of Process Abroad, http://travel.state.gov/law/judicial/judicial_2513.html.

US Department of State, Obtaining Evidence Abroad, http://travel.state.gov/law//judicial/judicial_2514l.

US Department of State, Service of Legal Documents Abroad, http://travel.state.gov/law/judicial/judicial_680.html.

US International Social Security Agreements (Social Security Administration), http://www.ssa.gov/international/agreements_overview.html.

US Trade Compliance Center, Bilateral Investment Treaties, http://tcc.export.gov/Trade_Agreements/Bilateral_Investment_Treaties/index.asp.

United States Senate, Treaties, http://www.senate.gov/pagelayout/legislative/d_three_sections_with_teasers/treaties.htm.

United States State Department, Current Treaty Actions, http://www.state.gov/s/l/index.cfm?id=3428.

United States State Department, http://www.state.gov/s/l/c8183.htm.

US Department of State, NAFTA Investor-State Arbitrations, http://www.state.gov/s/l/c3439.htm.

Vandevelde, Kenneth J., Bilateral Investment Treaties: History, Policy, and Interpretation (New York: Oxford University Press, 2010).

Vargas, Jorge A., Mexican Civil Code Annotated (Eagan, Minn.: West, 2009).

Vargas, Jorge A., *Mexican Law on the Web: The Ultimate Research Guide*, 32 Int'l.J. Legal Info. 34 (2004).

Vargas, Jorge A., Mexican Legal Dictionary (2009–10 ed., [St. Paul, Minn.]: West/Thomson Reuters, 2009).

Vaughn, John R., A Comparative Analysis of Disability Laws (New York: Nova Science Publishers, 2010).

Vedder, Anton, et al., NGO Involvement in International Governance and Policy (Leiden; Boston: Martinus Nijhoff Publishers, 2007).

Vervliet, Jeroen, *International Organizations and Legal Information, in* The IALL International Handbook of Legal Information Management 281 (Richard A. Danner & Jules Winterton eds., Farnham, Surrey; Burlington, VT: Ashgate Pub., 2011).

Vesnik Kanstytutsyinaha Suda Respubliki Belarus: VKS (Minsk: Belarus-Infarm-Servis, 1994–).

Vestnik Konstitutsionnogo Suda Rossiiskoi Federatsii (Moskva: Konstitutsionnyi Sud, 1993–).

Vietnam Laws Online, subscription database, http://www.vietnamlaws.com.

Villiers, Charlotte, The Spanish Legal Tradition: An Introduction to the Spanish Law and Legal System (Aldershot, UK; Brookfield, VT: Ashgate/Dartmouth, 1999).

Villiger, Mark Eugene, Customary International Law and Treaties: A Manual on the Theory and Practice of the Interrelation of Sources (rev. 2d ed., Hague; Boston: Kluwer Law International; Zürich: distributed in Switzerland by Schulthess Polygraphischer, 1997).

vLex Global, subscription database, http://vlex.com.

Von Glahn, Gerhard, Law Among Nations: An Introduction to Public International Law (8th ed., New York: Pearson/Longman, 2007).

War Crimes Studies Center of UC Berkeley, http://socrates.berkeley.edu/~warcrime/index
.html.
War Crimes Research Office, American University Washington College of Law, Basic Infor-
mation and Reports, http://www.wcl.american.edu/warcrimes.
War Crimes Research Portal (Frederick K. Cox International Law Center), http://law.case
.edu/war-crimes-research-portal.
WARD, IAN, A CRITICAL INTRODUCTION TO EUROPEAN LAW (2d ed., London: LexisNexis
UK, 2003).
WARD, RICHARD ET AL., WALKER & WALKER'S ENGLISH LEGAL SYSTEM (11th ed., Oxford;
New York: Oxford University Press, 2011).
WATSON, ALAN, COMPARATIVE LAW: LAW, REALITY AND SOCIETY (3d ed., Lake Mary, FL:
Vandeplas Pub., 2010).
WATT, ROBERT, CONCISE LEGAL RESEARCH (6th ed., Sydney: Federation Press, 2009).
Wayback Machine, http://www.archive.org/web/web.php.
WEEKLY COMPILATION OF PRESIDENTIAL DOCUMENTS [WCPD] ([Washington, DC: Office of
the Federal Register, National Archives and Records Service, General Services Administration:
Supt. of Docs., U.S. G.P.O., distributor], 1965–). 1993 to present available at http://www.gpo
.gov/fdsys/browse/collection.action?collectionCode=CPD and on HeinOnline.
WEBSTER, THOMAS H., HANDBOOK OF UNCITRAL ARBITRATION: COMMENTARY, PRECE-
DENTS & MODELS FOR UNCITRAL BASED ARBITRATION RULES (London: Sweet & Maxwell:
Thomson Reuters, 2010).
Weigman, Stefanie, Update to Researching Intellectual Property Law in an International Con-
text (2000), http://www.llrx.com/features/iplaw2.htm.
Welch, Tom, et al., *Witness Anonymity at the International Criminal Court: Due Process for
Defendants, Witnesses or Both?*, 2011 DENNING L.J. 29.
Wenger, Jean, International Commercial Arbitration: Locating the Resources–Revised (2004),
http://www.llrx.com/features/arbitration2.htm.
Wenger, Jean, ASIL Guide to Electronic Resources for International Law: International Eco-
nomic Law, http://www.asil.org/erg/?page=iel.
WEST'S LAW AND COMMERCIAL DICTIONARY IN FIVE LANGUAGES: DEFINITIONS OF THE
LEGAL AND COMMERCIAL TERMS AND PHRASES OF AMERICAN, ENGLISH AND CIVIL LAW
JURISDICTIONS (St. Paul, MN: West, 1985).
Westlaw China, subscription database, http://www.westlawchina.com.
Westlaw Gulf, subscription database, http://www.sweetandmaxwell.co.uk/westlawgulf.
Westlaw, AFRNEWS database.
Weatlaw, ALI-ABA database.
Westlaw, CMB-TREATIES (Combined Treaties) database.
Westlaw, CML-RPTS (Common Market Law Reports) database.
Westlaw, EHR-RPTS (European Human Rights Reports) database.
Westlaw, ENFLEX-INT (Environmental laws and regulations) database.
Westlaw, ENP-RPTS (European Patent Reports) database.
Westlaw, ETR-RPTS (European Trade Mark Reports) database.
Westlaw, EU-CS (European Court of Justice and Court of First Instance cases) database.
Westlaw, EU-TREATIES (EU treaties) database.
Westlaw, FLEET-RPTS (Fleet Street Reports) database.
Westlaw, IACHR-OAS (Inter-American Commission on Human Rights documents) database.
Westlaw, INT-ICJ (International Court of Justice) database.
Westlaw, INT-ICTY (International Criminal Tribunal for the former Yugoslavia) database.
Westlaw ICSID materials, ICSID-ALL, ICSID-AWARDS, ICSID-RULES, and ICSIDMODC.
Westlaw International Chamber of Commerce (ICC) materials, ICC-RULES, ICCMODC, and
ICC-ALL.
Westlaw, International Commercial Arbitration cases (ICA-CASES). [Note: This database
contains very few international cases.]
Westlaw, LH database.
Westlaw, NAFTA-AWARDS (arbitration awards) database.
Westlaw, NAFTA-BIP (NAFTA panel decisions) database.
Westlaw, NAFTA-LH (NAFTA legislative history) database.

Westlaw, PLI database.

Westlaw, SCHMP (South China Morning Post) database.

Westlaw, UDRP-ARB database.

Westlaw UNCITRAL materials, UNCITRAL-RULES, UNCITRAL-MODL, and UNCITRAL-ALL.

Westlaw, USTREATIES database.

Westlaw, WTO-DEC (selected WTO and GATT Panel decisions) database.

WHARTON, FRANCIS, DIGEST OF THE INTERNATIONAL LAW OF THE UNITED STATES (Washington, DC: U.S. G.P.O., 1886). Second edition (1877) available on HeinOnline.

WHITEMAN, MARJORIE M., DIGEST OF INTERNATIONAL LAW ([Washington, DC: US Dept. of State; for sale by the Supt. of Docs., US G.P.O.], 1963–1973). Available on HeinOnline.

WIKTOR, CHRISTIAN L., MULTILATERAL TREATY CALENDAR =REPERTOIRE DES TRAITES MULTILATERAUX, 1648–1995 (Boston: Martinus Nijhoff Publishers, 1998).

WIKTOR, CHRISTIAN L., TREATIES SUBMITTED TO THE UNITED STATES SENATE: LEGISLATIVE HISTORY, 1989–2004 (Leiden; Boston: Martinus Nijhoff, 2006).

WILLE, GEORGE, ET AL., WILLE'S PRINCIPLES OF SOUTH AFRICAN LAW (9th ed., Cape Town: Juta, 2007).

WILLETT, LINDA, U.S.-STYLE CLASS ACTIONS IN EUROPE: A GROWING THREAT? (Washington, D.C.: National Legal Center for the Public Interest, 2005).

WILLIAMS, ROBERT V., THE INFORMATION SYSTEMS OF INTERNATIONAL INTERGOVERNMENTAL ORGANIZATIONS: A REFERENCE GUIDE (Stamford, CT.: Ablex Pub., 1998).

Willyams, Karen, *Bibliography of Books and Articles on International Law Relevant to New Zealand*, 3 N.Z. Y.B. INT'L L. 281 (2006).

WIPO Arbitration and Mediation Center, http://www.wipo.int/amc/en/index.html.

WIPO Directory of National and Regional Industrial Property Offices, http://www.wipo.int/directory/en/urls.jsp.

WIPO, Geographic Indicators, http://www.wipo.int/geo_indications/en/about.html.

WIPO, Index of WIPO UDRP Panel Decisions, http://www.wipo.int/amc/en/domains/search/legalindex.jsp.

WIPO Lex, http://www.wipo.int/wipolex/en.

WIPO MAGAZINE (Geneva: WIPO, 1998–). Also available at http://www.wipo.int/wipo_magazine/en.

WIPO, Search WIPO Cases and WIPO Panel Decisions, http://www.wipo.int/amc/en/domains/search/index.html.

WIPO, WIPO Arbitration and Mediation Center, http://arbiter.wipo.int/domains.

THE WORLD ALMANAC AND BOOK OF FACTS (New York: Newspaper Enterprise Association [etc.], 1886–). Also available by subscription, http://firstsearch.oclc.org.

WORLD ARBITRATION AND MEDIATION REPORT (London: BNA International, 1990–).

WORLD ARBITRATION REPORTER: INTERNATIONAL ENCYCLOPAEDIA OF ARBITRATION LAW AND PRACTICE (2d ed., Loukas Mistelis et al., eds., Huntington, NY: Juris, 2010–).

World Bank, http://www.worldbank.org.

WorldCat, http://www.worldcat.org/ (free version); http://firstsearch.oclc.org/ (subscription version).

World Conservation Union [IUCN], http://www.iucn.org.

WORLD COURT DIGEST (Berlin; New York: Springer, 1993–). Available at http://www.mpil.de/ww/en/pub/research/details/publications/institute/wcd.cfm.

WORLD COURT REPORTS (Reprint of the 1934 ed., Washington, Carnegie Endowment for International Peace: 1935–1969). Available on HeinOnline.

World Courts, http://www.worldcourts.com.

WORLD DICTIONARY OF LEGAL ABBREVIATIONS (Igor I. Kavass & Mary Miles Prince eds., [Buffalo, NY]: W.S. Hein, 1991–).

WORLD E-COMMERCE & IP REPORT (London: BNA International 2000–).

THE WORLD FACTBOOK (Washington, DC: Central Intelligence Agency, 1981–). https://www.cia.gov/library/publications/the-world-factbook.

World Health Organization [WHO], International Digest of Health Legislation, http://www.who.int/idhl.

World Intellectual Property Organization [WIPO], Administered Treaties, http://www.wipo.int/treaties/en.

WORLD INTELLECTUAL PROPERTY REPORT (London: BNA International, 1987–2000). Also available as part of BNA Intellectual Property Library, http://www.bna.com.

WORLD INTELLECTUAL PROPERTY RIGHTS AND REMEDIES (Dennis Campbell ed., Eagan, MN: West, 2011–).

World Law Guide (Courts/Cases), http://www.lexadin.nl/wlg/courts/nofr/courts.htm.

World Legal Information Institute [WorldLII], http://www.worldlii.org. Includes: Australasia (AustLII), UK & Ireland (BAILII), Canada (CanLII), The Commonwealth (CommonLII), Cyprus (CyLaw), Droit Francophone, Hong Kong (HKLII), JuriBurkina, New Zealand (NZLII), Pacific Islands (PacLII), Southern Africa (SAFLII), and USA (LII(Cornell)), and others. Links to these sites are available at http://www.worldlii.org; see bottom of the homepage.

WorldLII, Intellectual Property Directory, http://www.worldlii.org/catalog/315.html.

WorldLII: International Courts & Tribunals Directory, http://www.worldlii.org/catalog/2561.html.

WorldLII: International Courts & Tribunals Project, http://www.worldlii.org/int/cases.

WorldLII, Treaties & International Agreements, by Country, http://www.worldlii.org/catalog/2322.html.

World News Connection, subscription database, http://wnc.fedworld.gov.

WORLD TRADE AND ARBITRATION MATERIALS (Geneva, Switzerland: Werner Pub. Co., 1989–). Also available on HeinOnline.

World TradeLaw.net, subscription database, http://www.worldtradelaw.net.

WorldTradeLaw.net, Links to Government Submissions in NAFTA and WTO Disputes, http://www.worldtradelaw.net/submissions.htm.

WorldTradeLaw.net, Tariff Schedules, http://www.worldtradelaw.net/tariffs.htm.

WorldTradeLaw.net, WTO Case Law Index, http://www.worldtradelaw.net/dsc/wtoindex.htm.

World Trade Organization [WTO], http://www.wto.org.

WORLD TRADE ORGANIZATION DISPUTE SETTLEMENT DECISIONS: BERNAN'S ANNOTATED REPORTER (Lanham, Md.: Bernan Press, 1997–).

World Trade Organization, Dispute Settlement, http://www.wto.org/english/tratop_e/dispu_e/dispu_e.htm.

World Trade Organization, Documents Online, http://docsonline.wto.org.

World Trade Organization, GATT Documents, http://www.wto.org/english/docs_e/gattdocs_e.htm.

WORLD TRADE ORGANIZATION, A HANDBOOK ON THE WTO DISPUTE SETTLEMENT SYSTEM (Cambridge, UK; New York: Cambridge University Press, 2004).

World Trade Organization, Principles of the Trading System, http://www.wto.org/english/thewto_e/whatis_e/tif_e/fact2_e.htm.

World Trade Organization, Settling Disputes, http://www.wto.org/english/thewto_e/whatis_e/tif_e/disp1_e.htm.

World Trade Organization, TRIPS, http://www.wto.org/english/tratop_e/trips_e/trips_e.htm.

World Trade Organization, Understanding the WTO: Settling Disputes, http://www.wto.org/english/thewto_e/whatis_e/tif_e/disp1_e.htm.

WORLD TREATY INDEX (Peter H. Rohn ed., Santa Barbara, CA: ABC-Clio, 1983). A beta version of this index is available at http://worldtreatyindex.com.

Worldwide Political Science Abstracts (CSA, 1975–), subscription database, http://www.csa.com/factsheets/polsci-set-c.php.

WRIGHT, CHARLES ALAN, ET AL., FEDERAL PRACTICE & PROCEDURE (St. Paul, MN: West Pub. Co., 1969–). Also available on Westlaw.

WTO ANALYTICAL INDEX–GUIDE TO WTO LAW AND PRACTICE (2d ed., Lanham, MD: Bernan, 2007). Available on the WTO websites at http://www.wto.org/english/res_e/booksp_e/analytic_index_e/analytic_index_e.htm.

WTO APPELLATE BODY REPERTORY OF REPORTS AND AWARDS, 1995–2010 (4th ed., Appellate Body Secretariat, comp., Cambridge; New York; Cambridge University Press, 2011).

WTO Dispute Settlement, Cases Involving the EU (European Commission), http://trade.ec.europa.eu/wtodispute/search.cfm.

WTO Dispute Settlement (USTR), http://www.ustr.gov/trade-topics/enforcement/dispute-settlement-proceedings/wto-dispute-settlement.

WTO REPORTER (Washington, DC: Bureau of National Affairs 2000–). Available on Lexis-Nexis and Westlaw through some subscription plans, otherwise as a web subscription on BNA, http://www.bna.com.

WTO BASIC INSTRUMENTS AND SELECTED DOCUMENTS [BISD] (Geneva: World Trade Organization; Lanham, MD: Bernan, 2003–).

THE WTO'S CORE RULES AND DISCIPLINES (Kym Anderson & Bernard Hoekman eds., Cheltenham, Glos, UK; Northampton, MA: Edward Elgar Pub., 2006).

WTO Tariff Schedules (US Dept. of Agriculture), http://www.fas.usda.gov/scriptsw/wtopdf/wtopdf_frm.asp.

YEARBOOK, COMMERCIAL ARBITRATION (Deventer: Kluwer, 1976–). Also available on Kluwer Arbitration.

YEARBOOK OF EUROPEAN LAW (Oxford: Clarendon Press; New York: Oxford University Press, 1982–).

YEARBOOK OF EUROPEAN ENVIRONMENTAL LAW (Oxford; New York: Oxford University Press, 2000–). Available online from publisher.

YEARBOOK OF INTERNATIONAL ENVIRONMENTAL LAW (London; Boston: Graham & Trotman, 1991–).

YEARBOOK OF INTERNATIONAL HUMANITARIAN LAW (The Hague, The Netherlands: T.M.C. Asser Press, 1998–).

YEARBOOK OF INTERNATIONAL ORGANIZATIONS (Munchen: K.G. Saur, 1983–). Available by subscription, http://www.uia.be/s/or/en.

YEARBOOK OF ISLAMIC AND MIDDLE EASTERN LAW (London: Published for CIMEL by Kluwer Law International, 1995–). Also available on HeinOnline.

YEARBOOK OF POLAR LAW (Leiden; Boston: Martinus Nijhoff Brill, 2009–).

YEARBOOK OF THE UNITED NATIONS (Norwell, MA: Kluwer, 1947–). Available online from 1946 to present, http://unyearbook.un.org.

YEARBOOK ON THE ORGANIZATION FOR SECURITY AND CO-OPERATION IN EUROPE (Baden-Baden: Nomos Verlagsgesellschaft, 1996–). Also available on the OSCE website from 1995/6–, http://www.core-hamburg.de/CORE_english/pub_osce_yearbook.htm.

YOUNG, RAYMOND, ENGLISH, FRENCH, AND GERMAN COMPARATIVE LAW (2d ed., London; New York: Routledge-Cavendish, 2007).

YU, GUANGHUA, THE DEVELOPMENT OF THE CHINESE LEGAL SYSTEM: CHANGE AND CHALLENGES (London; New York: Routledge, 2011).

ZACHARY, DOUGLAS, THE INTERNATIONAL LAW OF INVESTMENT CLAIMS (Cambridge, UK; New York: Cambridge University Press, 2009).

ZAMORA, STEPHEN, MEXICAN LAW (Oxford; New York: Oxford University Press, 2004).

ZIPPELIUS, REINHOLD, INTRODUCTION TO GERMAN LEGAL METHODS (Durham, N.C.: Carolina Academic Press, 2008).

ZWEIGERT, KONRAD, AND HEIN KÖTZ, INTRODUCTION TO COMPARATIVE LAW (3d rev. ed., repr, Oxford: Clarendon Press, 2011).

ZEITSCHRIFT FÜR EUROPARECHT, INTERNATIONALES PRIVATRECHT UND RECHTSVERGLEICHUNG (Wien: Manz, 2008–).

Index